ENCYCLOPEDIA
OF
SERMON
ILLUSTRATIONS

ENCYCLOPEDIA
OF
SERMON
ILLUSTRATIONS

Compiled
by
David F. Burgess

CONCORDIA PUBLISHING HOUSE · SAINT LOUIS

9 780570 042433

Copyright © 1988 Concordia Publishing House
3558 S. Jefferson Avenue, St. Louis, MO 63118-3968
Manufactured in the United States of America

Library of Congress Cataloging in Publication Data

Encyclopedia of sermon illustrations / compiled by David F. Burgess.
    p. cm.
    "Illustrations taken entirely from the Concordia pulpit from 1930–1985 editions"—
Pref.
  IBSN 0-570-04243-7
  1. Homiletical illustrations. I. Burgess, David F., 1946– . II. Concordia pulpit.
BV4225.2.E53 1988
251'.08—dc19   87-37941
                                                    CIP

---

6 7 8 9 10 11 12 13 14   08 07 06 05 04 03

PREFACE

This collection of sermon illustrations was compiled with the help of lay evaluators, who rated them for simplicity, conciseness, relevance, and clarity in making a specific point.

The illustrations differ in several respects from other collections of sermon illustrations:

1. A *specific moral or theological point* is made in each illustration. We have avoided naked illustrations that may be interesting anecdotes but do not clearly make a point.
2. *Multiple textual references*—an illustration is only as good as its availability for use when it is needed. When studying a text from Scripture for preaching or teaching, one needs to know exactly where to look for the appropriate illustrations if they are to be of much help. The illustrations in this book are all referenced to at least one and as many as eight passages from Scripture. Such references are listed in the Scriptural Index.
3. *Cross-references*—at the end of many of the categories listed in the table of contents, the reader will find a list of illustrations related to the specific topic being studied. Also, some of the categories are themselves cross-referenced to related categories (for example, in the category **Eternity** is the note "See also **Endurance of the Kingdom, Immortality**").
4. *Simplicity*—we used lay persons to help in evaluating the illustrations, because they are the ones for whom the illustrations are meant. If an illustration does not enhance a point or make it clearer, then what's the point of using it?

It is our prayer that we have succeeded in our efforts to produce a book that pastors and teachers will find useful in their ministry to the souls placed in our care.

CONTENTS

A

Absolution

1. The power of absolution is not dependent on the faith of him who is being absolved but on the promise of God. If a king presents you with a castle, but you refuse to accept it, the validity of the gift is thereby not affected. The absolution of even a godless preacher is valid. A pearl remains a pearl, even though it be in the hand of a thief. *References:* Is. 52:7; Luke 24:47; Rom. 10:15.

Abundant Life

See also **New Life**

2. A father once took his small son to visit a huge cathedral. As the two were walking down the aisle, the boy pointed at the cross on the altar and said: "Father, what is that big plus sign up there?" If we ever think that the Christian religion subtracts something from our lives, we are grievously mistaken, for the Christian religion is the big plus sign that adds the best there is to our lives. *References:* Job 22:21; Mal. 3:10; Matt. 6:33; John 10:10; Rom. 8:32; 2 Cor. 9:8; Eph. 3:20; Phil. 4:19.

Acceptance

3. Of God's Ways. While you cannot understand His wonderful ways and His unsearchable judgments, rest assured that His intentions are always good and His purposes never falter. Learn to say with St. Paul: "We know that in all things God works for the good of those who love him." When Magdalene, the 14-year-old daughter of pious Dr. Luther, lay sick unto death, her father prayed: "Lord, I love her very much and should like to keep her, but, dear Lord, since it is Thy will to take her away, I am glad to know that she will be with Thee." *References:* Ps. 30:5; 34:19–20; 41:3; Is. 43:2; Rom. 8:28; 2 Cor. 4:17; 1 Peter 4:12–13; Rev. 21:4.

4. Of Others. An old cartoon pictures what appear to be two wriggling worms sticking up from the ground, one of which was obviously enamored of the other. But to his expressions of love came the indignant reply, "Hey! I'm your other end." How are we handling that part of the church that seems on the opposite end of the spectrum from us? Is there cause for indignation at the loveless treatment of the brother? *References:* Matt. 22:39; Mark 12:33; John 13:35; 15:12; Rom. 15:1–2; Gal. 5:14; James 2:8; 1 Peter 1:22.

5. Of Self. In the "Peanuts" comic strip series, a small fry came up to Charlie Brown and said, "Yes, sir, Charlie Brown. Abraham Lincoln was a great man. . . . Charlie Brown, would you like to have been Abraham Lincoln?" He paused thoughtfully for a moment and said: "Well, now, I don't know. . . . I'm having a hard enough time being just plain old Charlie Brown!" *References:* Ps. 139; 1 Cor. 12:1–11; Gal. 2:20; Phil. 4:11.

6. Of Self. As Dr. George Muedeking says in his excellent study, *Emotional Problems and the Bible:* "Accept the limits of personality potential with which God has endowed you. . . . God is not interested in success as it is measured by competition. God is concerned that a man's life be developed to the fullness of its potential." *References:* Ps. 139:1–6; John 3:27; Acts 11:29; 2 Cor. 3:5; 8:12; 1 Peter 5:6.

Adversity
7. Adversity is like the period of spring rains—cold, gloomy, uncomfortable; yet from that season flowers and fruits have their birth. (W. Scott) *References:* John 15:2; 2 Cor. 4:17; Heb. 12:11.
8. Stars may be seen from the bottom of a deep well when they cannot be discerned from the top of a mountain. So many things are learned in adversity which the prosperous man dreams not of. (Spurgeon) *References:* Ps. 94:10–14; 119:67.
9. The strongest trees grow not beneath the glass of a conservatory or in the sheltered and sunny valleys. The stoutest timber stands on Norwegian rocks, where tempests rage and long, hard winters reign. So the trials to which piety is exposed impart to it robust and healthy character. (Guthrie) *References:* Job 23:10; Mal. 3:3; Heb. 12:11.
10. Leads to Patience. I have often wondered whether Franklin Roosevelt would have ascended to the presidency if he had not been crippled by polio. That apparent tragedy helped make him the person he became. Someone once asked him how he could remain so patient through the bitter and vicious attacks to which he was subjected by the press and radio. He simply replied, "Brother, if you had spent two years learning how to wiggle your big toe,

you would learn what patience is too." *References:* Rom. 12:12; Gal. 6:9; James 1:3–4; 5:10–11; 2 Peter 1:5–6. *Related illustrations:* 80, 320, 469.

Affliction
See also **Tribulation**
11. God proves us that He may improve us. *References:* Deut. 8:2; Zech. 13:9; James 1:2–3.
12. The American evangelist Dwight L. Moody used to say that a Christian must never be found living under his circumstances. He must live above them. *References:* 1 Cor. 4:11–13; 2 Cor. 6:10; Phil. 4:4–7.
13. The same affliction moves the unbeliever to blaspheme God and the believer to praise Him, just as the same motion releases the offensive stench of garbage in one case and the sweet odor of perfume in the other. Tribulation simply reveals what is in us. (W. F. Besser) *References:* Deut. 8:2; Luke 6:47–49; 1 Cor. 3:13.
14. In sickness let me not so much say, Am I getting better of my pain? as, Am I getting better for it? (Shakespeare) *References:* Job 23:10; Heb. 12:11; 1 Peter 1:7.
15. Affliction brings out the glory of a Christian's faith, as lightning shines brighter in the depths of night than in the glare of day. (Guthrie) *References:* Eccl. 7:2–3; Is. 48:10; Rom. 8:18.
16. In *The Great Texts of the Bible* James Hastings relates the story of Captain Allan Gardiner, who with three other men had gone to Tierra del Fuego to preach the Gospel. When winter was over, another ship touched the bleak shores and found the remains of all at the entrance of a cave. They had died of hunger, Gardiner being the last. Here were devout men filled with the desire to make known the love of Jesus to the miserable Fuegians, and they starved to death. But Gardiner's

faith never failed him. At the entrance of the cave he had painted the words: "My soul trusts still upon God." His daybook contained his last words: "I know not how to thank God for His marvelous loving-kindness." Had he died in vain? The sacrifices of this saintly hero brought about the Patagonian Mission, which Christianized these islands. *References:* Ps. 32:10; 37:5; 56; 57; 102; Hab. 3:17–18; 2 Cor. 6:10; 1 Peter 4:12–13.

17. In 1857, at the outbreak of the Sepoy Rebellion in India, the Hindus attempted to slaughter as many Englishmen as they could, especially officers and their families. One such officer and his wife had gone to a neighboring town, not knowing that any danger was threatening. They left their little daughter at home in the care of a native nurse, of whom the girl was very fond. When the uprising began, Ellen was in mortal danger in spite of her tender years, for she had a white skin and was an officer's child. But her father's countrymen did not forget her nor forsake her. One of them galloped to her home, snatched her from her dark-skinned nurse, and remounted his horse, holding little Ellen before him.

By this time shouting, frenzied people filled the street. They attempted to stop the horse and kill both the rider and the child. But the man drew his saber and fought them every foot of the way, all the time holding the child firmly with his left arm. Naturally, she was exceedingly frightened by all the noise and confusion. She kicked and struggled and cried. Several times she almost slipped from his arms. This multiplied the difficulties of his task enormously, but at last he won through and after a long, hard ride delivered his little charge to her mother.

Who can picture the frantic joy of the parents to have their little one safe with them? Their gratitude knew no bounds. But it was entirely different as far as their daughter was concerned. She felt deep resentment toward her rescuer. He had held her so roughly; he had shaken her so much while riding; he had refused to let her go back to her nurse. How could such a rude man be considered a friend and a benefactor? Under no circumstances could she be induced to kiss him or even thank him.

What was beyond the understanding of this child is clear and plain to *you* is it not? As Ellen grew older, she must often have been ashamed of her childish ignorance for failing to recognize that the officer risked his life for the sake of her safety and that the bumps and jolts she received during the wild ride were unavoidable factors in effecting her rescue. But at the time she judged by outward appearances and actually believed that the rider was mean to her and angry with her. *References:* Ps. 141:5; Prov. 3:11–12; Eccl. 7:5; Luke 17:3; Heb. 12:5; Rev. 3:19 (resenting our afflictions). Deut. 8:5; Ps. 66:8–12; 94:12–15; Prov. 3:11–12; 2 Cor. 4:17; Heb. 12:11; 1 Peter 1:6–7 (necessity of trials).

18. Lap dogs never get powerful; they are pampered too much. The wolf that has to run fast to get a meal, that has to fight hard to stay alive, gets real strong.

That's the way it is with people, too. History is full of the stories of people and of nations who failed because life became too easy. The great Roman Empire, which at one time dominated practically all the civilized world, fell when the people began to want nothing but bread and games. And then the barbarians swept down from the north and took over. Through trials and troubles God teaches endurance, and we need endurance in our spiritual life. *References:* Job 23:10; Ps. 17:3; 66:10;

Zech. 13:9; Mal. 3:3; Heb. 12:11; 1 Peter 1:7; 4:12.

19. Some years ago in an African mine the most magnificent diamond in the world's history was found. It was presented to the king of England to blaze in his crown of state. The king sent it to Amsterdam to be cut. It was in the hands of an expert lapidary. He took the gem, cut a notch in it, and with a hard blow split the superb jewel in twain. What recklessness! But nay, it was the climax of the lapidary skill. . . . So God sometimes lets a stinging blow fall on a Christian's life. The blow seems to be an appalling mistake. But it is not. God is the most skilled lapidary in the universe. He knows just how to deal with the Christians that some day may blaze in His diadem. (McConkey) *References:* Ps. 51:8; Rom. 8:28; 2 Cor. 4:17; 12:7–9; 1 Peter 1:3–7; 4:12–13; Rev. 2:10.

20. The early Christians counted suffering for Christ not as a burden or misfortune but as a great honor, a blessing, for in their suffering they could bear witness to their faith. Tacitus, a Roman historian, wrote of the early Christian martyrs: "Mockery of every sort was added to their deaths." Covered with skins of beasts, they were torn by dogs and perished or were nailed to crosses or were doomed to the flames and burned to serve as nightly illumination when daylight had expired. Nero offered his gardens for the spectacle. We are told that the martyrs went rejoicing to their deaths, as if they were going to a marriage feast. They bathed their hands in the blaze kindled for them and shouted with gladness. They marched into the arena as if marching into heaven. When Ignatius, an elderly martyr, was about to die for his faith in A.D. 110, he cried out, "Nearer the sword, then nearer to God. In company with wild beasts, in company with

God." Now we are not trying to be macabre, nor are we saying anyone should seek an adventuresome death. Rather, we are saying that the Christian life often involves suffering. *References:* Matt. 16:21–28; Mark 8:31–38; Luke 9:22–25; 1 Peter 2:19–21.

21. In a German picture gallery is a painting called "Cloudland." It hangs at the end of a long hall, and at first sight it looks like a daub of confused color, without design. As you approach it, the picture begins to take shape; it proves to be a mass of little angel faces.

One is reminded of the lines in Cowper's famous hymn:

> Ye fearful saints, fresh courage take,
> The clouds ye so much dread
> Are big with mercy and shall break
> In blessings on your head.

References: Job 5:17; 23:10; Eccl. 7:2–6; Zech. 13:9; Rom. 8:18; 2 Cor. 4:17; Heb. 12:11; 1 Peter 1:6–9.

22. In 1519, when Prince Frederick the Wise, one of Luther's protectors, was seriously ill, Luther wrote a little book for him, titled *Fourteen Consolations*. In addition to many other instructions and words of comfort, Luther told Prince Frederick, "Thus it is good for us always to be oppressed with some trouble, lest in our weakness we succumb to the offenses of the world and fall into sin." Without struggle there is no victory. His conflict with the evil influence of the Sodomites helped Lot, for example, make progress in his righteousness. So while trouble usually brings tension, it can for Christians also be the context for triumph. *References:* Gen. 19:1–22; Job 23:10; Ps. 119:67; Mal. 3:3; 2 Cor. 4:17; 2 Tim. 2:9–12; Heb. 12:11; 1 Peter 1:6–7.

23. Many have discovered that suffering is the avenue to nobler qualities and higher achievement. Cornelius

Ryan, author of the best selling books *The Longest Day, The Last Battle,* and *A Bridge Too Far,* which chronicled the fighting in Europe during World War II, collaborated with his wife in writing his last book, *A Private Battle.* In it they described his personal four-and-one-half-year struggle with cancer during which he finished *A Bridge Too Far.* Hope, alternating with despair, teased cruelly; pain became a constant companion; incontinence stripped away dignity; and increasing weakness gave birth to helplessness and dependence. Yet in the midst of this ordeal, without in any way minimizing its severity or becoming unrealistically Pollyannaish, Ryan observed, "No one seems to realize that pain makes the mind sharper. Ironically, I think I am writing better with cancer than I did without it." In reflecting on the impact the disease had on their marriage, his wife wrote, "I think I loved my husband in his years of sickness more than at any other time in our marriage. The way he handled his illness, the fierce courage with which he fought it, submerged my sexual desires as my pride in him increased." *References:* Is. 40:31; 41:10; 2 Cor. 12:9–10; Heb. 12:11.

Related illustrations: 12, 13, 164, 258, 279, 284, 319, 523, 536, 537, 790, 812, 936.

Aimlessness

24. There is a parable of life in the story of the farmer whose dog followed him to town one day. As he hitched his horse and buggy to a post in front of the country store, the storekeeper, seeing the panting dog, chided the farmer for making the dog run all the way while he rode. The farmer responded, "That dog is not tired from following me to town. What tired him was all his foolish zigzagging. There was not an open gate, a hole in the fence, or a tree stump that he did not explore. He is tired from all his zig-zagging." That's the way many people live. They zigzag from one diversion to another, from one pleasure to another, from one excitement to another. They wear themselves out but really don't know where they are going. They just chase everything that appears. Robert Burns, the famous poet, confessed late in life, "The misfortune of my life was want of aim." *References:* 1 Kings 20:39–40; Eccl. 1:14; 2:11; 4:8; Is. 55:2; Luke 15:14; John 6:27.

25. In chapter 37 of Gibbon's *Decline and Fall of the Roman Empire* is a description of the "Origin, Progress, and Effects of Monastic Life." When you read that, you are haunted by the weird, fantastic spectacle of men suddenly getting the idea that life would be happiest when one does nothing. They swarmed out into the desert and lived solitary lives. They took vows of perpetual silence and ceased to speak. They ate the most disgusting foods. They lived the lives of wild beasts. "Even sleep," says Gibbon, "the last refuge of the unhappy, was rigorously measured; the vacant hours rolled heavily on without business and without pleasure; and before the close of each day the tedious progress of the sun was repeatedly accursed." We can understand that this fad didn't last long and that not many were led to indulge in it. Where there is no real purpose in life, where nothing is achieved, there cannot be even the semblance of happiness. *References:* Eccl. 9:10; John 4:34; Phil. 3:7–8; 2 Thess. 3:10–13; Heb. 12:2–3; 1 Peter 4:7–11.

Related illustration: 773.

Ambassadors for Christ

26. When the president of the United States sends out an ambassador, that person represents the President of our country wherever he or she goes. If the president should slight the ambassador of a European country, that would be regarded as a slight to the country, its leaders and its people. Even so, when the ambassadors of Christ are heard, Christ Himself is heard, and when these are despised and slighted, Jesus looks on this as a slight to Himself and the Father in heaven, who authenticated Him to preach and to send out preachers in His name. *References:* Matt. 10:40; 28:18–20; Luke 10:16; John 20:21; 2 Cor. 5:20.

Ambition

See also **Covetousness, Greed**

27. Though the chimney is the highest part of the house, it is not the cleanest or the sweetest part. *References:* 2 Sam. 15:1–4; Matt. 23:12; Rev. 3:17.

28. There is a story about Alexander the Great that he conquered all the known world of his day and then sat down and wept; he was sorry because he had no more to conquer. *References:* Prov. 1:19; 15:27; 22:16; Eccl. 5:10; Hab. 2:9–10; 1 Tim. 6:6–10; 2 Peter 2:15.

29. Cineas, when dissuading Pyrrhus from undertaking a war against the Romans, said, "Sir, when you have conquered them, what will you do next?" — "Then Sicily is near at hand and easy to master." — "And what when you have conquered Sicily?" — "Then we will pass over to Africa and take Carthage, which cannot long withstand us." — "When these are conquered, what will be your next attempt?" — "Then," said Pyrrhus, "we will fall in on Greece and Macedon and recover what we have lost there." — "Well, when all are subdued, what fruit do you expect from all your victories?" — "Then," said he, "we will sit down and enjoy our-

selves." — "Sir," replied Cineas, "may we not do it now? Have you not already a kingdom of your own? And he that cannot enjoy himself with a kingdom cannot with the whole world." (Foster) *References:* Eccl. 2:1–11; 4:8; 5:10; 6:7; Is. 55:2; Matt. 16:26; Luke 15:14.

30. Take perhaps the four greatest rulers that ever sat on a throne. Alexander, when he had so completely subdued the nations that he wept because there were no more to conquer, set fire to a city and died in a scene of debauch. Hannibal, who filled three bushels with the gold rings taken from the slaughtered knights, died by poison administered by his own hand, unwept and unknown in a foreign land. Caesar, having conquered eight hundred cities and dyed his garments with the blood of one million of his foes, was stabbed by his best friends in the same place that had been the scene of his greatest triumph. Napoleon, after being the scourge of Europe and the desolator of his country, died in banishment, conquered and a captive. (Bowes) *References:* Gen. 11:4–9; 2 Sam. 15:1–6; Ps. 127:1–2; Eccl. 2:1–11; Is. 14:12–15; Obad. 4; Matt. 23:12.

Related illustration: 839.

America

31. Harold Bosley says, "America is today running on the momentum of a godly ancestry. When the momentum runs down, God help America." *References:* Is. 1:2–9; Jer. 2:11–13; 5:15–19.

32. Lord Macaulay, the brilliant historian, made this prophecy about America: "Your republic will be pillaged and destroyed just as ancient Greece and Rome . . . but the one to destroy your nation will be the citizens of your own country, the products of your own civilization." *References:*

Prov. 14:34; Jer. 2:11–13; Matt. 23:37–39.

33. From his field camp at White Plains, Aug. 20, 1778, George Washington wrote: "The hand of Providence has been so conspicuous in all this, that he must be worse than an infidel that lacks faith, and more than wicked, that has not gratitude enough to acknowledge his obligations." At another time he said: "There never was a people who had more reason to acknowledge a divine interposition in their affairs than those of the United States, and I should be pained to believe that they have forgotten that agency, which was so often manifested during our revolution, or that they failed to consider the omnipotence of that God, who is alone able to protect them." *References:* Ex. 19:4–6; Deut. 6:10–12; 8:7–14; 32:15; Prov. 30:8–9; Luke 12:16–21.

Related illustrations: 787, 835.

Angels (Ministering Spirits)
34. In *The Life of Florence Nightingale,* we find the angel nurse of the Crimea and the mother of modern nursing asking, "Who are the ministering angels?" She answers: "The angels are not they who go about scattering flowers; any naughty child would like to do that. The ministering angels are they who, like nurse or ward maid, do disgusting work, removing injury to health or obstacles to recovery, emptying slops, washing patients, and numerous other menial and often distasteful tasks, for all of which they receive no thanks. These are the angels." *References:* Mark 1:13; Acts 12:7; 27:23; Heb. 1:14 (ministering angels). Matt. 10:42; John 13:4–17; Acts 18:24; 2 Cor. 8:1–5 (humble service).

Related illustration: 622.

Anger
35. Divine Anger. As wet wood, though it be long in burning, yet will burn faster at the last, so the anger of God, although it be long in coming, yet will come the fiercer at the end. (Cawdray) *References:* Nah. 1:3–6; 2 Peter 3:8–10.

36. Human Anger. Anger is a poor gun. It has frequently burst at the breech and killed its holder. (M. Henry) *References:* Prov. 27:3; Eccl. 7:9; Matt. 5:22.

Ascension of Christ
37. Christ's ascension meant triumph and joy for His disciples. As a rule the departure of a beloved leader brings sorrow and grief to his followers. We think of Socrates, the great philosopher, when he was drinking the poisonous hemlock, how he tried in vain to banish the despair of his sorrowful followers. Most of us remember vividly Nov. 22, 1963, when President John F. Kennedy was assassinated. We remember particularly the bleakness and blackness of it all, the sorrow and sadness that filled our land.

The departure of Jesus Christ, however, meant triumph and joy to His followers. *References:* Matt. 28:16–20; Mark 16:19–20; Luke 24:50–53; John 16:6–7; Acts 1:6–14; Eph. 1:19–23; Heb. 4:14–16.

Assurance of Salvation
38. So many church people have the idea that you cannot really be sure of this. You ask them, "Are you a Christian?" and they answer, "I hope so. . . . I suppose I am." And, friend, that is not proper. If a man asks you, "Are you an American?" it does not occur to you to say, "I hope I am." No! You know that you are an American. *References:* 1 Thess. 1:4–6; Heb. 10:22–23; 1 John 3:1–3, 19–21; 4:13.

Atheism
See also **Infidels**

39. Plato says of atheism: "Atheism is a disease of the soul before it becomes an error of the understanding." *References:* Job 24:13; Ps. 10:4; 14:1; 36:1–4; 73:3–12; 2 Tim. 3:1–7; 1 Peter 3:3.

40. It is usually found that a freethinker is not a man who thinks freely but a man who is free from thinking. (Colton) *References:* Eccl. 10:3; Rom. 1:22; 2 Tim. 3:7–9.

41. An atheist will try to make proselytes even to a system so fatherless, so forlorn, and so gloomy as his. And he will try it on the same principle that causes children to cry at night for a bedfellow—he is afraid to be alone in the dark. (Colton) *References:* Ps. 10:4–11; Matt. 24:11; Acts 20:29–30.

42. To be an atheist requires an infinitely greater measure of faith than to receive all the great truths that atheism would deny. (Addison) *References:* Ps. 10:4–11; 14:1; Jer. 5:12.

43. When Dr. Johnson was asked why so many literary men were infidels, he replied, "Because they are ignorant of the Bible." *References:* Ps. 10:4; Matt. 22:29; Eph. 4:17–18.

44. A young woman walked into a pastor's office and said, "I'm an atheist." The pastor said, "Well, that's very interesting. Tell me what kind of God you don't believe in." And for an hour she told him. When the hour was over, the pastor said: "You know, I think I must be an atheist, too, because I don't believe in that God either!" Then he proceeded to tell her what kind of God we have—a God who is discoverable and contemporary, a God who reveals Himself and comes to us and lives in our lives if we but use the means of grace, the "tools," the channel by which He comes. *References:* Judg. 2:10; Job 21:14; Jer. 4:22; John 1:10; 8:19; 15:21: Acts 17:23; Rom. 1:28.

45. Atheism's Moral Bankruptcy. What has atheism and militant unbelief ever done for the world? Has it sent missionaries to the leper-ridden areas of India, China, or Africa? Has it built orphanages for abandoned children or homes for the aged poor? Has it given comfort and hope to the disconsolate and dying? Has it not added to human misery by trying to take from people their most priceless possession (i.e., Christ)? *References:* Ps. 10:4–11; 14:1–4; 36:1–4; 53:1–3; 73:6–11: 2 Peter 3:3–7; 1 John 2:22.

46. Atheists who did not live up to their convictions. There have been avowed atheists. Few have been consistent in their atheism. John Quincy Adams, the sixth president of the United States, saw the inconsistency of atheism in his day, and in a letter to Thomas Jefferson he wrote this review of the atheists who had been popular in his age: "Bolingbroke said his philosophy was not sufficient to support him in his last hours. D'Alembert said, 'Happy are they who have courage; but I have none.' Voltaire, the greatest genius of them all, behaved like the greatest coward of them all at his death." *References:* Ps. 10:4; 14:1; 53:1; 36:1–2.

Related illustrations: 53, 59, 649.

Attentiveness

47. The story of the youth at Troas who fell asleep in church has long been a favorite not only of those of us who still sometimes fall asleep in church but also of those of us who try not to. The old Pilgrims in Massachusetts used to hire a deacon to keep the congregation awake. He tickled the women under the chins with a feather. The men were rapped a sharper touch on the noggin with a pole. Fortunately we no longer encourage three-hour sermons, perhaps two or three in a single day. These taxed not only the ability of the worshiper to stay awake but also the ability of the preacher to say something worthwhile. *References:* Prov. 6:9–10; 20:13; 23:21; Matt. 26:36–45; Acts 20:7–12.

B

Backbiters

48. Writes Henry van Dyke: "Cannibalism is dying out among barbarous tribes, but it still survives among the most highly civilized peoples. . . . If you wish to serve up somebody's character at a social entertainment or pick the bones of somebody's reputation in a quiet corner, you'll find ready guests and almost incredible appetites." And we might add that among those guests you may find even Christians. *References:* Ex. 20:13; Ps. 15:1–3; 101:5; 2 Cor. 12:20; Eph. 4:31; Titus 3:2; James 4:11.

49. What does a buzzard find as it circles the countryside? A squirrel that has been run over on the highway or a dead rabbit under a bush. The land may be green with dew and pleasant with the song of birds. But the buzzard misses all these things because it is looking for something rotten. Some buzzards are human. They're always looking for something rotten to talk about—in the name of truth, mind you! *References:* Ex. 20:16; 2 Sam. 15:1–6; Ps. 15; Prov. 3:2–3; 2 Thess. 3:11; 1 Tim. 5:13; Titus 3:2; James 3:6; 4:11.

Backsliders

50. The blackest shadows are cast by the brightest light; the angel that falls becomes a devil. Sinning against light and conscience, the children of God, on becoming wicked, become far worse than others. (Guthrie) *References:* Luke 11:24–26; 2 Peter 2:20.

51. Children who forget their baptismal vows are doing what Noah's raven did; when that raven found a carcass, it forgot the ark. (Caspari) *References:* Gal. 4:9–11; Col. 2:10–22.

52. Life is no level plane but a steep incline on which there is no standing still; if you try to stand still, down you go. Either up or down must be the motion. If you are not more of a Christian than you were a year ago, you are less. (MacLaren) *References:* 1 Cor. 10:12; 2 Peter 1:5–6; Rev. 2:5.

53. Darwin, the great naturalist, is reported to have said toward the close of his life that he was completely untouched by the Gospel of the cross. He says, "When I, as a youth, went down into the Brazilian forests and saw the grandeur of those trees, I would say to myself, How wonderful is God! and I believed in the greatness and goodness of my Lord. But years after, when I returned to these same forests, I was completely unmoved. I no longer believed in God." So the last state of that man becomes worse spiritually. *References:* Matt. 12:43–45; 24:12; Luke 9:62; 11:24–26; 2 Tim. 4:10; Heb. 10:38; 2 Peter 2:20.

Related illustrations: 172, 766, 767, 794.

Baptism

54. Value It Highly. A great king of France received his crown at the city of Rheims, and it was a custom in those days that kings would call themselves after the city where they received their crown. But this king called himself Louis of Poitiers, because he was baptized there. We, too, should value our baptism highly because it is something important to us. *References:* Mark 16:16; John 3:3–6; Acts 2:38; 8:36; 22:16; Rom. 6:3–11; 1 Cor. 12:13; Gal. 3:27; Col. 2:12.

55. Belonging to Jesus. Years ago, in the wide open spaces of the West, a little girl was baptized. The next day at school her friends asked her why. She said, "I was a little maverick out on the prairie. When I was baptized, the Jesus mark was put on me, and now everyone knows that I belong to Jesus." The word *maverick* was originally a man's name. Samuel Maverick was a Texas cattleman who for some reason did not brand his cattle. Because of that, an unbranded animal, especially a lost calf, came to be known as a maverick, and such a maverick could then become the legal property of anybody who would catch and brand it.

We are *all* spiritual mavericks as we come on this human scene. We are lost as far as God is concerned, straying outside the boundaries of His ranch, far from the Father's house and home. But in His seeking love and mighty Word, the Spirit finds us and creates and implants within us the precious life that we call faith. . . . When the Spirit has branded us with this mark of faith, we are no longer mavericks but children in the family and household of God. *References:* Acts 10:44–48; 1 Cor. 12:13; Gal. 3:26–27; Col. 2:11–13; 1 Peter 2:10.

Related illustration: 51.

Bible
56. While the Bible has shallows through which a child may wade on its way to heaven, it has deep, dark, unfathomed pools that no eye can penetrate where the first step takes a giant beyond his depth. (Guthrie) *References:* Is. 2:3; Matt. 11:25; 22:29; John 5:39; Rom. 15:4; 2 Tim. 3:15–17.

57. "I thoroughly believe in a university education for both men and women," said Dr. William Lyon Phelps of Yale University, "but I believe a knowledge of the Bible without a college course is more valuable than a college course without the Bible. Every one who has a thorough knowledge of the Bible may truly be called educated, and no other learning or culture, no matter how extensive or elegant, can form a proper substitute." *References:* Ps. 19:7–11; Is. 34:16; 2 Tim. 3:15–17.

58. Sir Walter Scott one day asked his son, "Bring me the Book." His son asked him which book he meant. He answered, "There is only one." *References:* Ps. 119:105; 1 Peter 1:25; 1 John 5:13.

59. One evidence of the value of the Bible is the character of those who oppose it. (Luther) *References:* Ps. 50:16–19; Is. 5:18–24; Jer. 8:8–10.

60. When Chief Justice Jay was dying and was asked if he had any farewell address to leave to his children, he replied, "They have the Bible." *References:* Luke 16:27–31; Rom. 15:4; 2 Tim. 3:15–17.

61. When unbelieving Thomas Paine showed Benjamin Franklin the manuscript of *The Age of Reason,* Franklin advised him not to publish it, saying, "The world is bad enough with the Bible; what would it be without it!" *References:* Amos 2:4; Acts 13:27; Rom. 15:4; Heb. 4:6, 12.

62. We search the world for truth; we cull
The good, the pure, the beautiful,
From graven stone and written scroll
And all old flower fields of the soul;
And, weary seekers of the best,

We come back laden from our quest,
To find that all the sages said
Is in the Book our mothers read.
—John Greenleaf Whittier, in
Miriam.

References: Ps. 19:8; 119:105, 130;
Is. 40:8; John 5:39; 2 Tim. 3:15–17; 2
Peter 1:19.

63. The artist must go out into God's
nature to see colors as God made them.
Otherwise his paintings will become
murky. As he mixes his colors in the
studio, he finally loses the sense of true
green, true red, true blue. So he must
go out into the open spaces and see the
true colors as God made them. You and
I can become morally colorblind. We
need the Word to set us straight, to
guide us into noble and God-pleasing
living. *References:* Ps. 19:8; 119:9,
105; Prov. 6:23; John 17:17; Rom. 7:7;
Col. 3:16; 1 Peter 1:22.

64. Denied by the Ungodly. Holy
Scripture fares no better than Christ did
during His earthly sojourn. Since
Christ was "found in fashion as a
man," the Jewish public regarded Him
as a mere man, like John the Baptist,
Elijah, Jeremiah, or one of the prophets. People make the same mistake
where the written Word is concerned.
Since the Bible is written in ordinary
human language, it is not held to be
God's Word but is placed into one class
with human books and is even criticized by people. (F. Pieper) *References:* 2 Chron. 36:16; Ps. 50:16–17;
Is. 5:24; Jer. 6:10; Zech. 7:12; Matt.
15:1–9; Mark 7:5–13.

65. When the Americans recaptured
the island of Attu in the Aleutians, they
found a dead Japanese boy with a New
Testament inscribed by his father on
the flyleaf: "Son, you will probably
not come back. But if you will read
this book and heed its teachings, you
will live forever." *References:* Deut.

8:3; John 5:39; Rom. 1:16; Eph. 6:17;
1 John 5:13.

66. The captain of a large ship was a
skeptic, a man who doubted the existence of heaven, the person of Christ,
and many other doctrines of the Bible.
After his retirement from active duty,
he spent his declining years in a soldier's home. One day the chaplain,
who was deeply concerned about this
man's soul, surprised him with a challenge. Handing him a New Testament
and a red pencil, he asked the man to
mark everything that he could not believe. Periodically, the chaplain would
visit the man and would ask him if he
had found anything to mark. The man
never replied, only smiled. One morning the chaplain was informed that the
captain had died suddenly during the
night. The chaplain hurried to his room
and found the Bible clutched in his
hand as he lay dead on his bed. The
chaplain paged through the New Testament looking for red marks and found
none. Turning to John 3:16, he noted
that the man had written in red ink on
the margin: "I have cast my anchor in
a safe harbor; I am at peace, thank
God." Every child of God who rests
his whole weight on Christ has cast anchor in a safe harbor. *References:* John
3:16; 14:27; 16:33; Rom. 5:1; Phil.
4:7; Col. 1:20.

67. Lord Bacon tells us of a bishop
who used to bathe regularly twice every day and, on being asked why he
bathed that often, replied, "Because I
cannot conveniently do it three times."
If those who love the Scriptures were
asked why they read the Bible so often,
they might honestly reply, "Because
we cannot find time to read them of-
tener." (*Biblical Illustrator*) *References:* Deut. 11:18–20; Job 23:12; Ps.
1:1–3; 19:7–10; 119; Jer. 15:16; 2 Tim.
3:16–17; 1 Peter 2:2.

68. Difficult Passages. An old man

once said, "For a long period I puzzled myself about the difficulties of Scripture, until at last I came to the resolution that reading the Bible was like eating fish. When I find a difficulty I lay it aside and call it a bone. Why should I choke on the bone when there is so much nutritious meat for me? Some day perhaps I may find that even the bone may afford me nourishment." (Spurgeon) *References:* Ps. 119:169–70; Prov. 2:1–5; Rom. 15:4; James 1:5.

69. A young woman who purchased a book and read a few pages laid it aside as not interesting. But some time later she became acquainted with the author. Tender friendship sprang up, which ripened into love and betrothal. Then the book was no longer dull. Every sentence had a charm for her heart. Love was the interpreter.

Why is the Bible uninteresting and even distasteful to the natural human heart? Because it knows not the Author. But when by the Spirit of God the heart learns to know and love Him who gave the Bible and who reveals Himself in the Scriptures, then the pages of this Book become most interesting, and every sentence is interpreted by the Spirit of love. (W. G. Polack) *References:* John 14:15–23; 16:13–15; 1 Cor. 2:9–16.

70. Authority of the Word. To reassert vigorously the authority of the Word, Luther stated in the Leipzig Debate of 1519: "A simple layman armed with Scripture is to be believed above a pope or a council without it. As for the pope's decretal on indulgences, I say that neither the church nor the pope can establish articles of faith. These must come from the Scriptures." *References:* Deut. 4:2; 12:32; Prov. 30:6; Luke 21:33; Acts 17:11: Eph. 6:17; Heb. 4:12; Rev. 22:19.

71. The Book That Leads to Wisdom. A cartoon by a well-known artist of a large metropolitan newspaper depicts two students at their desks. One of the young men is occupied with a veritable mountain of books labeled "Books to prepare for life." The other youth is engrossed in but one Book, tagged "The Book to prepare for eternal life." And this is the thought-provoking caption of the cartoon: "Student, how wise are you?" *References:* Deut. 17:19; Ps. 19:8; Prov. 4:1–13; Hos. 14:9; Matt. 7:24; Rom. 15:4; 1 Cor. 2:1–10; 2 Tim. 3:15.

72. The Bible's Literary Attestation. Our present printed Bibles are based on older, hand-copied manuscripts. There are still a great many of these ancient Bible manuscripts in existence. Scattered throughout the libraries of the world are about 1,500 Old Testament manuscripts in Hebrew. Likewise about 4,000 New Testament manuscripts are in careful preservation. There are thousands of copies even of Jerome's Latin translation, one of the earliest made. Such providential preservation cannot be claimed for any human book.

You have probably heard of such ancient writers as Thucydides, Herodotus, Pindar, Euripides, and Aristotle. Hardly a copy of their writings exists that was produced less than 1,600 years after their death. One or two copies made more than a thousand years after death of these writers are accepted by scholars as evidence of their genuineness. We have original quotations of Scripture on first- and second-century documents. We have actual manuscripts written in A.D. 250 and 316. If we compare the dearth of classical manuscripts with the overwhelming wealth of Biblical manuscripts, we must say that he who doubts the truthfulness of the Bible despite such enormous evidence and yet accepts the classics as true and unimpeachable on such slight evidence is little less than foolish. *References:* Is. 2:3; 40:8; Matt. 24:35; Luke 21:33; Rom. 15:4; 2 Tim. 3:16; 1 Peter 1:25; 2 Peter 1:21.

73. How to Study the Bible. Luther said that he studied the Bible the way he gathered apples. First, he shook the whole tree, that the ripest might fall. Then he climbed the tree and shook each limb, and when he had shaken each limb, he shook each branch, and after each branch every twig, and then he looked under each leaf. Let us search the Bible as a whole, shake the whole tree, read it as rapidly as we would any other book; then shake every limb, studying book after book. Then shake every branch, giving attention to the chapters (when they do not break the sense). Then shake every twig by careful study of the paragraphs and sentences, and you will be rewarded if you will look under every leaf by searching the meaning of the words. (Selected) *References:* Ps. 119:105; Is. 28:9; 1 Cor. 14:20; 2 Tim. 2:15; 3:14–17; Heb. 5:12–14; 1 Peter 2:2; 2 Peter 3:18.

74. Ignorance of God's Word. During the Middle Ages before the Reformation, ignorance and superstition abounded within the visible church. Religion had been reduced to mere formalism in many quarters. It's true, great cathedrals were built, and mighty crusades were launched in Europe to regain possession of the Holy Land, but the hearts of most of the people were far from God. A self-seeking and indolent priesthood neglected the spiritual care of their parishes. The Bible had become practically an unknown book to many thousands in those dark days. Even the clergy knew little of it and often neglected to urge its study.

It is a tragedy today that the Bible is a lost book to millions. It is true that it is still the most widely distributed book in the world and reckoned as the best seller year after year. Yet while there may be more Bibles in the homes, few take the time to read the Bible and to heed its contents. *References:* Ps. 50:17; Is. 5:24; Jer. 6:10; Matt. 22:29; Mark 7:13; Acts 13:27; 2 Cor. 3:15.

75. Eternal Word. Addressing the clergy gathered at the Diet of Augsburg in 1530, Luther wrote, "God's Word is more ancient than you and will also be newer and more modern than either we or you, since it is eternal. So it shall rule and change all things, both old and new, and itself shall be neither ruled nor changed by anything, whether new or old." *References:* Ps. 119:89; Is. 40:8; Matt. 5:18; 24:35; Heb. 12:25–28; 1 Peter 1:25.

76. Our Spiritual Lifeline. When Admiral Byrd, exploring Little America many years ago, walked away from his camp during the long dark nights down there, he would set out stakes every few yards as he walked so he would be able to find his way back to his hut. This line of stakes became his lifeline back to safety. Had he lost contact with the stakes, he would have lost his life. In a sense the Bible is a lifeline like that—not because it sets down rules to show us how to live, but because it leads us to know God in Jesus Christ. *References:* Ps. 119:105, 130; John 5:39; Rom. 1:16; 15:4; 2 Peter 1:19; 1 John 5:13.

77. The Word's Power to Save. Dr. E. V. Rieu was a distinguished British scholar, well known for his translations of the works of Homer into English. The publisher of the Penguin Classics asked him to try his hand at the gospels. At the age of 60, having been a lifelong agnostic, Rieu agreed to try it. At that time his son said, "It will be interesting to see what father makes of the four gospels. It will be even more interesting to see what the four gospels make of father.'' Within a year Dr. Rieu was converted to Christianity. He observed, ''I got the deepest feeling that the whole material was extraordinarily alive. My work changed me. I came to the conclusion that these words bear the seal of the Son of Man and God'' (Quoted by E. M. Blaiklock, ''More and More Scripture Lives!'' *Christianity Today*, 17 [Sept. 28, 1973]: 18–19) *References:* Jer. 23:29: Ezek. 37:7; Luke 4:32; 24:45–47; John 6:63, 68; Rom. 1:16; Eph. 6:17; Heb. 4:12.

Related illustrations: 92, 103, 186, 465, 620, 775, 813, 962, 1016.

Blessings

78. God the Source of. Samuel Morse, an American painter turned inventor, tapped out a message on a new device called the telegraph in the capitol of the United States. The message was received in Baltimore, and these were the words chosen on that auspicious occasion: ''What hath God wrought!'' Without boasting about his own accomplishments, with deep humility, with a recognition that he was only putting God's laws to work, he wired the words that a hundred years later were sent around the world: ''What hath God wrought!'' *References:* Neh. 9:6; Ps. 31:19; 68:19; 107; John 3:27; Acts 14:15; 2 Cor. 3:5; 1 Peter 5:7.

79. Innumerable. Mark Guy Pearce writes, ''I was walking along one winter night, hurrying toward home with my little maiden at my side. Said she, 'Father, I am going to count the stars.' 'Very well,' said I. 'Go ahead.' By and by I heard her counting: 'Two hundred and twenty-three, two hundred and twenty-four, two hundred and twenty-five. . . Oh, dear,' she said, 'I had no idea there were so many.' Ah, dear friends, I sometimes say in my soul,

'Now, Master, I am going to count all Thy benefits.' I am like the little maiden. Soon my heart sighs—sighs not with sorrow but burdened with such goodness, and I say within myself, 'Ah! I had no idea that they were so many.' '' *References:* Lev. 26:3–13; Deut. 28:2–6; Ps. 23:5; 65:9; 68:19; 103:1–5; 116:12.

80. Blessed Through Adversity. ''God does not give us everything we want, but He does fulfill His promise, i.e., He still remains Lord of the earth and still preserves His church, constantly renewing our faith and not laying on us more than we can bear, gladdening us with His nearness and help.'' Thus wrote Dietrich Bonhoeffer to a friend on August 10, 1944, from a prison cell. One of the heroes of the faith during the last war, Dietrich Bonhoeffer—Lutheran pastor, teacher, lecturer, and writer, and a leader of the resistance movement against Hitler—was arrested and imprisoned on April 5, 1943, and hanged at Flossenburg on April 9, 1945. *References:* Ps. 34:19–20; 50:14–15; Is. 43:1–2; Rom. 8:18–39; 2 Cor. 4:17; 12:7–10; 1 Peter 4:12–13; Rev. 7:13–14.

Related illustration: 420.

Blindness
See also **Faultfinding**

81. Paul had enjoyed physical sight, but he had been soul-blind. At his conversion he was stricken physically blind that he might bend his mind on spiritual light and receive soul sight. Then he was given back his sight in order that he might go out and bring saving sight to sinners everywhere.

A man lost his sight but in this adversity found his Savior. One day a friend expressed his sympathy to him. But the blind man said, ''Do not pity me; I am fortunate. If I still had my eyesight, I might be blind yet. Now that I have become blind, I have learned to see. I could never see Jesus before, and I was not interested in Him. But I see Him now, and I am much happier today than I was before I became blind.''

Later an operation restored the man's sight. He said, "May God protect and keep me, so that the things these eyes now see may never again lead me away from the light my inward sight beholds!'' *References:* Matt. 5:29; 15:14; John 9:25, 39–41; Acts 9:1–22; 2 Cor. 4:4.

Related illustrations: 341, 342.

Brotherhood

See also **Love, Human**

82. Heathen people who observed the brotherly love of Christians toward one another marveled at what they saw and cried out, "Behold, how they love one another!'' The renowned Roman lawyer Marcus Minucius Felix, who lived in the second century, became a true Christian, and he testified of the early Christians: "They loved one another, even before knowing one another (personally).'' Of course, many heathen people remained what they were and scoffed at Christianity. For example, Lucian, who also lived in the second century, and sneeringly wrote of them: "Their Master (Jesus Christ) has made them believe that they are all brethren.'' *References:* John 13:34–35; 15:12; Gal. 6:1–10; 1 Thess. 3:12; Heb. 13:1–2; 1 Peter 1:22; 1 John 4:7–11.

Related illustration: 611.

Burdens

83. Released at the Cross. In *The Pilgrim's Progress* John Bunyan depicts the striking scene of a Christian fleeing from the world with a large bundle resting on his shoulders. He arrives at a place somewhat elevated above the surrounding area. On that hill there stands a cross, and below the hill there is a grave. As the man comes to the top of the hill with his heavy burden, the load is suddenly released from his shoulders, drops to the ground, rolls down the hill, and disappears into the empty grave. *References:* Is. 53:4; Matt. 6:31–33; 8:17; 11:28–30; Rom. 5:6; 8:32; 2 Cor. 5:4.

84. Christ's Yoke Not a Burden. You have watched a kite fly in the wind. Would you say the string that holds it is burdensome and is a heavy yoke? No, it is there to control the kite. The kite will not fly unless it is in partnership with the string. The string and the kite are yoked together. You cannot cut the string and expect the kite to soar right up into the heavens. When the restrictive yoke of the string is cut, the kite will crash to the ground. So the yoke that the Lord Jesus gives is not burdensome. He walks alongside and helps us carry that burden. When we accept the invitation to walk along with the Lord Jesus Christ, we receive so much consolation and strong hope that the yoke seems easy and light. *References:* Lam. 3:25–27; Matt. 11:28–30; Rom. 6:16–18; 1 Cor. 9:16–19; Eph. 4:3; Col. 3:24.

85. Christ bids us to cast our burdens on Him. Some may feel that we ought stoically to face our pains and sorrows without bothering God with them. Christ clearly urges us to come to Him with all our burdens and find relief. When Thorwaldsen, the famous Dutch sculptor, had completed the clay model of his statue of Christ with arms raised in blessing, he left it in his studio to harden overnight. It was an unusually humid night, and when Thorwaldsen returned in the morning, the arms raised in blessing had collapsed to the side of the statue. Suddenly the artist had an inspiration. He would make the statue with Christ's arms extended

BURDENS

openly at His side in welcome. The resulting "Come unto Me" figure of Christ is known and appreciated by millions. *References:* Lam. 3:25; Matt. 6:32; 11:28–30; Luke 12:7; Heb. 4:15–16; 1 Peter 5:7.

Related illustration: 493.

C

Carnal Security

86. Kierkegaard wrote that the Christians of his day were like a flock of geese living in a barnyard. Every seventh day they paraded to a corner of the yard, and their most eloquent orator got up on the fence and spoke of the wonders of geese. He told of the exploits of their forefathers, who dared to mount up on wings and fly all over the sky. He spoke of the mercy of the Creator, who had given geese wings and the instincts to fly. This deeply impressed the geese, who nodded their heads solemnly. All this they did. One thing they did not do. They did not fly. They went back to their dinners. They did not fly; for the corn was good, and the barnyard secure. (*Christian Century*) *References:* Is. 40:31; Rom. 13:11; 1 Cor. 3:1–3; Gal. 4:9; Heb. 5:12; 12:1; 1 Peter 2:9.

Catechism, Luther's Small

87. "Blessed are the hands that have written this book," exclaimed a Catholic cleric in Venice, not knowing it was Luther's Catechism that he was reading. *References:* Deut. 32:1–4; Matt. 7:15–20; 1 Tim. 4:6.

88. Martin Luther tells of his son coming home from school visibly thrilled by something. "And what's it all about?" inquired the father. "Well, today we finished the catechism," replied the son. "Then," said the great Martin Luther, "you are far ahead of me." Restudy your catechism. *References:* Deut. 17:19; Acts 17:11; Rom. 15:4; 1 Cor. 14:20; Heb. 5:12–6:3; 2 Peter 3:18.

89. The history of the church shows that in the first centuries a proper and thorough indoctrination of members was regarded as a matter of course. Clement of Alexandria, who lived about A.D. 150, tells of his catechumens, his students of the chief parts of Christian doctrine. Cyril of Jerusalem (died 386) became famous for his 23 catechetical lectures on Christian faith and practices. Around the year 1000 the church became steeped in the superstitions of medieval Catholicism, until Luther so marvelously revived thorough indoctrination by publishing his Small Catechism in 1529. *References:* Lev. 10:11; Deut. 6:6–7; Ps. 71:17; Prov. 1:8–9; Acts 18:26; 28:23; Rom. 10:14–17; Col. 3:16.

Ceremonies

90. All form in worship is like fire—it is a good servant, but it is a bad master. (MacLaren) *Reference:* Matt. 6:5–13.

Challenge to Faith

See also **Commitment, Consecration**

91. There are two kinds of church members: those who belong to St. Minimum congregation and those who belong to St. Maximum. The people who belong to St. Minimum ask questions such as: How often do I have to go to church? How many times a year must I commune? How much must I give? I pray three times a day; is that enough? I was on a committee last year; do I have to serve on another this year? But the people who belong to St. Maximum ask questions like: What can I do to help with Sunday school? How often will the Sacrament be available for our joy and comfort? What can we do to share the Gospel with people here and everywhere? All of us keep transferring back and forth between these two congregations. At times we surrender to the power of the Holy Spirit that works in us. At other times we resist by putting limits on the message of Christ that we know. *References:* Is. 7:10–13; Matt. 25:24–30; Luke 18:11–12.

92. A Challenge to Put Christ's Word to the Test. John Moser has been regarded as one of the most learned and upright jurists and judges of Germany. In his youth he was influenced by the writings of Voltaire, the Frenchman whom many consider to have been the worst scoffer the world has ever seen. But being a fair-minded man, Moser decided to hear the other side. He steeped himself in the study of the Bible. He came across this passage: "If anyone chooses to do God's will, he will find out whether my teaching comes from God or whether I speak on my own" (John 7:17). Moser said: "What! Jesus made the proof so simple? It would be a shame for a heart thirsting after knowledge not to make a trial of it. I'll try it." He did. He read and studied the teachings of Christ and put them to the test in his daily life. He became convinced that the teaching was of God and turned out to be a devout Christian. *References:* Deut. 4:29; Prov. 2:3–5; 8:17; Jer. 29:13; Matt. 5:6; Luke 11:9; John 7:17; James 1:5.

Character

93. Christian character is not an act but a process, not a sudden creation but a development. It grows and bears fruit like a tree; it requires patient care and unwearied cultivation. (Beecher) *References:* Luke 2:40, 52; 1 Thess. 3:12; 1 Peter 2:2.

Chastisement

See also **Affliction, Discipline**

94. God Loves Those Whom He Chastens. The oldest son of the late ambassador to Greece, though brilliant, was a spastic and hopelessly crippled. Queen Fredericka grew fond of the boy and invited him often to the royal palace to play with her children. One day young Prince Constantine said to his little American friend: "My sister and I have been talking about you, and we have decided that you must be the favorite pupil of Jesus." "What do you mean?" the crippled boy asked sadly. The prince replied: "Well, you know how it is. In school the best pupil is always given the hardest problem to solve. God gave you the hardest problem of all, so you must be His favorite pupil." *References:* Deut. 8:5; Ps. 94:12; 118:18–19; Prov. 3:11–12; Jer. 10:24; John 11:3; Heb. 12:6; Rev. 3:19.

95. That We Should Look Up. A Christian doctor who had helped many people on the road to recovery was suddenly stricken with illness. He lay on the bed of suffering many days. His many friends came and sympathized with him, saying, "It is too bad, doctor, that you must now be down." "Not at all," he replied, "the Lord brought me down that I might not forget to look up." It may appear unwise to prune a healthy grapevine by cutting off some of its good branches, yet every true gardener knows that such pruning helps the vine to bear more fruit.

The same is true of the child of God. *References:* Ps. 94:12; Prov. 3:11–12; John 15:2; 1 Cor. 11:32; Heb. 12:5–11; Rev. 3:19.

Children

96. Kahlil Gibran writes graphically of parents and children in *The Prophet:* "And though they are with you yet they belong not to you. . . . You are the bows from which your children as living arrows are sent forth." *References:* Ex. 20:5–6; Ps. 127; Prov. 22:6; 2 Cor. 12:14; Eph. 6:4.

97. Children may make a rich man poor, but they can make a poor man rich. (Whately) *References:* Gen. 33:5; Ps. 127:3–5; Prov. 17:6.

98. "If I could climb to the highest place in Athens," said Socrates (400 B.C.), "I would lift up my voice and shout: 'Fellow citizens, why do you turn and scrape every stone to gather wealth and take so little care of your children to whom one day you must relinquish it all.'" *References:* 1 Sam. 3:13; Prov. 22:6; Eccl. 2:18–19.

99. 'Twas a SHEEP, not a lamb, that strayed away
In the parable Jesus told—
A grown-up sheep, that had gone astray
From the ninety and nine in the fold.
OUT ON THE HILLSIDE, out in the cold,
'Twas a SHEEP the Good Shepherd sought;
And back in the flock safe in the fold,
'Twas a SHEEP the Good Shepherd bought.
AND WHY FOR THE SHEEP should we earnestly long,
And earnestly hope and pray?
Because there is danger if they go wrong
They may lead the lambs astray;
When the SHEEP go wrong, it will not be long

Till the lambs are as wrong as they.
AND SO WITH THE SHEEP we earnestly plead,
For the sake of the lambs today;
If the lambs are lost, what a terrible cost
Some SHEEP will have to pay.

References: Deut. 4:9; 6:7; Is. 28:9; John 21:15–17; Eph. 6:4 (our duty to the young and weak). Matt. 18:6; Mark 9:42; Luke 17:1–2 (Woe to those who lead lambs astray).

100. God Entrusts His Children to Us. A school superintendent was speaking one night to a parent-teacher meeting. Looking around, he saw a mother holding a sleeping child in the front row. "How much would you take for your child?" The mother hesitated. "Mister, I would not sell him for a million dollars. But you may hold him awhile." Our children belong to God. We hold them awhile for Him. We provide for them, love them, train them, and equip them so that one day they stand on their own feet and live their own lives for the Lord. *References:* Gen. 22:1–18; 1 Sam. 1:19–28; John 21:15.

101. Contrariness of Teenagers. Somehow our parents' advice was never as good as our buddy's. One young man was able to see himself clearly and admit, "There are conflicting pressures that seem to cause me to do and say things I don't plan to do or say." The result is often resisting adults. Bill McKee put it well when he wrote, "They pull some beauties and seem to enjoy just the opposite of what parents desire, like the teenage girl who asked a shoe salesman, 'If my parents like these shoes, can I bring them back?' They're just antiadult, that's all . . . but they'll come around." *References:* Deut. 21:18–21; Prov. 15:20; 30:11; Micah 7:6; 2 Tim. 3:2.

102. Good Parents Are No Guarantee of Good Children. The piety of the parent does not save the child. "We have Abraham for our father." Sunday school and Christian day school are no cure-alls. "I was baptized a Lutheran"—but what are you now? The reputation of the parent is a good recommendation in business, but the faith of the parent is no passport into heaven for the child. Often children of worthy parents are most ungodly. It is a notorious fact that people who go wrong after good training are often more wicked than others. Examine the leaders of infidelity today and see how many come from good families. *References:* 2 Sam. 15:1–6; 2 Chron. 32:33–33:2; Matt. 3:9; Luke 3:8.

Christ

See also **Jesus**

103. The Center and Heart of Scripture. A remarkable copy of the Constitution of the United States is in Washington, D.C. At first glance, it appears to be a confusion of irregular lines and unusual lettering. But visitors who look at it closely suddenly see the face of George Washington looking up at them. The lines and lettering form a good likeness of the father of our nation. As George Washington shines through all the history of this great nation, so Jesus Christ in a much higher way shines through all the Bible. From Genesis to Revelation, the central emphasis is Jesus Christ, the Savior of the world, the answer for all human needs. *References:* Luke 24:46–48; John 5:39; 20:31; Acts 4:12; 1 John 5:13.

104. A man on a jetliner was quietly reading his pocket New Testament. A man sitting next to him noticed this and said, "I don't go much for religion. . . . I don't see any sense . . . in following a Christ who has been dead 2,000 years." "What did you say?" asked the first man; "Christ—dead? Why, that couldn't be, for I was just talking to Him a few minutes ago!" *References:* Is. 43:2; Matt. 18:20; 28:20; Acts 4:13; Gal. 2:20; 1 John 1:3; Rev. 3:20.

105. The Rock of Ages. Off the southwestern tip of Great Britain, on a great boulder some distance from the shore, stands a tall and massive column of solid masonry known as the Eddystone Lighthouse. After several previous failures by others, John Smeaton, a pioneer civil engineer, built the present lighthouse, laying the foundation deep into the rocky core of the foundation boulder. In faith he engraved on the side of his lighthouse the words of Scripture: "Except the Lord build the house, they labor in vain that build it." Unshaken by wind or tempest, this lighthouse has stood for almost two hundred years, a tribute to the skill of a man who in humble faith built on the solid bedrock of Eddystone.

Eddystone Rock typifies Christ the Rock. He is our Rock of Ages. The Father has taken Him and made Him the Cornerstone of His church. *References:* Ps. 127:1; Is. 28:16; Matt. 21:42; Acts 4:11; Eph. 2:20; 1 Peter 2:6.

Related illustration: 321.

Christ the Savior

See also **Cross of Christ**

106. Behold in Christ the seeking God. He comes to seek and to save the lost. A China convert expressed that truth in this way: "A man fell into a deep pit, miry and slippery. As he lay injured at the bottom, *Confucius* looked in and said, 'My friend, I am sorry for you; if you ever get out of that place, take care that you never fall in again.' Then a *Buddhist* priest came along. 'I grieve to see your plight. If you can manage to climb up two thirds of the way, or even half, I might help you up the rest.' Unable to rise, such advice was mockery. Then *Christ* came by. *Descending into the pit, He lifted the man to safety.* That is the difference between Christ and the others.'' *References:* Luke 15:3–10; John 6:68; 10:7–18; 15:13; Acts 4:12; 1 Cor. 3:11; Eph. 5:2; 1 John 3:16.

107. His Death, Our Salvation. Shortly after the terrible crash of Air Florida's Flight 90 in Washington, D.C., in January 1982, *Time* magazine printed an essay entitled, ''The Man in the Water.'' The unnamed man in the water was a survivor clinging to the tail section of the plane in the Potomac River. Every time the rescue helicopter lowered a lifeline, he passed it to another passenger. When the helicopter had rescued all the others and finally came back to get him, it was too late. He had gone under the icy waters. He knew as he passed the lifeline, especially that last time as the helicopter pulled the passenger to safety, that he was giving up his chances for life. He sacrificed his life to a cold death in the river so that the others could live. Jesus Christ, God's Son, gave His life on the cross so that you and I do not have to perish but can have life—life that is indestructible, that never ends, that is eternal. *References:* John 3:16–17; 10:11; 12:23–24; 15:3; Rom. 5:6; 2 Cor. 5:15; Heb. 2:9–10; 1 John 3:16.

Related illustrations: 203, 276, 321, 404, 489, 826.

Christ the Victor

See also **Easter, Resurrection of Christ**

108. Our Victory Through Him. Near Milan, Italy, in A.D. 312 the Roman general Constantine had a vision that if he replaced the Roman eagle with a Christian cross at the top of his banners, he would be victorious in the military contest for the post of emperor. In this vision he saw a cross in the skies accompanied with the Latin inscription *''In hoc signo vinces,''* which means ''In this sign you shall conquer.'' He did conquer and became emperor of Rome.

We too are more than conquerors through Christ who loved us, died for us, and rose again for us. With complete confidence and assurance we can say with Paul, ''Neither death nor life, neither angels nor demons, neither the present nor the future, nor any powers, neither height nor depth, nor anything else in all creation, will be able to separate us from the love of God that is in Christ Jesus our Lord'' (Rom. 8:38–39). *References:* Ps. 20:7; 44:5; Mal. 4:2–3; Luke 10:19; Rom. 8:37–39; 1 John 5:4; Rev. 15:2.

109. Jesus and Alexander died at thirty-three,
One lived and died for self; one died for you and me.
The Greek died on a throne; the Jew died on a cross;
One's life a triumph seemed; the other but a loss.
One led vast armies forth; the other walked alone;
One shed a whole world's blood; the other gave His own.
One won the world in life and lost it all in death;
The other lost His life to win the whole world's faith.

Jesus and Alexander died at thirty-three.
One died in Babylon; and one on Calvary.
One gained all for self; and one Himself He gave,
One conquered every throne; the other every grave.
The one made himself God; the God made Himself less;

CHRIST THE LORD

The one lived but to blast; the other
but to bless.
When died the Greek, forever fell his
throne of swords;
But Jesus died to live forever Lord of
Lords.

Jesus and Alexander died at thirty-
three,
The Greek made all men slaves; the
Jew made all men free.
One built a throne on blood; the other
built on love,
The one was born of earth; the other
from above;
One won all this earth, to lose all
earth and heaven:
The other gave up all, that all to Him
be given.
The Greek forever died; the Jew for-
ever lives.
He loses all who gets, and wins all
things who gives.

(Charles Ross Weede)

References: Is. 53:12; Luke 22:69;
Acts 2:36; Rom. 14:9; Eph. 1:20–22;
Phil. 2:8–11; 1 Peter 3:18–22; Rev.
5:5–13.

110. King of Kings. When Queen
Victoria had just ascended her throne,
she went, as is the custom of royalty,
to hear the *Messiah* rendered. She had
been instructed about her conduct by
those who knew and was told that she
must not rise at the singing of the Hallelujah Chorus. When that magnificent
chorus was being sung and the singers
were shouting, "Hallelujah! Hallelujah! Hallelujah! for the Lord God Om-
nipotent reigneth," she sat with great
difficulty. It seemed as if she would
rise in spite of the custom of kings and
queens, but finally when they came to
the part of the chorus in which with a
shout they proclaim Jesus King of
kings, suddenly the young queen rose
and stood with bowed head as if she
would take her own crown from off her
head and cast it at her Master's feet.
(Wilbur Chapman) *References:* Ps.
51:15; Luke 19:37–40; Acts 4:20; 1
Cor. 9:16; 1 Tim. 6:5; Rev. 17:14;
19:16.

**111. His Victory over the Perse-
cutor.** Most of you have heard the
story of Julian, the apostate emperor of
Rome. Once a Christian, he turned pagan and made it his life's effort to wipe
out Christianity in the empire. In 363,
on his campaign against Phesia, a soldier in his army asked a Christian who
was being mocked by the others,
"Where is your carpenter now?"
Steadfastly the Christian soldier replied, "He is making a coffin for your
emperor." A few months later Julian
received a mortal wound in battle, and
according to the legend, when death
was approaching, he dipped his hand
into his own blood and threw it heavenward with the cry, "O Galilean,
Thou hast conquered!" *References:*
Mal. 4:1; Matt. 24:48–51; Luke 18:7–
8; 1 Thess. 5:1–3; 2 Thess. 1:6–10; 2
Peter 3:3–7; Rev. 6:9–11.

**112. Victory Through Christ's
Death.** In the battle of Sempach the
Swiss were facing defeat by the well-
armed charging line of the Austrians
when Arnold von Winkelried rushed
forward, grasped with outstretched
arms as many enemy pikes as he could
reach, buried them in his body, and
bore them by his weight to the earth.
Into the breach thus made the Swiss
soldiers charged and gained a decisive
victory. Thus Jesus Christ, by His
death, overcame the kingdom of the
devil and delivered humanity from its
bondage. *References:* Is. 53:4–5; John
10:11; 12:23–24; 15:13; Gal 2:20; 1
John 3:16; Rev. 5:9.

Related illustrations: 223, 283.

Christ the Lord
See also **Glory to God**

113. At God's Right Hand. You know how important the proper seating arrangement is in government protocol. Before a state dinner at the White House, who sits next to whom is carefully planned. And on the reviewing stand in Red Square in Moscow the placement of the officials is often the surest clue to the current balance of power in the Soviet hierarchy. The highest position that any human could even imagine attaining in the power structure of the universe is the seat next to God Himself, at the right hand of the Creator and Ruler of all. Only one person has ever sat down in that most exalted place: Jesus, our Savior and Lord. To Him God said: "Sit at my right hand until I make your enemies a footstool for your feet" (Ps. 110:1). *References:* Ps. 110:1; Mark 16:19; Luke 22:69; Acts 2:36; 5:31; Eph. 1:20; Phil. 2:9–11; 1 Peter 3:22; Rev. 5:12.

114. What Kind of King Is He to You? Suppose you saw an *earthly kingdom* in which the king's subjects felt free to ignore whatever they didn't want to hear. What impression would you have of their king?

Or suppose you saw an *earthly kingdom* in which the king's subjects spent one day a week honoring him and telling him how great they thought he was but then spent the other six days making a mockery of everything he had tried to do for them. What impression would you have of their king? *References:* Ps. 78:35–36; Is. 29:13; Ezek. 33:31–32; Matt. 7:21–23; 25:31–46; John 18:33–37; Titus 1:16.

115. No Other Ruler Like Him. Here is a kingdom in which the Lord of love reigns supreme. No earthly monarch ever established a domain like it. Napoleon the Great on St. Helena spoke truthfully: "You speak of empires and power. Well, Alexander the Great, Julius Caesar, Charlemagne, and myself founded empires, but on what did we found them? Force. Christ founded His on love, and at this moment there are millions ready to die for Him. . . . I see no army, no banner or battering-ram; yet a mysterious power is there, working in the interest of Christianity—men secretly sustained here and there by a common faith in the great Unseen. I die before my time, and my body will be given to the earth as food for worms. Such is the fate of him called Napoleon the Great. But look to Christ, honored and loved in every land. Look at His kingdom, rising over all other kingdoms. His life was not the life of a man; His death not that of a man but of God." *References:* Ps. 72; Is. 9:6–7; Dan. 7:14; Zech. 9:10; Eph. 1:22; 1 Tim. 6:15; Rev. 17:14–18; 19:16.

Related illustrations: 386, 387, 388, 562.

Christian Warfare

116. A Canadian scientist warns against the danger of developing the stingless bee. He says that such a seemingly desirable little creature would immediately become the helpless prey of every kind of marauder. The ant, wasp, moth, and other honey-consuming insects would overrun the hives, and the bear, the skunk, and the human robber would feast unmolested on the treasure therein stored.

There is a lesson here for those who are so anxious to rob the forces of righteousness of their God-given powers of resistance. Christians ought to be like the bee—industrious, productive, and devoted to peaceful pursuits amid the fairest and the sweetest of earth's blossoms. They are to live amid the beauties of God, draw honey, and store up sweetness. But God gave the bee a sting, and for a very good purpose. No one ever heard of bees giving up their honey business to go out on marauding expeditions. When they show a warlike front, it is for the single reason that they have been robbed, attacked, or wantonly aroused by alien forces bent on getting their honey. So God gave Christians the power of defense, and for the same purpose—to prevent the predatory "insect," the "bear," and the "skunk" from robbing them of His treasure. (*Moody Monthly*) *References:* Matt. 10:16; Eph. 6:10–18; Phil. 1:17; 1 Tim. 6:12; 2 Tim. 4:1–8; 1 Peter 3:15; Rev. 11:3–6.

Christianity

See also **Church**

117. If true Christianity is not the truth of God, then the richest vintage that ever the world saw and the noblest wine of which it ever drank did grow up a thorn. (MacLaren) *References:* 1 Kings 8:56; 1 Cor. 1:7–9; Heb. 6:18–20.

118. A well-known theologian once explained that to be a Christian is to share in something that has happened, that is happening, and that will happen. *References:* Ps. 118:22–25; Heb. 12:1–3.

119. Christian Mercy. The first public hospital was founded in Rome by a Christian woman, Fabiola, about A.D. 400. Down through the Middle Ages Christian organizations took the lead in making provisions for the sick, and even the modern hospital with all its ramifications had its origin in Christian institutions. *References:* Matt. 25:34–36; Luke 10:33–34; Rom. 15:1; Gal. 6:10; Col. 3:12; James 5:14.

120. The distinction between Christianity and all other systems of religion consists largely in that in the others, people seek God, while in Christianity God seeks people. (Thomas Arnold) *References:* Matt. 18:12; Luke 15:3–10; 19:10; John 1:43; 9:35.

121. Christianity's Early Progress. Within 70 years after the founding of the first Gentile Christian congregation in Antioch of Syria the church had already reached the remote province of Bithynia and had begun threatening the stability of heathen cults and religions. Seventy years later a complete circle of Christian communities stretched from Lyons in France to Edessa in Mesopotamia. After another 70-year period the Roman Emperor Decius wrote, "I would far rather have a rival ruler in Rome than the presence of a Christian bishop in that city." And 70 years later the cross was seen on the Roman colors. *References:* Ps. 72:16; Is. 9:7; 54:3; 55:5; 60:5, 22; Mark 4:31–32; Acts 1:8.

122. Christianity's Jewish Roots. Throughout Christian history, from the first century until modern times, many have tried to sever Christianity from its Jewish foundations. An early Christian named Marcion denied that the Old Testament any longer possessed validity for the church, but the church declared him to be in error. As part of his anti-Semitic program Adolf Hitler sought to eliminate the Old Testament from Christian churches, and today some clergy would attempt a similar exclusion. But throughout His ministry Jesus identified Himself with the proclamations of the patriarchs and prophets. After His resurrection He met the disciples en route to Emmaus, and "beginning with Moses and all the Prophets, he explained to them what was said in all the Scriptures concerning himself" (Luke 24:27). *References:* Is. 9:6–7; Matt. 1:1; Luke 2:32; 18:31; 24:25–27; Acts 3:22–26.

Related illustrations: 2, 407, 712, 785, 789, 840.

Christians

123. A true Christian is both a beggar

and an heir. (Luther) *References:* Rom. 8:14–15; Gal. 4:3–6.

124. The Christian is one to whom sin clings; the unbeliever is one who clings to sin. (W. F. Besser) *References:* Ps. 52; Rom. 5:19–6:6; 7:15–25.

125. In the World but Not of It. What the soul is to the body Christians are to the world. The soul dwells in the body but is not of the body. So Christians dwell in the world but are not of the world. The immortal dwells in the perishable tabernacle of the body. So Christians, heirs of immortality, dwell in a perishable world. The soul is the guardian of the body. Christians are the guardians of the world. Without the soul the body becomes a rotting corpse; without Christians the world is a mass of corruption. (Justin Martyr) *References:* Luke 10:3; John 15:19; 17:16; Rom. 12:2; 2 Tim. 2:4; Heb. 11:13–16; 1 John 2:15.

126. Our Christian Heritage. Many people make much of their family tree and ancestral history. The family tree in which any family may glory and to which it may proudly call the attention of every visitor to its home is the Tree of Life. The ancestral record of which no one need ever be ashamed is the history of those members of the family whose names are written in the Book of Life. *References:* Deut. 14:2; Is. 63:16; Matt. 12:50; Luke 8:19–21; John 1:12; Rom. 8:15–17; 1 Peter 2:9.

127. A Joyous People. In a letter written A.D. 250 by Cyprian to his friend Donatus: "This is a cheerful world as I see it from my garden, under the shadow of my vines. But if I could ascend some high mountain and look very far, what would I see? Brigands on the highways, pirates on the seas, armies fighting, cities burning, in the amphitheaters people murdered to please applauding crowds, selfishness and cruelty, misery and despair under all roofs. It is a bad world, Donatus, an incredibly bad world. But I have discovered in the midst of it a quiet and holy people who have learned a great secret. They have found a joy that is a thousand times better than any of the pleasures of our sinful life. They are despised and persecuted, but they care not. They are masters of their souls. They have overcome the world. These people, Donatus, are the Christians—and I am one of them." *References:* Deut. 33:27–29; Ps. 46; 71:1–5; Is. 25:1–5; Matt. 11:28–30; John 16:33; 2 Cor. 1:3–4; Rev. 7.

128. In a heap of rubbish, people found a block of marble; they saw a stone and nothing more. Michelangelo saw in that stone a statue, and he carved it out—his monumental Moses. Out of the persecuting Saul, God carved the apostle Paul. Out of the despairing monk God carved the heroic Reformer Luther. And so it is with many heroic multitudes. God saw Christians in their sin, cleansed them, and built them into His temple. (Dallmann) *References:* Ps. 51:5–13; 1 Cor. 1:26–29; 2 Cor. 5:17; Eph. 2:10; 4:24; Col. 3:10.

129. Imperfect Saints. A Sunday school teacher once taught a fine lesson on heaven, and some of the pupils disturbed the class a bit that day. When the teacher asked, "Who wants to go to heaven?" all raised their hands enthusiastically except one boy. When the teacher asked, "Why don't you want to go to heaven?" he responded, "I really do, but not with this crowd."

We can appreciate his remark because on this side of heaven "this crowd" is not perfect in living. "This crowd" of believers is under the construction of God's grace, living in repentance and reflecting faith in deeds of love. *References:* Rom. 7:22–25; 1 Cor. 1:26–31; Phil. 3:12; Rev. 3:2.

130. Double-Minded Believers.
What is said in 2 Kings 17:33 of the heathen colonists brought in from Assyria is remarkably descriptive of many professing Christians: "They worshiped the LORD, but they also served their own gods." (Guthrie) *References:* 2 Kings 17:33; Luke 16:13; 1 Cor. 10:21.
Related illustrations: 116, 312, 313, 500, 501, 944.

Christmas
131. Dick Shepherd, a noted minister in some circles a couple of generations ago, once stated, "I do love Christmas; to me it is like a Gothic ruin come to life for 24 hours." That minister may well have loved Christmas, but his assessment of it is vastly understated.

Christmas is more than a 24-hour event, for its influence, beyond the daylong festivities, goes on for a lifetime. It speaks of the unique way in which God brings into the world His promised kingdom through the "Son of the Most High." *References:* Is. 9:1–7; Matt. 1:20–23; Luke 1:31–33; 2:13–14; Gal. 4:3–7.

132. Christmas Without Christ?
My children banded together to bake sugar cookies for the school Christmas party. As they worked together and prepared the batter, they tasted it, but it wasn't right. Something had been left out, and even the raw batter could not hide it. Quickly they rechecked what they had done with the recipe and learned to their astonishment that they had left out the sugar. What a difference that addition made! Sometimes we leave that out of the Christmas Bread of life itself. We follow the recipe with cold assurance, only to discover that the most important ingredient has been forgotten. As sugar cookies cannot be sugar cookies without sugar, so Christmas Bread cannot be Christmas Bread without Christ. *References:* Matt. 2:1–2; Luke 2:10–11; Gal. 4:4.

133. The Fleeting Joy of Christmas.
In a "Peanuts" cartoon by Charles M. Schulz, little Lucy throws up her hands in utter despair and shrieks, "For months we looked forward to Christmas. We couldn't wait till it came, and now it's all over!"

Even Christmas is a fraud, it would seem. For a few brief moments there is a special glow in the air. Life is softer, gayer, more exciting somehow. For a few breathless moments the world is a magic land where everybody loves everybody and problems melt away.

But then the magic moment is past. The tinsel wasn't silver after all, only aluminum foil. The problems all return, and the gaiety and laughter turn out to be only whistling in the dark. The warm glow of friendship disappears, and people become strangers again, passing each other by, unknown and unrecognized. *References:* Matt. 2:1–11; Luke 2:8–20, 25–32.

134. Christmas Peace to God's People. During the early winter of 1755 the pioneers of the Lehigh Valley in Pennsylvania, threatened by Indian massacres, fled for refuge to Bethlehem (Pa.), where Moravian colonists had established friendly relations with the red men. But the Conestoga Indians had been aroused to such frenzy that they broke truce and planned a bloody attack on the village. As Christmas approached, the signal fires flared brightly on the surrounding heights. The tribal drums rumbled in fearsome rhythm. The war whoops, reechoing through the hills, filled the settlers with horror and trembling.

Christmas dawned, a Christmas of sinking fear. Yet enough courage triumphed in that crisis to perpetuate a time-honored custom, as young and old in Bethlehem gathered to sing their early morning praise to the newborn Christ Child. The chorales ended—seldom, perhaps, have Christmas anthems been intoned under more crushing weight—the worshipers returned to the grim suspense of watching and waiting for a Christmas Day attack. Hardly had the fighting men of the village resumed their guard when, to their unbounded joy and astonishment, they watched the Indians break camp and disappear from sight in the distant, wooded hillsides. Miraculously, it seemed, the feared bloody massacre was averted.

Later, when peaceful relations had been reestablished, the reason for the retreat was revealed: While the war council of chiefs prepared for the attack, the winds wafted the Christmas carols to the wigwams on the hills, and those sweet melodies soothed the enraged warriors. Thus on Christmas Day, as the settlers acknowledged allegiance to the Christ Child, they found deliverance and safety. And in that Pennsylvania Bethlehem God blessed their Christmas faith as their families were spared and their individual lives saved.

Even so our triune God directs our attention to His Son and says, "Turn to Me and be saved." *References:* Ps. 34:7; 91:112; 121; Prov. 3:24; Is. 45:22–25; Heb. 13:6.

135. God's Free Gift. Our Lord came to save us by grace, without demanding price or payment, condition or qualifications, reward or recompense. It may be hard for some of us to believe this when Christmas chocolates sell for $8.00 and more a pound, Christmas handkerchiefs at $225, Christmas dressing robes at $500, Christmas fur coats at $24,000 or when a New York jeweler tells newspaper readers of the "steady Christmas demand for the really expensive stuff from $75,000 and up." Thank the Lord on bended knees today that our salvation is the gift of His grace; that His blood has paid the whole price for our title to the prepared place in the heavenly mansions; that though we may be poor and unnoticed, no prince, prime minister, or president can have a costlier Christmas remembrance than we, once the Savior is ours. *References:* Is. 7:10–14; 9:6; Matt. 1:18–23; Luke 2:10–14, 25–32; John 1:14; Gal. 4:4–5.

136. Joseph: An Ordinary Man. A worried mother phoned the church office on the afternoon before the annual Christmas service to say that her small son, who was to play the role of Joseph in the Christmas play, had a cold and had gone to bed on doctor's orders. "It is too late now to get another Joseph," the teacher replied. "We'll just have to write him out of the script." And they did, and few of those who watched the play that night realized that the cast was incomplete. Joseph just is not that important to the Christmas story as it speaks of ancient prophecies fulfilled, angels' announcements, the virgin and her holy Son, a world receiving its Savior. But he was important to God. *Reference:* Matt. 1:18–25.

Related illustrations: 270, 520, 609, 632, 667.

Church

See also **Christianity**

137. If the church joins the world, there is no need for the world to join the church. *References:* John 15:19; 17:15–18; Eph. 5:11.

138. No matter how beautiful without, if Christ Crucified does not adorn the church within, is not the subject of its preaching, such a church is like that beautiful statue of Greek art, *Venus de Milo*—beautiful to look on but lacking the arms to reach out and help. *Ref-*

erences: Rom. 12:4; 1 Cor. 2:2; 12:27; Eph. 1:20–23; 5:23; Col. 1:18; 2:18–19.

139. Church Activities. Some may remember the days when DC-7s were the fastest planes flying across the country. Their engines could annoy the eardrums as they also vibrated the cabin. On a night flight out of Los Angeles one passenger was finding it difficult to get to sleep and made a derogatory remark about the noisy engines. His companion, almost asleep, slowly drawled, "Let's not complain unless we do not hear the noise at all." So it is with the organized church. We may wonder at the necessity of the hum and noise of activity, of programs and meetings to keep the church in operation. Yet if this hum ceased, what then? *References:* Neh. 8:18; Acts 2:46; 1 Cor. 15:58; Phil. 1:27; Heb. 3:13.

140. Church Universal: A Common Language of Grace. On Pentecost from prison Dietrich Bonhoeffer wrote to his parents: "At the tower of Babel all the tongues were confounded, and as a result men could no longer understand one another as they all spoke different languages. This confusion is now brought to an end by the language of God, which is universally intelligible and the only means of mutual understanding among men. And the church is the place where that miracle happens." (*Prisoner for God* [Macmillan], p. 41) *References:* Matt. 16:13–19; Acts 2:4–11; Rom. 12:5; 1 Cor. 1:10; 2 Cor. 4:13; Gal. 3:28; Eph. 2:13–22; Phil. 1:27.

141. Suffer with the Suffering. As we serve with the reconciling power of God, His presence will be known. Dietrich Bonhoeffer, the martyred German pastor, called the German confessing church back to a servant role. His words, contemporized by Alvin Porteous, summarize the servant's role in the world: "Only those who cry for the Negroes in their drive for freedom and justice; only those who weep for the poor in the urban tenements and rural shacks of our land; only those who share in the sufferings of the victims of war and social strife, and the more incalculable hurts of the lonely, the despised, and forsaken of our society; only these have the right to raise their voices in praise to God in the hymns and prayers of the church. For they alone represent the church in its true essence as the suffering servant-people of God." (Alvin C. Porteous, *Prophetic Voices in Contemporary Theology* [New York: Abingdon Press, 1966], p. 200) *References:* Matt. 22:39; Luke 10:33–37; Rom. 15:1; Gal. 6:2; Heb. 13:3; James 1:27; 1 Peter 3:8.

142. The Heavenward Voyager. It is reported that when Christopher Columbus was nearing the continent that he discovered, he saw floating toward him in the water the branch of a tree. Most wonderfully significant it was. That green sprig told him and his disheartened, mutinous crew that somewhere not far away was what they so frantically coveted—the goal of their agonizing suspense. Nor was it long before from the topmast rang out the cry that thrilled their hearts with a joy unspeakable: "Land ahead! Land!" For 1,900 years the ship of God's construction, the Christian church, has been making its way across the ocean of time. Its course is set. Unvaryingly its compass points to a distant shore. It sails confidently, for its Master has told it that it shall reach the goal and anchor on that new heaven and new earth in which righteousness dwells. But when that will be, it does not know. *References:* Matt. 24; Mark 13:32; Luke 17:26–30; 1 Cor. 15:51–52; 1 Thess. 4:13–5:6.

143. Servant of the World. Alan Paton, a Christian whose life and reputation have been dedicated to the cause of justice for all, wrote in *Instrument of Thy Peace:* "I have no higher vision of the Church than as the Servant of the World, not withdrawn but participating, not embattled but battling, not condemning but healing the wounds of the hurt and the lost and the lonely, not preoccupied with its survival . . . but with the needs of mankind." *References:* Matt. 5:13–16; 25:35; Luke 10:25–37; Rom. 15:1–2; Gal. 6:10; Heb. 13:2.

144. Worldliness in the Church. Emperor Constantine in the Edict of Milan (A.D. 313) had granted toleration of the Christian religion and begun bestowing court favors on the Christians. This new attitude produced a great change in the relationship between the church and the state. Multitudes now came into the membership of the church after professing repentance and faith in Christ and accepting baptism. But only the Searcher of hearts knows how many of these remained pagans at heart. Their harmful influence in the church soon became apparent. They demanded and obtained one concession after another. The forms of worship and Christian discipline and practice were brought into closer conformity with paganism. It was now popular to be a Christian. The offense of the cross had ceased. The reproach of the name of Christ was gone. As the church grew in favor with people, it lost power with God. The seed of the divine Word that was still sown by some faithful preachers was choked more and more by the tares of worldliness. *References:* 2 Kings 17:15; John 15:19; Eph. 5:11; James 4:4; 1 John 2:15–19 (worldliness in the church). Matt. 13:36–40; Mark 13:22; Acts 20:29–30; 1 Tim. 4:1–3; 2 Tim. 3:13–14; 4:3 (evil corrupters in the church).

145. Loyalty to the Church. An old legend about Zacchaeus, the little man who climbed a sycamore tree to see Jesus, says that after his great experience of having Jesus in his own home and of taking Jesus into his heart, he would leave his home early every morning. After a while his wife became curious, so one morning she followed him to see what he was up to. At the town well she saw him fill a jug with water and carry it to the sycamore tree outside the town walls. Setting the jug down, he cleared away the debris and rubbish that had accumulated at the base of the tree. Then he poured the water on the roots. After this he gently caressed the tree and stood there a few minutes, looking as if he were reminiscing about something wonderful. At this point his puzzled wife came out of hiding and asked, "Zacchaeus, what have you been doing?" His simple answer: "My darling, this is the tree that enabled me to see Christ." For most of us it is the church that has enabled us to see Christ. Once again, serve it! Let your love flow into it and through it! *References:* Ps. 23:6; 26:8; 27:4; 84:4; 122; Micah 4:2; Gal. 6:1–10; Heb. 10:25.

146. Great People of the Church. Gladstone: "As I grow older, my faith becomes stronger. . . . I was a member of the cabinet for forty-seven years and in that time had intimate dealings with sixty of the greatest men of the country; with but five exceptions they were Christians." Do not believe that only the uncultured find the church congenial. Only the half-learned would have people believe that. And only the half-learned believe it. *References:* Is. 60:3; John 3:1–2; 12:42; 19:38–39.

147. Called Out of the Wilderness. The story is told that when it became known that God was about to give the Law to Israel from a mountaintop, all the mountains appeared before God. Each one pleaded that God would choose it for this honor. Mt. Hermon pleaded, "Choose me. I am the tallest of all. I alone towered above the waters of the flood even as Your holy Law." "Choose me," said Mt. Carmel, "for I am lovely as a garden." "Choose me," said Mt. Lebanon, "for my cedars sing of Your greatness." But God said to Mount Sinai, "From your summit shall My Law go forth to My people, for you alone are set forth in the desert even as Israel alone is among the people of the earth and I am God alone." *References:* Ex. 19:1–6; Deut. 7:7–8; Hos. 11:1; 1 Cor. 1:26–29.

148. Religion in the Church. Horace Greeley once received a letter from a woman stating that her church was in distressing straits. She wrote, "We have tried every device we could think of—fairs, strawberry festivals, oyster suppers, a donkey party, turkey banquets, Japanese weddings, poverty sociables, mock marriages, grab bags, box socials, and necktie sociables," and then she asked what device he would suggest to keep her struggling church from disbanding. The editor briefly replied, "Try religion." (Theo. Graebner) *References:* Acts 2:42; 1 Cor. 9:16; 11:20–22; 1 Peter 2:9.

Related illustrations: 712, 831, 967, 969.

Church Attendance
See also **Fellowship**

149. When rain keeps people away from church, we see why the church is necessary. *References:* Luke 14:18–20; Heb. 10:25.

150. George Washington's pastor said, "No company ever kept him away from church. I have often been at Mount Vernon on a Sunday morning when his breakfast table was filled with guests. But to him they furnished no excuse for neglecting his God and losing the satisfaction of setting a good example. Instead of staying at home out of imaginary courtesy to them, he used constantly to invite them to accompany him." Washington did not forsake the assembling of himself with other Christians, as the manner of some is.

Hofmann, the famous German chemist, related the following experience: Arriving in Glasgow late on a Saturday night, he called on Lord Kelvin on Sunday morning. The door was answered by the maid, whom Hofmann asked if Lord Kelvin were home. "Sir, he most certainly is not." "Could you tell me where I might find him?" "You will find him in church, sir," was the reply, "where you ought to be." *References:* Ps. 84:4; Mark 1:21; Luke 4:16; 24:52–53; Acts 2:46; Heb. 10:25.

151. President Theodore Roosevelt, in spite of all the burdens that were laid on him, never missed a church service, because he had promised that at his confirmation. Even though he became an extremely busy man with all kinds of affairs of state, he always went to church. When he could not attend the worship service, he always sat down and wrote his pastor an excuse and told him where he was and explained why he had to be absent. *References:* Ps. 84:4; 122:1–4; Matt. 12:9; Mark 1:21; Luke 4:16; Acts 13:14; Heb. 10:25.

152. Years ago a man driving through Pennsylvania saw a large field of mules. On inquiring, he was told that the mules worked all week in the mine below the ground and must be brought up each Sunday so they don't go blind. After we struggle and strive all week in this hectic world, we too need to come to the Son once a week and let Him fill us with the rays of new light and hope. This is why the psalmist cries out, "My soul yearns, even faints, for the courts of the LORD; my heart and my flesh cry out for the living God" (Ps. 84:2). *References:* Ex. 20:8–11; Deut. 12:5; Ps. 84:1–4; Micah 4:2; Luke 4:16; Heb. 10:25.

153. The way to conserve the heat of glowing coals is to keep them together. So the religious fervor of Christians is kept alive by frequent "gathering themselves together." (A. H. Francke) *References:* Acts 2:42–47; 4:32–37; 1 John 1:3–7.

Related illustrations: 145, 348, 579, 633, 634, 1003.

Comforting

154. A Scottish preacher, Ian MacLaren, was asked what he would do differently if he had his preaching ministry to live over again. He replied, "I would comfort people more." *References:* Is. 40:1–2; 2 Cor. 2:7–8; 1 Thess. 5:11.

155. Comfort is not an armchair. Comfort is God leading, feeding, reassuring, inspiring, heartening us. *References:* Is. 51:3; 66:13; 2 Cor. 1:3.

156. The great missionary David Livingstone returned to England after serving in Africa for 16 years. He went to his old school and addressed the students. They saw a man with a face worn and thin, a man whose arm was disabled from the bite of a lion, and a man who had been inflicted with fever. Included in his words to those students was this testimony: "Do you know what sustained me during those 16 years of exile in Africa? The passage that helped me most was 'Lo, I will be with you always even unto the end of the world!' " Livingstone knew that Christ, the living Bread, would guide him every day in this world, as well as into everlasting life. *Reference:* Matt. 28:20.

157. Luther says: "The resurrection is comfort against the devil, sin, death, and hell. The first commandment not only to the women but to all baptized and believing Christians is: Fear not!" *References:* Matt. 28:5; Mark 16:6; Luke 24:36–38; 1 Thess. 4:14; 1 Peter 1:3; Rev. 1:17–18.

158. The Comfort to Overcome Defeatism. We are so often tempted to follow Elijah's example. How often don't we lament to one another that the world is getting worse, so what's the use? Many Christians have made their faith a matter of private concern and refused to speak out on important issues. They have turned their churches into Elijah's cave—a place of refuge to hide from the terrible conditions outside and to pity themselves because no one seems to listen anymore. Pierre Berton in *The Comfortable Pew* hit the nail on the head when he observed that Christians no longer want "comfort" in the Biblical sense of strength to go on. Rather they want "comfort" in the sense of making themselves comfortable while the world struggles alone. *References:* 1 Kings 19:9–18; Matt. 24:9–14; 2 Tim. 4:1–5.

159. Abide with Me. On September 4, 1847, Henry Francis Lyte, whose health had been undermined, preached a farewell sermon to his congregation at Brixham, South Devonshire, England. After holding other pastorates, this man had devoted himself for a quarter of a century to the pastoral care of uncultured but warm-hearted seamen and had gained their love and confidence in a high degree. He visited the fishermen and sailors, both on the ships and in their huts. He provided every outgoing ship with a Bible.

Toward evening of the day when he preached his farewell sermon, he went down the garden path to view the setting of the sun over Brixham harbor.

While this lovely scene of nature was before his eyes, the pastor in a long, fervent prayer, as he later told his family, asked his God for ability to write a hymn that might comfort his survivors. No sooner had the sun gone down than he returned to his study, as his children thought, to rest.

But an hour later the door opened, and the pastor came forth with the manuscript of the immortal hymn he had just written, the hymn we love so much:

> Abide with me, fast falls the eventide.
> The darkness deepens; Lord, with me abide.
> When other helpers fail and comforts flee,
> Help of the helpless, oh, abide with me.

The final stanza is the prayer:

> Hold thou thy cross before my closing eyes,
> Shine through the gloom, and point me to the skies;
> Heaven's morning breaks, and earth's vain shadows flee;
> In life, in death, O Lord, abide with me.

References: Is. 43:2; Matt. 18:20; 28:20; Luke 24:29; John 15:4–7; Heb. 13:5; Rev. 3:20.

Related illustration: 403.

Commitment

See also **Consecration, Discipleship, Following After God**

160. While on his way to his great missionary work among the Indians, St. Francis Xavier, returning from Italy, passed through Spain and came into his native country. As he and his party of travelers entered a rich and fertile valley, they saw the sun shining on the turrets of a noble castle. "What a lovely spot!" said one of St. Francis' traveling companions. Then suddenly stopping, he exclaimed, "Why surely, Father Francis, we must be in the neighborhood close to your home! Is not that the castle of Xavier we see yonder, just visible between the trees? We must make a halt hard by in order to give you time to pay a visit to your mother and your family."

"With your permission, noble sir," returned Francis, "we will pursue our journey. My dwelling is now wherever our Lord is pleased to send me; I have given up my earthly home to Him and have no intention of revisiting it.

"Such a visit and such a leave-taking would be productive only of useless pain and regrets. It would be like looking back after having put the hand to the plough and would tend perhaps to unnerve and unfit me for the labors which are before me." *References:* Matt. 10:37–39; 19:27–29; Mark 10:28–30; Luke 5:11; 9:61–62; 14:33; 18:28–30; Heb. 11:8–16.

161. When the Lord had determined to destroy Sodom, Lot and his family not only were told about it but were earnestly and sternly admonished to get out of Sodom as fast as possible and to flee to a small town in the mountains. And they all obeyed—except Mrs. Lot. Instead of keeping her eyes fixed on Zoar ahead, she began to slow down and to think of what she had to leave behind—all the joys and friendships of Sodom. It was just too much for her. She stopped, turned around, looked back, and became a lifeless pillar of salt. Friends, when you and I have declared to our Lord that we will follow Him, when we have put our hands to the plow of discipleship, let us keep our eyes fixed on the Holy City, the New Jerusalem, which lies at the end of the road. Beware of looking back! *References:* Gen. 19:15–26; Hos. 10:2; Luke 9:61–62; 16:13; 17:28–33; Heb. 12:1–2.

162. "In the future, the most important test of the Christian church may not lie in the wisdom of our planning or the skill of our preaching but in the plain, stubborn, devoted commitment of people like ourselves, who are not wise enough or good enough to deserve the name of Christians but who resolve to follow Christ in everything that we do." (Stephen F. Bayne Jr., *What Future for Christianity?* [New York: Friendship Press, 1967]) *References:* Mal. 4; Matt. 10:22; 1 Cor. 15:58; Gal. 6:9; 1 Peter 1:13; Rev. 3:11.

Complacency

163. When nations are to perish in their sins,

'Tis in the church the leprosy begins;

The priest, whose office is with zeal sincere

To watch the fountain and preserve it clear,

Carelessly nods and sleeps upon the brink

While others poison what the flock must drink. (Cooper)

References: Is. 56:10–12; Ezek. 34:2–3: Acts 20:27–31.

Complaining

164. A suburban commuter train was crowded on a hot day. The seats were all taken, and many people were standing. At one station a cripple was carried on. As the passengers made room and gave him a seat, one complained, "We've been standing here for an hour." The invalid looked up at the impatient man and said, "You are very fortunate." *References:* Deut. 8:1–6; Ps. 37:1–4; Matt. 6:30; Phil. 4:4–7.

Related illustration: 256.

Confessing Christ

165. It is a pity that many Christians are like the rivers that flow into the North Sea—frozen at the mouth. (Lyon) *References:* Matt. 10:32–33; Mark 8:38; John 7:13.

166. Courage. It takes courage to stand up and be counted in the classroom, in the office, in the shop—especially when we are in the minority. I cannot but think here of Angie Evans, a teenager who made national headlines and was hailed as one of the most courageous teenagers of our time because of her unpopular stand in the integration problem at Little Rock. In response to a group in our church who had invited her to speak, she said: "Your absolute surety that God *really* does care for each person and his problems helped my faith and trust a lot. I found I could pray more easily. This summer has been a good one for me. I'm not as fearful of people or things or circumstances as I was last year. I've found that I'm my worst enemy, and I am not afraid to talk with non-Christians about Christ." *References:* Mark 15:43; Acts 4:7–13, 31; 9:29; 14:3; 19:8; 28:30–31.

167. *Kurios Christos* (Christ is Lord) was the creed of a group of people in the Roman Empire in the late first century A.D. This Christian group was far more politically concerned than its simple faith formula might suggest. They lived in a time and place in which all loyal, patriotic citizens were required to assert once every year, "Kurios Caesar," which means "Caesar—the State—is Lord." So when these Christians pronounced their creed, "Kurios Christos," they were not only saying "Christ is Lord," but they were also saying, "the State—Caesar—is not Lord." They were affirming what the Lord had told their Israelite forebears on Mount Sinai: "You shall have no other gods before me." *References:* Ex. 20:3; Matt. 10:32; Luke 12:8; Rom. 10:9; 1 Cor. 8:6; 1 John 2:23; 4:15.

Confession of Sins

168. A faithful church member

46

wanted to know which word in the English language is the most difficult to say. His pastor suggested a few tongue twisters, but each time the old gentleman shook his head. Finally he answered his own question by spelling out the word w-r-o-n-g. Have you ever noticed how hard it is to get anyone to say, "I am wrong"? *References:* 2 Sam. 12:13; 24:10; Job 7:20; Ps. 51:3–4; Luke 15:18; 23:41; 1 Cor. 11:31.

169. Dr. C. F. W. Walther, in his well-known *Law and Gospel,* says: "Unless a Christian clearly understands this fact, he ceases to be a Christian. What constitutes a person a Christian is this believing knowledge that he is a miserable, accursed sinner, who would be lost forever if Christ had not died for him." *References:* 2 Sam. 12:13; Ezra 10:11; Job 33:27–28; Ps. 51; Prov. 28:13; Jer. 3:11–13; Luke 5:8; 1 John 1:6–10.

170. In *Seven Great Statesmen* Andrew D. White tells of the death of Hugo Grotius, the great Dutch and Swedish political figure during the early 1600s. His account touches the deep places of the heart. On his way back from Sweden Grotius was shipwrecked on the Pomeranian coast. Gravely ill, he managed to get as far as Rostock. There the famous scholar, jurist, and diplomat lay on his deathbed. The local Lutheran pastor, learning of his presence, came to see him. He greeted the dying man kindly, then simply read to him our Savior's parable of the Pharisee and the publican, ending with the words "God, be merciful to me, a sinner!" At that the dying statesman opened his eyes and exclaimed, "That publican, Lord, am I!" *References:* 2 Sam. 12:13; Prov. 28:13; Is. 55:6–7; Luke 15:21; 18:9–14; 1 John 1:9.

Related illustrations: 429, 549, 856.

Confirmation

171. Guard Your Faith. An English skipper's son had been confirmed on a Palm Sunday morning. Sitting in the cabin of the ship with his son that evening and anxious to deepen certain confirmation convictions within the heart of the son, the father said to him: "Light this cabin candle, go out on the deck, and return to the cabin with the candle burning." "But, Father," said the son, "if I go on the deck, the wind will surely blow it out." "Go," said the father; "do it." And the son did. With much shielding and maneuvering he succeeded in keeping the flame burning and returned the candle to his father. The father said to him, "Son, even so it is with life. You were confirmed today. Your faith is still small and frail. And you are getting into a big, tempting world that will surely snuff out the flame of your faith unless you properly shield it." *References:* Matt. 26:41; Luke 12:37; 1 Cor. 10:12; Eph. 6:10–18; 1 Peter 5:8; Rev. 2:10; 3:11.

172. Spiritual Casualties. Confirmands sometimes look so grand in new clothes or gowns, so sure, so full of bright hopes. But in the last century so did the grand Army of the Potomac as it crossed Virginia's Rapidan River. Dressed in the blue uniforms of the Union Army, with golden buttons gleaming, bands playing, flags flying, and horses neighing, this splendid army marched south to invade the Confederacy for the last time in the American Civil War. How full of hope they were! To be sure, within a year that army would march back in victory. But of those who crossed the Rapidan River that fine spring day, 6 out of 10 would become casualties in less than two months.

A staff officer watching them cross the river wondered: What if some mysterious hand placed badges on their chests that day, perhaps red badges to identify those who would be killed in the fighting ahead—in the Battle of the Wilderness or Spotsylvania Court House or Cold Harbor or Petersburg— and orange badges to identify those who would be wounded or maimed for life and green badges to identify those who would die of disease or starvation in a prison camp? Would these soldiers have marched out as if they were going to a picnic?

And if some mysterious hand placed badges on the robes of the confirmands in each church each year to identify those who would desert Christ and lose the life He has won for us, how many confirmation days would be turned from days of joy to days of tears and heartbreak? This is why I appeal to you: Stay with Christ. To His question: "You do not want to leave too, do you?" let Peter's answer be yours: "Lord, to whom shall we go? You have the words of eternal life." *References:* Prov. 1:7–8; John 6:66–69; 1 Cor. 10:12; 2 Tim. 4:10.

173. Why Confirmands Leave? Many confirmands leave because they think that confirmation day is graduation day, the end of the road. It is more like a lock in a canal, not the end of the journey but a step in raising the journey to a new and higher level. Life with Christ goes on—from adventure to adventure, from childhood dreams to adult responsibilities, from childhood joys to adult joys, from battles and scars to victories and triumphs. Confirmation day doesn't mean you're so grown up that it is safe now to walk without Christ. That is never safe. No, it means you have grown in your understanding so you can walk with Him no longer as an immature child but as a maturing student who is eager to learn more deeply and to shoulder larger re-

sponsibilities of the Christ-life. *References:* Luke 8:13; 9:62; John 6:66– 69; 1 Cor. 13:11; Gal. 4:9; 2 Tim. 4:10; Heb. 10:38; Rev. 2:4.
Related illustration: 151.

Conscience
See also **Guilt**

174. Conscience warns us as a friend before it punishes us as a judge. *References:* John 8:9; Rom. 2:15; 2 Cor. 5:11.

175. Conscience speaks lowest when it ought to speak loudest. The worst man is least troubled by his conscience. (MacLaren) *References:* 1 Cor. 5:2; 1 Tim. 4:2; Titus 1:15.

176. The memory of a man who has done some guilty deed is like a book with a broken back—it always opens at the same page. (W. Taylor) *References:* Ps. 44:15; 51:3; Jer. 23:40.

177. The Cranes of Ibycus. The ancient Greeks knew of the power of the conscience to rob a person of peace, and they referred to this power as "the cranes of Ibycus." They told of Ibycus, a merchant of Corinth, who was attacked by two robbers, Timotheus and another, who beat him to death and took his possessions. As he was dying, Ibycus saw some cranes flying overhead, and since there were no human witnesses to the crime, Ibycus appealed to the cranes to avenge his death and bring the criminals to justice. The next day, satisfied that they would escape detection, the robbers went to the stadium to witness the Corinthian games. There they imagined that suspicious eyes surveyed their every action. Because of their condemning consciences it seemed as though everyone in the stadium saw that their hands were red with the blood of Ibycus. Then a flock of cranes flew overhead, and when the one saw it, he called out in fear, "Look! Look, Timotheus! The cranes!

CONSECRATION

The cranes of Ibycus!'' This led to the arrest and execution of the men. So the cranes of Ibycus, as it were, fly over our heads also. Now and again little things happen to arouse the sleeping conscience and amplify the small voice of condemnation. *References:* Gen. 42:21; Ezra 9:5–6; Ps. 40:12; Zech. 12:10; John 8:6–9; Acts 2:36–37. *Related illustration:* 713.

Consecration
See also **Commitment**
178. Great Sacrifices Call for Great Devotion. In the days of Oliver Cromwell, a young soldier was sentenced to die at the ringing of the curfew. The woman who loved this soldier went to Cromwell to plead for his life. But he turned her down with a hard no. Then she rushed to the sexton of the church who was to ring the curfew, but he, too, refused to help her. The fatal hour came, and they marched her beloved out to be put to death. The sexton went to the church bell and began to pull the rope.

But no shot was fired. For up there in the belfry was the young woman hanging onto the bell, while the sexton below, deaf as he was, kept pulling the rope, thinking that the bell was ringing.

After the sexton left, having done his duty, the woman came down from the tower and hastened to Cromwell with her bleeding hands and bruised body. When Cromwell asked why the curfew had not rung, she told what she had done to save the life of that soldier.

Cromwell then said to her: "Curfew shall not ring tonight." Needless to say, from that day on that young man was devoted to that woman. Because she had saved his life, he would have even died for her.

Fellow redeemed, our Lord and Savior left heaven's glory, became a true Man only that He might lay down His life for us on that first Good Friday. He died that we might have life. *References:* 2 Cor. 5:14–15; Heb. 2:9–11; 12:1–3; 13:12–13; 1 Peter 2:21.

179. David H. C. Read writes in *The Christian Faith:* "Each of the New Testament writers speaks of Christ (whom most had known and seen in action) in staggering terms of religious awe and devotion and claims that in and through Him God acted uniquely and decisively in history." No one ever had to say to those people, "Your God is too small! Your Christ is insufficient!" *References:* Matt. 16:13–16; John 1:49; 6:68–69; 20:28–31; Rom. 10:9; Phil. 2:11; 1 John 4:15.

180. Queen Elizabeth asked a rich merchant to go on a mission for the crown. The merchant remonstrated, saying that such a long absence would be fatal to his business. "You take care of my business," replied the Queen, "and I will take care of yours." When he returned, he found that his business, through the patronage and care of the queen, had increased in volume, and he was richer than when he left. So every business executive can afford to place the interests of Christ's kingdom first; for the promise is clear and unmistakable, "Seek first his kingdom and his righteousness, and all these things will be given to you as well." (A. C. Dixon) *References:* Lev. 26:3–6; Mal. 3:10; Matt. 6:33; 19:21, 27–29; Luke 18:18–30.

181. The world would be amazed to see what would happen if we were truly consecrated to Him. Have you heard this story about Dwight L. Moody? When he was still a lad, he heard a sermon by a preacher in England. The pastor had said: "The world has not yet seen what God can do by His Holy Spirit in and through one man who will truly be consecrated to Him." Hearing that statement, Moody said to himself,

49

With God's help I will be that man! *References:* 2 Kings 23:3; 2 Chron. 15:15; Ps. 119:69; Matt. 22:37; Rom. 12:1; Phil. 3:7–8; 1 Thess. 5:23; 2 Tim. 2:21.

182. Put Christ at the Center of Your Life. In the Berlin art gallery there once hung an unfinished picture by Menzel of Frederick the Great talking to his generals. There was a small bare patch in the center of the picture where a charcoal sketch indicated the artist's intentions. He had painted in all the generals, but he had left the king to the last. That is so lifelike for so many of us. We carefully put in all the generals and leave the King to the last, with the hope that grows ever more faint that some day we may still get the King in the center. Poor Menzel died before he had finished his picture. Get the King into the center of the picture now, and His kingdom in your heart. *References:* Deut. 32:6; Matt. 6:31–33; Luke 18:28–30; Rom. 14:8; Eph. 3:17–19; Phil. 3:7–8; Rev. 3:20.

Related illustrations: 666, 1005.

Contentment

183. Contentment makes much of little; greed makes little of much. Contentment is the poor man's riches and desire the rich man's poverty. (Adams) *References:* Prov. 15:16; Phil. 4:11–13; 1 Tim. 6:6–10.

184. "Nevertheless not My will but Thine be done." Sidney Lanier, in his poem "A Ballad of Trees and the Master," expressed the result of Christ's prayer in Gethsemane in five beautifully chosen words. He wrote that when Jesus emerged from Gethsemane He was "content with death and shame." *References:* Matt. 26:36–46; Mark 14:32–42; Luke 22:39–46; Phil. 2:8; Heb. 5:7–9.

Related illustration: 29.

Conversion

185. The spiritually dead can convert themselves as little as a corpse can raise itself from the dead. As a stone rolling down the hill cannot by its own effort reverse its course, so fallen human beings cannot in their own strength return to God. (Stock) *References:* John 3:3; 6:44; Eph. 2:1; James 5:20.

186. As the sun cannot be seen but by its own light, so neither can God be savingly known but by His own revealing. (Leighton) *References:* Is. 60:1–2; John 8:12; 2 Cor. 4:6.

187. Coloring water as much as you please does not make it wine. It is not a change of habit but a change of nature that one needs to become truly good. An unbeliever whose habits have been reformed has simply given his Old Adam a change of clothing, but clothing does not make the person. *References:* Ezek. 36:26; John 3:3–6; 2 Cor. 5:17.

188. General Sam Houston, liberator and hero of the days of the Texas republic, came to accept Christ as his Savior in the later years of his life. When he was taken to the stream where the candidates for church membership were usually baptized, he was reminded to remove personal valuables before he went into the water. He took off his glasses, removed some papers from his vest pocket, and handed over his watch. The presiding pastor asked him whether he didn't want to remove his billfold lest the money become wet and unfit for use. The general is said to have replied that in his observation, if there was any part of the church member that needs Baptism more than any other part, it would be the billfold—and so he went into the water.

Luther is quoted as having said, "A man needs three conversions: first of the head, then of the heart, and finally of the pocketbook." *References:* Deut. 16:17; Matt. 10:8; Acts 4:32–37;

20:35; 1 Cor. 16:2; 2 Cor. 8:1–5; 9:6–7; 1 Tim. 6:17–19.

189. Cleansed Only by Christ's Blood. At the Portland navy yard a United States ship came in for repair and fumigation as yellow fever had broken out among its crew during its previous voyage. The ship was thoroughly scraped and repainted and then put into commission again, but it was less than a month at sea when the fever appeared again. It was decided to open the ship and expose the fever spores to a thorough freezing during the winter, as medical men said that the spores could not live in cold weather. In the spring the ship was again painted and refurnished, but the fever appeared again. Then it was realized that, though a noble-looking vessel, death was in it, and it was towed to sea and sunk. So is it with all who have not been born again; they carry within their hearts the seeds of a fatal fever, and unless they are cleansed from it by the blood of Christ, they will one day go down in the sea of the divine wrath. *References:* Is. 1:18; Ezek. 36:25; Zech. 13:1; Matt. 3:2; John 3:5–7; Eph. 5:25–26; Titus 3:4–8; Heb. 9:14; 1 John 1:7; Rev. 1:5.

190. St. Augustine was accosted on the street by a former mistress shortly after his conversion. He saw her and turned to walk in the opposite direction. Surprised, the woman cried out, "Augustine, it is I." But continuing on his way, Augustine cried back, "Yes, but it is not I." *References:* Rom. 6:6; 2 Cor. 4:11; Gal. 2:20; 5:24; Col 2:20; 3:3; 2 Tim. 2:11; 1 Peter 2:24.

191. An Indian who by the grace of God had been converted to Jesus was once asked by a white man how his conversion had come about. The Indian gathered several sticks, laid them on the ground in a circle, took a worm and placed it in the midst of the circle, and set the wood on fire. As soon as the worm began to feel the heat of the fire, it crawled to this and then to that side of the circle, trying to find a way of escape. Observing that all its efforts were in vain, it returned to the center of the circle and stretched itself out to die. In that moment the Indian put forth his hand, seized the worm, and lifted it to safety. "Thus," replied the Indian to the white man, "it was with my conversion. When all around me I beheld nothing but the flames of God's wrath, I tried to save myself, but all my efforts were useless and brought me no peace. Then the Lord Jesus caught me with His merciful hand and rescued me." (Rodemeyer) *References:* Ps. 34:18; Jer. 31:18; John 6:44, 65; 15:5; Rom. 5:6; 7:18–25.

Related illustrations: 77, 92, 441.

Conviction

192. An English cleric of a generation or two ago summed up that habit of thought, which we meet so generally now, in the comment: "People look at you with amazement if you suggest that there is such a thing as a fixed truth, and they eye you with supreme contempt if you dare hint that the opposite of truth must be a lie. You must be some old fogy or antediluvian, or you would never make such an observation. The sooner you are back in Noah's Ark, the better. A man says that black is white, and I say it is not so. But it is not kind to say, 'It is not so.' You should say, 'Perhaps you are right, dear brother, though I hardly think so.' " *References:* Deut. 32:4–7; Is. 59:4; John 8:31–32; 17:14–17; 18:38.

Related illustrations: 179, 195, 883.

Courage

193. Courage and Fear. "Fear," writes John Eddison in *The Troubled Mind,* "is a God-implanted instinct for self-preservation. It serves the same purpose in emotional makeup as pain does in the physical. It warns us of danger.'' Eddison goes on to explain, "Courage is not measured by the fear you never feel, but by the fear you manage to overcome." *References:* Deut. 31:6; 2 Chron. 32:7; Is. 12:2; 41:13; Matt. 17:7; Phil. 1:28; 1 John 4:18.

194. Courage to Proclaim the Gospel. On the night of 15 October 1940, 480 German aircraft dropped an estimated 386 tons of high explosive and 70,000 incendiary bombs on London. The incendiary bombs were something new, and while Londoners sought shelter in basements, important and historical buildings burned out of control above their heads. If this were to continue, nothing of London would be left. Winston Churchill became the chiding angel. " 'To the basement!' " he said, "must be replaced by 'To the roofs!' " With a courage born of near desperation the people no longer went into hiding when the nightly attacks began. With little or no protection beyond a tin hat, the able-bodied among them took to the streets and the rooftops as fire spotters and fire fighters and saved much of their city.

Has it ever occurred to you what might have happened in the history of the world and the church if the disciples of Jesus had not taken to the road? They could have stayed where they were, in Jerusalem or their native Galilee, simply waiting for the promised return of their Lord. But He had given them a Great Commission to carry the Gospel "to the ends of the earth," and that's how this blessed Gospel of God's loving forgiveness in Jesus Christ has managed to come down to you and me. *References:* Matt. 28:18–20; Mark 16:15–18; Luke 10:3; 21:15–18; Acts 1:6–11; 5:41; 2 Cor. 4:6–12; James 5:10.

195. Sir Edward Coke, a great English jurist, was a man of courage and conviction, who fearlessly refused to shade the law for anyone. Not even King James could swerve this eminent Christian man from the path of truth and uprightness. While Coke's colleagues among England's high justices cowered before their mighty king and ruler, Sir Edward, when asked to disregard the common law in the king's interest, removed his judicial mantle and, with a gesture of contempt, hurled it in James's face.

How differently Pontius Pilate acted when threatened by force! *References:* Matt. 27:19–26; Mark 15:1–15; Luke 23:13–25; John 19:1–16.

196. St. John Chrysostom, suffering under the Empress Eudoxia, tells his friend Cyricus how he armed himself beforehand. "I thought," said he, "will she banish me? The earth is the Lord's and the fulness thereof. Take away my goods? Naked came I into the world, and naked must I return. Will she stone me? I remembered Stephen. Behead me? John the Baptist came into mind." (Spencer) *References:* Deut. 31:6; 2 Chron. 32:7; Ps. 46; Matt. 10:28; Luke 12:4; Rom. 8:35–39; Phil. 1:28; Rev. 2:10.

Related illustrations: 166, 883.

Creed

197. The creed determines the deed. *References:* Prov. 4:1–9; 2 Tim. 3:16–17; 2 John 9.

198. A Christianity without a creed is a dream. Bones without flesh are dry, no doubt, but what about flesh without bones? An inert, shapeless mass! (MacLaren) *References:* 1 Cor. 15:3–6; 1 Tim. 4:6; 2 Tim. 3:16–4:5.

199. Living Your Creed. In Thayer's *Life of Theodore Roosevelt,* this single sentence occupies a paragraph by itself: "Anyone can profess a creed; Theodore Roosevelt lived his." *References:* Matt. 7:21; Col. 3:16–17; 1 John 3:18.

200. People say, "If our life is good, it is a small matter what we believe." Hm! and if the stream is pure, it is a small matter that the fountain is polluted; if the fruit is good, that the tree is bad; if the vessel is rightly steered, that both compass and chart are wrong. Why, who ever heard of such a thing? Who has gathered grapes of thorns or figs of thistles? (Guthrie) *References:* Deut. 32:1–2; Matt. 7:15–20; John 7:16–18; Gal. 1:6–12; 1 Tim. 4:16; Titus 2:7–8.

Cross of Christ
See also **Christ the Savior**

201. Christ *died*—that is history; Christ died *for us*—that is Christianity; Christ died *for me*—that is salvation. *References:* Rom. 5:6; Heb. 9:28; 1 Peter 2:24.

202. A century ago Mark Twain was traveling in Europe. Reports reached America that the famous author had died. Learning of this news, Twain cabled home, "The reports of my death are greatly exaggerated."

The reports of the death of Jesus were not greatly exaggerated. They rested on hard evidence. Christ was crucified in a public place. The crowd included both adversaries, such as the priests and scribes, and members of His family, including Mary, His mother. The identity of the Man on the cross was not in doubt. Nor was there any uncertainty about His death. *References:* Mark 15:43–45; John 19:33–34.

203. When men see that a prairie fire is coming, what do they do? Not the fleetest horse can escape it. They just take a match and light the grass around them. They take their stand in the burned district and are safe. They hear the flames roar as they come along, but they do not fear. They do not even tremble as the ocean of flames surges around them, for over the place where they stand the fire has already passed, and there is no danger. And there is one spot on earth that God has swept over. Nineteen hundred years ago the storm burst on Calvary, and the Son of God took it into His open bosom, and now, if we take our stand by the open cross, we are safe for time and eternity. (Moody) *References:* Ex. 12:1–13; Matt. 16:25; Luke 9:24; Rom. 6:3–10; 2 Cor. 4:11–12; Col. 3:3–4.

204. A tourist in New York took the trip to the top of the Empire State Building. As he was looking down from that view to the people on the sidewalks, they looked like ants running around. He said, "I imagine this is the way the people of the earth look to God." No way! God doesn't look down from a high pinnacle and watch people struggle and suffer. He Himself came down to them in the person of His Son Jesus Christ and went the way of the cross to help them. "He . . . did not spare His own Son." *References:* Ps. 103:13; Is. 43:1–2; Zech. 2:10; Matt. 1:23; 18:20; 28:20; Rom. 8:31–32; Heb. 4:15.

205. Divine Patience in the Cross. Once when Alexander the Great laid siege to a city, he had a great lamp set up, and he kept it burning night and day as a signal to the besieged. He sent word to the people in the city that while the lamp was burning, they had time to save themselves by surrender. But when once the lamp was put out, the city and all that were in it would be destroyed without mercy. So God has set up His light, the cross, and waits year after year, inviting people to come to Him that they might have light and salvation. Will you exhaust His patience until it is too late? Remember what happened to Jerusalem! Redeem the time! (W. M. Czamanske) *References:* Is. 48:9; Ezek. 33:11; Matt. 23:37–39; Acts 2:40; 17:30–31; Rom. 2:3–5; 1 Peter 3:20; 2 Peter 3:9.

206. The Cross Lies at the Heart of the Gospel. There is a strange legend of old St. Martin. One day he sat busily engaged in his sacred studies, when there came a knock at the door, and a stranger appeared of lordly look and princely attire. "Who art thou?" asked Martin. "I am Christ," was the answer. The confident bearing and the commanding tone of the visitor would have overawed a less wise man. But Martin simply gave his visitor one deep, searching glance and then quickly asked, "Where is the print of the nails?" He had noticed that this one indubitable mark of Christ's person was wanting. There were no nail scars on those jeweled hands. Confused by this searching test question and his base deception exposed, the Prince of Evil—for he it was—quickly fled.

That is only a legend, but it suggests the one infallible test that should be applied to all truth and life. There is much in these days that claims to be of Christ. There are those who would have us lay aside the old faiths and accept new beliefs and new interpretations. How shall we know whether to receive them? The only true test is that with which St. Martin exposed the false pretensions of his visitor: "Where is the print of the nails?" Nothing is truly of Christ that does not bear this mark on it. A gospel without a wounded, dying Christ is not the real Gospel. (E. Eckhardt) *References:* John 20:25; 1 Cor. 1:23; 2:2; Gal. 1:8–9; 6:14.

207. Letting the Cross Be Evident in Your Life. During World War II, when the Russians invaded Finland,

their planes bombed a hospital that according to international law should have remained untouched; it was clearly marked with a huge red cross on its roof. Investigation, however, revealed that shortly before the attack snow had fallen and covered the cross. So while the cross could be seen, all in the hospital were safe, but when it disappeared, many were killed. You see, don't you, the striking similarity in our spiritual lives? As long as we keep the cross in evidence in our lives and trust in it as our means of salvation, we are safe for time and eternity. But when it becomes obscure, we are lost. Always keep the cross and Him who hangs there in the middle of your life, at the center of your faith. *References:* Rom. 6:6; Gal. 2:20; 6:14; Col. 1:20.

208. Inspired by the Cross. When Michelangelo contemplated painting his great picture of the crucifixion, he had the story read to him from each of the gospels while he sat blindfolded. He listened till his spirit was imbued with the spirit of the narrative, and then he took palette and brush and did the work that made his name immortal. It was the sight and thought of the cross that inspired him. (Pittman) *References:* 1 Cor. 1:18; 2:2; Gal. 6:14; Eph. 2:16; Col. 1:20.

209. Freedom by the Cross. The Emancipation Proclamation of Abraham Lincoln changed the condition of human beings in bondage. It raised Blacks from slavery to liberty. Unfortunately, it could effect no miraculous change in the character or nature of those downtrodden slaves. It has taken the greater part of a century to effect a regeneration and to erase the damage of long enslavement of the mind and imprisonment of the spirit.

The cross does more than merely announce the legal acquittal of guilty sinners; it is a power that produces an inner transformation and creates a new and vital personal fellowship with God. The all-too-human point of view passes away, and we begin to look at life from God's point of view. Our philosophy, our outlook, our way of thinking and living become more and more divine because we are new creations in Christ. *References:* John 8:31–36; 2 Cor. 5:17.

210. I climb some lofty hill to survey the land that lies in beauty at its feet. And had I the universe to range over, where should I go to obtain the sublimest view of God? Shall I soar to heaven and listen to the angels' hymns? Shall I descend to the edge of hell and listen to the wail of the lost? No. Turning from both, I remain on this world of ours. Traveling to Palestine, I stand at the foot of the cross on Calvary. (Guthrie) *References:* Rom. 5:8; 1 Cor. 1:18–24; Gal. 2:20; Phil. 2:5–11; 1 John 3:16.

211. Our Enduring Foundation. One of the world's most fabulous cities is Venice, Italy. Built on water, this city has canals instead of streets and gondolas in place of automobiles. Each year tourists come to wonder at the beauty of that place and to visit ancient buildings that speak of stability and firmness in spite of being built over water and sand. What is the secret of their enduring quality? They were built long before the days of poured concrete pilings, which make it possible to erect skyscrapers and span rivers today. The early Venetians discovered a wood that grew harder and more enduring with time. They lay down great numbers of these to establish their city.

A wooden cross whose shaft was sunk on Calvary's hill is the foundation on which our hope is built. God had a hand in planting that cross. He sent His Son, who died thereon as the ransom for all people. That cross has lost none of its enduring qualities with the passage of time. Indeed, it is still the only hope of salvation for sinful humanity. All other ground is sinking sand. *References:* Is. 28:16; Matt. 7:24–25; 1 Cor. 1:18–24; 3:10–11; 1 Tim. 6:19; 2 Tim. 2:19; 1 Peter 2:6.

Related illustrations: 83, 366, 385, 429, 476, 749, 816.

Cross of Believers

212. Several Christian exchange students from our land were listening to a professor at a college in South America. He said, "You've probably seen many crosses in our land. Every church spire, many of our public buildings, even the rooms of our homes are decorated with a cross. Now it's your job as Christians to get the crosses off the church towers and into the hearts of the people." What did he mean? Simply that the cross is not merely a Christian symbol but a way of salvation. It is not merely an ornamental device but our hope for eternity. *References:* Matt. 16:24–25; Acts 4:32–35; Rom. 6:6; 2 Cor. 4:11; Gal. 2:20; 1 Peter 2:24.

Related illustrations: 141, 818.

D

Death of Believers

213. A noble Christian woman, as she lay dying, overheard the doctor whisper, "She's sinking fast." The dying woman smiled and replied, "I'm not sinking; I can't sink through a Rock." *References:* Ex. 17:6; 1 Cor. 10:4; Heb. 13:8; 1 John 2:17.

214. When the threat of death and pain does not bend people, they enjoy a new freedom. Then they can say with Bishop Becket in T. S. Eliot's *Murder in the Cathedral,* "I am not in danger, only near death," and mean it. *References:* Is. 25:8; Hos. 13:14; 1 Cor. 15:54–55; 2 Tim. 1:10; Rev. 21:4.

215. At death, Christ Himself will lead us, and when we open our half-bewildered eyes, the first thing we see will be His welcoming smile, and His voice will say, as a tender surgeon might to a child waking after an operation, "It is all over." (MacLaren) *References:* Ps. 23:4; John 14:1–3; Rev. 14:13.

216. There is one fact that we may oppose to all the wit and argument of infidelity, namely, that no man ever repented of being a Christian on his deathbed. (H. More) *References:* Acts 7:59; 2 Tim. 4:6–8; Heb. 11:13.

217. When President Garfield on his way to Williams College was shot by Guiteau, he showed his conquering spirit by saying, "God's will be done, doctor; I'm ready to go if my time has come." *References:* Is. 25:8; Hos.

13:14; 1 Cor. 15:55–57; 2 Tim. 1:10; Heb. 2:14.

218. In *Joy in Believing,* Vincent McNabb tells us, "When we come to realize that death that crushes is but the tender clasp of God that loves, it loses all its terror." I like the question asked by the *Old Farmer's Almanac:* "Feared of dying? Were you feared of being born?" *References:* Num. 23:10; Ps. 23:4; 116:15; Rom. 14:8; Phil. 1:21; Rev. 14:13.

219. It is sadness to our senses to look into the grave, but it is gladness to our faith to look beyond it. When a man is about to rebuild an old and tottering house, he first sends out its occupant, then tears it down and rebuilds a more splendid one. And this occasions no grief to the tenant and his friends. They do not brood regretfully over the ruins of the old house but look forward joyfully to the glories of the new. So the Savior removes the soul of the believer at death. The body is destroyed only to be rebuilt and to receive again its tenant, the soul, in purified glory. *References:* Rom. 8:22–23; 1 Cor. 15:42–44, 50–52; 2 Cor. 5:1–4; Phil. 3:20–21; Col. 3:14.

220. Peter Marshall told of a mother telling her little child about death: Son: "What is it like to die? Does it hurt?" Mother: "Remember when you were little, you liked to crawl into your big brother's bed? And around midnight big loving hands would carry you into your own bed. You would wake up in your own room. That's what death is, waking up in your own room.'' *References:* Luke 16:22; 23:42–43; John 11:25–26; 14:2–3; 2 Cor. 5:8; 1 Thess. 5:10; Rev. 14:13.

221. "Lord, as you have promised, you now dismiss your servant in peace. For my eyes have seen your salvation." That was the swan song of old Simeon. He speaks like a merchant who has all his goods on shipboard and now desires the master of the ship to hoist sail and be gone homewards. Indeed, why should a Christian, who is but a foreigner here, desire to stay longer in the world but to get his full lading in for heaven? (Gurnall) *References:* Ps. 39:4–13; Luke 2:25–32; 2 Tim. 4:6–8; Heb. 4:8–11; 11:13.

222. Death to a believer is like the wagon that was sent for old Jacob; it came rattling with its wheels, but it was to carry Jacob to his son Joseph. So the wheels of death's chariot may rattle and make a noise, but they carry a believer to Christ, the eternal Son of God, the Redeemer. (Watson) *References:* Gen. 45:27–28; Ps. 23:4; 116:15; Prov. 14:32; Is. 43:1–3; Luke 16:20–22; Rom. 14:8; Phil. 1:21.

223. Death Swallowed Up in Victory. There is a lovely old legend from Greek mythology about the hero Ulysses. One day he returned home from one of his adventures to find that the entire nation was in mourning. When he asked why, he was told, "Haven't you heard? Our queen is dead." When he hurried to the palace, he discovered that it was true. The lovely queen was dead. Ulysses then went on his most perilous adventure. He went out to the lonely tomb and wrestled with the ancient enemy, death, and fought death for the life of the queen. He snatched from death the life of the queen and

took her back to the palace in his arms, handing her to the king alive.

In ancient lore, there was never any hope that this story was true. But bring that story over into Christianity, and it is true! Our Christ went to that lonely grave and wrestled death and conquered it for us, and as He stands outside that tomb victorious, He says to us, "I am alive, and because I live, you shall live also.'' *References:* Is. 25:8; Rom. 8:35–39; 1 Cor. 15:20–28, 51–58; 2 Tim. 1:10; Heb. 2:14; Rev. 21:14.

224. "Some day you will read in the paper that D. L. Moody is dead,'' said the evangelist of himself. "Don't you believe a word of it! At that moment I shall be more alive than I am now; I shall have gone up higher, that is all— out of this old clay tenement into a house that is immortal.'' *References:* Luke 23:43; John 14:2–3; 2 Cor. 4:17; 5:1–8; Phil. 1:21–23; Heb. 4:9–11; 11:13–16; Rev. 7:13–17.

Related illustrations: 3, 184, 360, 361, 362.

Death in General

225. Some tombstones may be high and some low, but the dead beneath them all lie on the same level. Authors, orators, poets, and musicians sleep side by side with the ignorant. *References:* Ps. 49:10; Eccl. 3:19; 8:8.

226. All death is sudden to the unprepared. *References:* Ps. 37:35–38; Prov. 5:23; Luke 12:20–21.

227. In a sense, "It's too bad that dying is the last thing we do, because it could teach us so much about living.'' (Robert Herhold) *References:* Ps. 90:9–12; Luke 16:27–28; Heb. 9:27.

228. As a surgeon told some seminarians in a lecture on the progress of medical science, "Do not forget . . . that with all this advancement, the mortality rate remains at 100%." *References:* Ps. 90:10; Eccl. 8:8; Rom. 5:12.

229. Alexander the Great ordered that at his death his hands should be exposed to public view to show that he could take with him not one single penny of his great wealth. We can take nothing with us when we die. Our shrouds will have no pockets. *References:* Job 1:21; 20:28; Ps. 49:10; Prov. 23:5; 27:24; Eccl. 2:18; Jer. 17:11; 1 Tim. 6:7.

230. "I have studied all my life to be ready for this hour; yet I did not think it would be as serious and severe as this." (Matthias Claudius, on the pain of death). *References:* Job 30:23; Ps. 49:10; 90:7–11; Eccl. 8:8; 9:10; 11:8; Heb. 9:27.

231. No Place for Euphonies. Oh, the lying that is practiced beside many deathbeds! All are engaged in a conspiracy to deceive the victim. Truly, the tender mercies of the wicked are cruel. Every hint of death is forbidden; everything that could excite alarm is forbidden; a dying-chamber is turned into a stage for players who wipe away their tears before they enter and wear a lying mask of ease and smiles and hopes when hope itself is dead. The whole scene is like that old pageant of heathen worship in which they crowned the lambs with garlands and then led them to the slaughter with dances and music. (Guthrie) *References:* 1 Kings 22:1–38; Job 8:13; Prov. 11:17.

232. Death Exposes the Folly of the Infidel. Years ago, Robert Ingersoll, the infidel, delivered a funeral oration at the grave of the child of an intimate friend. There was deep sorrow in that home, and a word of cheer and hope was sorely needed, but the infidel Ingersoll had to content himself with vague sayings clothed in beautiful rhetoric. He spoke on human affection. And his thoughts could wing their flight to no higher realm, could offer no better comfort than was expressed in his one sentence, much quoted since: "It is better to have loved and lost than never to have loved at all." How pitifully inadequate, yea, bankrupt, unbelief proves to be when confronted by death and the grave! *References:* Ps. 73:17–20; Prov. 14:11–13; Eccl. 9:10; Eph. 4:17: 1 Thess. 4:13 (empty human comforts fail). Prov. 5:21–23; Eccl. 8:10–13; Luke 12:20 (human folly exposed).

233. An Unspeakable Experience. Dr. Maurice S. Rawlings writes in *Before Death Comes,* "The occurrence of uniformly 'good' experiences in the next life sounded, even to me at the time that I first read of these cases, entirely too good to be true. As I reported in *Beyond Death's Door,* the turning point in my own concepts occurred when a patient experienced cardiac arrest and dropped dead right in my office. Of course, that alone didn't change my thinking, but the fact that this 48-year-old postman was screaming, 'I'm in hell! Keep me out of hell!' each time he responded to resuscitation efforts did cause me some concern" (p. 19). Further studies are now showing that people witnessing others dying without God and without hope are inclined to forget as quickly as possible such a harrowing experience, and they are not inclined to want to talk about it. *References:* Ps. 37:35–38; 55:23; 73:16–19; 112:10; Prov. 5:21–23; Matt. 8:12; Heb. 6:8; Rev. 21:8.

234. A Powerful Preacher. Death is the most powerful and effective preacher the children of this world have. Though they avoid all churches and despise all preachers of God's Word, yet one preacher—death—they are compelled to hear. His church is

DEPRAVITY

the earth, his pulpit the deathbed, the casket, the hearse, the grave, and the cemetery. With a heart-rending voice He cries out, "O man, it is appointed unto you to die; you have no continuing city in this world, this earth is not your home, this life does not finish your course; in an hour unknown to you, you will have to leave this world with all its treasures. Oh, repent, repent!" (C. F. W. Walther) *References:* Job 10:20–22; Ps. 39:5; 89:48; 90; Is. 40:6–8; Heb. 9:27; James 4:14.
Related illustrations: 515, 720, 830.

Delay
See also **Opportunities**
235. "Almost saved" is just another expression for "altogether lost." (Guthrie) *References:* Luke 9:61–62; 18:18–23; Acts 24:25.
236. When Alexander the Great was asked how he conquered the world, he replied, "By not delaying." *References:* Is. 55:6; Luke 19:41–42; John 9:4.
237. Delaying One's Repentance. Hannibal, after the grand victory at Cannae, could have taken the city of Rome with comparative ease. But he neglected to improve that opportunity. When some time later he attempted to take Rome, a terrible storm prevented him from doing so. Then he is said to have exclaimed with chagrin, "When I could, I would not, and now when I will, I cannot." So it is with all those who delay their repentance from day to day. Having time to be reconciled to God, they will not; but if they continue to resist the grace of God, the time will come when they cannot. (Stock) *References:* Jer. 8:20; Matt. 23:37–38; 25:10; Luke 9:61–62; 14:16–24; Acts 24:25; Heb. 12:17.
Related illustration: 413.

Denial of Christ
238. It is a shame for any man to be married to a woman and to wish to keep the marriage a secret. It is not honorable for a person to belong to a society or organization and have to conceal membership in it. For anyone to be convinced of the truth as it is in Christ, to possess love for Christ, to regard His religion and church as the means of salvation to a fallen, sinful world and not to espouse the cause of Christ is a shameful, ungrateful attitude. Such a one is in danger of losing his or her discipleship. *References:* Matt. 10:32; Luke 12:8–9; John 3:1–2; 7:13; 9:22; 12:42; 19:38.

Depravity
See also **Original Sin**
239. It is commonly said that "all people are good at heart." But are they? In the summer of 1970, Delaware experimented with the honor system for 20 days on the Delaware Turnpike. Motorists without exact change at the automatic toll booths were allowed to take return envelopes and mail in the money. But in 20 days, of more than 26,000 envelopes taken, only 582 were returned, according to the Associated Press. And of those that were returned, some had stamps and pieces of paper instead of money. The experiment cost the state about $4,000 before it was discontinued. And that didn't include lost tolls. *References:* Gen. 6:5; Ps. 53:3; Prov. 20:9; Is. 53:6; 64:6; Rom. 3:23; 1 John 1:8.
240. Hearts of Stone. Ezek. 36:26 says that the natural heart is as hard as stone. Fire melts ice but not stone. Water softens clay but not stone. A hammer bends the stubborn iron but not stone. A stone resists these influences. It may be shattered into fragments or ground to powder, yet its molecules are as hard as ever. It is with the dust of diamonds that the diamond is cut. With such a heart, a person can

59

DESIRES

be saved only because there is nothing impossible to God. (Guthrie) *References:* Ps. 95:8; Jer. 5:3; Ezek. 11:19; 36:26; Zech. 7:12; Mark 6:52; John 12:40.

241. No Limit to Their Sins. The heart of the unregenerate is the same sin-encrusted heart from age to age. During the closing days of World War II, a Nazi official of the Belsen concentration camp, known as the "Bitch of Belsen," made lamp shades from the tattooed human skin of some of the prisoners. There is no limit to the actions of the unregenerate. *References:* Gen. 6:5; Jer. 17:9; Rom. 3:10–18.

242. A person is sick before showing signs of sickness, and the signs of sickness appear because the person is sick. The symptom is not the sickness nor the cause of it, but the result, the effect, the revelation of it. The infection comes before the fever, the smallpox before the pustule, the obstruction of the pores before the cough. So there is original sin in the heart before it manifests itself in life. (Krauth) *References:* Matt. 15:19; John 3:6; James 1:15; 4:1.

Related illustrations: 861, 862, 873, 875.

Desires

243. The stoical scheme of suppressing our wants by lopping off our desires is like cutting off our feet when we want shoes. (Swift) *References:* Matt. 5:27–30; Rom. 13:14; Gal. 5:16.

Related illustration: 244.

Devil

244. Satan, like a fisherman, baits his hook according to the appetite of the fish. (Adams) *References:* Gen. 3:1; James 1:14; 2 Peter 2:18–19.

245. To God the people limp, to the devil they run. *References:* Job 15:14–16; Prov. 2:12–14; Jer. 14:10.

246. The devil is a clever debater.

Grant him one false premise, and he will draw thousands of false deductions from it. (Nitzsch) *References:* Gen. 3:1–5; Matt. 4:3–10; Luke 4:3–13.

247. Overly Preoccupied with the Devil. A front-page headline flippantly asked, "Are more worshipers going to the devil?" Nearly every major magazine and newspaper in the land has had one or more features on devil worship and black magic. *Time* magazine did a cover story on the "Occult Revival" (June 19, 1972), and a subheading on the cover gave this ominous warning: "Satan returns."

People are unpredictable, aren't they? Either they overdo Satan, or they underdo him—and either is bad. C. S. Lewis hit the nail on the head in his preface to *The Screwtape Letters:* "There are two equal and opposite errors into which our race can fall about the devils. One is to disbelieve in their existence. The other is to believe, and to feel an excessive and unhealthy interest in them. They themselves are equally pleased by both errors, and hail a materialist or a magician with the same delight." *References:* Luke 4:1–13; 10:17–20; Rom. 16:20; Eph. 6:11; James 4:7; Rev. 2:9–11.

248. A popular novel tells the story of a young girl who was possessed by a demon. One of the scenes takes place outside the room in which the child is imprisoned. Two priests are discussing the horrifying experience. The younger priest asks why such possessions occur. The older priest says that he thinks the demon's target is not the possessed but those who watch. Its purpose is to make us despair, reject our own humanity, and see ourselves as without dignity. *References:* 2 Sam. 12:14; Matt. 23:13; Rom. 2:23–24; 14:13; 1 Cor. 5:6; Gal. 6:1; 2 Peter 2:1–2.

Related illustrations: 531, 887, 925, 961.

DISCIPLESHIP

Diligence
See also **Labor, Disappointment**
249. Karamin, the Russian traveler, observing Lavator's diligence in studying, visiting the sick, and relieving the poor, was greatly surprised and said, "Whence have you so much strength of mind and power of endurance?" "My friend," replied he, "one rarely lacks the power to work when he possesses the will. The more I labor in the discharge of my duties, the more ability and inclination to labor do I constantly find within myself."
The greatest reward is not the pay received for services rendered, but the consciousness of having done a good thing well. A dog does not watch more faithfully because of a dainty morsel given to it, nor does the bird sing more sweetly in return for the grain thrown out to it. Service for the joy of serving is the faithful servant's greatest satisfaction and highest reward. *References:* Prov. 6:6–8; 17:2; 27:18; Matt. 24:45–47; Gal. 6:9; 2 Peter 3:14.
250. Diligence to Finish Our Task. We have reason to work with every power and with unflinching zeal until the Master Himself shall bid our labors to cease.
Only doing can help, the kind of doing that must be forever linked with the name of one who in the seventh century after Christ was called "The Venerable Bede." One of the greatest Christian scholars of his time, he was devoted to the task of translating the Latin Bible into English. In the last year of his life he had been working hard on the translation of St. John's gospel. A disease had fastened itself on him, and he could hardly go on. At last, on the morning of Ascension Day, his pupil encouraged him by saying, "Dear master, there is but one chapter yet to do." Though scarcely able to work, Bede commanded him, "Take

your pen and write quickly." He continued at intervals throughout the day in great weakness and pain. When night came, the pupil bent over his deathbed and whispered, "Master, there is just one sentence more." Bede wasted no words: "Write quickly." Once more the pupil spoke: "See, dear master, it is finished now." Once more the master answered, "Yes, you speak truly; it is finished." And thus he died. *References:* John 4:34; 17:4; 19:30; Acts 20:24; Gal. 6:9; 2 Tim. 4:6–8; Heb. 12:1–2; 1 Peter 1:13.
Related illustrations: 556, 557, 898.

Disappointment
See also **Diligence**
251. You have seen Christian men and Christian churches so dispirited and discouraged that you knew at once that they could not hope for success at that rate. What a pity to labor zealously for years in the kingdom of God and then to give up, just because we do not seem to be making much headway—possibly none at all. Humanly speaking, what would have become of that little band of Saxon immigrants in 1839 when their leader went wrong if Dr. Walther and his colleagues had given up in despair? *References:* 1 Kings 19:9–18; Ps. 43:5; 73; 1 Cor. 9:24; 2 Cor. 4:1, 16–18; Gal. 5:7; 6:9.

Discipleship
See also **Commitment, Following God**
252. When Cortez disembarked his 500 men on the east coast of Mexico, he set fire to the ships that had brought them. His warriors, watching their means of return going up in flames, knew that they were committing everything, even their lives, to the cause of conquering a new world for Spain. So also with you and me. When Christ says, "Follow Me"—when the call of the Spirit comes to set foot on the

61

shores of discipleship—we are also called to burn our ships in the harbor, to set ourselves free from all worldly loves and loyalties that might come between us and our Christ. *References:* Matt. 8:21–22; 10:37–38; Luke 9:59–60.

253. Cost of Discipleship. In Jesus' story of the sower, the seed fell on at least four different kinds of soil. Some of it fell where the soil was very thin, and of this soil Jesus said, "Those on the rock are the ones who receive the word with joy when they hear it, but they have no root. They believe for a while, but in the time of testing they fall away" (Luke 8:13). To use another picture, they are like people watching soldiers on parade. The smart uniforms, the shining weapons, the glittering medals—all these are so impressive that suddenly they feel a great urge to get into the parade. But actually to get into the army itself, to join the service as a full-time undertaking—that is something different! And so there are also folks who at one time or another, for one reason or another, are very much impressed by the idea of becoming a Christian. To such our Christ still says, "I have no comfortable place to lay My head in this world, for My way leads to Jerusalem and to the cross and to death and to the tomb. If this is the kind of Christ you truly want, the Savior-Christ, then come and follow Me." *References:* Matt. 8:19–20; Mark 4:5–6, 16–17; Luke 8:13; 9:57–58.

254. *Newsweek* magazine once published a little piece on "The Toughest Job in the World," a reference to making decisions. I share it with you here, replacing the words "making decisions" with "being a disciple." It reads:

It can be more fatiguing than a day of stonecutting. It can be more nerve-racking than a day of heart surgery. It can bring success, happiness, life . . . or failure, unhappiness, death. In today's security-conscious society, it's a job fewer people want to tackle. It's not for the faint-hearted who are afraid to fail. It's not for the reckless who can be dangerous. It invites ridicule, criticism, and unpopularity. But without it the world stands still. It is the lonely, ulcerous, precarious job of being a disciple. *References:* Matt. 5:11–12; 10:22, 38–39; 16:24–25; Luke 14:33; 2 Cor. 4:8–10; James 5:10; 1 Peter 2:21.

Discipline

255. A child must not be permitted to argue, pout, or make a great ado when told to do this and that, and yet when a command is given, there must be kindness, gentleness, a disposition to attract. As Luther aptly expressed it, "Next to the rod must lie the apple." *References:* Prov. 13:24; 19:18; Eph. 6:4; Col. 3:21.

Discontent

256. Dissatisfaction with our condition is often due to our false idea of the happiness of others. *References:* Job 12:6–8; 21:7–21; Ps. 73:3–22.

257. A container full of water, if struck, will make no great noise. So it is with the heart. A heart full of grace will bear a great many strokes and never make a noise. But an empty heart, if that be struck, will make a noise. (Burroughs) *References:* Ps. 73:3–28; 2 Cor. 12:7–10.

Divine Guidance

258. A lax church member had been visited by a series of misfortunes, and on a bed of illness he called for his pastor. After an almost endless tale of woe he finally said, "Pastor, I sometimes feel that the devil has been hounding me. He has upset one plan after another, and now here I am, at the end of the road, a miserable failure.'' The pastor looked at his wayward sheep knowingly but sympathetically and said, "No, John, that was not the devil. That was the Savior, but you did not recognize His voice!" *References:* Deut. 32:11–12; Ps. 16:10–11; 23:1–4; 25; 27:11; Is. 55:2–3; Matt. 14:22–27.

259. Jesus Our Sure Guide. When a mariner has lost his path on the lone and trackless ocean—when his vessel is tossed by the angry winds and waves, no shore appears in sight, and no compass can fix his location—if he can succeed in discovering one particular star, the polestar, he can secure his bearings.

People may be compared to such a storm-beaten mariner. Seated in a frail canoe, they are being irresistibly carried forward on the whirling current of the stream of time; the shore from which they set out in infancy has long faded from sight; no map tells the location of the land to which they are steering on the broad expanse of time. Yet if they can focus the telescope of Christian faith on one bright luminary, the guiding polestar, then no matter how the waves of life's dispensation may rise and the winds rage, they have a definite aim, a safe and solid mooring, and can continue their route with cheerfulness and confidence of heart. That star—the unchangeable One—is Jesus. *References:* Luke 1:78–79; John 14:6; Rom. 5:1–2; Eph. 2:18.

260. Jesus Our Guide. Visitors to Switzerland who plan to climb the Alps are always warned that it cannot be done without a guide. The presence of a guide spells safety and confidence. When climbers reach a fork in the road, everyone looks to the guide for instruction. When the path leads by a steep precipice around the side of a mountain, each one gladly grasps the guide's hand and passes safely by the dangerous corner. When the path becomes very narrow and stony, the guide warns each one to follow closely in his footsteps. When a member of the party tires of the burden of the knapsack, the guide willingly lends a hand and takes over part of the load. And so it is with our journey through life. Jesus warns us in His Word: "Apart from me you can do nothing" (John 15:5). And after a few tries many learn to appreciate that warning; they entrust their lives to His competent guidance and leadership. *References:* 2 Chron. 20:12; Ps. 23:1–4; Jer. 10:23; Matt. 28:20; John 3:27; 10:27–28; 15:5.

261. Christ's Guidance Alone Is Unfailing. The famous poem "The Charge of the Light Brigade" contains these unforgettable lines:

> Into the valley of death
> Rode the six hundred. . . .
> Someone had blundered.
> Theirs was not to reason why,
> Theirs but to do and die.

People give wrong orders, make wrong decisions, or give wrong advice, and often a tragedy ensues for those who follow. But the religion of Christ is from God. It is truth. It is not fallible. Our religion is right, because it comes from God. *References:* Joshua 1:5; Ps. 20:7; 121; Is. 40:30–31; 2 Thess. 3:3; Heb. 10:23; 13:5–6.

Related illustration: 156.

Divine Patience
See illustrations 35, 205.

Divine Possibilities

262. A TV preacher sent out the call to gather $1,000,000 per day for seven days and then put the burden squarely on the shoulders of the almighty God, because "with God all things are possible." Incredibly, one of the four men who assassinated Anwar Sadat in 1981 said in an interview, "We knew it would be difficult to pull off, but we believed in what we were doing, and 'with God all things are possible.' "

No! A thousand times no! Resist every temptation to list our material and emotional desires and demands for happiness and wholeness and then believe that God will respond accordingly because "with Him all things are possible." No wonder we are so often disappointed and even disillusioned in matters of faith when we don't get what we want! Frankly, most of what we want and think we need is impossible for God to give to us because He knows better than we do what we need for happiness and wholeness. *References:* Micah 3:2–4; Matt. 6:10; 26:39–42; John 5:30; James 4:3.

263. He Turns Ugly into Beautiful. A man in Scotland spent the day fishing and stopped at an inn in the evening for refreshments and also for an audience with which to share his fish stories. As he described the one that got away with the usual hand gestures to indicate the size of the fish, he flung his hands out without watching where they were going. As he did so, he struck a waitress who was about to set a cup of tea on the table. The cup and its contents were dashed against the wall and immediately an ugly brown stain appeared on the white surface.

The fisherman was embarrassed and apologized profusely. But one of the guests got up from the table and said, "Never mind." He took a pen from his pocket and began to sketch around the brown spot. Soon there emerged a picture of a magnificent royal stag with huge stately antlers. The artist was Sir Edward Landset, famous painter of animals in England.

In a way, that is what God does with us. In our faults and sinfulness we are like that ugly brown spot on the white wall. But God, like the painter, takes us for what we are and makes us into something beautiful. *References:* Eph. 4:24; Phil. 2:13; Col. 1:25–28; 3:10; 1 Thess. 3:12–13; Heb. 13:20–21; 1 Peter 2:9–10; 1 John 3:2.

264. One day Michelangelo came into the studio of Raphael and looked at one of Raphael's early drawings. Then he took a piece of chalk and wrote across the drawing, "Amplius," which means "greater" or "larger." Raphael's plan was too cramped and narrow. So it is that God looks down on our plan of life today and, knowing what He can do through us, writes over the plan, "Amplius!" Greater! Larger! *References:* Ps. 91:14; Is. 58:14; Jer. 1:7–10; Hab. 3:19; Matt. 25:20–23; Luke 19:16–19; 1 Peter 2:9; Rev. 3:21. *Related illustration:* 240, 939, 967.

Divine Presence

265. Admiral Nelson of the British navy is said to have been a wizard of naval tactics, one from whom students of seamanship were able to learn much. Sir Robert Stopford was once sailing with Nelson in the West Indies and wrote to a loved one, "We are half starved and otherwise inconvenienced by so long out of port, but our reward is that we are with Nelson." We, too, may be half starved or otherwise inconvenienced, but our reward is God's promise that we are ever with Jesus. *References:* Gen. 28:15; Ex. 33:14; Deut. 20:1; Is. 43:2; Matt. 18:20; 28:20; Acts 4:13; Rev. 3:20.

266. A missionary to India wrote: "It was night when we (I on my motorcycle and a native catechist in the sidecar) entered the forest road leading into the jungle. A ranger had warned me of the presence of a herd of wild elephants, which, he said, were somewhere in the thicket near the road ahead pulling down trees. I also had reason to fear other wild animals.

"But I could not stop. A storm came up. Soon the lightning flashed cruelly, and the thunder rolled incessantly. I did not dare stop to light my carbide lamp for fear of being charged by some lurking beast but kept right on into the jungle, seeing the road only by the ever-repeated streaks of lightning. Suddenly there came out of the darkness to my right the piercing, terrifying trumpet of an elephant. Had the beast seen us? Was he going to charge? My hairs stood on end. With the throttle opened wide, I raced on through the night. All at once the catechist reached out his hand, laid it on my arm, and said, 'Jesus is with us.' How comforting was that word in that moment! Yes, Jesus was indeed with us and brought us safely through the terrors of that ride." *References:* Matt. 28:20; John 10:28; Rom. 8:38–39.

Related illustrations: 156, 159, 204, 547, 598.

Divine Providence

267. We are apt to believe in Providence so long as we have our own way. But if things go awry, we think that if there is a God, He is in heaven and not on earth. (Beecher) *References:* Job 11:7; Hos. 6:1; 1 Cor. 2:14–16.

268. The eagle, according to naturalists, has a most tender affection for her young and shows it in a very peculiar manner. When she thinks them strong enough to fly, she disturbs their nest, breaks it up, and makes it so disagreeable for them that they must leave it. Then she flutters over them and shows them how to fly in order to encourage them to try their own wings.

If she fails in this, she will spread her wings, take her young ones on them, and soar aloft. Then suddenly gliding from beneath them, she will leave them for the moment to their own resources. But if they are unable to bear themselves up, she will dart beneath them, receive them again on her wings, and bring them back in safety to the rock on which the nest was built.

According to Moses, as an eagle trains, leads, and guides her young, so the Lord lovingly dealt with His chosen people. He was ever faithful to His promises: "If you follow my decrees and are careful to obey my commands, . . . I will walk among you and be your God, and you will be my people" (Lev. 26:3, 12). His enduring love and preserving care was continually with them, granting them every blessing in temporal and spiritual things. And whenever they were in danger of forgetting Him, neglecting His service, and losing sight of the glorious hope and expectation of their promised inheritance, God stirred up their nest, that is, sent them needful trials and afflictions. *References:* Ex. 19:4–5; Lev. 26:3–12; Deut. 32:11–12; Is. 40:31.

269. A Frenchman, imprisoned in a dungeon, seemed to be forsaken by everybody. In loneliness and despair he took a stone and scratched on the wall of his cell: "Nobody cares."

One day a green shoot came through the cracks in the stones on the floor and began to reach up toward the light in the tiny window at the top of the cell. It grew until at last it became a plant with a beautiful blue flower. The prisoner then scratched out the words previously written on the wall and above them scratched: "God cares." *References:* Gen. 28:15; Ps. 115:12; Is. 41:10; 49:14–16; Luke 12:7; 2 Tim. 1:12; 1 Peter 5:7.

270. Christ the Bread of Life. During the siege of Leningrad, the populace made bread out of anything they could find. They used wallpaper paste and sawdust. Thousands starved to death, because their meager diet afforded them no nutrients to maintain life. Christ comes in fulfillment of Micah's prophecy to nourish us to a spiritual strength that will never know death. Christ, the Good Shepherd, feeds His flock in the very strength of God Himself. *References:* Micah 5:2–4; Matt. 14:15–21; Mark 6:34–44; Luke 9:12–17; John 6:35, 48–51.

Related illustrations: 33, 80, 897.

Divine Security, Protection

271. A Christian, persecuted by his enemies, took refuge in a malthouse; he crept into the empty kiln and lay down. Soon he saw a spider lower itself across the narrow entrance by which he got in, fixing the first line of what was soon to be a large and beautiful web. Not long after this, his pursuers also came. He noted their steps and listened to their cruel words as they looked about. When they came close to the kiln, he overheard one saying to the other, "It's no use to look in there; the old villain can never be there. Look at that spider's web; he could never have gotten in there without breaking it." They went to search elsewhere, and he escaped safely out of their hands. (Spurgeon) *References:* Ps. 34:7: 91:4; 125:2; Is. 43:1–3; Luke 21:16–18; Rom. 8:28.

Related illustrations: 134, 156, 203, 207, 894.

Doctrine, False

272. The hearts that are tenderest towards the wandering sheep will be severest against the seducing shepherd who leads them astray. *References:* Is. 56:8–12; Ezek. 34:2–3; Matt. 23:13–15.

273. We shall not have the Biblical view of false doctrine until we regard it as the devil's work. (Rudelbach) *References:* John 8:44; 1 Tim. 4:1; 2 Peter 2:1–2.

274. All false religions are alike in instructing people to gain God's grace and salvation through something good in themselves. (F. Pieper) *References:* Prov. 12:15; 30:12; 2 Cor. 10:12.

Doctrine, True

275. Some say, "Pure doctrine! Pure doctrine! That can only lead you into dead orthodoxy. Pay more attention to your life, and you will raise a growth of genuine Christianity." That is exactly like saying to the farmer, "Don't worry forever about good seed; worry about good fruits." (C. F. W. Walther) *References:* John 8:31–37; 2 Tim. 3:16–17; 2 John 9–11.

276. As a clean window lets the sunlight pour through it so that the room is bathed in light, so should Christians by the clarity of their confession and the purity of their lives let Christ shine through them so that the world might be flooded with light, with the knowledge that in Christ there is salvation. *References:* Dan. 12:3; Matt. 5:13–16; 2 Cor. 3:18.

Related illustration: 511.

Doubt

277. Too many people reserve their skepticism for the sphere in which religion is the teacher, while in the presence of scientific research they are as innocent and simple as infants in their receptivity. (Theo. Graebner) *References:* 2 Tim. 3:14–17; Titus 1:9–2:1; Jude 3–5.

278. A famous historian of the Reformation period relates that in his student days he was seriously bothered by doubts about the Christian religion. He recited his troubles to a minister, but the minister told him, "If I were to rid you of your doubts and difficulties, others would soon arise. There is a simpler way of getting rid of your vexations. Let Jesus Christ really be the Son of God and the divine Savior to you, and no doubts will be able to disturb the serenity of your mind.'' The person who comes to the Lord Jesus Christ and says,

> Just as I am, though tossed about
> With many a conflict, many a doubt,
> Fightings and fears within, without,
> O Lamb of God, I come, I come,

will find that the Lord will erase doubts and will fill the heart with a sure faith. *References:* Matt. 14:29–31; 21:21–22; Mark 9:24; John 8:24; 20:24–28; Heb. 3:12–15.
Related illustration: 803.

Dropouts
See also **Backsliders**
279. Some church members seem to have enlisted only for the parade, not for the battle. At the first alarm of war, they disappear from the ranks. They seem to have been allured only by the uniform and the accessories of military life. When affliction or persecution arises, while the enthusiasm of others comes out, theirs goes out. (W. Taylor) *References:* Matt. 13:5–6, 20–21; 24:9–13; Mark 4:5, 16–17; Luke 8:6, 13.

Duty
See also **Responsibility**
280. Our Duty to Our Neighbor. A great theologian (Thomas Aquinas) said centuries ago, ''Patiently to endure wrongs done to yourself is a mark of perfection. But patience over against the wrongs done to others is a sign of imperfection; in fact, it is sin.'' *References:* Prov. 21:13; 25:20–21; Amos 1:11; Matt. 25:41–46; Luke 10:30–32; Rom. 15:1.

281. Our Duty to Missions. Surely it is not a very exalted degree of virtue to pay our debts. We ought not expect to be praised for that. Nor are we at liberty to choose whether we shall do it or not. We are simply dishonest if we do not. Just so mission work is our sacred duty. As Paul says, we are ''debtors'' to all people; we owe the Gospel to all. (MacLaren) *References:* Matt. 28:19; Mark 5:18–20; 13:10; 16:15; Luke 24:47; Acts 1:8; Rom. 1:14–15.

282. Duty in Danger. When the plague came to Wittenberg, Luther wrote to his friend, a friar of the Augustinian cloister at Erfurt: ''The plague is here and is beginning its destructive work, chiefly among the dear youth. You advise me to flee from Wittenberg. I am confident that the world will not collapse even if Brother Martin were to die. Because of my duty to remain here, I cannot flee till the duty that has called me here commands me to depart.'' (Rodenmeyer) *References:* Dan. 3:18; Acts 4:19–20; 1 Cor. 15:58; 1 Peter 5:9; Rev. 2:10; 20:4.
Related illustration: 180.

E

Easter

See also **Resurrection of Christ**

283. Jesus Defeated . . . the Enemy. While the Battle of Waterloo was being fought, all England waited breathlessly for news. At last the message came slowly across the channel. "Wellington defeated" had just been spelled out when a sudden blanket of fog obscured the signals. News of the disaster quickly spread, and the deepest gloom settled on the land. Then the message was completed: "Wellington defeated the enemy!" Sorrow was turned into great rejoicing. In the gloom of Good Friday the disciples could only read: "Jesus defeated!" But in the new light of Easter Day the glorious truth broke in on their sorrow: "Jesus defeated the enemy!"

> He giveth us the victory
> O'er Satan, self, and sin;
> O hearts, make room for Jesus,
> Arise and let Him in.
> This glorious Easter morning
> Come, greet your risen King
> And to His praise and honor
> Triumphant anthems sing.

References: Is. 53:4–12; Matt. 28; Mark 16; Luke 24; John 20; 1 Cor. 15:51–58; Heb. 2:14.

284. There once was a family that lost three of its four children within just two weeks from a virulent disease. One child was left, a four-year-old boy. The family had buried the third child just two weeks before Easter. On Easter morning the parents and the remaining child went to church. The mother told her Sunday school class about the resurrection of Christ. The father read the Easter story in Sunday school as he led the devotions. People who knew of their great loss wondered how they could do it. On the way home, a 16-year-old youth asked his father, "Dad, that couple must really believe everything about the Easter story, don't they?" "Of course they believe it," said the father. "All Christians do." "But not as they do," said the youth. *References:* John 11:25–27; Rom. 5:1–5; 10:9; 1 Cor. 15:1–8; 2 Cor. 4:8–14 (believing in the Resurrection). Job 23:10; Ps. 119:67; 2 Cor. 4:17; Heb. 12:11 (strengthened in faith through tribulations).

285. Our Over-Familiarity with the Story. An old minister who had conducted Easter services for 50 consecutive years was one day asked by a young minister, "Tell me, which one of the 50 Easter seasons gave you the biggest thrill?" Promptly the old pastor, with a broad smile, replied, "My first." When asked, "Why the first?" he said, "Because it was all so new to me." He continued, "It is regrettably sad but unfortunately true that with the years we are inclined to miss much of the terror and the triumph of those momentous days in Jerusalem because we know the end before we begin to read the story." *References:* Is. 6:9; Jer.

6:10; Matt. 28:1–15; Mark 16:1–13; Luke 24:1–12; John 20:1–18.

286. Easter Joy. Martin Luther, having pondered the facts of Easter, once exclaimed: "One can never speak of Easter without rising to his feet. The pulpit is never so cramped and crowded as it is on Easter day. Hearing its message and assurances is like Jacob hearing that Joseph was still alive. It is almost incredible. It appears too good to be true." *References:* Gen. 45:27–28; Matt. 28:8; Luke 24:41; John 20:16–17.

Related illustrations: 157, 223.

Education, Spiritual

287. When a woman once told her pastor that she would not give her children religious instruction until they had attained the years of discretion, the pastor replied, "Madam, if you do not teach them, the devil will." (A. Ahlquist) *References:* 1 Sam. 3:13; Prov. 22:15; 29:15.

288. Need for Repetition. No wise teacher is ever afraid of repeating himself. The average mind requires a repetition of truth again and again before it can make this truth its own. One coat of paint is not enough; it soon rubs off. *References:* Phil. 3:1.

289. Value of a Christian Education. A legend tells of a young lad who was picking flowers on a hillside. When he picked one special flower, a large cave opened up before him. He walked in and found the place filled with precious gems. He laid the magic flower on a rock and began filling his pockets with the costly stones. Thereupon he started walking out of the cave. A voice said to him, "Don't forget the best," but he failed to heed the warning. The cave closed behind him, and the gems in his pocket turned to ashes.

"Don't forget the best!" These words may well serve as a slogan for Christian education, since it is the key for the present as well as the future life. It alone has permanent value. It alone has promise "for both the present life and the life to come." *References:* Prov. 2:3–5; 3:13; 6:23; 12:1; 23:23; 1 Tim. 4:7–9; 2 Peter 1:5.

290. Have you ever seen a picture of what the imaginary inhabitants of Mars are supposed to look like? They are usually pictured as being all head and eyes and ears with miniature bodies and spindly arms and legs. And that would probably be a good picture of one who has been trained only in mind, ignoring the physical development of the body. And we have seen pictures of what Mars, the Roman god of war, might look like if he existed. He is not exactly handsome with his bullet-shaped head, neck and shoulders like an ox, and bulging muscles. And that is probably a good picture of one whose only development has been physical.

But it is just as unnatural to think that one can be a whole person without spiritual development, a knowledge of the things of God. Someone once said: "To educate a man in mind and not in morals is to educate a menace to society." And the man who spoke these words was not a preacher but a former president of the United States, Theodore Roosevelt. An English philosopher, who was also practical enough to be an engineer and an architect, once said, "When a man's knowledge is not in order, the more of it he has, the greater will be his confusion." *References:* Prov. 9:10; Jer. 5:3–4; John 8:31–32; Rom. 10; Eph. 4:17–24; 2 Tim. 3:7.

291. In an address delivered at the opening of a rescue mission for homeless children, a noted educator asserted that if only one child were saved by means of that mission, all the expenses of erecting and maintaining it would be well worth it. After the service, a guest went to the speaker and said to him in a derisive tone, "Sir, you surely did not mean what you said. Did you not exaggerate when you declared that the salvation of one child will exceed the cost of the erection and maintenance of this school?" "No, I did not. This school is not too expensive if that child were my child," was the prompt and terse reply. (Rodenmeyer) *References:* Deut. 31:13; Prov. 22:6; Eph. 6:4; 2 Tim. 1:5; 3:14.

Related illustrations: 57, 71, 306, 370, 496.

Education, Secular
292. Public Schools. A public school system in itself is indeed of enormous benefit to the race. But it is of benefit only if it is kept healthy at every moment by the absolutely free possibility of the competition of private schools. A public school system that becomes monopolistic is the most perfect instrument of tyranny that has yet been devised. (Machen) *References:* Jer. 4:22; Acts 17:18; 1 Cor. 8:1–2.

293. The president of the University of Minnesota told the graduating class at Notre Dame that nearly every offender in Watergate was a graduate of a university such as Harvard. He posed the question, Where did we go wrong? Answering his own question, the president observed, "The sad fact is that there is no moral guidance anywhere in our public schools from kindergarten up to high school. The fear of contamination by religion is so great that there is no place in our schools for teaching what is right or wrong." *References:* Job 28:28; Prov. 1:7–9; 4:7; Hos. 14:9; Matt. 7:24; 2 Tim. 3:15; James 3:17.

294. When Education Forgets Its Purpose. Much of the decline in morality in our country is due to the fact that many of our educational programs have forgotten God. For centuries the Bible had been the wellspring of culture and education in our land. We need but glance at our great universities of the past for proof. Harvard University had as its motto "For Christ and the Church." The seal of Yale recalls the office of the high priest, who was a mediator between the people and God. Princeton's first president, John Witherspoon, declared, "Cursed be all learning that is contrary to the Cross of Christ!" The teaching of the religion of Jesus was the underlying motive for the establishment of these and many other great schools of our land. The sad fact must be recognized today that too many schools have forgotten their primary purpose. *References:* Deut. 4:9; 6:6–9; Prov. 1:7, 22; 5:7–14; Jer. 32:33; 2 Tim. 4:3–4; Heb. 6:4–6.

Related illustrations: 406, 981.

Election by God
295. "God's choice of Israel did not imply election to privilege so much as election to responsibility," says Alan Richardson (*The Gospel and Modern Thought*, p. 109). *References:* Gen. 12:1–3; Ex. 19:4–6; Deut. 26:16–19; Jer. 31:31–34; Matt. 3:9–10; John 1:11–13; Rom. 9:1–7.

296. An aerospace engineer . . . talks and writes about the capabilities of a supersonic bomber; although he discusses speed, bomb loads, range, and flying altitude, the plane is still on the drawing board. Such predictions of a plane's capabilities are no second guesses; even though the plane is only on the drawing board, the engineer can inform the public of the plane's abilities as well as its limitations. Before we were off the drawing board, before Israel was a nation, and before any of us were walking around, God selected us to receive the Spirit of Pentecost.

References: Deut. 7:6–8; Is. 44:1–2; Jer. 1:5; Rom. 8:28–30; Eph. 1:4–6.
Related illustration: 353.

Enemies, Love for
See also **Love, God's; Love, Human**
297. When Abraham Lincoln espoused the cause of a Confederate, someone asked him how he could be so kind to his enemies. He replied, "They are no longer my enemies when I love them." *References:* Prov. 25:21–22; Matt. 5:43–44; Rom. 12:20.
298. Christians want peace and pursue peace not only in the circle of relatives or fellow church members but also in a much wider circle of acquaintances. How can we hope to bring Christ to our neighbors if we have already antagonized them? Edwin Markham once wrote of an opponent:

> He drew a circle that shut me out—
> Heretic, rebel, a thing to flout.
> But Love and I had the wit to win;
> We drew a circle that took him in.

References: Lev. 19:18; Prov. 24:29; Matt. 5:39–48; Rom. 12:17–21; 1 Thess. 5:15; 1 Peter 3:9.

Endurance of the Kingdom
See also **Eternity, Kingdom of God**
299. Paintings and books that were acclaimed a few years ago are now almost forgotten; others, spurned in their day, are now firmly enshrined in hall of fame. Schubert could not find steady employment in his day; Rembrandt died a bankrupt; Mozart was obliged to work himself into a state of tuberculosis; Paderewski was scorned by German critics; Van Gogh's paintings were spat on by respectable Dutch burghers in his native land; Giuseppe Verdi was refused admission to the Milan Conservatory of Music (from *Van Loon's Lives*). Jesus was the classic example of all of these. He represented more than education and

culture. He was "the way and the truth and the life" (John 14:6). He was rejected more completely than any. Yet 2,000 years have not been able to dim His glory or His teachings. The genuine endures. *References:* Matt. 7:15–27; 1 Cor. 3:11–15; 2 Cor. 4:18; 1 Peter 1:24–25 (only the genuine endures). Ps. 118:22; Mark 12:10; John 1:11–12; 12:48; 15:25–27 (Christ rejected).
300. We are reminded of the inscription on the monument of the Wesleys in Westminster Abbey: "God buries the workers, but He carries on the work." *References:* Num. 20:23–29; Joshua 1:1–9; 2 Kings 2:1–14; Matt. 9:37–38; 2 Tim. 4:1–8.

Envy
301. Envy is like a fly that passes over all a body's sounder parts and dwells on the sores. (Chapman) *References:* Esther 5:12–14; Prov. 14:30; James 3:14.
302. A wrestler was so envious of Theogenes, the prince of wrestlers, that he even wrestled with his statue, until one night he threw it, and it fell on him and crushed him to death. (Dallmann) *References:* Esther 5:12–7:10; Dan. 6:24.

Epiphany
303. History of. We mark the ancient festival of Epiphany, a festival older than Christmas itself. From the earliest beginnings of the Christian church this festival was celebrated in remembrance of the coming of the Wise Men from the East, who presented to the Christ Child their rich gifts of gold and frankincense and myrrh. Church history tells us that this festival had a fixed date, January 6. In more recent times many churches celebrate this festival on the Sunday nearest that date, remembering it as "the Gentiles' Christmas," since the Wise Men were non-Jews, or Gentiles. In England it was called "the

Twelfth Night," signifying its date after the Christmas festival. On that day the king of England would enter Westminster Abbey and place on the altar there his gifts of gold and frankincense and myrrh, remembering the homage of the Wise Men, who came to worship the Christ Child, presenting their gifts to Him. *References:* Is. 9:2; 42:1–9; 49:6; 60:1–7; Mal. 1:11; Matt. 2:1–12; Luke 2:32.

304. In the cathedral of Cologne one can see the Shrine of the Three Kings. Visitors are told that their number was three; that their names were Caspar, Balthazar, and Melchoir; that Caspar was from Tarsus, Balthazar from Ethiopia, and Melchoir from Arabia. But the Scriptures tell us nothing of that—no number, no names, no place of origin. All they tell us is this: "After Jesus was born in Bethlehem of Judea, during the time of King Herod, Magi from the east came to Jerusalem and asked, 'Where is the one who has been born king of the Jews? We saw his star in the east and have come to worship him' " (Matt. 2:1–2). *References:* Is. 60:1–6; Matt. 2:1–12.

Equality

305. When the Duke of Wellington once took the Sacrament at his parish church, a poor old man knelt down close by his side. A warden came and touched the poor man on the shoulder, motioning him to move farther away. When the great commander noticed this, he clasped the old man's hand and said in a whisper, "Do not move; we are all equal here." *References:* Prov. 22:2; Acts 10:34–35; Rom. 10:12; 1 Cor. 10:17; Gal. 3:28; 1 Tim. 5:21; James 2:4–5.

Related illustration: 225, 479.

Eternity

See also **Endurance of the Kingdom, Immortality**

306. One of America's most famous statesmen, Daniel Webster, orator, jurist, humble Christian, once said: "If we work on marble, it will perish; if on brass, time will efface it; if we rear temples, they will crumble into dust; but if we work on immortal souls and imbue them with principles, with the just fear of God and love of our fellowmen, we engrave on those tablets something that will brighten to all eternity." *References:* Deut. 7:9; Ps. 1; 103:17–18; Is. 40:29–31; 2 Cor. 3:1–3; Heb. 11:24–26.

307. Ascending one of the magnificent stairways in the Library of Congress, one reads at the top this inscription on the wall: "Too low they build who build beneath the stars." (Young, *Night Thoughts*). In building your life, build with God for eternity. In building the church, build to the glory of Christ and for the salvation of souls. *References:* Matt. 6:19–21; 6:33; 7:24–27; 1 Cor. 3:9–15; Eph. 2:20–22; Col. 2:6–7; 1 Peter 2:5.

Evolution

308. A minister's little girl one day came home from school and said, "Do you know folks used to live up in trees like monkeys?" "Not your folks," replied her father. "Your folks came down from God, not up from slime." *References:* Gen. 1:26–27; 5:1; Ps. 8:4–6; James 3:9.

309. The doctrine of evolution is as deadly as leprosy; it may aid a lawyer in a criminal case, but it would, if generally adopted, destroy all sense of responsibility and menace the morals of the world. An evolutionist would never write such a story as the prodigal son. (W. J. Bryan) *References:* Rom. 1:18–25; 1 Cor. 1:19–24; 3:16–20.

310. Evolution is not truth; it is merely a hypothesis—it is millions of guesses strung together. (W. J. Bryan)

References: Ps. 82:5; 1 Cor. 3:20; 2 Tim. 3:7.

311. The worst sort of clever people are those who know better than the Bible and are so learned that they believe that the world had no Maker and that people are only monkeys with their tails rubbed off. Dear, dear me, this is the sort of talk we used to expect from Tom of Bedlam, but now we get it from clever people. If things go on in this fashion, a poor plowman will not be able to tell which is the lunatic and which is the philosopher. (Spurgeon) *References:* Ps. 53:1; Prov. 12:23; 26:12; Eccl. 10:1; Is. 29:14; Rom. 1:22; 1 Cor. 8:2.

Example
See also **Influence**
312. Bad Examples of Christians. Friedrich Nietzsche, German philosopher of the 19th century, once said, "The greatest hindrance to Christianity are the Christians." *References:* 1 Cor. 1:10–12; 3:3; 5:1; 11:18; 2 Cor. 12:20; Phil. 4:2; James 2:1–7.

313. When the famous military leader General Gordon tried to hire a Muslim as his servant, the man refused and gave as his reason: "You will make me a Christian." Gordon promised that he would never speak to him about religion. And still the man refused because, as he said: "By my daily association with you I would become a Christian without a word from you. Your conduct speaks plainer than words, and I wish to avoid it. I will not be a Christian." God give us more such Christians—Christians who by daily living will be a powerful means of influencing others so that they, too, may be attracted to His Word and through the Word be drawn into the Kingdom. *References:* Matt. 5:13–16; Acts 13:47; 2 Cor. 9:2; Phil. 2:15; 1 Thess. 5:5–9; 2 Thess. 3:9; 1 Tim. 4:12.

F

Faith

314. There is something better than understanding God, and that is trusting God. (G. L. Knight) *References:* Ps. 37:5; Prov. 3:5–6; Is. 26:3; 50:10; Nah. 1:7.

315. A small diamond is a diamond no less than a large one; a drop of rain is water no less than a great sea. So weak faith is as truly faith as is strong faith and has the power to save a sinner. (Caspari) *References:* Is. 42:3; Matt. 17:20; Luke 17:6.

316. Martin Luther describes faith as being like glue—it glues the heart to God's promises. *References:* Ps. 125:1; Is. 26:3; Nah. 1:7; Heb. 4:1–2.

317. Quasi-Faith Saves No One. How many there have been and are still today who approach Christ, apparently brush up against Him, yet never truly touch Him! Unless the final contact of faith is achieved, all is lost. Should an electric wire stretch 20 miles to a remote outpost and yet lack one foot of reaching its destination, for all the benefit gained, the electric power used, it might just as well stretch only half the way or a quarter of the way or no part of the way at all. *References:* Matt. 19:16–26; 25:11–12; Luke 9:61–62; 18:18–27; Acts 24:25; 26:28. (*See also* 235.)

318. A man once came to Dwight L. Moody and asked, "How can you accept the Bible with all its mysteries and its contradictions, you with your fine mind?" Moody answered, "I don't explain it. I don't understand it. I don't make anything of it. I simply believe it." *References:* Hab. 2:4; John 12:46; Rom. 1:17; 4:3; Gal. 3:26; Eph. 6:16; Phil. 3:9; Heb. 11:1–6.

319. Believing Without Seeing. In a bunker near Cologne some hunted men had hidden for a time during World War II. This inscription was on the wall:

> I believe in the sun even if it is not shining!
> I believe in God even if He is silent.
> I believe in His love even if it is hidden.

This is how a sorely afflicted person hallows the name of the heavenly Father. But Christ, who taught us to pray in trust to His Father and ours, grants us grace to say:

> I believe in the light, for Christ is the light in the darkness;
> I believe in God, for He spoke in Christ and is not silent;
> I believe in love, for love appeared on the cross.

References: John 14:8–11; 20:29; 1 Cor. 13:12; Heb. 11:13; 1 Peter 1:8–9; 1 John 3:2.

320. The Anchor of Our Souls. Ships nearing a dangerous shore in a violent storm throw out an anchor. This has a twofold effect. It keeps the vessel from being driven toward the rocks that line the shore and from being dashed to pieces on them, and it holds the nose (or bow) of the vessel straight into the wind, so that the onrushing waves are cut in two and do not strike the ship sideways and swamp it. The faith of Christians holds safely in the midst of storms of life, so that they are kept from being swamped by the waves of adversity or dashed to pieces on the rocks of despair. *References:* Ps. 125:1; Is. 26:3; Matt. 8:23–37; Mark 4:37–41; Luke 8:22–25; Heb. 11:1.

321. Faith in Christ Makes More Sense of Life. One rainy Sunday afternoon, a father was babysitting his children and had the task of keeping them entertained. He assigned specific tasks to each child. To keep his 10-year-old son busy, he had torn a full-page map of the United States out of a magazine, cut it into small pieces, and told his son to reassemble it as a jigsaw puzzle. To the father's amazement, his son presented him with the completed puzzle in just a few minutes. "How did you do it, son?" he asked. "It was easy," the boy replied. "At first, when I tried to fit together all those little lines and dots and the small print on the map, it looked like an impossible job. Then I saw part of a man's face on the back of one of the pieces. So I turned the pieces over, and when I got the man together, the United States took care of itself."

The jigsaw puzzle of life makes sense and we get it all together when we live our life against the background of Christ. That is, faith in Christ as Redeemer and Lord makes all the pieces fit. *References:* Matt. 7:24; John 8:31–36; 17:3; 1 Cor. 2:2; Phil. 4:13.

322. Saved by Faith Alone. Some years ago Walter Carlson of Chicago's WMBI took his roving microphone into the city's Union Station and asked passers-by the question, How does a person go to heaven? For half an hour a parade of travelers responded with such answers as "Obey the Golden Rule," "Be good to your neighbor," "Go to church," "Do good," "Pay your bills." These answers are natural for all people, also for us. We are born with a good opinion of ourselves, with the idea that we are able to satisfy God with our own efforts. This is our natural bent—we think that we are something.

How can I get right with God? Paul answers this question with a God-given answer that will cause the human heart to rebel. People can get right with God not through good works but only by faith. *References:* Hab. 2:4; Rom. 1:16; 4:1–5; 4:13–17; Eph. 2:8–9.

323. Faith Active in Love. After the Battle of Lookout Mountain, when the Federal troops cleared the heights with an irresistible dash, General Grant sent to General Woods and asked, "Did you order the charge?" He said, "No." To Hooker and to Sheridan the same inquiry was put, and from them the same response was received. The men had been filled with such enthusiasm that nothing could have stopped them. They leaped to the fray, defying danger and death, and when the victory was gained, they were filled with glad wonder at it. So it is with Christians. When their hearts are filled with faith, it will be active in love and good works. *References:* Mark 9:23; Acts 4:18–20; Gal. 5:6; Eph. 2:8–10; Heb. 11:6; James 2:18.

324. Alexander had great confidence in his friend and physician. When the physician had mixed him a potion for his sickness, a letter was put into Alexander's hand warning him not to drink the mixture, since it was poisoned. He held the letter in one hand and the cup in the other and in the presence of his friend and physician he drank up the draught. After he had drained the cup, he bade his friend look at the letter and judge of his confidence in him. Alexander had unstaggering faith in his friend that did not admit of doubt. "See now," said he, "how I have trusted you."

This is the assurance that the believer should exercise toward his God. The cup is very bitter, and some tell us that it will prove to be deadly, that it is so nauseous that we should never survive the draught. Unbelief whispers in our ear, "Your coming tribulation will utterly crush you." Drink it, my brother, and say, "If He slay me, yet will I trust in Him." It cannot be that God should be unfaithful to His promise or unmindful of His covenant. (Spurgeon) *References:* Gen. 22:1–18; Job 13:15; Ps. 25:1–2; 56:1–3; Is. 26:3; 2 Tim. 1:12.

325. Confidence of Faith. A poet and an artist examined the great painting representing the healing of the blind men of Jericho. To the poet everything was excellent—the form of Christ, the grouping of the individuals, the expressions on the faces of the leading characters. The artist saw it in a different light. "Do you see the discarded cane laying there? When the blind man heard of Christ, he was so sure of being healed that he let his cane lie there, firmly believing that he would need it no longer." To the artist he hastened to the Lord as if he could already see. That is the confidence of faith. So often we hold on to canes and crutches and all sorts of other means instead of coming directly to the Savior and helper. *References:* Matt. 20:29–34; Mark 10:46–52; Luke 18:35–43. *Related illustrations:* 16, 171, 278, 284, 399, 400, 401, 590, 620, 881.

Faithfulness
See also **Commitment, Conviction**
326. The termite, or white ant, of the tropics takes so firm a hold of an object

that, rather than let it go, it permits you to pull its body from its head. With equal determination we ought to cling to Christ, choosing to lose our life rather than Him. (Guthrie) *References:* Matt. 10:39; 2 Cor. 4:11; Rev. 2:10.

327. The flower that follows the sun does so even in cloudy days. (Leighton) *References:* Job 13:15; Is. 26:3; Prov. 3:5–6.

328. Faithful Amidst Chaos or Death. Most of us are familiar with the fate of the city of Pompeii on the Bay of Naples in Italy; it was destroyed in A.D. 79. During recent years the ruins of that city have been excavated. There are numerous evidences that many tried to flee from the catastrophe. But one man did not. At the city gate was found the skeleton of a Roman guard. There he had remained, both hands clutched about his weapon, while the very ground on which he stood trembled and the fiery ashes were gradually burying him; after these many centuries, he was found at his post of duty. So you must perform the task Jesus has given you, yes, be so busy that, even though the world goes to pieces under your feet, you still will be found striving to please God. *References:* Ps. 90:12; Matt. 16:25; Mark 8:35; Rom. 13:11–14; 1 Cor. 7:29–31; Eph. 5:15–16; Rev. 2:10.

329. Unquestionable Loyalty. It is said that when the famous Garibaldi led an infantry attack against the Austrians, he never looked about to see if his men were following him; he was absolutely certain that at the moment when he reached the enemy columns, he would feel his men's breath hot on the back of his neck. May we, along with the Syrophoenician woman, offer to the Captain of our salvation the same utter loyalty, the same unquestioning obedience, the same persistent faith. *References:* Matt. 10:22, 39; 15:21–

28; 19:29; John 11:16; Acts 21:13; Heb. 12:1–2; James 5:10.

330. Faithfulness May Often Be Accused of Being Unloving. Of that stalwart defender of the faith Athanasius his biographer, Dr. Hagenback, wrote, "It was his vocation with unfaltering boldness to stand up for the church's exact and orthodox belief, to resist the course of error, a duty as difficult as it was important. He was accused of pride, harshness, stubbornness. Certain it is that in that breast of iron, which he ever offered to the enemies of truth, he hid a royal measure of love to the flock that he led and to the whole church of Christ." Luther was named a "severe, sharp physician," "a bold, rebellious, contentious spirit," "a wild, drunken swine." *References:* Luke 17:3; Acts 20:28–30; Gal. 2:11; Eph. 5:11; 1 Thess. 2:3–5; 1 Tim. 5:20; Titus 1:13; 2:15; Jude 3–4.

331. General Jackson feared God, and he feared nothing else. When the Confederates were falling back at Bull Run, or Manassas, General Lee rallied his men by calling out, "Look to Jackson! There he stands like a stone wall!" That made Jackson famous in the South and in the North and in history. So Christians should stand as firm as a wall over against the temptations in the battles of life. *References:* 2 Kings 22:2; Job 23:11; Dan. 3:18; Acts 20:24; 1 Cor. 15:58; Heb. 10:23; Rev. 2:10.

Related illustrations: 282, 557, 833, 834, 883, 908, 910.

False Gods
See also **Money**

332. Ambrose Bierce, cynic that he was, was not wholly wrong when he wrote, "Mammon is the chief god of America's leading religion." *References:* Prov. 15:27; Eccl. 5:10; 1 Tim. 6:9–10; James 5:3; 2 Peter 2:15.

333. *Newsweek* magazine once had a stack of silver dollars as its cover picture. On them were printed the words "In Oil We Trust." *References:* Luke 12:15; 1 Tim. 6:9–10; 2 Peter 2:15.

334. In 1929 people jumped out of windows for religious reasons. Their god, money, had failed them. *References:* Eccl. 5:10; 1 Tim. 6:9–10; James 5:3.

Related illustrations: 130, 661.

False Teachers
See also **Heretics**

335. Mr. Seton Thompson, who spent years watching the lives of wild animals, declares that the instinct to recognize danger that some of them have is so extraordinary that it really seems as if there must be an angel who warns and protects them. Defended by this instinct only, they will not touch poisonous grasses, and they unerringly avoid the presence of their foes. But people are not like that. They open their doors and their hearts to false prophets, who hide the hook of falsehood with a bait of truth (cf. 2 Tim. 3:5). There is hardly a person in the world so mean as to lie to another about the right road to the next town. But how many folks mislead others about the right road to heaven! *References:* Matt. 7:15–23; Gal. 1:6–10; 2 Thess. 2:9–12; 2 Tim. 3; 4:3–5.

Family

336. The family is like a book—the children are the leaves; the parents are the cover that protective beauty gives. *References:* Ps. 127; 2 Cor. 12:14; Eph. 6:4.

337. A man in a dream found himself on Judgment Day at the wrong side of the Judge. The terror of his situation grew when he saw his children, whom he had always dearly loved, near him. He implored the Judge to save at least his children, even though he might hope for no change of his own fate.

But he was told that if he had felt the same concern for his family when he and they were still on earth, the end would have been altogether different; now it was too late. He awoke and without delay sought salvation for himself and his family. *References:* Deut. 4:9; 1 Kings 22:52; 2 Chron. 22:3; Prov. 22:6; Jer. 9:14; Amos 2:4; 2 Tim. 1:5.

Faultfinding

338. Faults are always thick where love is thin. *References:* Prov. 17:9; 1 Cor. 13:5; 1 Peter 4:8.

339. How frequently we point out our neighbor's faults but ignore our own! And yet how inconsistent and unwise that is! Or have you ever observed a person weeding his neighbor's garden to the neglect of his own? (Scriver) *References:* Matt. 7:1–5; John 8:3–9; Rom. 2:1–3.

340. A family was on its way home from church. The father was criticizing the sermon, the mother was finding fault with the choir, and the sister was running down the organist. They all quieted down in a hurry when little Jimmy piped up and said, "I thought it was a pretty good show for a dime." *References:* Matt. 7:1–5; Rom. 2:1, 21; 1 Tim. 6:4.

341. From Aesop's Fables: "Jupiter, making man, gives him two wallets, one for his neighbor's faults, the other for his own. He threw them over man's shoulders, so that one hung in front and the other behind. The man kept the one in front for his neighbor's faults, and the one behind for his own, so that, while the first was always under his nose, it took some pains to see the latter." Then Aesop adds: "This custom, which began early, is not quite unknown at the present day." (Phaedrus, *Fables* 4.9.1).

So we see that the beam in our own eye blinds us to our faults, sins, and oddities. *References:* Matt. 7:3–5; John 8:3–10; Rom. 2:1–3; 14:12–13; Gal. 6:1–4; James 4:10–12; 1 John 1:8.

342. We look at our neighbor's errors with a microscope and at our own through the wrong end of a telescope. We have two sets of weights and measures, one for home use and the other for foreign. Every vice has two names; we call it by its flattering and minimizing name when we commit it and by its ugly name when our neighbor does it. (MacLaren) *References:* Prov. 20:6; 30:12; Matt. 7:1–5; Rom. 2:1, 21–24; 2 Cor. 10:12; 1 John 1:8.

Fear of God, Filial

343. To live with fear and not be afraid is the final test of maturity. (Edward Weeks) *References:* Deut. 31:6; 2 Chron. 32:7; Ps. 91:5; Prov. 3:24; Is. 12:2; 1 John 4:18.

Related illustration: 193.

Fear of God, Slavish

See also **Superstition**

344. Superstitious Fear of God. Have you ever met someone who, when something good comes along, starts wondering when God's going to take it back? Pagans of long ago in Germany and Holland used to think that way. If Johann met Hans in the forest and said, "Hey, Hans! I got that horse I wanted—good price, too!" in a second both men would gasp, and Johann would run to the nearest tree and start pounding on it. People believed that the gods lived in trees, and if the gods heard about any human happiness, they would become angrily jealous; they would cause mischief. So Johann, realizing his mistake in the listening forest, would rap on trees to drive the gods away. "Knock on wood!" Quite a custom, don't you think?

Is that our custom with God? It's either "Thy will be done" or "Knock on wood." Either God is out for our good, or we must be out for our own, on our own. There is a community of folks around us who are afraid of losing jobs and afraid that God may punish them in that way. *References:* Gen. 3:8; Is. 40:25–31; Jer. 10:1–2; Luke 24:38; Acts 17:22–31; Heb. 10:27; 1 John 4:18.

345. Irrational Fears. A magazine cartoon shows a psychiatrist with his filled-up pad in hand saying to his patient, "Now, my friend, besides your fear of nerve gas, irritating tars, sonic boom, human wolf packs, hexachlorophene, rock music, Wall Street, DDT sprays, plastic bombs, the Birch Society, labor unions, riots, intercontinental missiles, urban sprawl, inflation, unemployment, Red China, street crimes, and revolving credit, do you have any IRRATIONAL fears?" *References:* Num. 13:31–14:1; Matt. 14:30; Luke 24:37–38; 1 John 4:18.

346. When Hamburg was stricken with the plague and large numbers were dying, the healthy, in mortal dread of being called in to swell the ranks of death, flocked to the churches of the city, which they would not do previously. It was not the fear of God that drew them to church but the fear of the cholera; as soon as the pest abated, the zeal for the worship of God also abated. (Dallmann) *References:* Judg. 2–3; Ps. 78:35–36; Ezek. 33:31; Matt. 3:7–9; Mark 7:6; Luke 6:46–49; John 6:66.

347. Fear's Destructive Effects. There is an old Arab tale about Pestilence overtaking a caravan on the desert way to Baghdad. "And pray," said the chieftain of the caravan, "what are you going to do in Baghdad?" To which Pestilence replied, "I shall claim 5,000 lives." Actually, some 50,000 died in Baghdad. Later, when meeting Pestilence again, the chieftain said to him,

"But you were unfair. You promised to take only 5,000." Pestilence replied, "I kept my word. I took only 5,000. The other 45,000 died of fear." *References:* Ps. 3:6; 27:1–3; 46:1–3; 55:4–5; 91:5; 118:6; Prov. 3:24.
Related illustrations: 193, 343, 938.

Fellowship
See also **Church Attendance**
348. In the arid parts of the western United States the early settlers made their homes along the streams. Anyone doing otherwise would have been thought very foolish. But there are individuals and families who establish themselves far away from their church or otherwise arrange their home affairs in a way that gives them no time or opportunity to draw water from the stream of life, thus inflicting on themselves the greatest possible harm. *References:* Ps. 26:8; 27:4; 84:10; 122:1; Is. 55:1; Zech. 8:21; Luke 4:16; Heb. 10:25.
Related illustration: 4.

Flattery
349. "In your church you hear nothing but sin and sin and more sin." Well, we would all rather be flattered than censured. But when it is a matter of life and death, flattery doesn't go far, does it? You wouldn't appreciate it very much if your doctor would try to make you forget your fever by telling you that your red cheeks improved your natural beauty. You would tell him, "I'm paying you to cure me, not to flatter me." All the remedies in the world cannot help you if he cannot diagnose your disease and apply the right remedy, and you do not care how terrible the disease is that he fixes on you if he has a remedy to cure you.

Well, here is the universal malady, sin, and here is the universal remedy, the blood of Jesus Christ, God's Son, that cleanses us from all sin. And blessed is everyone who does not take offense at this "blood-and-wounds theology" but takes refuge in the wounds of Christ. *References:* Prov. 24:24; 26:28; 28:23; 29:5; Matt. 11:6; Luke 7:23; 1 Thess. 2:5; 1 John 1:7.

Flesh

350. Our affections must not rise to become unruly passions; for then, as a river that overflows the banks, they carry much slime and soil with them. (Sibbes) *References:* Prov. 25:16; Rom. 6:12; James 3:2.

351. A mile or two above Niagara Falls, the river widens into a lake, where an oarsman may enjoy himself as if no cataract were near. But as it moves on, the river reaches a slope and the current gets so fearfully strong that, if a person gets into it, there is practically no human possibility of escaping from the falls. Little more than a line divides the sphere of safety from the sphere of danger. In the moral world also, there is little more than a line between the service of Christ and the service of the flesh. A person may drift into the sowing of the flesh very easily, but one cannot drift into the sowing of the Spirit. *References:* Matt. 6:24; Acts 20:28–31; Rom. 8:1–9; 1 Cor. 10:6–12; Gal. 3:3; 5:17; 6:7–8. *Related illustration:* 617.

Following God

See also **Discipleship**

352. Letting Jesus Lead Us. One evening at a mission station in the Belgian Congo a converted native prayed, "Lord Jesus, Thou art the needle, and I am the cotton." To the missionary this seemed strange language, and so he asked the man what he meant by his unusual words. It turned out that the native had visited the mission school that day and watched the girls sewing. What interested him most was that the thread always followed the needle. In

the same way, he wanted to follow Jesus wherever He led.

When Jesus tells us "Follow Me," He wants to have us so close to Him at all times, so completely yielded to Him, that we follow Him as directly and dependently as the thread follows the needle. *References:* Hos. 6:3; Matt. 4:18–20; 9:9; John 8:12; 10:27–28; 21:22; 1 Peter 2:21; Rev. 14:4.

353. The Elect Follow Him. A traveler relates that one day he came to a well at the time when the shepherds watered their flocks. Many different flocks came there at the same time. The sheep of the various flocks mingled, and no attempt was made to keep them separated. The traveler thought that the shepherds would have a tedious and difficult job separating them. But when the time came, each shepherd went his way calling his sheep, and every sheep followed its shepherd. Every sheep of Christ knows and follows His voice. *References:* Ps. 77:20; Jer. 31:34; John 10:4, 16, 27; 18:37.

354. Look Onward and Upward. A man walking along a narrow ledge on a mountain has only one chance of safety. He must not look at his feet or at the yawning gulf beneath into which his dizziness will hurl him if he gazes down. He must look onward and upward. Look onward and upward at Christ and not at the waves, as Peter did. If you turn your eyes away from Him and fasten them on your troubles and afflictions, down you will be sure to go. (Maclaren) *References:* Gen. 19:15–26; Matt. 8:26; 14:28–33; Luke 21:28; John 3:15; Heb. 12:2. *Related illustrations:* 811, 819.

Forgetting God

355. Bennett Cerf told about a traveler for a big publishing house who couldn't wait to get to St. Louis, where his oldest friend owned a prosperous bookstore. "Sam," he said to the owner the moment they were alone, "I want you to lend me $2,000." "The answer, Joe," said Sam, "positively is no." "But, Sam," protested the salesman, "in 1929, when Bond and Share broke from 189 to 50, who gave you $10,000 to keep you from being wiped out?" "You did," admitted Sam. "And in 1931, when your daughter Shirley had the tropical disease, who took her to Florida because you couldn't get away from business? Who did, Sam?" "You, my friend, you did." "And in 1935, when we were fishing together, who dove into the rapids and saved you from drowning at the risk of his own life?" "You did, Joe. It was wonderful" "Well, then, Sam, in heaven's name, why won't you lend me $2,000 now when I need it?" "All the things you say are true," said Sam, nodding his head slowly, "but what have you done for me lately?" (Bennett Cerf, *Try and Stop Me* [Garden City, N.Y.: Garden City Books, 1944], pp. 189–90).

How much does God have to do for you before you trust Him? *References:* Deut. 6:10–12: 8:11–14; Is. 7:10–13; 51:13; Jer. 2:11–13; 31:32.

356. Savior, I've no one else to tell,
And so I trouble Thee.
I am the one forgot Thee so.
Dost Thou remember me?
(Emily Dickinson)
References: Is. 1:3; 43:16–26; 64:7–9; Dan. 9:13.
Related illustrations: 33, 294.

Forgetfulness
357. Forgetting the Needy. A boy in a poverty-stricken section of a large city found his way into a Christian day school. There he learned to know Jesus and was led to faith in Him. One day, long after, one of those wicked grown-up people who take special pleasure in

doing the work of the devil tried to shake the poor boy's faith by asking, "If God really loves you, why does He not tell somebody to give you a pair of shoes or enough coal to keep your home warm in winter?" The lad thought a moment and then, squaring his shoulders, looked at the speaker and said, "Jesus does tell somebody, and somebody forgets." Shall it be said of us that, when Jesus calls to service for the needy, we forget? *References:* Prov. 21:13; Ezek. 34:4; Matt. 25:44–45; Acts 20:35; Rom. 15:1; 1 John 3:17–18.

Forgiveness, Divine
358. Sin is forgiven not so that we may continue in it but that we might break loose from it; otherwise it would be called a permission and not a remission of sin. (Luther) *References:* Rom. 6:1–2; 2 Cor. 5:15; 1 Peter 2:24.

359. Fear of Forgiveness. Hydrophobia is said to be a very dangerous disease in animals because it will, for example, drive a dog mad with a desire to bite and tear when all the while it dreads the thing it really wants, a drink of water. So there are people who rush madly about, taking their spite out on everything and everybody, trying to find satisfaction in one thing or another, whereas they are afraid of the one thing they need, the forgiveness and mercy of God. As St. Augustine once put it, "O Lord, our souls come from Thee, and they know no rest until they rest in Thee." *References:* Prov. 28:1; Is. 2:19; 9:13; 33:14; 66:4; Ezek. 33:11; Rev. 9:20–21; 16:11.

360. Forgiven and Forgiving. Not far from New York is a cemetery with a grave that has just one word on the headstone: "FORGIVEN." There is nothing else—no name, no date of birth, no date of death, no word of praise for the departed—just the one word, "FORGIVEN." And yet what greater word could possibly be written above our own last resting place? To the word "FORGIVEN" I would want to add just one other: "FORGIVING." "Forgiven" and "forgiving" belong together, just as He placed them together when He taught us to pray: "Forgive us our trespasses as we forgive those who trespass against us." *References:* Ps. 130:4; Matt. 6:12–14; Mark 11:25; Luke 11:4; Eph. 4:32; Col. 3:13.

361. Freely Forgiven, We May Approach God's Throne. One night a condemned conspirator on the life of the premier of Ceylon sat alone in his cell waiting for dawn and his own execution. Suddenly he roused himself from apparently somber despair to ask that a certain Christian missionary he named be summoned to his cell as quickly as possible. When the astonished missionary arrived, knowing that the condemned man had been a Buddhist monk all his adult life, he was even more surprised to hear the man ask that he might be baptized immediately in the Christian faith. Assured that the man knew and understood the basic implications of his request, the missionary finally asked why he wanted to be baptized at that moment. The man replied with patent conviction that, since he must die, he "wished to die in a faith by which he could come freely to God—unrestrained by personal unworthiness and confident that he could entreat forgiveness simply out of love and mercy." *References:* Ps. 88:11–13; 103:1–4; 130; Luke 23:43; 2 Tim. 4:18 (dying with God's forgiveness). Heb. 4:14–16; 10:19; 1 John 4:17 (freely approaching God's throne).

362. When the great church father Augustine was near death, and his strength was ebbing away, he begged one of his friends to paint on the wall opposite his bed the words of Psalm 32: "Blessed is he whose transgressions are forgiven, whose sins are covered. Blessed is the man whose sin the Lord does not count against him." And the dying Augustine lay there, gazing at those words as the darkness closed in. There will be, dear friend in Christ, nothing else worth clinging to at last than those words to the repentant sinner. *Reference:* Ps. 32.
Related illustration: 992.

Forgiveness, Human
See also **Reconciliation**
363. Forgiving and Forgetting. There is too much of the spirit of the Highland man who, having been persuaded on what was supposed to be his deathbed to forgive a neighbor who had been led into his chamber for a formal reconciliation, called after him as he was leaving the room, "Remember, if I get better, this will all be off!" (W. Taylor) *References:* Is. 43:25; 1 Peter 3:9.

364. C. S. Lewis points out, "Everyone says forgiveness is a lovely idea until they have something to forgive." *References:* Matt. 6:12; Mark 11:25; Luke 11:4; 17:4; Eph. 4:32; Col. 3:13.

365. Jeanette Lockerbie in *The Image of Joy* tells about having overheard a Christian say about a fellow believer, "I've buried the hatchet—but I've left the handle sticking up." *References:* Matt. 18:21–22; Luke 17:3–4.

366. Forgiving One's Enemies. When Louis XII became king of France, he caused a list to be made of his persecutors and marked against each of their names a large black cross. When this became known, the enemies of the king fled. But the king, hearing of their fears, caused them to be recalled with the assurance of pardon and said that he had put a cross beside each name to remind them of the cross of Christ. He intended to follow the example of Him who prayed for His murderers, "Father, forgive them, for they know not what they do." *References:* Matt. 6:12–14; Mark 11:25; Luke 11:4; 17:4; 23:34; Eph. 4:32; Col. 3:13.

367. The first missionaries to Labrador found no word for forgiveness in the Eskimo language. They had to coin one, and they made a glorious choice: "not-being-able-to-think-about-it-anymore."

This is the quality of God's mercy to us. It determines the nature and measure of our merciful forgiveness person to person. *References:* Is. 43:25; Matt. 18:15; Heb. 10:17; James 5:20.

368. Forgiveness Through God's Love. Booker T. Washington, one of the great American Black leaders, wrestled at one period in his life with the gross difficulties of forgiveness but found the path to victory. He said, "When I saw the injuries and insults hurled against my people, I grew to hate white men. I hated them until my soul dried up. Then I took my hatred to Jesus Christ. He took the hatred out of my heart. He showed me how to forgive and how to love white men." That's the path to forgiveness, whether someone has snubbed you or hurt your business or killed your loved one. Stand at the foot of the cross, look to Him who hangs there, ask Him to give you His love. *References:* Matt. 5:43–48; Luke 6:27–36; 23:34; Acts 7:59–60; 1 Thess. 5:15 (forgiving one's enemies). John 13:34; 15:9; 1 Thess. 3:12; 1 John 3:16 (loving others with Christ's love).

Related illustrations: 360, 398, 595, 777.

Free Will

369. Free will in conversion is a downright lie. Like the woman in the gospel, the more it is taken in hand by physicians, the worse it is made. (Luther) *References:* John 6:44; 15:6; 1 Cor. 1:27–28.

370. A friend of mine thought it very unfair to influence a child's mind by inculcating any opinion before it had come to the age of discretion to choose for itself. I showed him my garden and told him it was my botanical garden. "How so?" said he; "it is covered with weeds." I replied, "That is only because it has not yet come to its age of discretion and choice. The weeds, you see, have taken the liberty to grow, and I thought it unfair of me to prejudice the soil towards roses and strawberries." (Coleridge) *References:* Deut. 4:9; 6:6–7; Prov. 22:6; Is. 28:9; Amos 2:4; John 21:15; Eph. 6:4.

Friends

371. False Friends. Have you ever seen ants swarm over the flower bud of the opening peony? How they cling to it! How nursingly they go round and round it! Is it because they love flowers? No! It is so that they may lick up the sugary secretion of the bud. So there are many who cling to people and call themselves their friends not because they love them but because of what they can get out of them. (Beecher) *References:* Job 19:19; Ps. 41:9; 55:12–13; Micah 7:5; Matt. 26:56; 2 Tim. 4:10.

Related illustration: 17.

Fruitfulness

372. Only What Is Alive Can Be Fruitful. If I planted my watch, dare I hope for a crop of watches? Why not? The watch is the product of the trained human mind and skillful human hand, but there is no life in it that could germinate and bring forth fruit. Christ alone by His indwelling can bring forth fruit in our life that is pleasing to God. *References:* Matt. 5:36; 6:27; John 3:27; 15:4–5; 2 Cor. 3:5.

373. Unfruitfulness of Hypocrisy. There is a counterfeit olive tree in Palestine. It is called the wild olive, or the oleander. It is in all points like the genuine tree, except that it yields no fruit. When I see a person taking up a large space in Christ's spiritual orchard and absorbing a vast amount of sunlight and soil and yielding no real fruit, I say, "Ah, there is an oleander." (Brown) *References:* Matt. 3:10; 7:15–23; John 15:1; Rom. 11:17–25.

G

Giving

See also **Stewardship**

374. I never knew a child of God being bankrupted by his benevolence. What we keep we may lose, but what we give to Christ we are sure to keep. (Cuyler) *References:* Ps. 41:1; Mal. 3:10–12; Luke 6:38.

375. Liberal givers are like trees, which, after their lower branches have been cut, grow all the better and bring a larger amount of fruit. (Stock) *References:* Prov. 3:9–10; Luke 6:38; 2 Cor. 9:7.

376. Christians ought to give more liberally. They ought to be more like a mirror. Instead of taking beams of light and selfishly absorbing them and keeping them, they should reflect them and give them out again. (Beecher) *References:* Prov. 11:24; Matt. 10:8; 2 Cor. 9:7.

377. Obligatory Giving. Christian giving does not need to be commanded. It is poor virtue that only obeys a precept. Gifts given because it is duty to give them are not really gifts but taxes. (MacLaren) *References:* Ex. 25:2; Matt. 10:8; 2 Cor. 8:8.

378. Complaining About Giving. Two members of the same congregation were leaving a church service one Sunday morning. As they started walking away from God's house, the one lifted up his voice in bitter complaint. "Well," he said, "we heard it again this morning. We're supposed to give

willingly, give regularly, give generously. Give, give, give! When are all these appeals for money going to stop?" His friend turned to him and said, "Bill, you remember my son Jim, don't you? When Jim came into the world he cost me quite a tidy sum. I had to pay the doctor bill and the hospital charges, buy a crib for the little fellow, and the like. Moreover, money had to be spent for medicine, food, clothing, and other such items. As Jim began to grow up, expenses increased. When he started school, additional money was required for transportation, books, and certain school activities. In due time we were told that he should have braces on his teeth. That was a rather expensive undertaking. He entered high school, and it took more money to support him. And then he went away to college. You can well imagine what that cost! Well, as you may remember, just a few weeks before he was to graduate he became critically ill. We did everything we could for him, but the good Lord was pleased to call Jim home to heaven. Bill, since we buried our boy, he hasn't cost us a single additional cent. No, not one cent!" *References:* Gen. 28:22; Prov. 11:24; Mal. 3:8–10; Matt. 25:34–40; Luke 6:38; 12:15–21; 2 Cor. 9:7.

379. Giving Liberally. An Indian once heard that white people slept on feathers and enjoyed it. So he thought that he would also try this. He took

85

three feathers, placed them on a rock for his pillow, and lay down to sleep. But he had a poor night's rest. In the morning he awoke with a headache and exclaimed, "How is it possible for white people to sleep on feathers and enjoy it?" What was his trouble? He had not taken enough feathers. Had he put thousands of them in a bag and used that for a pillow, he would have experienced how satisfactory it is to sleep on feathers. So it is with many Christians. They do not enjoy giving because they do not give freely. (L. H. Schuh) *References:* Deut. 16:17; 1 Chron. 29:9; Matt. 10:8; Luke 21:1–4; Acts 4:34–35; 11:27–30; 2 Cor. 9: 6–7.

380. Our Financial Responsibility.
Through someone's neglect a sheep
  has been lost;
Lord, is it I?
Some of us failed to figure the cost;
Lord, is it I?
The needy have suffered, the orphan
  has cried,
The kingdom of God to heathen
  denied,
Because some of us laid our funds
  aside;
Lord, is it I?

References: 2 Chron. 29:7; Prov. 28:27; Is. 43:24; Mal. 3:8–9; Matt. 26:22; Acts 5:1–2.

381. Giving with Love. God's great action is the eternal reminder that, though you may give without loving, you cannot love without giving. As someone has phrased it:

God made the sun—it gives.
God made the moon and stars—
  they give.
God made the air—it gives.
God made the clouds—they give.
God made the earth and sea—
  they give.
God made the trees—they give.
God made the flowers—they give.
God made the fowls—they give.
God made the beasts—they give.
God made the PLAN—He gives.
God made man—he . . . ?

References: Deut. 16:17; Matt. 10:8; 1 Cor. 16:2; 2 Cor. 9:7; 1 John 4:10–11.

382. A public meeting was held in a certain English town in the interest of foreign missions. The chairman was reading a list of donors. "Mr. So-and-so, a hundred guineas." Tremendous cheering! "Mr. So-and-so, 50 pounds." Great cheering. "Mr. So-and-so, 6 pennies." No cheering. Not being pleased with the cold reception of a gift that probably involved as much sacrifice, possibly more, than any of the foregoing, the chairman in the breathless silence exclaimed: "Hush! I think I hear the clapping of the pierced hands." The audience keenly felt the rebuke. *References:* Prov. 11:25; Mark 12:41–44; Luke 21:1–4; Acts 4:34; 20:35; 2 Cor. 8:1–6; 9:6.

383. God Blesses Unselfish Giving. Some years ago a boy of 16 left home because his parents were too poor to keep him any longer. He was not well educated but knew something about making soap. As he trudged along, he met an old canal captain who prayed with him and gave him this advice: "Be a good man, give your heart to Christ, pay the Lord all that belongs to Him of every dollar you earn, and make an honest soap." When the boy arrived in New York, he found employment making soap. He soon became a partner, later sole owner of the business. At first he gave two-tenths, then three-, four-, five-tenths. After his family was educated and plans for life were settled, he gave all income to the Lord's work. The Lord blessed him more than ever. This is the story of William Colgate, who has left a name that will never die. We are not as poor as the Macedonians or as wealthy as William Colgate, but we have one beautiful thing in common: "You know the grace of our Lord Jesus Christ, that though he was rich, yet for your sakes he became poor, so that by his poverty you might become rich" (2 Cor. 8:9). *References:* Prov. 22:9; Mal. 3:10–12; Luke 6:38; Acts 4:32–35; 20:35; 2 Cor. 8:1–9; 9:6.

384. Using What You Have Wisely While You Still Have It. Henry Thornton, always a generous supporter of his church, once sent a check for $100 to the church treasurer. A telegram informed him shortly thereafter that he had lost $10,000. Feeling the sting of his loss, he asked for the return of the check—and made out another for $1,000. "For," said he, "God has just informed me that I may not possess my property much longer and that I must use it well." It is not so much what we give to the Lord but what we keep from Him that makes us poor. *References:* Ex. 36:5; 1 Chron. 29:3; Mal. 3:10; Luke 21:1–4; Acts 4:34–35; 11:29–30; 2 Cor. 8:1–5.

Related illustrations: 188, 657.

Glory to God
385. His Glory Seen Through Jesus' Death. Some of the world's greatest and most noble men and women gave evidence of a deep inner strength and displayed a measure of real glory at the time of their death. They may have been misunderstood, unjustly judged, criticized, or condemned in their lifetime, but in the hour of death their true nobility and place in the scheme of things was seen. Abraham Lincoln had his enemies during his lifetime, but even those who complained about him and held him in a low regard recognized something of his glory and greatness when he died. Someone came out of the room where

Lincoln died saying, "Now he belongs to the ages." Joan of Arc was burned as a witch and a heretic in a city square. A secretary of the king of England who witnessed all left the scene of Joan's burning saying, "We are all lost because we have burned a saint."

Jesus Christ glorified His Father in His death. A Roman soldier who was present on that Friday saw it as he stood looking up to the cross. Do you recall what he said? "Surely this man was the Son of God" (Mark 15:39). *References:* Matt. 27:54; Mark 15:39; Luke 23:47.

386. When Arturo Toscanini was conducting a rehearsal of the New York Philharmonic Orchestra in Beethoven's Ninth Symphony and had judged that all were ready, he had them play the entire work without interruption. When the finale had reached its stirring close, there was silence. "Who am I?" he asked. "Who is Toscanini? I am nobody. It is Beethoven . . . he is everything!" To a Christian a similar question comes: Who am I? Who are you? We are nobody! Christ is everything! (*Christian Clippings*). *References:* Mark 1:7–8; Luke 3:16; John 3:27–30; Gal. 2:20; Phil. 3:4–8; Rev. 22:8–9.

387. To Deny Christ's Deity Is to Deny His Glory. During the reign of Theodosius the Great in the fourth century, the Arians made their most vigorous attempts to undermine the doctrine of the divinity of Jesus Christ. But when Theodosius made his son Arcadius partner with himself on his throne, it became the happy opportunity for him to see the God-dishonoring character of their creed.

Among the bishops who came to congratulate Theodosius on the occasion was the famous and esteemed Amphilochus, who suffered much under Arian persecution. He approached the emperor, made a very handsome and dutiful address, and was about to leave. "What!" said Theodosius. "Do you take no notice of my son? Do you not know that I have made him a partner with me in the empire? Is this all the respect you pay to a prince that I have made of equal dignity with myself?" At this the bishop rose and looking the emperor in the face said, "Sir, do you so highly resent my apparent neglect of your son because I do not give him equal honor with yourself? What must the eternal God think of you, who have allowed His coequal and coeternal Son to be degraded in His proper divinity in every part of your empire?" (Jeffers) *References:* John 5:23; 14:7–9; 17:5; Acts 2:36; Phil. 2:9–11; Col. 2:9; 1 Tim. 3:16; Heb. 1:5–13.

388. People still offer good and favorable opinions about who Christ was. The German atheist Fichte even wrote of Him: "Till the end of time all the sensible will bow low before this Jesus of Nazareth, and all will humbly acknowledge the exceeding glory of this great phenomenon."

Richter the pantheist calls Him "the purest of the mighty, the mightiest of the pure, who still continues to rule and guide the ages."

Hegel the philosopher wrote: "Among the improvers of ideal humanity He stands in the very first class and remains the highest model of religion within the reach of our thought."

Renan, the French rationalist, said: "Jesus is unique in everything, and nothing can compare with Him. He is a man of colossal dimension."

Such answers are complimentary, but they express nothing about the true nature or mission of Jesus Christ. Our verdict on His person is inadequate if we merely elevate Him to the highest rank among the sons of men. *Refer-ences:* Matt. 16:13–20; Mark 15:39; John 1:49; 4:29; 11:27; 20:28; Acts 8:37.

God

389. Luther declares: "Whoever knows that God is gracious to him walks through life along a path of roses, even in tribulation, and for him the land flows with milk, honey, and precious wine." *References:* Rom. 8:28–39.

390. People Long for God Even When Ignorant of Him. A child feels that its wants are taken care of when food and drink are offered, though it may not be able to explain why it cried for them. People who are unhappy because they are not at peace with God desire such peace, though they cannot analyze their desires. *References:* John 4:22; Acts 17:23.

391. What kind of proof does God offer us that He exists and that He loves? Could it be that the signs of God's presence are so plentiful that we don't recognize them as footprints of the Divine but see them only as part of the ordinary? We normally think of the suspension of the laws of nature, such as the parting of the Red Sea, as a miracle offering proof of God's existence and care. But isn't there more proof in the predictability and precision with which the law of nature works? Rabbi Harold S. Kushner in *When Bad Things Happen to Good People* observed:

Our human bodies are miracles, not because they defy laws of nature, but precisely because they obey them. Our digestive systems extract nutrients from food. Our skins help to regulate body temperature by perspiring. The pupils of our eyes expand and contract in response to light. Even when we get sick, our bodies have built-in defense mechanisms to fight the illness. All these wonderful things happen, usually without our being aware of them, in accordance with the most precise laws of nature.

References: Ps. 19:1–6; 97:6; Acts 14:17; Rom. 1:19–20.

392. The Hidden God. God is everywhere, yet He is so elusive that He seems to be nowhere. A modern writer one evening said to a group of friends as they sat around a table together, "I've been trying to catch up with God all my life, but I've never quite made it. Often I've come into a room and had the strong feeling that God was there until just one second before I arrived." *References:* Job 23:8–9; Ps. 10:1; 13:1; 89:46; Is. 45:15; Hos. 5:6; Acts 17:22–31.

393. Paltry Conceptions of God. What do the people with whom you live and work think of Jesus? As J. B. Phillips notes in *Your God Is Too Small,* perhaps they view Him as a sort of "resident policeman"—that troublesome, gnawing conscience within them that gives them so much trouble all the time. Perhaps they view Christ as the "gentle Jesus meek and mild"— the "pale Galilean" who wouldn't hurt a fly and who died a tragic martyr's death to uphold His principles. Maybe they know Christ as a "secondhand God" or as "God in a box"—neatly wrapped up with all the answers in a little pocket Bible they carry with them. But all these are muddy conceptions of the true nature of our blessed Lord. *References:* Is. 9:6–7; Matt. 16:27: 28:18; John 3:31: Phil. 2:9–11; Heb. 1:1–11; Rev. 5:12.

394. When St. Augustine was trying to encompass the mystery of the Holy Trinity with his finite mind, he was rebuked for his vain attempt by a little boy who was trying to dip the water out of the ocean with a little shell into a little hole in the sand. This story teaches us to put our finger on our lips

and to hold our reason in captivity. Our God, who has revealed Himself in the Bible, is inscrutable and unsearchable in His being. *References:* Job 11:7; 33:12–14; Ps. 145:3.

Related illustrations: 78, 262, 395, 677, 908.

God's Name

395. The sun is always equally hot and luminous in itself, but it is not so to us. Sometimes it is hotter, and sometimes it is colder; sometimes brighter, sometimes less bright; and for several hours each day we do not see it at all and are left in night and darkness. So it is with God and His name. In itself it is always holy, yet it is not always so among us. It is more revered, more hallowed, at one time than at another, and by some it is not hallowed at all. And the prayer is that it be becomingly revered, sanctified, and hallowed— that *we* render to Him the glory due His name. *References:* Lev. 22:2; Dan. 2:20; Matt. 6:9; Luke 11:2.

God's Will

396. A picture by a Dutch artist represents the interior of a kitchen, and the figure in the picture is an angel handling pots and pans and doing all the work connected with the situation. It is not hard to see what the artist intended to convey by his picture, namely, that our Christian calling may be fulfilled in the commonest surroundings, and that wherever our lot is cast, if the right spirit possesses us, our service may be in the sight of God like that of the angels, who in doing His will, do it well. *References:* Matt. 10:41–42; 25:23; Luke 16:10; 19:17; 1 Cor. 15:58.

397. When the Crusaders heard the voice of Peter the Hermit bidding them go to Jerusalem and take it from the hands of the invaders, they cried out at once, *"Deus vult!"* God wills it! And every man plucked his sword from his scabbard and set out to reach the holy sepulchre, believing that God had willed their mission. God has willed that we should not die in our sins; God has willed that we should be saved; God has willed that we should be with Him eternally in heaven. As we hear the voice of Jesus urging us to come to Him and be saved, let us with God's weapons go forth to capture the citadel of sin and make our salvation sure. *References:* Ezek. 33:11; Matt. 11:28–30; Mark 16:15; John 1:12–13; Rom. 10:13; 1 Tim. 2:3–4; 2 Peter 1:10–11; 3:9.

Related illustration: 262.

Good for Evil

398. Stephen Douglas insulted Abraham Lincoln in many caustic speeches, but Lincoln gave him a place of honor at his inauguration. Edwin Stanton humiliated and grieved Lincoln in lawsuits and politics, yet the president made him secretary of war. Much pressure was brought to bear on Lincoln to have General Lee and his staff and other Confederate prisoners tried as war criminals and shot. Lincoln declared a general amnesty and thus permanently reunited the North and the South. *References:* Ex. 23:5; Prov. 25:21–22; Matt. 5:43–48; Luke 6:27–36; Acts 7:60; Rom. 12:17–21; 1 Thess. 5:15.

Related illustration: 809.

Good Works

399. Faith and works are like the light and heat of a candle; they cannot be separated. (C. F. W. Walther) *References:* Eph. 2:8–10; James 2:17–18; 1 Peter 2:12.

400. A Follow-through to Faith. In many sports much is made of the "follow-through." In baseball, in golf, and in basketball coaches teach their athletes that it is necessary that they develop the "follow-through" if their stroke or shot is to be correctly carried out. It seems senseless that something one does after hitting or shooting the ball will affect the shot. And it doesn't! But that is not the correct way of looking at it. The point is that the stroke or the shot can't be executed properly without the type of action that will result in the desired "follow-through." Similarly, good works are the necessary "follow-through" of faith. *References:* Matt. 7:21–23; 25:31–46; Eph. 2:8–10; Titus 3:4–8; James 2:17–26; 1 Peter 2:12.

401. Faith: The Power of Good Works. A woman was being shown through a corn mill powered by a river that ran close by the wall. But all the wheels were silent and still. "Where is the power?" she asked. She was shown a handle and told to press it. She did, and the mighty force was instantly turned on, the wheels were moved, and the place was alive with activity. So the power of God moves in on us at the touch of faith, so that we can be active in good works. *References:* Matt. 8:13; 17:20; Mark 9:23; Rom. 1:16–17; Eph. 2:8–10; Phil. 3:9.

402. Mothers will hoard up trifles belonging to their children that everybody else thinks are worthless. Jesus Christ has in His storehouse a cup of cold water, the widow's mite, and many other things that the world counts of no value, but that He recognizes as precious. (MacLaren) *References:* Matt. 10:41–42; 26:7–10; Luke 21:1–4; 2 Cor. 8:12.

Related illustration: 323.

Gospel

403. Only the Gospel comforts. Christ has the only hand in all the universe that can touch a broken, bleeding heart without hurting it. (MacLaren) *References:* Is. 42:3; Mark 2:17; Luke 4:18; Heb. 4:15–16.

404. Isaac Newton, the renowned English astronomer, lay on his deathbed. His lifework was done, and he occupied himself more fully with the future. "I have learned two great facts," he confessed. "One is that I am a great sinner, and the other, that Jesus Christ is an even greater Savior." *References:* Ps. 23:4; 116:15; Prov. 14:32.

405. In Aesop's Fables, the wind and sun prepared to make a man shed his coat. The wind used its violence and force to tear off the coat, but the man only bound himself all the more within it. The sun gradually used its warmth on the man, and he voluntarily shed the coat himself. The gentle and gradual warmth of Christ's love brings about change much more effectively than intimidation or force. *References:* John 13:34; 15:9–12; 2 Cor. 5:14; Gal. 2:20; 1 Thess. 3:11–13; 1 John 3:16.

406. The Gospel's Superiority. I challenge anyone to show me anything better, anything more suited to humanity and its wants, than the Gospel of Christ. It is better than philosophy. Philosophy can only disclose, only describe and classify. It cannot heal or cure. It is like the physician who knows the disease but has no remedy, but the Gospel of Christ prescribes an infallible and universal cure.

It is better than education. Education can only call out and develop what is in fallen human beings; the Gospel recreates the human heart and nature and lifts the person up to the fulness of the stature of Christ. Education stops at the surface; the Gospel, which is the power of God for salvation, penetrates to the center of human necessities.

It is better than morality. Morality is conformity to law. When perfect, it is a star rolling on its God-appointed course. But humanity has broken law—the star has swerved from its course. Morality cannot bring it back and keep it in its course. The Gospel can. It brings people back to God, makes them one with Him, gives them a new start, and keeps them safe on their heavenward course.

The Gospel is better than philanthropy. Philanthropy is the love of one person for another; the Gospel is the love of God for people. The one would better the human condition here; the other would not only save people now, but would lift them where they belong—to heaven and to God. (F. A. Noble) *References:* Is. 55:1–11; Matt. 13:44–46; 1 Cor. 1:18–24; 2:2; 3:11; Phil. 4:9.

407. The Gospel Is Christianity. The Nile is Egypt; it had deposited its soil, and by an annual overflow it maintains its fertility. The limits of that flood are the limits of life. Without the Nile, Egypt would be just another desert, a vast expanse of barren sands. Just so the Gospel is Christianity. Its limits are the limits of spiritual life. Without the Gospel, Christianity would be like all other religions, a spiritually dead and barren desert. (Guthrie) *References:* Mark 16:15; Luke 24:47; Rom. 1:16–17; 5:1; 2 Cor. 5:17–21; Phil. 3:9; Rev. 14:6.

408. Freedom from Sin. A wealthy Hindu boarded a ship at Bombay loaded down with chains; he could move about only with the help of servants and could never know peace or comfort. Squatted on deck in the midst of chains, he explained that while still a young man, he had vowed to put on a link for every sin he committed; now he was helpless under the cruel weight of 600 pounds. It is a blessed message of the Gospel that Christ has broken the dreaded fetters of superstition, fear, sin, and hell. *References:* Ps. 130:1–4; Luke 15:1–10; 1 John 1:9.

409. Perfect Spiritual Food. Some years ago two men named Crumbine and Tobey wrote a book about milk. They called it *The Most Nearly Perfect Food*. And so it is. Milk is indeed an astounding gift of God for physical nourishment. Scientists point out that milk contains all the essentials of a human diet. It has fat, proteins, salts, a form of sugar, and all the known vitamins. What is more, these ingredients are in the proportions needed by the human body. Milk is the one thing in nature that seems to have been intended specifically for human food, and there is no entirely satisfactory substitute for it. The milk producers of America have adopted a slogan: "You never outgrow your need for milk." This is more than a slogan. Experts say that milk is the most nearly perfect food for people of all ages, young and old. How very fitting that the apostle should choose milk as the symbol for the perfect spiritual food, the grace of God, which we need daily to nourish us in the risen life. *References:* Deut. 8:3; Is. 55:2; Matt. 4:4; 1 Cor. 3:2; Heb. 5:12; 1 Peter 2:2.

Related illustrations: 194, 206, 650, 673, 1003.

Government

410. Although just government protects all in their religious rights, true religion affords its surest support. (Washington) *References:* Prov. 14:34; Rom. 13:1–7; 1 Peter 2:17.

411. If the Gospel could be promoted or maintained by worldly powers, God would not have committed it to fishermen. (Luther) *References:* Zech. 4:6; John 1:13; 1 Cor. 1:26–29.

412. Half of the calamities with which the human race has been scourged have arisen from the union of church and state. (Cobb, historian) *References:* Matt. 11:12; John 8:36.

Grace

See also **Mercy**

413. Matthew Henry remarks, "Grace despised is grace forfeited. They that will not have Christ when they may, shall not have Him when they would." *References:* Ezek. 33:9; Luke 14:16–24; Acts 24:25; Heb. 2:1–3; 12:25.

414. No rich person in this world has enough money to buy a single moment of divine grace, and no poor person has so little that he cannot get all the grace he needs if he will but ask for it penitently and receive it believingly. *References:* Is. 55:1–2; Dan. 9:18; Rom. 11:6; Eph. 2:8–9.

415. On the tombstone of the great and learned scientist and renowned astronomer Copernicus, who was also a devout Christian, this Latin inscription, composed by himself, is engraved: "Not the grace of a Paul do I ask for nor for the pardon once shown unto Peter; only the forgiveness bestowed upon the thief on the cross do I petition." Beautiful epitaph! When the scenes of this earth fade from our mortal vision, may our eyes be fixed on Christ as our only hope and comfort and may our lips whisper the heartfelt petition: "Lord, remember me and take me into Your kingdom." The same cheering and precious response will greet you: "I tell you the truth, today you will be with me in paradise." *References:* Is. 55:7; Matt. 8:8; 15:22–28; Luke 18:13–14; 23:40–43.

416. In one of England's famous churches a grave marker, written by the man who lies there, reads: "John Newton, once an infidel and libertine, a servant of slavery in Africa, was by the rich mercy of our Lord and Savior Jesus Christ preserved, restored, pardoned, and appointed to preach the faith he had long labored to destroy." John Newton heard Christ's liberating words, "Be opened!" He gives his grateful testimony in his hymn, "Amazing Grace":

Amazing grace! How sweet the sound
That saved a wretch like me!
I once was lost, but now am found—
Was blind, but now I see.

References: Deut. 9:5; Dan. 9:18; John 9:25; Eph. 1:7; 1 Tim. 1:15; Titus 3:5.

417. Grace Not to Sin. On October 25, 1517, six days before he gave his 95 theses to the world, Luther delivered a sermon in the chapel of the castle of Duke George the Bearded in Dresden, Saxony. He said in part: "Our salvation must ever remain our foremost concern. Man can obtain it only through faith in Christ Jesus, not by his own good works."

At the dinner table the duke asked Barbara von Sala, his wife's companion, "How did you like Brother Martin's sermon?" "Ah," she replied, "let me hear just one more like it, and I can die in peace." This moved the duke to fiery indignation. He exclaimed, "I'd give much money not to have heard it. It makes men secure and reckless in sin." Here's the old thought: "Will not men sin if told they are not under the Law?" My friends, is this the effect of grace? Not at all. It is, on the contrary, the grace of God alone that makes alive from sin. *References:* John 8:31–36; Rom. 6:12–18; 1 Cor. 8:9; 2 Cor. 5:17; Gal. 5:13, 24; 1 Peter 2:16.

Related illustrations: 135, 257, 389, 409, 558, 856.

Gratitude

418. In St. Mary's Church, Cambridge, England, there is a hassock with these words embroidered on it: "Think—thank!" If we, the children of God by faith in Jesus Christ and the heirs of eternal life, stopped to think more of God's mercy and love toward us, we would thank Him more. *References:* Deut. 4:3–9; 6:10–12; 8:2–14; Col. 1:12–17.

419. Dr. William L. Stidger told in *Guidepost* (November 1953) that he decided one evening years ago to write to his boyhood schoolteacher and thank her for awakening in him a love for English poetry. Weeks later the lonely woman wrote him: "I want to let you know what your note meant to me. I am an old lady in my eighties, living alone in a small room, like the last leaf on a tree. I taught fifty years, yet in all that time yours is the first letter of appreciation I have ever received. It came on a blue, cold morning and cheered my lonely heart as nothing has in many years." From that time on until his death, Dr. Stidger wrote thank-you notes to many for the little things and many favors shown to him over the years. *References:* Ruth 2:10–11; Luke 17:15–19; 1 Thess. 5:18 (appreciating the gratitude of others). Neh. 9:26; Eccl. 9:15; Is. 1:2–3; Luke 17:11–19; Rom. 1:21 (so few are grateful).

420. If one should give me a dish of sand and tell me there were particles of iron in it, I might look for them with my eyes and search for them with my clumsy fingers and be unable to detect them. But let me take a magnet and sweep through it, and it will draw to itself the almost invisible particles. The unthankful heart, like my finger in the sand, discovers no blessings. But let the thankful heart sweep through life, and as a magnet finds the iron, so it will find in every day some heavenly blessing. (Beecher) *References:* Ex. 34:24–26; Ps. 92:1–6; 95; 100; 107; Luke 17:11–19; 1 Cor. 2:14.

421. The early Pilgrims after those first hard years had a custom for a while that at their Thanksgiving Day there would be five kernels of corn on each plate. Before the big meal each person would have to mention five things for which to be thankful. The five kernels reminded them that at one time that was the daily allotment of corn—five kernels per person per day. *References:* Deut. 6:10–12; 8:1–14; Ps. 63:3–8.

422. Grateful People Are Appreciated People. The newspaper editor in a fairly large town (according to *Guideposts,* November 1953) said that too often he feels that his time is too precious to have people come in to talk to him about their gripes. Therefore, he instructed his secretary to tell all who came and asked to see the editor that he was in conference at that moment. One day a woman came in to see the editor and received the same brushoff. As she left, she said to the secretary that she just wanted to thank Mr. Editor for the excellent editorial he had written the day before. This was something new, and the secretary thought that she might be able to contact the editor. He came out and talked more than 15 minutes to the woman who had taken time out to say "thank you." *References:* Ruth 2:10–11; 2 Sam. 9:1; 10:2; Acts 2:47; 28:10; Col. 3:15; 1 Thess. 5:18; Heb. 13:15.

423. The hymn "Now Thank We All Our God" was written by Martin Rinckart, who was born at Eilenburg, Germany, in April 1586, forty years after Martin Luther's death. His hymn has been called the German Te Deum and is considered by many as second only among German hymns to the Reformer's magnificent "A Mighty Fortress Is Our God." Rinckart was minister of the Gospel in Eilenburg during the terrible Thirty Years' War. Eilenburg was a walled town and therefore a place of refuge for thousands who had lost everything in the war. The overcrowded condition of the city brought on famine and pestilence. At times Rinckart was the only minister in the city. To serve thousands suffering from hunger and dying from disease was a Herculean task. Often he read the burial service for from forty to fifty persons a day. At last the number of dead each day was so great that it became impossible to bury them singly, and they were interred in groups in trenches.

Altogether, 8,000 persons died in Eilenburg during this time, including Rinckart's wife. At the same time Rinckart suffered several financial losses and failed to receive the proper consideration at the hands of the authorities of the city in spite of his unselfish and tireless efforts in behalf of the sick and the dying. And yet he wrote during this time that wonderful hymn of praise and thanksgiving to the Lord. (W. G. Polack) *References:* Hab. 3:17–18; Eph. 5:20; Phil. 4:6; 1 Thess. 5:18.

Related illustrations: 79, 468, 525, 640, 722.

Greatness

424. In Westminster Abbey there are a number of monuments bearing names of people about which no one seems to know anything. The persons who bore these names were probably famous when they ended their earthly careers, but through the years they have been forgotten. When a visitor to Westminster Abbey asked a custodian for information about a man who had been accorded the honor of a memorial in the stately edifice, the officer replied that he had not the slightest idea who he was. Such is earthly fame. People toil hard to make names for themselves, but in the majority of cases they are soon forgotten.

> After a while a vanished face,
> An empty seat and vacant place;
> After a while a man forgot,
> A crumbling headstone, an unknown spot. (*Junior Messenger*)

References: Job 18:17; Ps. 103:15–16; Eccl. 6:3–4.

Greed

See also **Ambition**

425. Avarice reigns most in those who have few good qualities to commend them; it is a weed that will grow only in a barren soil. *References:* Luke 12:16–20; Acts 16:19; 2 Peter 2:15.

426. You Can't Take 'Em with You. Some have been so wedded to their riches that they have used every conceivable means to take their wealth with them. Athenaeus reports of one who at the hour of his death devoured many pieces of gold and sewed the rest in his coat, commanding that they should be all buried with him. Hermocrates, being loath that any man should enjoy his goods after him, made himself heir of his own goods. (Grey) *References:* Job 1:21; Ps. 49:10; Prov. 23:5; 27:24; Eccl. 2:18; Jer. 17:11; Matt. 6:19–21; 1 Tim. 6:7.

427. Years ago when men went to Alaska to search for gold, some penetrated far into the interior. There they discovered a miner's hut that seemed as quiet as a grave. Entering it, they found the skeletons of two men and a very large quantity of gold on a rough table. There was also a letter that told about their successful hunt for gold. They were so eager to get gold that they ignored the early coming of winter. The more they mined, the more gold they found. Suddenly one day a fierce snowstorm struck. They could not escape because of blizzard conditions. Their food ran out. They were unable to move about in their cabin. They became so weakened that they lay down to die—surrounded by all that gold.

There are many people like those two foolish miners. They labor for wealth, property, and the status symbols on earth. Suddenly the icy hand of death is on them and what have they to show for their labors? What have their labors accomplished? Jesus asks a very important question, and all of us need to consider and answer it: "What good will it be for a man if he gains the whole world, yet forfeits his soul?" (Matt. 16:26). *References:* Prov. 27:24; Matt. 16:26; Luke 6:25; 12:13–21; 1 Tim. 6:9; Rev. 3:17.

428. A Theology of Greed or of Meekness? Books urging readers to look out for number one make the best seller lists. Dallas-based firms sell success in three-day seminars costing participants $900 apiece. These seminars teach self-confidence, enthusiasm, and goal setting. There's nothing wrong with drive and objectives, but the success is financial, and goals are defined by dollar amounts. In the words of one of the success merchants, "God created Cadillacs, Lincolns, and Mercedes for His followers, not for sinners." When challenged with "But I thought the meek were to inherit the earth," he replied, "They may inherit it, but they'll have to work like hell to gain title to it." *References:* Rom. 16:17–18; Phil. 3:17–19; Col. 3:2; Titus 2:11–12; 1 John 2:15; Rev. 3:17 (a theology of greed). Ps. 22:26; 37:11; 147:6; Is. 29:19; Zeph. 2:3; Matt. 5:5; 1 Peter 3:4 (the meek shall inherit the earth).

Related illustrations: 29, 183, 686.

Guilt

See also **Conscience**

429. An African convert put it this way: "When the story of Christ's death was first read to me, I cursed Judas and Pilate, the Jews and the soldiers. But when I understood it, I cursed myself, for I, too, have crucified Christ." *References:* Ps. 53:3; Is. 53:6; Acts 2:36–37; Rom. 3:23; 1 John 1:6–10.

Related illustration: 177.

H

Habits
430. I have seen in the autumn, when the trees have shed their leaves, that two or three leaves have stuck fast on the branches and have clung to them all the winter through. Storms have beaten them, frosts have bitten them, snow and rain have blackened them, yet they have held fast to the tree. But when the spring has come and the sap has begun to ascend and push its way through every branch and every twig, the leaves have disappeared. They were pushed off by the rising tide of new life; for death can never stand before life. So it is with us. Those old, inveterate habits that belong to our fallen nature are tough to get rid of. We battle with them and try to beat them off, but again and again we are defeated. But when the Spirit of the Lord fills and possesses us, these habits disappear almost unconsciously, because death cannot stand before life. *References:* Matt. 3:11–12; Rom. 8:9–14; 2 Cor. 3:5–6; 1 John 3:24.

431. William James, the well-known American psychologist, wrote a famous and brilliant chapter on habit. Habit, he pointed out, is extremely important and useful. It is the great flywheel of society, which keeps things in regular motion. It is supremely important for people to make habits serve them instead of letting habits master them. Cultivation of good habits puts great resources at one's disposal. Letting bad habits grow puts a ball and chain on one's feet.

Habits are important also for our religious life. To appoint and cultivate regular hours for prayer, Bible reading, and churchgoing serves to promote our Christian life. Such habits simplify matters. They facilitate and promote devotion. *References:* Jer. 13:23; 22:21; Dan. 6:10; Luke 4:16.
Related illustration: 633.

Happiness
432. One day a man came to a rationalistic, unbelieving preacher for comfort and peace of conscience. Said the preacher to him, "Forget about those things! Go to see and hear that famous comedian who is now playing in our city and is keeping his audience in a constant roar. That man will dispel these morbid broodings of yours." There was a moment of silence. Then the visitor groaned, "I am that comedian." So shallow and artificial is the joy of the world. Many people's hearts are bleeding and breaking while their lips are made to laugh. *References:* Job 20:5; Prov. 14:13; Eccl. 7:6; Luke 6:25.
Related illustrations: 25, 445, 466, 537.

Hardness of Heart
433. Voltaire expressed the typical attitude of unbelievers when he said, "Even if a miracle should be wrought in the open marketplace before a thou-

sand sober witnesses, I would rather mistrust my senses than admit a miracle." *References:* Luke 16:31; 22:66–71; John 4:48; 6:64; 10:25; 12:37; Acts 7:51.

434. Dr. Samuel Johnson, the celebrated English author, once proposed to a distinguished company of men and women of a literary club, at a time when infidelity was the mode of the day, to entertain them with a story that was a work of rare merit and charm. Without telling them the details, he read to them. They were delighted with its beautiful simplicity and the charm of its heroine. All were eager to learn the name of the author, who, all agreed, could grace any circle of literature and fashion. But they were confounded and dismayed when told that this narrative was found in the neglected and despised Bible (the story of Ruth). *References:* Ruth; 2 Chron. 36:16; Prov. 1:7; Jer. 6:10; Mark 7:13.

435. On a winter evening, when the frost is setting in with growing intensity, and when the sun is now far past the meridian and gradually sinking in the western sky, there is a double reason why the ground grows every moment harder and more impenetrable to the plow. On the one hand, the frost of evening with ever-increasing intensity is indurating the stiffening clods; on the other hand, the genial rays that alone can soften them are every moment withdrawing and losing their enlivening power. Take heed that it be not so with you. As long as you are unconverted, you are under a double process of hardening. The frosts of an eternal night are settling down on your souls, and the Sun of Righteousness, with westering wheel, is hastening to set for you forevermore. If the plow of grace cannot force its way into your ice-bound heart today, what likelihood is there that it will enter tomorrow?

(McCheyne) *References:* Ps. 95:7–11; Prov. 29:1; Ezek. 33:11; Rom. 2:4–5; 2 Cor. 6:2; Heb. 3:13; 4:1–7.

Hatred

436. A Product of Ignorance. With spiritual ignorance and unbelief goes opposition to God and hatred of all that pertains to God and godliness. The Soviet State Publishing House once issued a new dictionary of 20,000 "foreign," that is, non-Russian, words and phrases. The definition of the word "Bible" was: "A collection of fantastic legends without any scientific support . . . full of dark hints, historical mistakes, and contradictions." The word "religion" was defined as follows: "A fantastic faith in gods, angels, and spirits, a faith without scientific foundations. Religion serves for the subjugation of the working people and for building up the power of the exploiting bourgeois classes. The superstition of out-lived religion has been surmounted by the communist education of the working classes." *References:* Job 21:14–15; Is. 59:8; Jer. 5:4; Zech. 7:11–12; John 15:21; 16:3; Rom. 10:3; Eph. 4:18.

437. We Suffer from Our Own Hatred and Are Rewarded by Our Love. In Chicago's West Side residential district two neighbors who had lived side by side in perfect harmony for years became involved in a quarrel. Their anger took on grave proportions. One of them built a spite fence of brick 20 feet high, only to find that it shut out much of the sunshine and light he had previously enjoyed and that it was illegal. The man who hates often suffers more than the one who is hated.

At another place two neighbors were at peace, and there was no fence at all to separate the front yards. In fact, at the property line, the lawn appeared to be better kept and greener than any-

where else. Asked about this, one of the men explained: "When I water my lawn, I make sure that the sprinkler reaches well over the line so that I may do my full share. My neighbor always does likewise. The result? Instead of a spite fence we have a greener lawn." *References:* Prov. 10:12; 25:8; Matt. 5:25–26; 7:1–5; 1 John 2:9 (we suffer by our own hatred). Prov. 12:20; Matt. 5:9; Rom. 12:16–21; 14:19 (they enjoy peace who make peace).
Related illustrations: 48, 359.

Healing

438. Dr. Charles Mayo of the Rochester, Minn., clinic early adopted the ancient physician Galen's motto: "I bound his wounds, but God healed him." *References:* Ex. 15:26; Ps. 103:3; Jer. 8:22; 17:14; Hos. 6:1; Matt. 4:23; 1 Peter 2:24.

439. Luther: "Our burgomaster here at Wittenberg lately asked me if it were against God's will to use physic; for, said he, Dr. Carlstad has preached that whoever falls sick shall use no physic, but commit his case to God, praying that His will be done. I asked him, 'Did he eat when he was hungry?' He answered, 'Yes.' Then said I, 'Even so you may use physic, which is God's creature, as well as meat and drink, or whatever else we would use for the preservation of life.' " *References:* Luke 10:34; Col. 4:14; 1 Tim. 5:23.
Related illustration: 441, 736.

Heart

440. Parable of the Sower. Someone has wisely said that in this parable we have four pictures of human hearts hung in a single frame: "The hardhearted, the faint-hearted, the halfhearted, and the truehearted." *References:* Matt. 13:2–23; Mark 4:1–20; Luke 8:4–15.

441. Changing People's Hearts. One doesn't slap a bandage on a serious wound without first cleansing the wound, lest the infection or bleeding continue. When one has a virus, the symptoms of a fever or headache can be temporarily relieved, but it is for nothing unless the virus is combatted. Often society has attacked the externals of evil with armies, police forces, prisons, and new laws. It realizes, however, that it can do nothing good until the human heart is changed. *References:* Jer. 17:14; Matt. 7:18; 23:24–28; Luke 6:45.
Related illustrations: 240, 241, 257, 931.

Heaven

442. A youth in heaven will know more than an aged theologian on earth, just as a child standing on the top of a mountain can see very much farther than a giant at its base. (Guthrie) *References:* John 16:12; 1 Cor. 13:12; 1 John 3:2.

443. Turn your eyes up to the sun. Once the eyes have been bathed in its dazzling beams, how do other objects appear? All are changed. They have grown dim, if not dark and invisible. The treasures and pleasures of this world look different after a person has caught a glimpse of heaven. (Guthrie) *References:* Ps. 17:15; 1 Cor. 13:12; Heb. 11:13–16; 1 John 3:2.

444. Secure Only in Heaven. When Alexander von Humbolt, the German traveler and naturalist, experienced his first earthquake, the house he was in began to crack and fall around him. Hastily he sought refuge in another house, but found that it too was in ruins. Lifting his eyes to the hills, he saw that they were reeling and staggering like drunken men. Looking to the sea, he saw the bare keel of a ship in the mud, for the waters had fled. The ground under his feet trembled; there was no place of security any-

HELL

where. In his despair he looked up, and there above the ruins he saw that the heavens were unmoved. There let us lift our eyes in every hour of trial and trouble, and like King Hezekiah, let us seek our help from the Lord, who made heaven and earth. *References:* Deut. 33:26–27; 2 Kings 19:14–19; Ps. 20:6–7; 46:1–2; 121; Rev. 6:12–17.

445. Can Heaven Be Found? Some years ago a pastor one Sunday morning delivered an eloquent sermon on the joy of the saints in heaven. The next day he met one of his wealthy parishioners, who said: "Pastor, you delivered a very fine sermon on the bliss of heaven, but you neglected to show us *where* heaven is to be found. Can you perhaps tell me now?" The pastor quickly replied:

"It affords me great pleasure. Only a few minutes ago I came from yonder height visiting a sheep of my flock. There in a small dilapidated cottage dwells a poor widow with two little children. All three are ill, confined to their beds. They are without fuel, flour, and other necessary things. I would advise you to buy at once a supply of food and then to go to that distressed family and offer them your help. When you arrive, read to them the Twenty-third Psalm and kneel down before their beds to pray with them for their speedy recovery, and if you do not find heaven, I shall pay the bill."

The parishioner did as advised by his pastor. The next day he returned to his pastor, his face beaming with joy, and said: "Pastor, I have for 15 minutes experienced the happiness of heaven. I wish only that others would follow my example." (*Die Abendschule*) *References:* Matt. 5:7–9; Luke 18:22; John 21:15–18; 1 John 3:14.

Related illustrations: 552, 997.

Hell

446. Hell is truth seen too late. *References:* Matt. 25:44–45; Luke 13:25; 16:19–31.

447. Loneliness of Hell. In "The Cocktail Party," T. S. Eliot describes three people waiting in the anteroom of hell; each talks, but only of himself. No one listens to another or responds. Gradually they become aware that they need not expect the devil to come and lead them to a worse place. They are in hell, each utterly alone. When people's lives close in on themselves, when communication with God and other people is cut off, that is the aloneness of hell. *References:* Is. 59:2; Matt. 13:49; Luke 16:23; Jude 13.

448. A pious pastor one day had preached on future punishment. The next morning a young man called on him and said, "There is a small dispute between you and me, Pastor, and I thought I would call and settle it right away." "What is it?" asked the pastor. "Why," said the young man, "you say that the wicked will go into everlasting punishment, and I do not think that they will." "Oh, if that is all," said the minister, "there is no dispute between you and me. If you turn to Matthew 25:46, you will find that the dispute is between you and the Lord Jesus Christ, and I advise you to go immediately and settle it with Him." (Herzberger) *References:* Is. 33:14; Matt. 3:12; 18:8; 25:46; Mark 9:44; Rev. 14:10–11; 20:10.

449. It has been said that "the doctrine of hell should be preached in all its terribleness. It is no kindness to spread a pretty covering of leafy branches over a pit into which many have fallen and broken their necks. That may be the cunning hunter's business, as it is the business of him who hunts the world for souls. But it is not the business of preachers to ruin people's souls in order to spare their feelings." *References:* Matt. 25:41; Mark 9:43–48; Luke 16:19–31; 2 Peter 3:7; Rev. 14:11.

450. Hell: Attractive but . . . A father and son were walking along the streets of Paris one night. They passed a place that was brilliantly lighted. It was decorated with all the colors of the rainbow. Soft music emanated from within, and the fragrance of Arabian spices floated outward from the open windows. "What is that?" inquired the boy. The father replied, "Son, that is hell!" This surprised the boy. Hell—with all the glitter and glamor? He thought that hell was something ugly. He thought that the belch of sulphur would greet one at its entrance. But here it all looked so nice! What is more, the sign read, "Free admission." But although it costs nothing to get in, it costs much to get out: character blasted, conscience burdened, one's soul in a lost condition. *References:* Gen. 3:3–4; Prov. 4:14–19; 5:3–5; 9:13–18; 14:2; Matt. 4:1–11; James 1:14–15.

451. Two soldiers on an American troopship crowded around their chaplain and asked him, "Do you believe in a hell?" "I do not," was his answer. "Well, then," they said, "will you please resign, for if there is no hell, we do not need you, and if there is a hell, we do not wish to be led astray." (*Christian Beacon*) *References:* Is. 33:14; 66:24; Matt. 5:22; 13:42; 23:33; Luke 16:22–23.

Heretics

See also **False Teachers**

452. A comet is a star that runs, not being fixed like a planet, but being a bastard among the planets. It is a haughty and proud star, engrossing the whole element, and carrying itself as if it were there alone. Such is the nature of heretics, who desire to be superior to others and in a class by themselves, bragging and boasting, and thinking they are the only people endued with understanding. (Luther) *References:* Is. 56:10–12; Ezek. 34:2–3; 1 Tim. 1:6–7; 4:1–3; 6:3–5; 2 Peter 2:1–3; 1 John 4:1.

Related illustration: 458.

Hiding from God

453. Robert Louis Stevenson said that one of the most powerful lessons of his life was learned when as a child he locked himself in a closet to hide from his father. It was terribly dark in that closet, and he soon became panicky and began to scream and cry for help. It was a long time before his father finally came, and then a locksmith had to come and open the door. It was a very grateful and chastened little boy who was finally let out of the closet! Are you hiding from God in your heart, my friend? *References:* Gen. 3:8; Is. 29:15; 30:1; Jer. 50:6; Ezek. 8:12; Luke 15:11–16; John 3:19–21.

Historical Backgrounds

454. Parable of the Pounds. William Barclay, the great English New Testament scholar, claimed that our Lord's parable of the pounds is unique among the parables because it may be the only parable that is based in part on an actual historical event. The parable speaks of a king who leaves to receive a kingdom and whose subjects protested his receiving it. Such an event did occur in Judea. Herod the Great died in 4 B.C., leaving his kingdom to be divided among Antipas, Herod Philip, and Archelaus. The division had to be ratified by Rome, to which Palestine was subject. Judea had been parceled out to Archelaus, who left for Rome to have his inheritance confirmed. A delegation of 50 Jews also went to Rome to protest to Caesar

Augustus that they did not want Archelaus to rule over them as king. In the end, Augustus did confirm the legal rights of Archelaus without granting him the title of king. The incident was indelibly impressed on the memory of Judea, and the people must have given rapt attention to Jesus when He included such an event in His parable. *Reference:* Luke 19:11–15.

455. The Samaritan Temple. Contrary to the will of God, the Samaritans had erected an altar on Mount Gerizim as the place where God was to be worshiped. Jeroboam, the son of Nebat, who made Israel to sin, really started this sinful and schismatic worship (1 Kings 12, 32; 2 Chron. 11:13–15; 13:9). The Samaritans, in part, were descendants of the lost 10 tribes. They accepted only the Pentateuch. They spoke of "our father Jacob" (John 4:12). Josephus says that Manasseh, brother of Jaddua, the high priest in the time of Alexander the Great, had married the daughter of a foreigner, Sanballat. The elders at Jerusalem commanded him either to divorce her or no longer to approach the altar. Manasseh thought of divorcing her, though she was still dear to him, but her father, Sanballat, deprecating his step, promised to build for his son-in-law, if he retained his wife, a temple to rival that of Jerusalem. He kept his word, erecting one on Mount Gerizim. This was the origin of the Samaritan temple on that mountain and must be dated before 330 B.C. (John D. Davis, *Dictionary of the Bible,* p. 255.) *Reference:* John 4:19–23.

456. It is now high noon. Suddenly an ominous darkness spreads over the scene of this revolting judicial murder. This supernatural darkness was recorded in the archives of Rome. When Dionysius observed this phenomenon in Heliopolis, Egypt, he is reported to

have exclaimed: "Either God Himself is suffering, or He mourns over the sad condition of a great sufferer, or the world is going to ruin." *References:* Matt. 27:45; Mark 15:33; Luke 23:44–45.

457. The Church of Philippi. Philippi had a very interesting history. In 42 B.C. Octavian and Antony defeated the Senate Party at Philippi. In 31 B.C., after Octavian had defeated Antony at Actium, Augustus founded Philippi, settling it with Roman soldiers, many of whom had surrendered to him with the defeat of his rival. In this way Philippi was by tradition linked very closely to the affairs of the empire. Its Gentile inhabitants were at the time of St. Paul for the most part perhaps grandchildren of Octavian's veterans. It was a Roman colony, and it was proud of it (Acts 16:12, 20–21). That is to say, its inhabitants enjoyed all the rights and responsibilities of Roman citizenship.

Philippi, moreover, was the site of the first Christian church in Europe. The record of its founding is contained in Acts 16. The first converts there were Lydia and her household, the slave girl delivered from an evil spirit, the jailer and his household, Euodia and Syntyche, and others. In every sense, therefore, the church at Philippi was an important congregation. It was located on an important highway; it was an outpost of imperial Rome, and in terms of church history was the first to accept the Gospel of our Lord Jesus Christ. *References:* Acts 16; Phil. 1:1.

458. Who Were the Nicolaitans? The church hates the work of the Nicolaitans. The New Testament does not mention this sect except in Rev. 2:6, 15. In fact, it is somewhat doubtful whether a real sect or party with its own specific tenets is meant. It is possible that the name denotes a wrong tendency that was exemplified in the lives of some of the members of the church.

Irenaeus is the first of the post-Apostolic writers whose works we possess to comment on these people. According to him they were a sect founded by Nicolas, one of the seven deacons mentioned in Acts 6. He calls them heretics who show affinity with the Gnostic Cerinthus. Clement of Alexandria (*Stromata* 3.4.25) informs us that the Nicolas of Acts 6 advocated the principle "abuse the flesh," using these words in an ascetic sense, while the sect that called itself by his name gave this slogan an immoral, licentious meaning. From all we can gather, we conclude that these people were servants of the flesh. It may be that they tried to justify their immoral conduct by quoting Scripture passages removed from their context. (See for instance, 1 Tim 4:4: "Everything God created is good, and nothing is to be rejected.") The express reference to their works seems to indicate that not only their teaching but also their way of life was obnoxious. *References:* Acts 6:5; Rev. 2:6, 15.

459. Forerunners of the Reformation. Although history has properly fixed October 31, 1517, as the beginning of the Reformation, there were before that date several men in various countries who are considered the forerunners of the Reformation. It is hardly conceivable that in the church of the Middle Ages, which groaned under the supremacy of the bishops of Rome, there would not have been men whose eyes were opened to the corruption of the church.

Already in the 12th century Peter Walden of Lyons, France, recognizing the errors of the Roman Catholic Church, felt constrained to bring the sweet Gospel of Christ to lost souls. He preached with remarkable success,

but his followers, known as the Waldensians, were persecuted and perished by the thousands as the result of the most frightful tortures.

In England, John Wyclif directed strong attacks against the godlessness of the monks; spoke emphatically against indulgences, the adoration of relics, and other popular errors; and translated the Bible into English. He, too, incurred the wrath of the pope; after his death in 1384, the Council of Constance (1415–1418) condemned his doctrines, and the bones of this valiant confessor were exhumed and burned.

Through the writings of Wyclif, which had become known in Bohemia, Jan Huss was moved to lift up his voice against the abuses prevalent in the church. Since he continued to preach in Prague in spite of his excommunication, he was cited to appear before the Council of Constance; because of his refusal to recant, he was condemned to die at the stake.

One more forerunner of the Reformation was Jerome Savanarola. Living in Italy, he startled the pope and the clergy out of their security by eloquently denouncing the depravity of his time. As the result of his fearless testimony, he cheerfully met death at the hand of the executioner on Ascension Day 1498, 15 years after the birth of Luther. *References:* Matt. 10:17–18; 11:12–15; 23:34–35; Luke 7:24–28; John 16:2; 2 Tim. 3:12; Heb. 11:37–12:1; Rev. 2:10.

Related illustrations: 630, 631.

Holiness

See also **Sanctification**

460. A former missionary in India once told of needing assistance in transferring a critically ill man from his house to the local hospital. She requested help from two "holy men" who were sitting not far away, intoning their devotions. She said she would never forget the fire of resentment that blazed up in the eyes of one of them as he replied: "We? We are holy men. We never do anything for anyone." What a twisted and dangerously false concept of holiness. *References:* Hos. 6:6; Micah 6:8; Mark 12:33; Rom. 13:10; Gal. 6:7–10; Eph. 4:23–25; James 1:27.

461. Many have heard the story of Simon Stylites, who had himself hoisted to the top of an ancient column to get away from the world of people and to live there in pious meditation. The legend says that after some time an angel appeared to the hermit and urged him to come down. As he did, the angel led him to the home of a gooseherd, who was tending his geese under rather adverse conditions. In the frugal home of the herder, Simon found a girl whose parents had been killed when the girl was but a tiny tot. The gooseherd had taken her to his home and heart, had shared with her his bare necessities, and given her his love and devotion. There the angel left Simon, who caught the meaning of it all. He too should remain in the valley to help, to serve, to sacrifice in the commonplace lives of discouraged people. This would be more pleasing to God.

We must help people where they are. That is why Jesus came down physically from the mountain to help the mentally sick and the physically handicapped. *References:* Ps. 113:5–8; 138:6; Matt. 8:1–4; 17:9–15; Luke 9:37–38; 1 Cor. 9:19–23.

462. Holiness should have a right and not a wrong place in our system of doctrine. The fruitfulness and beauty—the very life—of a tree depends not only on its having roots and branches but on these being placed in their natural, God-created order. Let a tree be planted upside down, the roots in the air and branches in the earth, and I need not ask how much fruit it would yield nor how long it would survive such barbarous and blundering treatment. Place sanctification below and justification on top—expect this to flow from that—and a similar catastrophe will occur. (Guthrie) *References:* Luke 1:74–75; Rom. 12:1–2; 2 Cor. 7:1; Gal. 2:16; Eph. 2:8–10; Heb. 11:6; James 2:17–18.

Holy Spirit

463. The noted evangelist Dwight L. Moody said that he had been a church member for seven years before he learned that the Holy Spirit is a Person of the Holy Trinity. *References:* John 14:17, 26; 16:13; Acts 5:3–4; 10:19–20; 13:2.

464. His Power over Evil. Dwight L. Moody, the American evangelist, once used a glass as an object to teach that the love of God overcomes our evil nature and controls our lives. He asked his audience, "How can I get the air out of this glass?" One person said, "Suck it out with a pump." But Moody insisted that this would create a vacuum and break the glass. He listen to a couple of other suggestions and then picked up a pitcher of water and filled the glass. "There," he said, "all the air is removed. We cannot overcome evil and enmity, bitterness and temptation, simply by fighting against it. We must let the Holy Spirit fill our hearts, let Him pour in love until it overflows." *References:* Rom. 8:9–10; 1 Cor. 6:18–20; Eph. 5:18–21; 1 John 3:24; 5:4–6.

465. His Ministry Through the Word. Rabbi Slostowski, a professor of the Talmud in the rabbinical seminary at Tel Aviv, hated the Lord Jesus Christ. So great was his resentment that he sharply criticized a young Jewish convert reading a Hebrew New Testament. The young man replied by giving him the copy. That night the rabbi, alone in his room, stayed up until three o'clock in the morning reading about the Nazarene who claimed to be the Messiah. The Holy Spirit guided him into all truth, and later he confessed, "I have already found more than 200 passages of the New Testament that prove beyond a doubt that Jesus is truly the Messiah." (Walter A. Maier, *For Christ and Country* [CPH, 1942], p. 99) *References:* Neh. 9:19–20; John 14:26; Acts 10:44; 1 Cor. 2:13; Gal. 4:4–6; 2 Peter 1:19–21; 1 John 2:27.

Related illustrations: 653, 711, 743, 795, 827, 874.

Home

466. A noted preacher once said: "A cottage will not hold the bulky furniture and sumptuous accommodations of a mansion, but if God be in it, a cottage will hold as much happiness as might stock a palace." *References:* Prov. 15:16–17; Song of Songs 8:7.

467. The beauty of the home is order; the blessing of the home is contentment; the glory of the home is hospitality; the crown of the home is godliness. *References:* Joshua 24:15; Prov. 15:16–17; Song of Songs 8:7.

Hope

468. No Situation Is Hopeless. When Robinson Crusoe was wrecked on his lonely isle, he listed in two columns what he called the evil and the good. He was cast on a desolate island, but he was still alive—not drowned, as all his ship's company were. He was separated from humanity and banished from society, but he was not starving. He had no clothes, but he was in a hot climate where he didn't need them. He was without means of defense, but he saw no wild beasts, such as he had seen on the coast of Africa. He had no one to speak to, but God had sent the ship so near to the shore that he could get from it all things necessary for his wants. So he concluded that there was no condition in the world so miserable that there was not something negative or something positive to be thankful for in it. (*Macartney's Illustrations*) *References:* Gen. 28:15; Ps. 34:17–22; 37:28; Prov. 2:8; Matt. 6:32; 1 Cor. 10:13; 1 Peter 5:7.

469. One of the first adventurers on the mighty oceans who sailed to South America went around a cape on a stormy sea. His ship threatened to go to pieces; so he called the place the Cape of Storms. But Vasco da Gama, who came later, changed the name to the Cape of Good Hope, for he saw ahead of him the jewels and treasures of India. You can call this a life of storms if you wish. But if you can see the glorious redemption of eternity ahead of you, you can call it what it is only in Christ—a life of good hope. *References:* Rom. 8:18–25; 2 Cor. 4:17; Col. 3:3–4; Heb. 11:13–16; 1 Peter 1:6–7; 1 John 3:2.

Related illustrations: 805, 936.

Humanism

470. The Folly of. One of the most amazing phenomena of our day is "New Humanism," a revived faith in humanity. As Joel H. Nederhood describes it in *The Church's Mission to the Educated American,* "in an atmosphere of brooding fatalism, his heart flushed empty of confidence, man reminds himself that there are tremendous, unused virtues slumbering within the human race which may yet prove man's salvation" (p. 114). Some people maintain this optimism today in the face of all the facts and lessons of history. In spite of the record of Genghis Khan, who slaughtered tens of

HUMILITY

thousands in his sweeps across Asia; in spite of a Tamerlane, who piled 90,000 heads outside a city gate in 1215; in spite of a Hitler, a Mussolini, an Eichmann, and heinous atrocities in recent conflicts, there are still those who cheerfully say: "I still believe in man!" *References:* Ps. 118:8–14; 146:3–5; Is. 2:17–22; 30:1–3; 31:1–3; Jer. 17:5–7; Matt. 16:21–23.

Related illustration: 715.

Humility

471. They that know God will be humble; they that know themselves cannot be proud. (Flavel) *References:* John 9:39–41; Rom. 12:3; 1 Tim. 1:15.

472. Saintliness and humility go hand in hand. The more fruit-laden the branch, the farther it bends to earth. (Scriver) *References:* Prov. 16:19; Matt. 18:4; Luke 22:26.

473. Humility is a virtue all preach and few practice, and yet everybody is content to hear. The master thinks it good doctrine for his servant, the laity for the clergy, and the clergy for the laity. (Selden) *References:* Prov. 16:19; Matt. 18:4; Phil. 2:3.

474. When asked, What is the first step in religion? Luther replied: "Humility." What is the second? "Humility." What is the third? "Humility." *References:* Gen. 18:27; 32:10; Job 40:4; Is. 6:5; Mark 1:7; Luke 5:8; 1 Peter 5:5.

475. An old writer has said that God has two thrones: one in the highest heaven, the other in the humblest heart. *References:* Ps. 147:3–4; 1 John 4:4.

476. In a painting of the crucifixion by the famous Dutch artist Rembrandt, attention is first drawn to the cross and to Christ who died there as our ransom. Then we notice the many people at Calvary and their various attitudes and actions. Then as our eyes drift off to the edge of the painting, we see a little figure of a man in the shadows. This is Rembrandt himself. He is saying, "My sins nailed the Savior there, but He died for me and I believe it." What humility of heart and what blessings of grace! *References:* Gen. 32:10; Is. 53:4–6; Luke 7:47; 23:43; Rom. 5:8; 1 Tim. 1:12–17; 1 John 2:2.

477. I used to think that God's gifts were on shelves, one above the other, and the taller we grew in Christian character, the easier we could reach them. I find now that God's gifts are on shelves, one beneath the other, and that it is not a question of growing taller but of stooping lower, and that we have to go down, always down, to get His best gifts. *References:* Prov. 16:19; 22:4; Matt. 18:4; Luke 14:10; 18:14; James 4:10; 1 Peter 5:5.

478. In nature the strongest powers of attraction do not always belong to the great things but often to the little. The snowcapped peak of a lofty mountain will overawe us, but the soft green outline of a lowly hill will tempt us to build a cabin on its ground. We admire the huge, fragrant magnolia blossoms and the gorgeous sunflower—and leave them where they are. But we stoop to pick the humble violet and adorn our persons and our tables with it. Heroes shine in the brilliant light of great deeds; we gaze in admiration and pass on. But the soft glow enveloping a faithful mother with her children on her knees tempts us to linger and abide. *References:* Prov. 16:19; Is. 57:15; Matt. 5:3–5; Rom. 12:3; Phil. 2:3; James 4:10.

479. Humility: Conquering Self-Righteousness. John B. Gough, eloquent orator, tells that one Lord's Day, when he entered his church, he was placed in the same pew with a pitiful cripple. This man was so repulsive that Gough slid to the other end of the pew. But when the congregation sang "Just as I Am, Without One Plea," the cripple joined heartily, and Gough moved closer, even though there was little tune or beauty in the poor man's song. Before the second stanza, the deformed sufferer bent toward Gough and whispered, "Can you please give the first line of the next verse?" Gough answered, "Just as I am, poor, wretched, blind." "Ah, that's it," the man replied. "I am blind—God help me!— and I am a paralytic." Then with twitching lips and shaking frame the sufferer again glorified the Savior with his halting song.

Later Gough declared that in his whole life he had never heard a hymn sung so beautifully as the handicapped cripple's response "O Lamb of God, I come, I come!" If with the Holy Spirit's help you and I can conquer self-righteousness and selfish racial or class pride, can place ourselves shoulder to shoulder with our fellow human beings, can look with them to the Almighty's Son as our Savior, can join them in singing

> Just as I am, Thou wilt receive,
> Wilt welcome, pardon, cleanse, relieve,

then we shall find a new and greater joy than any self-centered life could ever give us. *References:* Is. 57:15; Matt. 25:40; Rom. 12:3–5; 2 Cor. 5:14–16; Gal. 3:28; Phil. 2:1–4.

480. It is said that Peter the Great of Russia once laid aside his royal garments and traveled to Holland to learn the art of shipbuilding for his people. Dressed in working clothes like any other worker in the shipyards, he kept his identity a secret as he learned his trade and labored as a commoner for the eventual benefit of his people. He willingly assumed the most menial tasks to preserve his anonymity and to learn the full measure of laborious toil.

Although this may be a faltering illustration of Christ Jesus' assuming the role of an obedient and suffering Servant, it gives us a measure of insight into His humiliation. *References:* Zech. 9:9; Luke 22:37; John 13:5; Acts 8:33; 2 Cor. 8:9; Phil. 2:5–8; Heb. 4:15.

481. When the last grand review of Sherman's army was held in Washington at the close of the Civil War, the commander-in-chief summoned General Howard to him and appealed to him as a Christian to let a certain other general supplant him at the head of his corps. Howard replied that, if it was put to him in that way, he must yield. And he yielded. Then Sherman said that as commander-in-chief he ordered Howard to ride by his side at the head not of a corps but of the whole army. And so it happened, as it generally does where there is genuine worth, that the last was first and he who humbled himself was exalted. (Dallmann) *References:* Ps. 75:4–7; 147:6; Mark 10:31; Luke 1:51–52; 14:7–11.

482. Perhaps you have read the famous story of George Washington. As a general, with his coat covering the insignia of his rank, he was riding past a detail where a corporal was commanding his men to lift a heavy log beyond their capacity. He was shouting at them and commanding them to heave ho. Since they could not do it, Washington dismounted quickly, walked over, and with his strong and tall body gave the log a quick push, and it went into its place. Turning to the corporal, he asked him why he had not helped his men. The man said, "Sir, do you not see that I am a corporal?" George Washington humbly opened his coat and said, "Yes, sir, I see you are a corporal, but I wish for you to see that I am the general." *References:* Ps. 113:5–6; 138:6; Is. 53:9;

Matt. 9:10–13; John 13:4–15; Rom. 12:3; 2 Cor. 8:9; Phil. 2:5–8.

483. There is a moment in the history of the heroes of this world, of such as Charles XII or Napoleon, that decides their career and their renown; it is the moment when their strength is suddenly revealed to them. An analogous moment exists in the life of God's heroes, but it is in contrary direction; it is when they first recognize their helplessness and nothingness before God. (D'Aubigne) *References:* Job 40:42; John 21:15–19; Acts 9:1–22.

Related illustrations: 78, 170, 396, 533, 548, 549, 960.

Hypocrisy

484. Shallow rivers are frequently the noisy rivers, and the drum is loud because it is hollow. Fluency and sincerity do not always go together. (Guthrie) *References:* Ps. 78:35–37; 1 Cor. 2:1–4; 13:1.

485. Are hypocrites members of the church? Yes, in the manner in which perspiration, excrement, boils, rash, smallpox, and other diseases may be said to be part of the human body. (Luther) *References:* Matt. 23:1–4; Rom. 2:21; Titus 1:16.

486. In the Church but Not of It. Did you hear about the man who was going to a masquerade ball in a devil's costume? It was a thundering, rainy, stormy night, and the man was driving along a country road. The car went off the road into the ditch. He couldn't get the car started again, so he got out and made his way across a cornfield to a small country church.

The people were inside the church having their evening prayer meeting, singing hymns and praying. And just as the man got to the front door of the church and opened it—dressed in his devil's costume—there was a bolt of lightning and clap of thunder. All the

people looked around in amazement and saw the devil standing there, and they went out of the doors and windows as quickly as they could—except for one little old lady standing in the center aisle.

With her cane in hand and shaking from head to toe, she said, "Mr. Devil, I don't know what you want here, but I've got only one thing to say. I've been a member of this church for 40 years, but I've really been on your side all the time!" *References:* Jer. 3:10; Matt. 3:7–12; Luke 8:13; John 6:63–66; 2 Tim. 4:10; 1 John 2:19.

487. One secret enemy in a camp may do more harm than 50 men who are open foes. A single unholy and inconstant member in a church may do more injury than many who are avowedly opposed to religion. It is not so much by infidels and scoffers and blasphemers that injury is done to the cause of religion; it is by the unholy lives of its professed friends—the worldliness, inconsistency, and want of the proper spirit of religion among those who are in the church. (Barnes) *References:* Matt. 23:13–15; Luke 11:52; Rom. 16:17–18; 1 Cor. 5:1–6; Gal. 5:7–12.

488. Pretentiousness. Orders were given by the authorities of Paris to have all that is unsightly and all persons in rags removed from the streets through which Mary Louise was to pass as she arrived in the capital city to become the bride of Napoleon. Nothing disagreeable or distasteful or shocking should cross her path. But all the pomp and extravaganza did not mitigate the misery and wretchedness of human life. Even that very day many in Paris did not have food or shelter. Jesus does not want to belittle the doing of nice things in society or discredit those who wear clean garments. What Jesus wants to emphasize is that much of this activity is sinful show and pretense if the

heart is loveless, brutal, and wicked.
References: 1 Sam. 16:7; Matt. 23:27–28; John 8:6–7; 2 Cor. 5:12; 10:7; James 2:2–4.

Related illustrations: 312, 373, 995.

I

Identity

489. Jesus' Identity with Sinners. In *The Deputy* by Rolf Hochhuth, a young priest discovers the truth about the Jewish extermination camps. He makes it his mission to stop the awful orders that began and are keeping in motion the slow extermination of a whole people. He appeals to everyone in authority, finally even to the pope, but all turn a deaf ear to him or plead excuses that remove them from any responsibility. When all avenues of protest have been exhausted, the hero of the play sews the identifying six-pointed star on his sleeve and presents himself at an extermination camp, where he moves to the ovens with the people whose cause he had taken on himself. So Jesus, being baptized by John, identifies Himself with sinners. He will accept their punishment, their death. Unlike Hochhuth's hero, Jesus will go into death so that all sinners could have life and have it more abundantly. *References:* Gen. 3:15; Is. 53:4–6; 2 Cor. 5:21; Heb. 2:9; 1 Peter 2:24 (Christ's identity with sinners through punishment). Matt. 3:13–15; Mark 1:9–11; Luke 3:21; John 1:32–34 (baptism of Christ).

490. Loss of Identity. After World War II thousands of boys and girls were gathered by the Swedish government into concentration camps because they were homeless and nameless. Many of these children did not know their name or remember from what part of the country they had come. Anxiously they would ask, "Who am I? Who are my parents? What is my real name?" And no one could come up with the answer. *References:* Prov. 27:8; Lam. 4:14; Matt. 7:23; 1 Cor. 15:10; 1 Peter 2:25; Jude 13.

Idleness

491. Use me, Lord, use me—in an advisory capacity. *References:* Luke 14:18–20; Phil. 2:30.

492. When Cecil Rhodes, who added Rhodesia to the British Empire, was about to die at 49, he said, "So much to do; so little done." If we must give account for idle words, how much more for idle lives! *References:* Prov. 6:6–10; 2 Thess. 3:11–13; Heb. 6:12.

493. In New England during the hurricane of 1938, the railroad bridge at White River Junction was in danger of being swept away by the floods simply because it hadn't anything to do at the moment that was worthy of it. So they backed a long string of heavily loaded freight cars onto it until both tracks were filled. And it stood! The only kind of religion that is in any peril at all is the kind that carries no load. *References:* Matt. 10:38; 16:24–25; Mark 10:21; Luke 14:27; Rom. 15:1–3; Gal. 6:1–2.

494. God is dissatisfied with, and angered by, human idleness because it represents such a deep humiliation of His highest creatures on earth. It places humanity beneath the ant and the little honeybee. It places us in the same class with the insects that destroy people's gardens and harvests. For the idle person, like these insects, lives off the toil of others. (C. T. Spitz) *References:* Prov. 6:6–11; 13:4; 18:9; 2 Thess. 3:10–13.

Related illustrations: 25, 86.

Idolatry

495. Astrology: The Fashionable Occult. The most respectable and fashionable outlet for occult propensities is astrology. Prominent figures in the entertainment world have long inquired of the stars say about their prospects for stardom. J. P. Morgan, the great financier, is rumored to have relied on the American mother of astrology, Evangeline Adams. The pagan Nazis, who persecuted the church, were inconsistently superstitious in using astrological guides. *References:* Is. 8:19; 44:24–25; 47:12–15; Dan. 2:27–28; 4:7.

Related illustrations: 130, 332, 333, 334, 527, 602, 654, 906, 989.

Ignorance

496. Someone has said that God does not need our learning to further His cause. Of course not, but He needs our ignorance still less. (MacLaren) *References:* Prov. 2:3–5; 3:13; 2 Tim. 2:15.

497. A recent survey revealed that over 50 percent of the people interviewed, all of them professing belief in the Bible, could not name the first four books of the New Testament. *References:* Zech. 7:11–12; Matt. 13:15; Rom. 10:1–3; 2 Tim. 3:5.

498. At Princeton College there is a tradition that one night, when the student body was greatly stirred by a religious revival, Aaron Burr shut himself in his room, saying that before the night was over he would settle the

matter of his relationship to God. Later that night the students living nearby heard the shutters of his room thrown open and a loud voice exclaimed, "Good-bye, God!" That cry has been re-echoed in our present generation, though not in so many words, for few people want to stop believing in God. They simply ignore Him. *References:* Job 21:14; Jer. 4:22; Zech. 7:11–12; Matt. 13:15; John 9:26–30; Rom. 1:28; 2 Peter 3:3–5.

Related illustrations: 43, 74, 512, 513, 554, 951.

Imitation

499. Copying the Imperfections of Others. A gentleman had a lovely Chinese plaque with curious raised figures on it. One day it fell from the wall on which it was hung and was cracked right across the middle. Soon after, the gentleman sent to China for six more of these valuable plates, and to ensure an exact match, he sent his broken plate as a copy. To his intense astonishment, when he received the six plates six months later, including his injured one, he found that the Chinese had so faithfully followed his copy that each new one had a crack right across it. If we imitate even the best of people, we are apt to copy their imperfections, but if we follow Jesus and take Him as our example, we are sure of a perfect pattern. (A. Webb, *Sunday at Home*) *References:* 1 Sam. 8:19–20; Ezek. 20:18; Matt. 23:2–3; John 1:19–27; 13:15; 1 Cor. 1:12–13; 1 Peter 2:21; 2 Peter 3:17–18.

500. Imitating Christ. An Indian catechist at the end of the last century was dismissed from the church for some misdemeanor. Burdened with shame, knowing he would never again dare to preach, the man left the area and went to some far-off, non-Christian area, where he settled down as a stranger and made his living as a potter. The church never heard of him again, and he died there.

Later it was decided to send a team of evangelists to the distant area. They rented a house and started to tell the stories of Christ. They were amazed when the crowd of villagers responded eagerly, exclaiming, "We know the man you are talking about; he lived here for years." "Oh, no," said the preacher, "you don't understand. We are talking about Jesus Christ." "Well," answered the people, "he never told us his name. But the man you've described was our potter without a doubt." (John Taylor, *In Perilous Ways* [Seabury], p. 77) *References:* Matt. 11:29; 20:25–28; John 13:15; Rom. 15:5–7; Phil. 2:1–8; Col. 3:12–17; Heb. 3:1–2.

501. Imitating Christ, but Not in External Ways. In the early days of Christianity, devout men thought that they, as followers of Christ, should also imitate our Savior in external circumstances. Jesus lived in Palestine, yet men like St. Jerome found that they were no whit nearer to Him by taking up their abode in Bethlehem or Nazareth. Jesus was poor, yet the wealthy Joseph of Arimathea and the wealthy Nicodemus were nearer to Him than Judas. Christ was homeless, yet Aquila and Priscilla were nearer to Him than hermits Anthony and Macarius. Francis of Assisi tried, on the wild hills of Umbria, to reproduce the life that Jesus lived on the burning fields of Galilee, and before a generation was over, the begging friars who adopted his mode of life became the pests of Europe. No, no, my friends, the imitation of the life of Christ stands not at all in outward things. *References:* Matt. 16:24; John 13:15; 2 Cor. 10:7; 1 Thess. 1:6; Heb. 12:2; 1 Peter 2:21; 1 John 2:6.

502. Henry M. Stanley, the news-paperman, in his account of his association for a brief time with David Livingstone, great missionary to Africa, wrote, "Had my soul been of brass, and my heart of tin, the powers of my head surely compelled me to recognize, with due honor, the Spirit of goodness which manifested itself in him. Had there been anything of the Pharisee or the hypocrite in him, or had I but traced a grain of meanness or guile in him, I had surely turned away a skeptic. But my everyday study of him, during health and sickness, deepened my reverence and increased my esteem. He was, in short, consistently noble, upright, pious, and manly all the days of my companionship with him." What Stanley saw in Livingstone was the imitation of the inimitable, for the love of Christ was part of the man. *References:* Matt. 5:16; Eph. 5:1–9; Phil. 4:9; 1 Thess. 1:5–7; 2 Thess. 3:6–9; Titus 2:7.

Immortality

See also **Eternity**

503. Even heathen believe in the immortality of the soul. Cicero calls those who deny its immortality coarse men with minds of lead. Socrates, in one of his books, asks the question, "Do you not know that the soul is immortal and does not perish?" And the poet Ovid exclaims, "For the souls there is no death." (Stock) *References:* Eccl. 12:7; Luke 16:22–23; Rev. 20:4.

Immutability of God

504. Unlike the stars, God is not subject to revolutions and mutations. The so-called fixed stars are not fixed at all. Nothing in nature is stable. Every orb is on the wing. Some stars are so far away that they do not appear to move. For instance, two stars in the Great Dipper, one at either end, are flying in a direction opposite to that of the other five stars; but not before a thousand

years will anyone be able to note much difference in their relative positions. Someday the North Star will be out of position, and Vega, the arc light of the skies in the constellation Lyra, will be used by mariners as the polestar. In the case of stars there is variation. *References:* Ps. 102:25–27; Is. 24:4; 34:4; 2 Cor. 4:18; Heb. 1:10–12; 13:8.
Related illustration: 532.

Impenitence
505. One day near Excelsior Springs, Mo., a passenger train was rushing along at a terrific speed. The fireman, alarmed because there was no slowing up at the crossings and curves and because all signals were being ignored, leaned over to call the engineer and grasp him by the arm, only to find him dead at his post, his rigid fingers clutching the wide-open throttle. The mighty engine was brought under control, and disaster narrowly averted. We can hardly think of a more dramatic situation. A long train with hundreds of carefree passengers unaware of any danger thunders along the rails at a perilous speed with no guiding intelligence at its head, only a lifeless form.

Multitudes are going through life like that. They have the priceless treasure of an immortal, blood-bought soul aboard; yet they race madly onward, passing by the fountain of grace, despising the warnings of the Law, taking curves of sin at top speed, and ignoring the villages and crossings where fellow human beings must pass their way. *References:* Is. 47:8–11; Jer. 23:9–12; Luke 12:19–20; 19:41–44; 1 Thess. 5:3.

506. A pastor was called to see a man dying of a terrible disease. In his youth the man had received a good Christian training, but later he had turned his back on the church. His story was the story of the prodigal son. Poverty and disgusting disease brought him low. In his misery he thought of "his Father's house." The pastor shared with him the words of our merciful God, which are able to save for eternity every repentant sinner. The man accepted the pardoning hand of God extended in the Word and fell asleep in Jesus. His case was well known in the community in which he lived.

One of the prominent members of the church met the pastor shortly before the funeral and said to him, "Pastor, you are not going to bury that good-for-nothing scoundrel, are you?" The pastor replied, "Do you mean Brother John Smith (referring to the man who had died)? Certainly I am going to bury him." Whereupon the "good church member" retorted, "Well, if this man went to heaven, I do not want to go there." The pastor answered, "Never fear, Mr. Goodman, you are not going there." "What!" said the good church member, "this miserable wretch, John Smith, is to go to heaven, and I am not to go there?" "Not if that is the sentiment of your heart which you have just now expressed. Remember, brother, there is no difference, for all have sinned and come short of the glory of God." *References:* Matt. 21:28–32; Luke 7:47; 15:1–32; 23:42–43; Rom. 3:22–23.
Related illustrations: 823, 824.

Inconstancy
See also **Hypocrisy**
507. A communist was denouncing capitalism and the English government on the Commons at Hyde Park in London and extolling Russia, telling how much better the common people fared there. He was asked why he did not go to Russia. He answered that he enjoyed more freedom in England. *References:* Luke 6:46; Gal. 2:14.
Related illustration: 487.

Indecision

508. A great weakness of many persons is indecision. Napoleon once said, "In any battle there is a crisis, ten or fifteen minutes only, on which the outcome depends. To make proper use of this short space of time means victory; it's neglect, defeat." *References:* 1 Kings 18:21; 2 Kings 17:41; Hos. 10:2; Matt. 6:24; Luke 9:62; Acts 5:34–42; James 1:8; 4:8.

509. Mugwumps. According to the encyclopedia, the term is originally from an Indian language. It became famous—or at least common—during the presidential campaign of 1884. A newspaper editor picked it up, and soon everybody was using it. But Teddy Roosevelt gave it a definition that is perhaps most easily remembered: "A *mugwump*," he said, "is a bird that sits on a fence with its mug on one side and its wump on the other." It is someone who can't make up his mind. *References:* 1 Kings 18:21; 2 Kings 17:41; Hos. 10:2; Matt. 6:24; Luke 9:62; James 1:8; 4:8.

Indifference

510. God's truth can fight opposition far better than it can contend with indifference. (MacLaren) *References:* Amos 6:1; Zeph. 1:12; Rev. 3:15–16.

511. He who is indifferent to pure doctrine will also be indifferent to false doctrine. *References:* Acts 17:11; 2 Tim. 3:14; Jude 3.

512. A rabbi once summoned the townsfolk to meet in the town square for an important announcement. The merchant resented having to leave his business. The housewife protested against leaving her chores. But obedient to the call of the spiritual leader, the townspeople gathered together to hear the announcement their teacher was to make. When all were present, the rabbi said, "I wish to announce that there is a God in the world." That was all he said, but the people understood. They had been acting as if God did not exist. While they observed ritual and recited the correct order of prayers, their actions did not comply with the commandments of God. Their daily bread was sought and taken with little thought and reverence for God.

This parable is timely for our day. We may not openly deny God so much as try to confine Him to some remote corner of life away from our daily doings, associations, experiences, joys, heartaches, and all commonplace things. *References:* Deut. 8:11–14; Is. 43:22; 64:7; Hos. 10:2; Matt. 22:5; Luke 14:15–24; Acts 28:27.

513. Christ Weeps for the Indifferent. Apathetic, indifferent people bring great sorrow to the heart of Jesus Christ. Listen to this poem by G. A. Studdert-Kennedy:

When Jesus came to Golgotha, they
  hanged Him on a tree,
They drove great nails through hand and
  feet and made a Calvary;
They crowned Him with a crown of
  thorns, red were His wounds and deep,
For those were crude and cruel days, and
  human flesh was cheap.

When Jesus came in modern day, they
  simply passed Him by,
They never hurt a hair of Him, they only
  let Him die;
For men had grown more tender, and
  they would never give Him pain,
They only just passed down the street
  and left Him in the rain.

Still Jesus cried, "Forgive them, for
  they know not what they do;"
And still it rained the winter rain that
  drenched Him through and through;
The crowd went home and left the
  streets without a soul to see,
And Jesus crouched against a wall and
  cried for Calvary.

References: Is. 47:8; 64:7; Amos 6:1;

Zeph. 1:12; Matt. 22:5; Luke 14:15–24; Rev. 3:15–16.

Related illustrations: 86, 158, 498.

Infidels

See also **Scoffers**

514. The printing press from which Voltaire's infidel works were issued has been used to print the Word of God. Chesterfield's parlor, once an infidel clubroom, is now a vestry where Christians meet for prayer and praise. Hume predicted the death of Christianity in 20 years, but the first meeting of the Bible society of Edinburgh was held in the room in which he died. Paine, on landing in New York, predicted that in five years not a Bible would be found in the United States, but there are more Bible societies in America than in any country in the world. *References:* Ps. 2; 59:6–8; Is. 5:24; Jer. 6:10; Zech. 7:12.

515. Death of the Infidel. The French nurse who was present at the deathbed of Voltaire, being urged to attend an Englishman whose case was critical, asked, "Is he a Christian?" "Yes," was the reply, "he is a Christian in the highest and best sense of the term, a man who lives in the fear of God. But why do you ask?" "Sir," she answered, "I was the nurse who attended Voltaire in his last illness, and for all the wealth in Europe I would never see another infidel die." (Geo. F. Pentecost) *References:* Prov. 11:7; Is. 48:22; 59:8; 66:24; Ezek. 7:25; Matt. 3:12.

Related illustrations: 43, 61, 102, 216, 232, 950.

Influence

See also **Example**

516. One day a gentleman in India went into his library and took down a book from the shelves. As he did so, he felt a slight pain in his finger, like the prick of a pin. He thought that some careless person had stuck a pin in the cover of the book. But soon his finger began to swell, then his arm, then the whole body. In a few days he died. It was not a pin among the books but a small and deadly serpent.

There are many deadly serpents among the books nowadays; they nestle in the foliage of some of our more fascinating literature; they coil around the flowers whose perfume intoxicates the senses. People read and are charmed by the plot of the story, the skill with which the characters are sculptured and grouped, and the gorgeousness of the word painting so that they hardly feel the pinprick of the evil that it insinuates. But it stings and poisons. When the record of ruined souls is compiled, on what multitudes will be inscribed "poisoned by serpents among books"! *References:* Matt. 16:12; Acts 19:19; Col. 2:8; 1 Tim. 4:1–3; 2 Tim. 4:3.

517. Christian Influence. One of God's gifts is the example of a mature Christian, not to mention the gift of other "peers" with whom we search. William Glasser in *The Identity Society* says that "involvement with at least one successful person is a requirement for growing up successfully, maintaining success, or changing from failure to success." To be a "successful" and growing Christian person probably requires contact with at least one "Gospel-oriented" Christian. And still, in the Lutheran *Study of Generations,* 50% of those between the ages of 15 and 23 agreed that "hardly anyone in the congregation would miss me if I stopped going." *References:* Prov. 13:20; 1 Tim. 5:1–4; 2 Tim. 1:5; Titus 2:1–7.

Related illustrations: 99, 702, 703, 704.

Ingratitude

See also **Gratitude**

518. Luther: "He who would be a Christian must learn to remember that with all his benevolence, faithfulness, and service he will not always reap gratitude, but must also suffer ingratitude. But this should not move us to withhold help and service from others." *References:* Matt. 5:38–48; Luke 6:29; 17:11–19; 1 Cor. 4:10–13.

519. People in need readily recall that God has granted them the privilege of prayer; those helped out of their need by a merciful God are inclined to forget the God who has helped them; as Billy Sunday once phrased it, they in effect say to God: "I'll see You later." *References:* Deut. 8:11–14; 32:6; Neh. 9:26; Ezek. 16:17–18; Luke 17:17–18; Rom. 1:21.

520. A postal clerk in the dead-letter office in Washington, D.C., studied the mail that came during one Christmas season. Before Christmas thousands of letters came addressed to Santa Claus asking for toys and gifts, whereas after Christmas there was only one postcard saying thank-you to Santa for the gift received. *References:* Neh. 9:26; Eccl. 9:15; Is. 1:2–3; Luke 17:11–19; Rom. 1:21.

521. A doting grandmother, against her daughter's better judgment or wishes, took the daughter's little boy to the beach one day. She would take care of him—yes, she would! But in an unguarded moment the lad waded into the water, and the tide carried him toward certain death. The grandmother prayed for a miracle. A wave, greater than any she had ever seen, splashed across the sands, broke in front of her, and deposited the little one safe and sound at her feet. Was there a cry of thanks from the lips of the fortunate grandmother? No! Lifting her angry eyes toward heaven, she screamed, "OK, God, You brought my grandson back to me! But where is the cap that the child was wearing?" Have we ever blamed God for the caps that we lost—and failed to thank Him for the boys who were saved? *References:* Deut. 32:6; Neh. 9:26; Ezek. 16:17–18; Luke 17:17–18; Rom. 1:21.

522. Carlyle had a very devoted wife, who sacrificed everything for his sake, but he never gave her a single expression of appreciation, for which her heart yearned. She came to regard herself as the most miserable woman in London and evidently died of heart hunger. After her death, Carlyle, reading her diary, realized the truth. Froude found him at her grave suffering intense remorse and exclaiming, "If only I had known." (Ahlquist) *References:* Deut. 32:6; 1 Sam 25:21; 2 Chron. 24:22; Neh. 9:26; Matt. 22:37; Luke 17:11–19; Rom. 1:21.

523. By nature we can easily endure it if God blesses us for 10, 20, or 30 years, but when He sends us an evil year with famine, war, or epidemic, we begin to despair and lament as though He were no longer with us in our homes. But when God sends us 10 prosperous years, nobody seems to notice it or thank Him for it. Thus our human nature can endure the blessing but not the hardship and begins to murmur in spite of the fact that we have deserved nothing but the wrath of God. But God in His grace overlooks our shortcomings, so that He shows us much more mercy than wrath. (Luther) *References:* Joshua 7:7; Job 10:1; 1 Thess. 3:3–4; Heb. 12:5–8; Rev. 16:11.

524. In Shakespeare's *King Lear,* the father exclaims:

How sharper than a serpent's tooth it is
To have a thankless child!
Ingratitude, thou marble-hearted fiend!

How many the heartaches of mothers and fathers as they pine away in loneliness because their sons and daughters forget! Too much is taken for granted and accepted as a matter of course. Today a large majority of people, young and old, feels that the world owes them a living. Why should they say thank-you? *References:* Gen. 40:23; Judg. 8:33–35; 2 Chron. 24:22; Eccl. 9:15; Luke 17:17–18; Rom. 1:21.

525. An old legend tells of two angels sent to earth, each with a basket, the one to gather up the prayers of the people and the other their thanksgivings. When they returned, they were grieved to find that the first basket was filled to overflowing, while the other was nearly empty. (Deems, *Holy Days and Holidays*) *References:* Neh. 9:26; Ezek. 16:17–18; Luke 17:11–19; Rom. 1:21; 2 Tim. 3:2.

526. Like ancient Israel, we live in a good land. We have only 6% of the world's population, but we occupy 7% of its land surface, own 71% of it autos, use 56% of its telephones, listen to 50% of its radios, ride 29% of its railroads, and enjoy 83% of its television sets. Our cornucopias are overflowing. But how much of the overflow is used as a way of saying thank-you to God, the giver of all these things? *References:* Deut. 8:11–17; 32:6; Neh 9:26; Ezek. 16:17–18; Luke 17:17–18; Rom. 1:21; 2 Tim. 3:2.

Related illustrations: 17, 33, 355, 419.

Irreverence

527. A Universal Problem. Even the ancient heathen lost regard for their gods. The ancient Greek statues in existence today have hollow, staring eyes because through the ages the precious stones have been stolen from the eyes of virtually every Greek statue. The gods of the fathers became the victims of less reverent children. *References:* Gen. 6:5; Ps. 14:1–3; Jer. 16:12; Rom. 3:9–18; 2 Tim. 3:1–5; 2 Peter 2:10–12.

Related illustration: 512.

J

Jesus

See also **Christ**

528. John Dyer has said, "A man may go to heaven without riches, without honor, without learning, without friends, but he can never go there without Jesus Christ." *References:* Mark 10:21; Luke 10:41–42; Phil. 3:7–8.

529. He Alone Should Be Adored. When Leonardo da Vinci (died 1519) was working on his famous painting *The Lord's Supper*, he had but one object in view—that the person of the Savior should attract and hold the attention of all who beheld the painting. But in one part of the picture there was a tiny ship that he had painted with great care for three weeks. When the painting was exhibited and the people came to see it, Leonardo noticed that they all crowded together to look especially at the one corner of the picture with the small ship that had cost him so much pain and labor. "Just see how grand that is! Truly, he is a master artist!" he heard them exclaim. Chagrined at this, he took his brush when they were all gone and with one sweeping stroke blotted out the little ship, declaring, "No one shall find reason for admiring anything except Christ alone." (Walther League Messenger) *References:* Matt. 17:8; Mark 9:8; John 1:29–36; 12:21; 1 Cor. 2:2; Rev. 5:6–14.

530. The Imprints of His Love for Us. In an English cathedral the effigies of a crusader knight and his lovely lady lie side by side. On the effigy of the lady the right hand is missing. The record indicates that in one of the wars of the Crusades this English knight, fighting under Richard the Lion-Hearted, was taken prisoner. When he begged Saladin, the Muslim conqueror, to set him free and spare his life for the sake of the love that his lady in England had for him, Saladin scoffed at him and said that before long she would forget him and marry someone else. But the knight assured him that she would never do that and would always remain faithful to his memory as long as there was hope of his being alive.

Saladin asked for proof of that and said that if the lady would send her right hand as evidence of her love for her husband, he would set the knight free. When the letter reached the lady in England, she promptly had her right hand removed and sent in a bag to the Muslim conqueror. When Saladin saw that hand, he set the soldier free and sent him back to England. That amputated hand was the proof of the lady's devotion to her husband.

And so today Christ our Lord can open His hand and show to the Father and to us the nail prints and bare His side to show the wounds that are the signs of His perfect love in atoning for our sins. *References:* Luke 24:38–40; John 20:20–27.

JOY

531. Satan's Snare. I often delight myself with that analogy in Job of a hook that fishermen cast into the water, putting on the hook a little worm; then comes the fish and snatches at the worm and gets therewith the hook in his jaws, and the fisherman pulls him out of the water (Job 41). Even so has our Lord God dealt with the devil; God has cast into the world His only Son as the hook and on the hook has put Christ's humanity as the worm; then comes the devil and snaps at (the man) Christ and devours Him, and therewith he bites the iron hook, that is, the godhead of Christ, which chokes him, and all his power is thereby thrown to the ground. This is called *sapientia divina*, divine wisdom. (Luther) *References:* Gen. 3:15; Job 41; Ezek. 38; Rev. 12:1–9.

532. Jesus Always the Same. A Lutheran church magazine called for suggestions for a slogan that might be definitely suggestive of the confessional position of the Lutheran church. The slogan selected was "A Changeless Christ for a Changing World." This position has been vehemently attacked. But we hold that the Savior of the world does and must stand as the eternal Rock of Ages in the midst of the rapid mutations of an ever active world. *References:* Ps. 102:27; Mal. 3:6; John 8:58; Heb. 1:12; 13:8.

533. C. S. Lewis once said, "The Eternal Being, who knows everything and who created the whole universe, became not only a man but before that a baby and before that a fetus inside a woman's body. If you want to get the hang of it, think how you'd like to become a slug or a crab." *References:* Luke 1:31; 22:37; John 1:14; Rom. 1:3; 2 Cor. 8:9; Phil. 2:5–8.

534. Every moral reformer, every great philosopher, every preacher of ethics in the history of the world has pointed to some ideal outside himself. Our Lord did not. He pointed to Himself.

When Socrates was asked by one of his disciples what he should ask of the gods, Socrates told him to "wait for some greater teacher" to show him the way to God. When Buddha was asked by his dying follower, Ananda, for help and consolation, he told him, "Be a lamp to yourself and a refuge for yourself." And the same acknowledgment of personal insufficiency, the same recourse to an ethical or moral system is common to all the world's great moralists and religionists and philosophers from Confucius to John Dewey.

But Christ is different. There is no ideal apart from Him; He is the ideal. *References:* Matt. 11:28–30; John 3:14–18; 10:9–14; 14:5–9; 15:4–5.

Related illustrations: 202, 259, 270, 393, 465, 480, 535, 573, 677, 902, 919.

Joy

535. In one of his great writings called *Orthodoxy*, G. K. Chesterton writes about Jesus and why he became a Christian. He was once an avowed atheist, who fought Christianity with all his might. He said that there was a mystique about Jesus that no one understood and that was hidden from all people. It was something that was too great for God to show us when He walked this earth. "Then," he said, "as I have studied and restudied the life of Jesus, I have discovered that the great secret He kept hidden from everyone was His great joy."

Christianity without joy is a betrayal of the One we follow. We are a forgiven, redeemed people, who belong to the faithful flock on the way to heaven. We are people with great joy. *References:* Ps. 126; Is. 12:3; 61:10;

118

Jer. 15:16; Rom. 14:17; Phil. 2:1–2; Heb. 12:2; 1 Peter 1:8.

536. Joy for the Afflicted. An English officer once told this story: "In Belgium I met a converted Brahmin, whose confession of Christ, as I knew, had cost him everything. No sooner had he been baptized than his possessions were taken from him, and his friends deserted him. 'Are you able to bear your troubles?' I asked him. 'Many ask me that,' he answered, 'but they never ask me whether I am able to bear my joys; for I enjoy a happiness in my heart since I know that Christ has forgiven me that nobody has been able to take from me.' " *References:* Acts 5:41; Rom. 8:28; 2 Cor. 6:10; 12:9; Col. 1:24; Heb. 10:34; 1 Peter 4:12–13.

537. The man who writes and draws the comic strip "Archie" had the privilege of seeing his father come to faith as an adult. This gave him an entirely new outlook on life. His father was the late Senator Fred A. Hartley Jr., coauthor of the Taft-Hartley Act. The cartoonist's new outlook became dramatically evident when his father became sick and for months was paralyzed in a hospital bed. He was unable to do a single thing for himself and knew that slowly he was coming nearer to the time of his death. In that condition he could say to his son, "I am very happy." *References:* Rom. 8:31–39; 2 Cor. 6:10; Phil. 4:4–7; 1 Peter 1:3–7; 4:12–13.

Related illustrations: 127, 283, 722.

Judgment Day

538. Judgment Day is God's day of settlement with a world that has had a long credit. It is the winding up of this earth's bankrupt estate and each person's individual interests. It is the closing of an open account that has been running on ever since the Fall. *Refer-*

ences: Matt. 25:31–46; 2 Cor. 5:10; Jude 14–15.

539. No One Will Escape It. In the early 19th century, a native of Hanover, Germany, to show his contempt for the Easter message, provided in his will that great slabs of marble be laid across his grave, bound together with iron bands and covered with a granite boulder weighing nearly two tons. It bore the inscription: "This grave is purchased for eternity; it shall never be opened." But a poplar seed began to sprout within the tomb and press its way up toward the light. Gathering strength with the years, it broke the bands, moved the boulder, and opened the grave. *References:* Dan. 12:2; John 5:28–29; Acts 24:15; Heb. 9:27; Rev. 20:13–15.

Related illustrations: 337, 924.

Justification
See also **Salvation**

540. F. E. Mayer wrote, "The doctrine of justification is, as it were, the string on which all the pearls of Christian revelation are strung." (*Concordia Theological Monthly* 24 [Aug. 1953]) *References:* Gen. 15:6; Rom. 5:1; Gal. 3:24.

541. In Aledo, Ill., some years ago a circuit court jury convicted James Gibson, an 18-year-old high school senior, of voluntary manslaughter for stabbing his teacher to death. The jurors fixed the punishment at one to seven years in the state penitentiary. Then all went to shake his hand and wish him well. Seven jurors were weeping. Some embraced him, and one said, "God bless you, my boy." The farm-raised student, who had remained poker-faced during the nine-day trial, had tears in his eyes. The jurors were moved to sympathy and compassion over the fate of the boy, but not one of them said, "Let me serve your sentence." But this is just what Jesus Christ did. He served our sentence, dying a terrible death on the cross, suffering the agony of hell, and then rising victorious from the grave. God can now say to us, "You are free; your punishment and your guilt have been transferred from you to Jesus Christ. You are free." This is what justify means. We are declared righteous by grace through faith on account of the work of Christ. *References:* Matt. 8:17; Rom. 4:5; 5:18–19; 2 Cor. 5:21; Gal. 4:4–5; Heb. 9:28; 1 Peter 2:24; 1 John 3:5.

542. An Asiatic Christian of our times, David T. Niles, in his engaging little book *That They Might Have Life,* points out the real point of distinction between being a Christian and being a Hindu. He tells how "a leading Brahmo Samajist in India once delivered an address on the subject 'Jesus, my Ishta Devada'—'Jesus, the God of my choice.' 'I worship Jesus,' he said; 'I worship Jesus, but I am a Hindu. I am a Hindu because I accord the right to every man to worship the God he chooses.' " "That," writes Niles, "is true Hinduism. Christian faith, on the other hand, is not built on my choice of Jesus; it is built on my response to Jesus' choice of me. The initiative is His, and He claims me by the right that He made me." And by the right that He redeemed me and that the Holy Spirit has sanctified me. *References:* John 6:44, 65; 15:16; Eph. 2:8–9.

Related illustrations: 322, 462, 631, 824.

K

Kindness

543. If there are any kind words to be spoken, let us speak them now, while our loved ones are yet with us. If there are loving deeds to be done, let us do them today. Flowers on the lid of a coffin and a nice epitaph on a tombstone bring no cheer to the dead. *References:* Gal. 6:10; Col. 3:12; 2 Peter 1:5–7.

Kingdom of God

544. Prepare to Receive Your King. Some years ago a yacht landed one evening at the wharf of Inverness, Scotland. Two young men disembarked and set out on a walking tour. They got lost. Late that night they knocked at the door of a farmer's cottage, but though they pleaded that they were both hungry and cold, the farmer kept the door shut. They went to another cottage a mile or more away. Though it was past midnight, the farmer took them in. To his surprise he found that one of the young men was the prince who later became George V, the beloved king of England. What must have been the shame and humiliation of the other neighbor when he found that unwittingly he had shut the door in the face of his king! *References:* Ps. 24:7–10; Matt. 10:40; 22:4; Mark 9:37; John 1:12; Rev. 3:20 (prepare to receive your king). Matt. 25:37–45; Luke 19:41–44; John 4:10; Heb. 13:2 (unexpected visitors).

545. The Kingdom Grows. As it issues from the cool clear waters of Lake Itasca in Minnesota, the Mississippi River is only a little stream 10 or 12 feet wide and about 2 feet deep. By the time it reaches the Gulf of Mexico, it has flowed nearly 4,000 miles and at some points is many miles wide and reaches great depths. Fifty million people live in the states drained by this mighty river. Like this river, the kingdom of God begins small, but by the time it reaches Judgment Day it is tremendous. The kingdom is like the seed growing until it is many times its original size. *References:* Job 17:9; Matt. 13:31–32; Mark 4:20, 26–32.

546. Unlike Earthly Dominions. An earthly ruler gathers taxes from the people. The heavenly Ruler gives His Son to the people. An earthly ruler demands; the heavenly Ruler offers. God spared not His own Son but delivered Him up for us all. "God so loved the world that He gave His only begotten Son." An earthly Caesar fills his coffers with the coins of the people, but the heavenly Ruler sends His Son that people might have treasures in heaven. *References:* Is. 9:7; Matt. 20:25–28; Luke 2:10–14; 23:42–43; John 18:36.

547. The Presence of the Kingdom. Jerome of Stridon, known as St. Jerome, was a very learned and industrious man who, around A.D. 400, spent about 35 years at Bethlehem. Among other labors while he was there, he translated the Bible into Latin. His translation came to be

121

known as the Vulgate and was the standard version for many centuries. But when he heard of a man who wanted to make the arduous pilgrimage to Bethlehem, perhaps to die there, he sent him a message advising him not to do so. "For," he said, "heaven is as near to you in Britain as it is here, for the kingdom of God is within you." *References:* Ps. 34:18; Jer. 23:23; Matt. 18:20; 28:20; Luke 17:20–21; Acts 17:27–29; Eph. 2:12–13.

⟹ **548.** Frederick the Great of Prussia was in the habit of visiting the schools of his country to satisfy himself that they were doing the right kind of work. On one occasion he singled out a little girl, held up a stone in front of her, and asked, "To which kingdom does this stone belong?" "To the mineral kingdom," came the quick reply. "And to which kingdom does this apple belong?" "To the plant kingdom." Next the king pointed to the picture of a horse and asked her to classify the horse. "It belongs to the animal kingdom," said the girl. Then, after a pause, the king demanded, "And to which kingdom do I belong?" Now the girl hesitated. Finally, she answered, "You belong to the kingdom of God." The king was deeply moved by this unexpected reply and said to the girl, "Pray God that I may be found worthy of such an honor." *References:* Ps. 8; Matt. 6:10; Luke 11:2; Rev. 17:14.

Knowledge, Spiritual

549. Look at a mathematician and physicist like Sir Isaac Newton. Consider his invention of the telescope, his study of gravitation, his famous *Principia.* Yet when he was asked as an old man, "What do you consider your greatest discovery?" Newton humbly replied, "I have made two important discoveries in life: the one, I know I am a very great sinner; the other, I

know Jesus is even a greater Savior." *References:* Prov. 4:7; Jer. 9:24; Hos. 14:9; John 17:3; Phil. 3:8; 1 John 1: 7–9.

550. Dr. Alfred Adler, in an address to a Conference of Science, Philosophy, and Religion in New York City, correctly stated the foundation of the conquering spirit when he said, "Religion rests upon supernatural knowledge." To be more specific, faith in the conquering Christian is based on divine truth as revealed in our Bible. *References:* Ps. 19:8; Zech. 7:12; 2 Tim. 3:16; 1 Peter 1:25; 2 Peter 1:19–21.

551. The Chinese have a saying that there are five points to the compass: north, south, east, west, and where you are. The last of these is the most important. We cannot know which way we should go until we know where we are. *References:* Luke 18:9–14; John 9:35–41; Rev. 2:5.

552. Charles Dickens shared his faith with his eight children when for their use he wrote *The Life of Our Lord,* stating that he wanted them to know Jesus Christ as he knew Him. He wrote, "You never can think what a good place heaven is without knowing who He was and what He did." *References:* Jer. 9:24; John 17:3; Phil. 3:8–10; Col. 1:10.

Related illustrations: 69, 677, 1013, 1014.

Knowledge, Worldly

553. Ever Knowing, Yet Lost. An old farmer up in New England stood outside his place one day, leaning on a fence. A smooth young fellow from New York City rolled up in a shiny car and asked the way to half a dozen different places, one after the other. To each inquiry the farmer had nothing but a monotonous and gruff reply: "I don't know." Finally the young fellow, thoroughly exasperated, muttered as he started to drive away, "You don't know much, do you?" Whereupon the farmer straightened up with a twinkle in his eye and drawled, "Anyway, I ain't lost!"

More people know the answers to more questions today than ever before in the history of humanity. But for all that, a great many of our world leaders are quite willing to admit that ours is the most completely lost generation the world has ever known. *References:* Jer. 5:3–4; Matt. 13:13–14; Luke 12:56; John 3:10–12; 9:24–41; Acts 28:27; Rom. 10:3; 2 Tim. 3:7.

554. A long time ago someone suggested that all human knowledge could be compared to a fire burning in the night in a large open place. Around the fire is a circle of light and warmth; beyond the edge of the circle, the cold and the darkness. As we add to our knowledge, to our understanding of ourselves and the world around us, we add fuel to the fire. The area of light and warmth become larger and larger, but so does the circle of darkness. The more we learn—the more knowledge we accumulate and the more books we write—the more it becomes evident how small a fraction of knowledge we really possess. *References:* Job 11:7, 38; Ps. 73:22; Eccl. 3:11; Matt. 11:25; John 3:8–12; 1 Cor. 13:12; 2 Tim. 3:7.

555. Natural Knowledge of God. The Aztec king Nezahualcóyotl (1431–72): "Verily, the gods that I am adoring, what are they but idols of stone without speech or feeling? They could not have made the beauty of the heaven, the sun, the moon, the stars, which light the earth, with its countless streams, its foundations and waters. . . . There must be some God, invisible and unknown, who is the universal Creator." (Quoted in *Theological Quarterly* 10:82, 84–85) *References:* Ps. 19:1–6; 97:6–7; Acts 14:15–17; 17:22–31; Rom. 1:18–23.

Related illustrations: 551, 955.

L

Labor

556. There are three kinds of Christian workers—canal barges, sailing ships, and Atlantic liners. The canal barges need to be dragged to the work. Often they do wonderfully well, but on the whole one volunteer is better than three pressed into service. The sailing ships make fine going as long as wind and tide are with them, but when things get hard, when "the winds are contrary," when the work is discouraging, they turn tail and sail away. But give me the Atlantic-liner type of worker, the person who can fight through wind and tempest, because within there burns the mighty furnace of the love of Christ. *References:* John 4:34; 17:4; Acts 20:24; 1 Cor. 15:58; 2 Tim. 4: 7–8.

557. Elton Trueblood writes, "God is just as much interested in the life plans of carpenters as He is in the life plans of preachers." And again, "Secular work done well is a holy enterprise." (*Your Other Vocation* [New York: Harper & Brothers, 1952], pp. 67–68). *References:* Mark 9:41; Eph. 6:5–9; Col. 3:22–4:1; 1 Tim. 6:1–2; Titus 2:9; 1 Peter 2:18.

Related illustrations: 249, 250.

Law, Divine

558. "Knowledge of grace presupposes the Law," says Emil Brunner. "Without the Law there is no experience of the grace of God." *References:* Rom. 5:20; 7:7; Gal. 3:21–24.

559. Did you ever see the point of a needle under a microscope? However finely it is polished, the microscope discloses that it is still very rough and irregular. Our lives look like that when viewed through the lens of God's law. (MacLaren) *References:* Rom. 3:20; 7:7; Gal. 3:19.

560. The ceremonial laws were indispensable to Old Testament times, but they no longer apply to us who were freed by Christ. An eggshell is essential before the chicken is hatched, but would it not be absurd to insist that the chick should always wear the shell? (Beecher) *References:* Gal. 3:21–25; Col. 2:16–17; Heb. 8:6–13.

561. The Whole Law Must Be Kept. There are Ten Commandments, but there is only one Law. The Ten Commandments are like ten links in a chain. Suppose you were suspended from a chain having ten links and your life depended on that chain. If one link of the chain would break, down you would go to certain death, though all the other links were still good. So it is with the law of God, the Ten Commandments. If you break only one in desire, thought, word, or deed, you have violated the whole Law, and the curse rests on you; "for whoever keeps the whole law and yet stumbles at just one point is guilty of breaking all of it." (L. Wessel) *References:* Deut. 6:4–5; Joshua 23:6; Matt. 5:19; James 2:10.

562. Melanchthon, an associate of Martin Luther, found in the introductory statement of the Ten Commandments, "I am the Lord, your God," a wonderful Gospel proclamation. First, he says, you must discover that our God is a personal being, not merely a force or an urge, not merely a helpless statue like some of the images that were constructed in days of old or the devising of the human mind in our day. "I am the Lord, your God." The "I" reminds us that God is a personal being, intimately involved with His people. Second, he said, this God is eternal: "I am" the God who was, who is, and who ever shall be. He is not the product of human wisdom, but people are the product of His wisdom.

Third, He has the power to judge, for He says, "I am the Lord." In the Old Testament this title always referred to the God who moved in and called His people to judgment. But at the same time His judgment is always "judgment in love," for He adds: "I am the Lord, your God." He relates Himself to His people. He shows Himself to be concerned about their welfare. He remembers them in their need and comes to their rescue. And finally He has the power to say: "I am the Lord, your God." *Reference:* Ex. 20:2.

563. A stone hits a glass window in only one place, but it shatters the entire window. A chain may be broken in only one link, but it renders the entire chain worthless, no matter how good the other links are. Even in our courts this general truth applies. When a person has done a wrong, the judge does not ask how many right things he has done but condemns him for the wrong. You do not have to touch an electric wire in several places to get a shock; just one will do. So it takes only one sin, one breaking of God's commandments, to make us guilty of the whole

Law. *References:* Deut. 6:5; Joshua 23:6; Rom. 3:19–20; James 2:10.

564. An interviewer once asked several people, "What do you think of the Ten Commandments?" One person just stared at the questioner and gasped, "Are you kidding?" Another said, "Well, I don't take them literally." One person replied with a laugh, "Well, I think rules were made to be broken." Another said, "It's fortunate we don't have to keep them anymore." But one woman replied, "What do I think of the Ten Commandments?" Then she paused a moment and mused quietly, "Well, I think God loved us an awful lot to give them to us—to protect us from ourselves." *References:* Ex. 20:1–17; 1 Sam. 12:15; Ps. 1:1–3; Rom. 1:11–18; 3:11–18; Eph. 5:6; 2 Tim. 3:1–7.

Related illustrations: 417, 565, 817.

Law and Gospel

565. A man was preaching in the slums of a great Scottish city. He had been exhorting his listeners to make a new start, to use their will power to the utmost, to turn over a new leaf, and the like. On the outskirts of his crowd stood a poor fallen woman of the street. She stood this preaching of the Law as long as she could. Then from the depths of her despair and failure she cried out, "Your rope's not long enough for me!" No rope of the Law is long enough to reach down into the abyss of despair where the struggling soul is fighting its desperate battle against the power of indwelling sin. Only the far-flung lifeline of Jesus Christ, "the power of God for salvation," is sufficient for that. (James McConkey) *References:* Rom. 1:16; 3:19–28; 5:20; 7:7; 8:1–5; Gal. 3:19–24.

Related illustrations: 405, 562.

Laziness

566. Goofing-off America. This

125

country is experiencing the great era of the goof-off, the age of the half-done job. It is populated with laundry workers who won't iron shirts, waiters who won't serve, carpenters who will come around someday maybe, executives whose minds are on the golf course, teachers who demand a single salary schedule so that achievement cannot be rewarded, students who take cinch courses. The land from coast to coast has been enjoying a stampede away from responsibility. (Charles Brower, president of Batten, Barton, Durstine, and Osborne; quoted in *Reader's Digest*, August 1958) *References:* Prov. 6:6–10; 13:4; Is. 47:8–9; Jer. 48:10; Amos 6:1; Luke 12:19; James 4:17.

567. C. S. Lewis once said, "When our Lord and Master said that we were to be wise as serpents and harmless as doves, He did not mean for us to lay eggs. God does not like intellectual slackers any better than He likes any other kind of slacker." *References:* Neh. 6:1–4; Prov. 18:2; Matt. 7:24; 10:16; Luke 16:1–9. 2 Tim. 2:15. *Related illustrations:* 920, 987.

Learning

568. A young man was promoted to fill the position of a senior officer with a brilliant record who had just retired from the company. The young man asked his predecessor for the secret to his success. The old man answered, "Two words: right decisions." The young man then asked, "But how do you make right decisions?" Again the older man answered, this time even more tersely than before, "Experience." "And how do you get this experience?" The young man asked once more. "Two words—" answered the older man, "wrong decisions." *References:* Prov. 9:8–9; Jer. 10:23–24; 1 Cor. 13:11–12; 2 Peter 3:18.

569. He who stops learning should stop preaching or teaching. People like to drink from running streams, not from stagnant waters. *References:* Prov. 13:4; John 8:31–32; 2 Tim. 2:15. *Related illustrations:* 496, 567, 687.

Lent

570. A Time for Reconciliation. A man was separated from his wife and living in a different town for a number of years. On a business trip he stopped to visit the grave of his son. While standing there reflecting on his former relationship with his wife and the home they had made for their son, he heard steps behind him. Turning, he saw his wife, who also had come to visit the grave. His first impulse, because of the hostility that had built up between them, was to leave. But something about standing by the grave of their son held him, and he stayed and began to talk. Slowly the enmity and bitterness emptied out of his heart as they talked about their son. You and I come in Lent to stand at the grave of the Son of God, to see Him laid there and rise out of it with new life. Lent is the time for us to be reconciled—to God and to other people. *References:* Dan. 9:24; 2 Cor. 5:18–21; Eph. 2:13–19; Col. 1:20–22.

Liberty, Civil

571. When the founders of the United States drew up the Declaration of Independence and framed the Constitution, they adopted Luther's principles. This has been freely admitted by many great leaders of our country. Daniel Webster said, "The Reformation of Martin Luther introduced the principles of civil liberty into the wilderness of North America." President McKinley said, "Luther gave us civil and religious liberty." Henry Ward Beecher said, "Our civil liberty is the result of the open Bible, which Luther gave to us." In other words, "where the Spirit of the Lord is, there is liberty." *Ref-*

erences: John 8:31–32; Rom. 8:2; 2 Cor. 3:17; Gal. 5:1.

Related illustration: 507.

Liberty, Spiritual

572. Christ's yoke is like feathers to a bird—not a burden but a help for motion. (Jeremy Taylor) *References:* Matt. 11:29–30; John 8:31–32; 2 Cor. 5:14.

573. Christ Our Liberator. Warren Christopher, deputy secretary of state in the Carter Administration, concentrated his best efforts for long, trying months on the complex, sensitive mission of freeing the American hostages held in Iran. Shuttling back and forth between Washington and Algiers, he often endured long stretches without rest and prolonged absences from home. The mission of gaining freedom for 52 Americans was everything.

God is calling you to catch the significance and deep meaning of a mission that means everything for your life and for our life together in this parish. On this mission our Lord Jesus shuttled from the mansions of heaven to the poverty of earth. It became a preoccupation with Him because it was the freedom of hostages that was really at stake—your freedom. *References:* Is. 9:2–7; 42:6–7; 61:1–3; Luke 4:16–21; Rom. 8:2.

Related illustrations: 209, 408, 417.

Life, Physical

574. We truly live with the sword of Damocles ever suspended over our heads. And it is only by the good providence of God that the fragile hair by which it has been suspended all these years has not been severed. *References:* 1 Sam. 20:3; Ps. 103:15–16; Prov. 27:1; James 4:14.

575. Humanity is a highly temporary episode on a most petty planet. (H. E. Barnes) *References:* Job 14:1–5; Ps. 39:5; 103:15–16; James 4:14.

576. Shakespeare: "Out, out, brief candle! Life's but a walking shadow, a poor player that struts and frets his hour upon the stage, and then is heard no more; it is a tale told by an idiot, full of sound and fury, signifying nothing." Francois Rabelais: "Draw the curtain, the farce is played." *References:* 1 Chron. 29:15; Job 9:25; Ps. 39:5; James 4:14.

577. Depersonalization of Life. A science-fiction writer penned a story about a pedestrian in the coming mechanical age. He told of a man going out for a walk as people do today. A robot policeman eased up beside him, demanding to know why he was walking. "To breathe some air," was the answer. And the robot said mechanically, "But you've got an air conditioner." "I want to see things," the man said. "But you've got a television set," replied the robot—and the policeman hurried the pedestrian off to an insane asylum.

We sometimes contribute directly to the mechanistic age by the way we live and act. We are more concerned about an air conditioner than about the conditioning of the soul. We are more interested in seeing the funny side of life on television than in seeing the reality of human need around us. We certainly will have no one to blame but ourselves if the whole world is eventually run by robots and mechanical brains and our activity is confined to pushing buttons and twirling dials. *References:* John 10:10; Rom. 1:31; 1 Tim. 6:6–10; 2 Tim. 3:3.

Life, Spiritual

578. Grammatical Lessons for Life. And speaking of grammar, one of the most helpful bits of advice I have ever heard was from William DeWitt Hyde of Bowdoin. "Live," he said, "in the active voice rather than in the passive, thinking more of what you can do than of what may happen to you. Live in the indicative mood rather than in the subjunctive, concerned with facts as they are rather than as they might be. Live in the present tense, concentrating on the duty at hand without regret for the past or worry for the future. Live in the singular number, seeking the approval of your conscience rather than popularity with the many. Live in the first person, criticizing yourself rather than condemning others." *References:* Matt. 6:25–34; John 10:10; Rom. 6:4; Eph. 3:17–19.

Light Bearers

579. In a small English town it was the custom that at evening vespers the deacon would light a candle as each family of the parish entered to worship. Naturally, the more families worshiping, the more candlelight there was in the church. The more the children of God let their light of faith shine in this darkened world, the more light of the Gospel there will be. *References:* Matt. 5:16; Eph. 5:8; Phil. 2:15; 1 Thess. 5:5 (being light bearers for one another). Gal. 6:2; 1 Thess. 3:12; 1 Peter 1:22 (our duty to our brothers and sisters in Christ).

Light of Truth

580. At the zoo in Fort Worth, Texas, is a building where the tropical birds are kept. The hallway where the people walk is dark; the birds are in lighted cases of glass. All along each side of the building is a long case that looks like a tropical rain forest. It has a miniature waterfall, a pool, trees, and all sorts of plants. Among the trees and rocky ledges the small, brightly colored birds fly. As people watch this, they eventually become aware that there is no glass between them and the birds. They could reach in and touch them. Why don't the birds fly out? A

sign above the cage explains that the birds are afraid of darkness, and when it gets dark, they go to sleep. They love the light and will not deliberately fly from the light into the darkness.

So it is with Christians. We are in the light of the kingdom of God. We have been called out of darkness. We will not deliberately fly back into the darkness, for we love the light. *References:* Ps. 27:1; John 1:4–13; 3:19–21; 12:35–36; Eph. 5:8; 1 Thess. 5:5; 1 John 1:5–7.

Listening

581. The Greek writer Zeno once said, "We have two ears but only one mouth so that we may hear more and speak less." *References:* Prov. 18:15; 20:12; 25:12; Matt. 11:15; 13:13–17; James 1:19.

Related illustration: 258.

Literature

582. With the invention of the printing press John Gutenberg conferred a greater blessing on the world than Christopher Columbus did with his discovery of America. *References:* Is. 52:7; Matt. 24:14.

583. Much of modern literature is so filthy that Christian homes cannot be too careful in selecting reading material. As to telling stories, remember what General Grant said when a person was about to tell a shady story and asked, "Are there any ladies present?" Grant replied, "No, but there are gentlemen present." *References:* Prov. 1:10; 28:10; 2 Peter 2:18–19.

584. Witnessing Through Christian Literature. For years Mrs. Bernard Shaw tried to get her famous author husband to write a biography of Joan of Arc, but he never was interested until she brought book after book on the life of the Maid of Orleans home and placed them within arm's reach of his favorite reading chair. In the course of

time Shaw became so enthused about Joan of Arc that he wrote one of the finest dramas about her life. Countless Christian husbands and wives have, by putting Christian literature in convenient places in their homes, gotten their unbelieving partners in marriage to read themselves into the Christian faith. *References:* Is. 52:7; Matt. 5:16; 1 Cor. 7:14; Gal. 6:6–10.
Related illustration: 516.

Locusts

585. The Bible repeatedly speaks of countless locusts (Ps. 105:34; Judg. 7:12; Jer. 46:23). An ancient writer, describing an alighting swarm, says that they descended like falling snow (Ecclus. 43:17). A vast cloud of these insects that crossed the Red Sea in 1889 was estimated to be 2,000 square miles in extent. In other words, this single swarm, flying in a column wide enough to cover the whole city of Cleveland, would have reached all the way to Toledo. Official reports from Cyprus state that 1,300 tons of locust eggs were destroyed in 1881 on that island. Locust swarms have been seen at sea as much as 1,200 miles from land. *References:* Ex. 10:12–15; Deut. 28:38; Judg. 7:12; Ps. 105:34; Jer. 46:23.

Loneliness

586. Loneliness! A husband may accompany his wife to the delivery room, but she alone in all the universe must labor for the birth of her baby. *References:* Ps. 38:11; Luke 22:39–44; John 16:32.

587. Dr. Paul Morentz, Lutheran pastor and psychiatrist, says, "Loneliness is still mankind's greatest problem. And it stems from the 'original sin' of man's self-imposed loneliness and isolation from God back in the Garden of Eden." *References:* Ps. 58:3; Jer. 2:5; Eph. 2:12.

588. The story of Benedict Arnold's betrayal on the television program "You Are There" some time ago illustrated what the steward (Luke 16:1–9) feared. In a poignant ending Arnold is portrayed as a tragic figure. He has returned to England and is an officer in the British army. But whenever he or his wife would enter a room where there were other officers, the others would turn their backs and walk away. Arnold was completely ostracized, and that was a punishment far worse than if he had been imprisoned. *References:* Matt. 8:11–12; 22:13; 25:30; 27:3–5; Luke 16:1–9, 23; 1 Cor. 9:27.
Related illustration: 447.

Lord's Supper

589. The pelican feeds her young with her own blood when serpents have bitten them. So Christ gives us, who have been mortally wounded by the sting of Satan, His blood in the blessed Sacrament, that our souls may be delivered from death and destruction. (Stock) *References:* Matt. 26:27–28; Luke 22:20; 1 Cor. 11:24–26.

590. Faith does not put the body and blood of Christ into the Lord's Supper; it finds them there. (Krauth) *References:* Matt. 26:26–28; 1 Cor. 10:16; 11:23–28.

591. In her wanton frenzy Cleopatra is said to have offered a guest a goblet of rich wine in which she had dissolved a pearl of great value. But how insignificant Cleopatra's pearl is when compared with the pearl of Christ's body and blood in the Sacrament, which gives untold benefits! *References:* Matt. 26:26–28; 1 Cor. 10:16; 11:23–26.

592. In Remembrance of Me. The Taj Mahal in India, considered by some to be one of the most beautiful buildings in the world, was erected in memory of a faithful and loving wife.

Stanford University in California, renowned for its magnificent buildings, was built by some parents in loving memory of their only son, who had died. Today when someone thinks of Stanford University, they no longer think of the son; a tourist to the Taj Mahal does not think of the faithful and loving wife unless someone explains about her.

Our Lord, on that night in the Upper Room when He gave bread to His disciples and said, "This is My body," added, "Do this in remembrance of Me." When He gave them the cup that was His blood, He said, "Do this, as often as you drink it, in remembrance of Me." *References:* Luke 22:19; 1 Cor. 10:16; 11:23–26.

593. A Personal Encounter with Christ. In Westminster Abbey well over 500 years ago, King Henry V of England was found one day by a courtier receiving Holy Communion at an almost-deserted altar in a quiet part of the building, while a great crowd of people filled the vast nave of the abbey and listened to an address by a talented preacher. When the courtier asked why he was not with the larger congregation in the nave, the king replied, "I would rather meet with my Friend than merely hear Him talked about." *References:* Matt. 26:26–28; Mark 14:22–25; Luke 22:19–20; 1 Cor. 10:16; 11:23–26.

594. In a small park in a small Canadian town stands a beautiful war memorial, erected in honor of those who died for the cause of freedom. A light is kept perpetually burning in the small park. The place is called "the Garden of the Unforgotten." Our Communion services are in a real sense a memorial of the unforgotten Christ, who gave His life for our eternal freedom. *References:* Luke 22:19; 1 Cor. 11:23–26.

595. Where Love and Forgiveness Reign. When someone invites guests for dinner, it is not so that they quarrel with one another, but that they be friendly to one another and forgive one another any sins that may have been committed. Jesus had the same purpose in mind when He instituted the Lord's Supper. The Lord's Supper was to keep Christians in the bonds of love. Our old teachers therefore have said, "Jesus used bread and wine in the Lord's Supper to show that, as many kernels of grain, though they have their own body and form, are ground into flour and baked into one loaf of bread, in a similar way we, though each one of us has his own body and his own individuality, are one body and one bread because in the Sacrament we all are partakers of one bread." (Caspari) *References:* Acts 2:42; 1 Cor. 10:16–17; 11:17–34; Eph. 4:32; 1 John 1:7. *Related illustrations:* 305, 634, 1010.

Love, God's

596. Love is not a quality that God has but rather the all-embracing totality of what He is. (Besser) *References:* Jer. 31:3; John 3:16; 1 John 4:7–8.

597. God's Universal Love. The great Bible translator Richard Baxter once observed that if the name "Richard Baxter" appeared in John 3:16, he might wonder if another man by that name were meant. The "whosoever" makes it absolutely unquestionable that he was meant. *References:* John 3:16; Rom. 10:12; 1 Tim. 2:4.

598. One reaction to the "Death of God" movement appeared on an automobile bumper sticker that read: "God is not dead; He just doesn't want to get involved." But God is not only alive; He is also deeply involved in human affairs. People of faith know that God lives and is present in their concerns, not merely to watch them but actually to control them. *References:*

Ps. 8:4; 34:18–19; 113:5–8; 145:18–19; Is. 57:15; John 1:11–14.

599. National television showed twin brothers about eight or nine years old. One, because of kidney disease, was considerably smaller than the other. Once he had been weak and sickly, but now before the cameras he played and chattered away. Why the improvement? Because his brother had given him his kidney and saved his life. His brother was asked what kidney he gave. He replied, "My right one . . . because I am right-handed, and I figured that my right kidney was my best kidney."

What an example of love! His parents said that it was his own idea to give his kidney and that his love was free and generous toward his brother. Yes, for a good man, for a bishop, or for his brother a person might be willing to die. But God shows His love for us in that "when we were God's enemies, we were reconciled to him through the death of his Son" (Rom. 5:10). *References:* John 3:16; Rom. 5:6–11; 2 Cor. 5:14.

600. God's Special Love for Each of Us. When the small daughter of the distinguished sculptress Sally Farnham was once asked which child was her mother's favorite, the little girl promptly replied, "She loves Jimmy best because he's the oldest, and she loves Johnny best because he's the youngest, and she loves me best because I'm the only girl."

It would be difficult to find a better illustration of God's all-embracing love for His children. It is wonderful to know that God loves us personally, no matter what our experience has been. His love transcends all barriers, and each one of us is most precious in His sight. *References:* Is. 43:1; Jer. 31:3; John 15:13; Gal. 2:20; 1 John 3:1.

601. Language fails to express the love of God manifested through Christ to us. Motherly love is the nearest approach to this divine passion. Mr. Gladstone announced in the House of Commons the death of Princess Alice with the following pathetic story: "The little daughter of the princess was critically ill with diphtheria. The mother was forbidden by the physician to kiss her because of the almost certain danger of contracting the disease. In one of the paroxysms of delirium to which the child was subject, the mother was so distressed that she took her in her arms and gently soothed her into quietness. When reason returned, the little sufferer looked up into the mother's face and cried, 'Mama, kiss me.' This was too much for the mother's heart. Without stopping to think, the princess pressed the little one to her bosom and kissed her lips. But it was the kiss of death. Before many days had passed, the child was well, but the mother lay pale and cold in her splendid shroud. The sacrifice of life was prompted by an impulse of love. Even so Christ loved us. Taking no account of the cost, He just lived and died." (Walther League Messenger) *References:* Is. 53:4–11; John 3:16; 13:1; 15:13; 2 Cor. 5:14–15; Gal. 2:20; Eph. 5:2.

602. A traveler tells of being shocked one night during a trip through China when he awoke and looked out in the moonlight at a row of Chinese gods. The faces were hideous and terrifying. One can look at any heathen religion, and the gods are the same: subject to human passion, cruel, and sometimes frightening. There are among them some gods called gods of mercy and pity, but there is never a real god of love. Only the God of the Bible, the triune God, is a God of love. *References:* Deut. 7:7–8; Is. 40:18–31; Jer.

31:3; John 3:16; Rom. 5:8; Eph. 2:4–5; 1 John 3:1; 4:9–16.

603. God Loves Even His Foes. Rita Snowden related that in 1915, as Col. T. E. Lawrence was crossing the desert with some Arabs, they rode with their hoods covering their heads for protection from the wind and sand. With the food supply low and their water on a minimum ration, one Arab noticed an empty camel. "Where is Jasmin?" he asked. "Who is Jasmin?" another Arab answered. A third explained, "Jasmin is that yellow-faced man from Mann. He killed a Turkish tax collector and fled into the desert." It soon became evident that Jasmin had fainted in the heat and fallen off his camel. Finally, one Arab said, "What does it matter? Jasmin was not worth half a crown." So they hunched down on their camels and rode on. But Lawrence turned and rode back in the blazing heat. After an hour and a half he found Jasmin, blinded and almost mad from the heat and thirst. Lawrence shared some of his precious water, put him on his camel, and brought him back. That night when they reached the others, the Arabs were amazed. Jasmin, not worth half a crown, was saved by Lawrence at the risk of his own life.

It was not for good people that Christ died. It was for people like Jasmin—for the sinner, the ungodly, the enemies, those hostile to God. This is love. *References:* Matt. 5:45; Luke 23:39–43; Rom. 5:6–8; 1 Tim. 1:15 (God's love for His enemies). Ex. 2:5–6; Luke 10:30–37; James 2:1–4 (our duty to be compassionate).

604. Our Helper in Need. In the TV movie "Eric" we watch young Eric struggle with cancer. There is a scene in which he stands on the beach of the family's summer home with his father. "Daddy," he says, "remember how I wanted to swim across the bay with you? We got halfway across, and I said I couldn't make it. Remember how you reached out and helped me? Well, Daddy, I don't think I can make it now." Eric's father quickly spread his arms around him and said, "I'll help you." That's God's promise to us. *References:* Ps. 40:17; 57:1; 121; Is. 41:10; 46:4; Heb. 4:16; 13:6; 2 Tim. 4:18.

605. When Michelangelo came down from the scaffolding from which he had for some weeks been painting the frescoes of a high ceiling, he had become so accustomed to looking upward that it caused real pain to turn his eyes to the ground. Would that we might evermore be so arrested and held by the confidence of God's love that we could never be satisfied to turn our eyes from His face. *References:* Jer. 31:3; Acts 1:10; 2 Thess. 3:5; Titus 2:11–14; 1 John 3:1; 4:7–17; Jude 21.

606. God's Unqualified Love. A large family with 11 children accidentally left one of them behind in a motel in Denver. They traveled several hundred miles before they discovered that one was missing. They didn't just continue on, saying, "Oh well, we still have 10 kids left; what's one child?" They drove back, and out near the Kansas border they met the state police, who had brought the child that far. God is like those parents. His love includes all people—the rich and the poor, the reputable and the outcasts, those society accepts and those it rejects. That's what He was trying to get across to the Pharisees and scribes who figured that the tax collectors and sinners should be rejected by Jesus as worthless scum. *References:* Ps. 113:5–7; Matt. 9:10–13; Luke 4:17–21; 7:36–50; 15:1–10; John 3:16; 1 John 2:2.

Related illustrations: 94, 115, 204, 368, 502, 530, 609, 610, 613, 639.

Love, Human

See also **Brotherhood**

607. The soul of charity is charity for the soul. *References:* 1 Peter 1:22; 1 John 4:7.

608. Love is the little golden clasp
That bindeth up the trust;
Oh, break it not lest all the leaves
Shall scatter and be lost.

References: Rom. 12:9; 1 Thess. 3:12; 1 Peter 1:22.

609. Our Need for Love. Our world desperately needs to be loved. At the close of World War II an American soldier was on sentry duty on the outskirts of London on Christmas morning. Later in the day, as he walked to the city with a few other GIs, he came to an old gray building with a sign: "Queen Anne's Orphanage." To see what sort of Christmas party might be going on inside, the soldiers knocked on the door. An attendant told them that all the children in the orphanage had lost their parents in the London bombings. The soldiers went inside, and seeing no tree, no decorations, and no gifts, they gave out as gifts whatever they had in their pockets—a stick of gum, a coin, a stubby pencil. One soldier saw a boy standing alone in a corner. He went to him and asked, "My little man, what do you want?" Turning his face up to the soldier, the little boy answered, "Please, sir, I want to be loved." That's our world—in desperate need of love. God loves it and wants to love it through us. *References:* Jer. 31:3; John 3:16; 13:34–35; Rom. 5:8; Eph. 2:4–5; Col. 3:14; 1 John 3:1; 4:9.

610. What Is Love? In the movie *Arthur* a filthy rich young man, who had never in his life had to care for anyone, suddenly falls in love. It is a feeling he cannot describe. In order to determine if it is the real thing, he asks a total stranger, "How can you tell if you are in love? Does it make you feel funny? Does it make you whistle all the time?" The stranger, unimpressed by the joy of new love, tells him, "You could be in love; then again, you could be getting sick."

Arthur's dilemma of not knowing what love feels like is unfortunately typical. In fact the problem is even worse than that. Not only do we not know what love feels like, but it is difficult for us even to know what love is. The word itself covers such a broad range of emotions—I love pizza, I love my children, let's make love—that it is no help at all in getting to know what love is.

Scripture tells us that "God is love" and that "we love, because He first loved us" (1 John 4:8, 19). From God we learn what love is by experiencing it in the gift of His Son. The more we can know about how God loves, the more we will know what love is and the more we will be able to love. *References:* John 15:9–17; 1 Cor. 13:1–8; 2 Cor. 5:14; Gal. 2:20; Eph. 5:1–2; 1 John 3:16; 4:8–19.

611. Back in the fourth century of the Christian era, Julian the Apostate charged the Christians with seeking to obtain followers by bribing the sick and suffering and needy. He said, "These Christians give themselves to this kind of humanity. Now we see what it is that makes them such powerful enemies of our gods. It is the brotherly love that they manifest towards the stranger and the suffering and the poor." That's quite a charge—a charge of which we must be continually guilty. *References:* Matt. 22:39; John 13:35; 15:12; Rom. 12:9; 13:9; 1 Thess. 3:12; Heb. 13:1–2; 1 Peter 1:22.

612. Love Not a Respecter of Persons. Love is heavenly. The world cannot understand it. A story from the

Christian leper hospital in India illustrates this clearly. The doctor in charge received a report that one of the patients was dying by the roadside a few miles away. "It can't be," the doctor said. "We have all our patients here." But the doctor sent out four other patients to see. Two miles out along the road they found an emaciated leper who had collapsed just short of the hospital toward which he had traveled many hard miles. He was dying of starvation and weariness. The men carried him tenderly back to the hospital, washed, fed, and cared for him. A few days later, as he lay on his clean white hospital bed, the superintendent of the hospital came to see him. Again and again the leper said: "When they brought me in, those men, they never even asked my name!" In India the name indicates the position and social caste, by which all of life is governed. *References:* Matt. 5:46; Acts 10:34; 15:7–9; Rom. 2:11; 10:12; Gal. 2:6; Eph. 6:9.

613. For the Love of God! A man driving on a dark highway one night accidentally struck a hitchhiker who had been near the roadside. Hearing the sickening thud on his front fender, he stopped to see what had happened. When he saw the injured fellow on the ground, he wanted to jump into his car and drive away. But as he started toward his car door, the injured man moaned, "For the love of God, help me!" The driver resisted his fearful temptation and returned to help. "For the love of God" we can resist temptation. And "for the love of God" we can go beyond temptation with His power to show that love to our neighbor, who also needs the power of His love. *References:* Matt. 4:1–11; John 14:22–23; 2 Cor. 5:14–15; Gal. 2:20.

614. Much More Than an Attraction. To be in love, according to the modern notion, "is something quite irresistible, something that just happens to one, like measles." C. S. Lewis points this out in one of those excellent little essays of his and goes on to say, "Because they believe this, some married people just throw in the sponge and give up when they are attracted by a new acquaintance." There is nothing else to be done about it; one cannot control one's falling in love or out of it any more than one can control the rain. If fate or the gods or whatever it is that ordains these things switches the emotion off, there is no sense in continuing to live with the other person, is there? *References:* Rom. 12:9; 1 Cor. 13:4–8a; 2 Cor. 6:6; 1 Thess. 3:12.

615. Hugh Latimer in England, in the days of the Reformation, said to his large congregation, "You can build a hundred churches and fill them with gold statues and with candles as big as oaks, but if you do not love your neighbor and feed the hungry and clothe the naked, you will go to hell in spite of all." *References:* Matt. 7:21–23; 25:41–46; John 13:35; 21:16; 1 Cor. 13:1–2; 1 John 3:14; 4:20.

616. When Carey landed on the virgin mission soil of India, he said, "Now let me burn out for God." Is the measure and degree of your love of Christ like that? *References:* Matt. 16:25; 19:21; Luke 14:26–27; 18:28–30; Phil. 3:7–8.

Related illustrations: 69, 82, 297, 298, 338, 381, 437, 502, 599, 603.

Lust

617. The Enemy Within. When Francisco Franco was leading the revolution in Spain, he originated the phrase "the fifth column." He was trying to capture Madrid. He said that he had four columns marching on the city, one from the north, one from the south, one from the east, and one from the west. And most important of all, he had a "fifth column" within the city. "Each one is tempted when, by his own evil desire, he is dragged away and enticed. Then, after desire has conceived, it gives birth to sin; and sin, when it is full-grown, gives birth to death" (James 1:14–15). As surely as Judas's betrayal led to the crucifixion of Christ, so surely will your flesh, if uncontrolled, lead to your eternal death. *References:* Ps. 41:9; Rom. 5:12; 7:14–24; James 1:14–15. *Related illustration:* 824.

Luther

618. The inscription on Luther's tombstone in Wittenberg reads, "If it is God's work, it will endure; if it is man's work, it will perish." (Caspari) *Reference:* Acts 5:34–39.

619. The Meaning of Luther's Seal. In 1530, while Luther was still at Coburg, Prince John Frederick ordered a signet ring for him. This gave the Reformer occasion to express himself in a letter to his friend Spengler at Nuremberg on the significance of the seal. It was to be characteristic of his theology. He wrote: "There should be a black cross in the naturally red heart; for in our heart we must believe in the Crucified One in order to be saved; the cross, indeed, causes pain and mortification, yet it does not kill, but rather promotes the vital energy of the heart. Such a heart should stand on a white rose, to show that faith imparts joy, comfort, and peace; and should be white because that is the color of spirits and of angels and the joys not of this world. The rose, finally, should be placed in a sky-blue field, as this joy is already the beginning of the heavenly and is comprehended in the hope of heaven; and that field should be encircled with a golden ring; for heavenly

salvation endures forever and is more valuable than all other possessions, as gold is the highest, noblest, and most precious of all metals." Early reproductions of Luther's coat of arms were accompanied by the inscription: "Des Christen Herz auf Rosen geht, Wenn's mitten unterm Kreuze steht." *References:* Rom. 6:6; 2 Cor. 4:11; Gal. 6:14; Eph. 2:13–18; Phil. 2:5–15; 2 Tim. 2:11.

620. A Man of Faith. If every angel in heaven had passed before Luther and each one had assured him of the truth of God, he would not have thanked them for their testimony, for he believed without the witness of either angels or people; he thought the Word of divine testimony to be more sure than anything that seraphim could say. Most of us are not as big as Luther's little finger; we do not have as much faith in our whole souls as he had in one hair of his head. (Spurgeon) *References:* Matt. 8:8–10; 15:28; Rom. 1:16–17.

621. A Man of Prayer. Veit Dietrich, a close friend of Luther, wrote to Philip Melanchthon, "Not a day passes during which he does not spend in prayer at least three hours, such as are most precious for study. On one occasion, I chanced to hear him pray. Good Lord, what a spirit, what faith spoke out of his words. He prayed with such reverence that one could see he was speaking with God, and with such faith and confidence as is shown by one who is speaking with his Father and Friend" (*Luthers Werke,* St. Louis Edition, 16:1763). *References:* Ps. 91:15; Luke 18:1; Eph. 6:18; Phil. 4:6; Col. 4:2; 1 Thess. 5:17; James 5:13.

622. A Messenger of God. John Bugenhagen, pastor of the town church in Wittenberg, where Luther preached most of his powerful sermons, preached at Luther's funeral in 1546. Like Luther a former priest and now a

Lutheran pastor, Bugenhagen delivered the sermon over Luther's body, which had been brought back on roads crowded with mourning multitudes from the little town of Eisleben, where Luther had been born and to which he had made a trip in the middle of the winter to resolve a family quarrel between the counts of Mansfeld. After reading the text, "I saw another angel flying in midair, and he had the eternal gospel to proclaim to those who live on the earth—to every nation, tribe, language and people. He said in a loud voice, 'Fear God and give him glory,' " Bugenhagen commented, "Luther was without doubt the angel of whom the Apocalypse speaks."

Even those who disagree with this interpretation of the text must admit that Luther was an angel, a messenger of God, a prophet, a modern apostle of Jesus Christ, calling the church back to the apostolic faith and to true worship, a teacher raised up by God to say what had to be said at that moment— the right thing at the right time. *References:* Mal. 3:1; Rev. 14:6–7.

Note: For related illustrations, see "Luther" in the topical index.

Lying
See also **Slander**

623. It is easy to tell a lie but hard to tell only one. One must be thatched with another, or it will soon rain through. (Fuller) *References:* Ps. 5:6; Prov. 12:22; Col. 3:9.

Related illustration: 231.

M

Mankind

624. Selfishness is native in human beings, not phenomenal. I read somewhere of a church convention that had a large banner with the legend "JESUS ONLY" hung over the entrance of the convention hall. Along came a strong wind and tore away the first three letters of the banner, so that it read "US ONLY." *References:* Is. 5:8; 14:13–14; 53:6; Luke 12:16–21; 22:24; John 5:44; Phil. 2:3–4.

Related illustration: 390.

Marriage

625. "He is half part of a blessed man, left to be finished by such as she; and she, a fair divided excellence, whose fulness of perfection lies in him." (Shakespeare) *References:* Gen. 2:18, 23–24; Eph. 5:31.

626. A good marriage resembles a pair of scissors; they are so joined that they cannot be separated; at times they might move in opposite directions, yet they always punish anyone who comes between them. (Sydney Smith) *References:* Gen. 2:24; Matt. 5:32; Mark 10:9.

627. Love Your Wife to Gain Her Respect. John Chrysostom, one of the early church fathers, speaking to husbands, said, "Do you want your wife to obey you as the church obeys Christ? Then care for her as Christ cares for the church. If it be needful that you should give your life for her or be cut to pieces a thousand times or endure anything, don't refuse it. Christ brought the church to His feet by His great care, not by threats or fear. So conduct yourself toward your wife in like manner." *References:* Eph. 5:21–31; Col. 3:18–19; 1 Peter 3:1–7.

628. Mixed Marriages. Another thing that will keep your married life happy is that you are both of the same faith. This is very important. I know that in exceptional cases mixed marriages turn out to be happy marriages. But I want to insist that there is danger in mixed marriages. If both parties want to be absolutely loyal and true to their own faith and their own church in every way, there is bound to be conflict. If church services are held at different times, family life or social arrangements are likely to be disturbed, and this will often cause argument and conflict. If both parties wish to contribute liberally to their church, dissatisfaction may creep in, and if both parties want to raise the children in their own faith, as a loyal church member should, then altercation and dissension cannot be avoided. Of course, it is possible to keep clear of any conflict by a compromise in these things, if each one gives up something for the other. But right there is the danger I am speaking of. A true and loyal member of the church cannot compromise. Loyalty knows no compromise. (F. Niedner) *References:* Gen. 24:1–4; 28:1; Deut. 7:3–4; Joshua 23:12–13;

MARTYRDOM

Ezra 9:12; Neh. 13:25; 2 Cor. 6:14.
Related illustration: 772.

Martyrdom

629. It is more difficult and calls for higher energies of soul to live a martyr than to die one. (Horace Mann) *References:* 2 Cor. 4:8–12; 2 Tim. 4:6–8; Rev. 2:10.

630. During the bloody reign of Queen Mary of England, Archbishop Cranmer became odious to her persecuting spirit. So she decided to bring him to the stake. Before carrying out her wicked plan, she engaged emissaries, who by flattery and false promises prevailed on him to renounce his faith. The good man was overcome and subscribed to the errors of the Church of Rome. But soon thereafter his conscience smote him, and he returned to his former persuasion. When brought to the stake, he stretched forth his hand, the hand that made the unhappy signature, held it in the flames till it was consumed, and exclaimed, "That unworthy hand!" Relying on the Lord, he suffered martyrdom and entered his reward. *References:* Matt. 26:69–75; Mark 14:66–72; Luke 22:56–62; John 18:15–27; 21:15–17.

631. John Hus of Prague, Bohemia, was summoned to appear before the Council of Constance. Emperor Sigismund guaranteed him a safe conduct. This council was called to reform the church in head and members. Hus had taught justification by faith in Christ Jesus. He insisted that forgiveness could not be bought with money and that the Scriptures are the highest authority in the church. At the council he was asked to recant. Instead he confessed his faith. On July 6, 1415, without being offered an opportunity for defense, he was led from the church where he had been condemned to die by fire. His hands were tied behind him with ropes. His neck was chained to the stake around which wood and straw were piled and set afire. Hus sang: "Christ, Thou Son of the living God, have mercy upon me." His ashes were thrown into the Rhine. Members of the council evidently believed that they were doing God a service. *References:* Matt. 10:16–22; 23:29–35; John 16:1–3; Heb. 11:32–40; Rev. 6:9–11. *Related illustrations:* 20, 112, 943.

Means of Grace

632. It has been well said that we must seek Christ not only *while* He may be found, but also *where* He may be found. The shepherds were given this direction: "This will be a sign to you:"—a proof that you have found Him whom you were seeking—"You will find a baby wrapped in cloths and lying in a manger." Luther says: "Word and Sacrament are the manger and the swaddling-clothes into which it has pleased Christ to lay Himself." The lowliness may seem incongruous to the superspirituality of some, but our Lord will be found nowhere else. *References:* Matt. 26:26–28; Acts 2:38; Rom. 1:16–17; 10:6–9; 1 Cor. 10:16; 11:23–29; Gal. 3:26–27.

633. We're not very good at taking advice, are we? The doctor tells us, "Stop smoking." Yet many of us would rather fight than switch. Some would rather die than stop. Doctors say, "Watch your diet." And we do—with Julia Child on TV! Doctors advise, "Exercise 15 minutes a day for better health." But it's so hard to find those 15 minutes. It's so easy to skip one day, then another. We start today and quit tomorrow. Or else we say we'll start tomorrow and never do. Good habits are so elusive, while bad habits are like glue—hard to shake.

We find ways to avoid the doctor's advice, but we're even worse about taking God's advice. We know that daily Bible study and weekly worship contribute to our spiritual health. But the epistles are seldom as interesting as the sports page, and worship can be so dull and wearisome. Movies are almost always more entertaining than Holy Communion, and many people are more inclined to lose sleep because of a Saturday night party than they are to get up early Sunday morning for church. *References:* 1 Sam. 8:10–22; Ps. 81:11–13; Prov. 4:14–23; Rom. 7:15.

634. During the memorable retreat of the French from Moscow, the soldiers froze to death by the hundreds. It is said that at night they gathered together such combustible material as they could find and made a fire. Then, gathering round it as closely as possible, they lay down to sleep. In the morning, after a bitter night, those in the outer circles would be found dead, frozen to death. They were too far away from the source of the heat. So the Christian's strength in the warfare of life lies in close and constant communion with Christ by the means of grace. To withdraw from them may—and will eventually—prove fatal. *References:* Ps. 73:25–28; John 3:27; 8:31–32; 15:4–7; 2 Cor. 3:5; Gal. 3:27.

Meditation

635. Along the Amazon River in South America there is said to be a tribe of Indians who at certain times of the year squat on the ground and refuse to move, saying that they are waiting for their souls to catch up with their bodies. Those Indians make good sense. We, too, need times of quiet, of stillness, of silence, so that the soul may catch up with the body. God Himself demands that when he says, for example, "Be still, and know that I am God!" *References:* Num. 9:8; 1 Sam.

9:27; 12:7; Job 4:16; 37:14; Ps. 4:4; 46:10; Hab. 2:20.

Memorial Day

636. Its Origin. Mrs. Mary Cotton Redpath, who had moved with her husband from Massachusetts to South Carolina, noted many unkempt and unkept soldier graves in Charleston. Hoping to remedy this distressful situation, she appealed to her friends. She proposed to them that they decorate these graves. Her friends in turn appealed to others, and on May 30, 1865, scores of interested persons marked these neglected graves and decorated them with myrtle, yellow roses, and other dainty blossoms.

Early in May 1868 General John A. Logan, commander-in-chief of the Grand Army of the Republic, officially designated May 30 as "a day for decorating the graves of the comrades who died in the defense of their country." For many years this annual event was known as Decoration Day. About the time it became a holiday, it also acquired its present and much more symbolic designation of Memorial Day. *References:* Joshua 24:26–28; Judg. 5:9; 2 Sam. 1:12; Ps. 20:7; 112:6; 1 John 3:16.

Mercy, Divine

See also **Grace**

637. The depths of our misery can never fall below the depths of mercy. (Sibbes) *References:* Ps. 103:17; 108:4; Lam. 3:22–23; Micah 7:18; Luke 1:50; Rom. 5:20; Eph. 2:4.

638. When Thomas Hooker was dying, someone said to him: "You are going to receive the rewards of your labors." He replied: "I am going to receive mercy." *References:* 2 Sam. 24:14; Ps. 108:4; Joel 2:13; Micah 7:18; Titus 3:5.

639. When Commander Scott Carpenter returned from his space travels, the highest dignitaries in the land honored him. In the middle of the ceremonies, his five-year-old daughter, Candace, tugged at his sleeve. She wanted to show her daddy the scratch on her right elbow that happened while he was gone. What did he do? Yes, he turned away from the honors, away from the acclaim of a proud nation to give his attention to the concerns of his little daughter. A scratch on the elbow was important to her, and so it was important to him. That is a parable of God's relationship to us, His sons and daughters. Whatever hurts us, whatever our needs and problems, we bring them to our Father, and He who is the Creator of the world, the Lord of the universe, turns to us and comforts us with the assurance of His presence and His love. *References:* Ps. 40:17; 136:23; Is. 49:14–16; Luke 12:7; Rom. 8:31–39; Heb. 4:14–16; 1 Peter 5:7.

Related illustrations: 418, 523, 604, 666.

Mercy, Human
640. A Roman lord had a servant, Androclus, whom he treated very unmercifully. When the servant no longer was able to bear the mistreatment, he fled into a large forest and lay down in a cave to sleep. He was greatly terrified when a great lion came into the cave, which had also been its home. But the lion came whining to the man and showed him a large thorn in its paw, which had become infected. The man extracted the thorn, which pleased the lion so much that it became the friend of Androclus, brought him food, etc. After about three years the man became tired of this wild life and wanted to return to civilized living, but a band of soldiers captured the runaway servant. He was sentenced to be thrown to the wild beasts at a coming festival. Meanwhile the lion was captured also. And

so it happened that when Androclus was thrown to the lions, his recent friend and host came to meet him, recognized him, and bounced about him like a pet dog. The spectators, who now heard the story of Androclus, begged for his life. *References:* Prov. 11:17; Eccl. 11:1; Matt. 5:7; 25:40; Luke 6:38 (the merciful shall obtain mercy). 1 Sam. 15:6; 2 Sam. 9:1; 10:2; 1 Kings 2:7; Luke 17:11–19 (gratitude for mercy shown).

641. Justice Knows No Partiality. Pastor Martin Niemoeller said in 1945, "When the Nazis came for the communists, I did not speak up because I was not a communist; when they came for the Jews, I did not speak up because I was not a Jew; when the came for the trade unionists, I did not speak up because I was not a trade unionist; when they came for the Catholics, I did not speak up because I was a Protestant. And then they came for me, and by that time there was not one left to speak up for anyone." *References:* Ps. 103:6; Prov. 21:13; 24:17; 25:21–22; Matt. 5:43–48; 25:41–45; Acts 10:34; Rom. 12:20.

Related illustrations: 119, 445, 460, 461, 682.

Ministers, Pastoral
642. Ministers are like alarm clocks; they get most of their abuse for doing their duty—waking people up. *References:* Matt. 10:22; John 15:18–21; 2 Tim. 4:1–5.

643. Dietrich Bonhoeffer's observation about the "cost of discipleship" pertains doubly to the special ministers of Jesus: "When Christ calls a man, He bids him come and die." Indeed, the man who says: "He must increase, but I must decrease," does not belong to himself. *References:* Matt. 16:24–25; Luke 14:26; 17:33; John 3:30.

644. Belgian Father Damien, on the

Hawaiian island of Molokai, contracted leprosy, but God kept him alive for 16 long years for the sole purpose of preaching to others similarly afflicted. *References:* Is. 38:1–5; Phil. 1:21–25.

645. Admonishing the Flock. Even if I preach correctly and shepherd the flock with sound doctrine, I neglect my duty if I do not warn the sheep against the wolves. For what kind of builder would I be if I were to pile up masonry and then stand by while another tears it down? The wolf does not object to our leading the sheep to good pastures. The sheep that have been fattened are the more eagerly sought by him. What he cannot tolerate is that the watchdogs stand on guard, ready to give him battle. (Luther) *References:* Matt. 7:15; 15:7–9, 14; Acts 20:29–31; Rom. 16:17; 2 Tim. 4:1–2.

646. A preacher must be both soldier and shepherd. He must nourish, defend, and teach; he must have teeth in his mouth and be able to bite and fight. (Luther) *References:* Acts 20:27–31; 1 Tim. 6:11–12; 2 Tim. 2:1–3, 15; 4:1–5; Titus 2:1–7.

647. One of the most colorful and helpful pictures was offered by Hans Rudi Weber, who suggested that the job of the clergy is to serve as "kitchen troops in the divine army." This is a great image for pastors and people in that it places the work of pastors in perspective. We need kitchen troops or the army would starve. But when kitchen troops begin to confuse the fighting men by suggesting that they spend more and more time in the kitchen or become arrogant enough to suggest that the kitchen troops are the most important part of the army, the only "full-time" members, perhaps they should be court-martialed. *References:* Jer. 3:15; 23:4; Ezek. 34:2–

3; Zech. 11:15–17; John 21:15–17; Acts 20:28; 1 Peter 5:2. *Related illustrations:* 154, 569.

Miracles

648. Miracles in the early days were a necessary accompaniment of revelation, as picture books are of childhood. (MacLaren) *References:* Matt. 16:1–4; Mark 8:11–12; Luke 11:29–32; 1 Cor. 13:8–11.

649. Robert Ingersoll, the famous atheist of some decades ago, traveled widely across the country, lecturing to large groups of people. It is said that at one time he sought to show how Jesus' raising Lazarus from the dead was just a trick to bolster Jesus' waning fortunes. Lazarus was a good friend of Jesus, and he would pretend to have died, Ingersoll said, be dressed in grave clothes by his friends, and secretly "buried." Then as Jesus would pass by the sepulcher some days later, He would give the clue by calling Lazarus's name. Lazarus would come out of the tomb, and everybody would think that Christ had performed a miracle and that He was really God. To clinch his point, Ingersoll asked the audience, "Can anyone tell me now why Jesus said: 'Lazarus, come forth'?"

An old Christian in the back got up and said, "Yes, I will tell you why my Lord said, 'Lazarus, come forth.' Because if He had not said 'Lazarus,' He would have had the whole graveyard of Bethany coming out to Him!" *Reference:* John 11:1–46.

Missions and Evangelism

650. Our Mission: The Gospel. Picture a father away on a business trip. Before coming home, he buys a gift for his little boy—a billfold with a $5 bill hidden inside. He walks into the house, calls his son, and gives him the gift. The boy is so excited that he grabs the billfold and runs to show his friends before his father is able to explain that there is more to the gift. It was good the boy was excited about the gift, but he should have contained his enthusiasm until he fully understood and appreciated *the total gift.* Even so, our mission is to the whole person: healing, yes, but with the even greater gift of the Good News of Jesus Christ and the new life He brings. *References:* Is. 55:1–3; John 4:13–14; 5:1–21; 6:22–27.

651. A Missionless Church Is a Dead Church. An artist was asked to depict a ruined church. He painted a beautiful structure equipped with all that modern taste and invention has devised. The nave contains a richly carved chancel, a magnificent altar, an elaborate organ, and beautiful colored windows. Many fashionable, well-dressed worshipers fill the pews. The elders, immaculately garbed, are in their places. But in a corner, attached to a wall, is a little box on which we read: "For Missions." A spider web has been woven over the opening of the mission box. That church had no mission helpers. Therefore it was a ruined church. *References:* Is. 52:7; Matt. 28:19–20; John 4:35–36; Acts 1:8; Rom. 10:12–15; 1 Peter 2:9.

652. Our Mission Is Still to Save Lives. A parable is told of a group of concerned citizens in Maine who organized a lifesaving station to assist those who were shipwrecked on the rocky coast. Into horrendous storms brave men rode to save the lives of the oppressed. In time they put up a building with an infirmary to care for the survivors. Interest in the mission grew, and others joined the endeavor. And before long a fellowship room and dining facility were added. More and more the lifesaving station became an exclusive club, until one day opportunities for assisting the distressed went unheeded.

In protest, a small band left the club and started another station several miles away. Before long it too became a club. Today the entire coast of Maine is lined with exclusive clubs. The church can suffer the same fate. *References:* Ezek. 3:17–21; 33:7–16; Matt. 20:23–28; 28:19; Mark 16:15; 2 Cor. 5:15–20; 1 Peter 2:9.

653. A humble cobbler named William Carey set out over a century ago to India. It seemed a foolish and futile enterprise, yet William Carey and his successors, "empowered" by the Holy Spirit, brought many to Christ. Just over a century ago Robert Morrison set sail for China. It seemed foolish. "Do you think," said the captain of the ship on which he sailed, "that you are going to convert China?" "No," replied Morrison, "but I believe that God will." It was not Robert Morrison alone who was going to China, but Robert Morrison "fortified" by the Holy Spirit. *References:* Zech. 4:6; Matt. 28:18–20; Luke 4:14–21; Acts 1:8; 2; 4:33; 1 Cor. 2:1–5.

654. It is said that every Muslim is committed to be a missionary for his religion. As we look at the record of our mission activity, the facts tell us that in Africa the Muslims win 14 pagans for Allah to every one that is won for Christ. *References:* Ex. 19:5–8; 1 Peter 2:9.

655. Everyone a Missionary. It is said that Dr. Wilfred Grenfell, who rendered outstanding service as a medical missionary in Labrador, was a guest at a dinner in London, England. A number of socially prominent individuals had been invited to the dinner. During the course of the evening a lady came up to the missionary and asked, "Dr. Grenfell, is it really true that you are a missionary?" After a moment's silence, this servant of the Lord replied, "Is it true, Madam, that you are not?" Is it possible that any of us assembled here in God's name this day are not witnessing for the Savior? *References:* Is. 62:6; Matt. 5:13–16; 28:19; Mark 5:18–19; Acts 1:8; 1 Peter 2:9; 3:15.

656. James Chalmers, missionary to New Guinea and other islands of the South Seas, near the close of his long career as a missionary said, "Recall the 21 years, give me back all my experiences, give me its shipwrecks, give me its standing in the face of death, give me surrounded with spears and clubs, give it me back again with spears flying about me, with the club knocking me to the ground, give it me back— and I will still be a missionary." *References:* Matt. 5:11–12; 10:39; 19:29; John 21:15–19; Acts 9:15–16; 2 Cor. 4:6–18; 12:10; Phil. 3:7–8.

657. Lip Service in Missions. Politicians sometimes play a shrewd game. They glibly and with much fanfare vote for certain bills coming out of committees and then very quietly refuse to allow the necessary appropriations of money or manpower to enable the bills to be put into effect. Is it possible that we Christians are guilty of such chicanery at times? We celebrate our mission rally days, we sing with lusty voice the beloved mission hymns, we listen with due respect to the mission message, we make much ado about our mission topics and mission discussions, but when it comes to giving the mission program its legs and hands and voice, we tighten our purse strings, and God's program goes begging. *References:* Ps. 78:34–35; Prov. 28:27; Is. 29:13; Mark 7:6; Acts 5:1–2; 2 Cor. 8:1–8; Titus 1:6.

658. Each time we see Andrew in action he is bringing someone to Jesus. An old preacher in England talked to a boy about Jesus. That boy grew up to be a shoemaker, a teacher, a lay preacher, and then a pioneer Christian missionary to India. His name was William Carey. Through the interest and influence of a Sunday school teacher, another boy grew up to be a great preacher and evangelist. His name was Dwight Moody. These boys were brought to Jesus by some Andrew, and like the boy whom Andrew brought, Jesus used these boys, when grown to manhood, to feed thousands with the Bread of life. *References:* John 1:35–42; 6:5–13; 12:20–22.

659. Missions: A Ministry of Patience. Swiftness in reaching souls does not necessarily bring lasting results. This is demonstrated from an effort on the part of Otto, bishop of Bamberg, who in 1124, as missionary to Pomerania, in half a year built eight churches and baptized 22,165 persons. These were not real converts, for people cannot ordinarily be brought to the knowledge of the truth in such numbers in so short a time. Although we are living many centuries later, we still have found no shortcut to bring people to the knowledge of the truth. This makes the task of missions one of patience and consecration, requiring many workers to bring the souls of sinners to the knowledge of the truth. *References:* Eccl. 7:8; Rom. 12:12–20; 1 Thess. 5:14; 2 Tim. 2:24–26; James 5:7.

Related illustrations: 194, 281, 821, 893, 902, 979, 983.

Money
See also **False Gods, Wealth**

660. To many people money is like a shoe: if the amount they have is too small, it pinches and irritates, but if it is too large, it causes them to stumble and fall. (Colton) *References:* Prov. 30:8–9; Mark 4:19; 1 Tim. 6:6–10.

661. Where did you place your trust in the year past? Was the American god your god, the largest of round coins, made of silver, bearing the inscription "In God we trust," of which someone has said that it ought to read: "In this god we trust"? *References:* Eccl. 5:10; Matt. 6:24; 26:15–16; 1 Tim. 6:10; 2 Peter 2:15.

662. We are told that 11 millionaires went to a watery grave with hundreds of other people on the ill-fated *Titanic* in April 1912. Their combined wealth totaled nearly $200,000,000. Yet if they could have sent a message to the living about the most important things in life, not one would have mentioned money. Newspapers reported that Major A. H. Peuchen of Toronto, who was saved from the ship, left more than $300,000 in money, jewelry, and securities in his cabin. He started back for the box, thought an instant, then turned away without it. Later he said, "The money seemed a mockery at that time. I picked up three oranges instead." (W. H. Brown, *Illustrative Incidents,* p. 163.) *References:* Job 20:28; Ps. 49:10; Prov. 23:5; 27:24; Is. 55:1–2; Hag. 1:6; 1 Tim. 6:7; Rev. 3:17.

663. Love of Money. There is perhaps no greater witness to financial tragedy than the case of Howard Hughes. Surrounded by millions of dollars, he certainly did not have an enviable life-style. Indianapolis widow Marguerite Jackson lived in paranoia that her money would be stolen. She was found dead with over $5 million dollars in her home. The money, concluded *Time* magazine, "had brought Mrs. Jackson nothing but a life of private terror." *References:* Eccl. 2:18; Luke 12:15–21; 1 Tim. 6:10.

Related illustrations: 98, 188, 332, 334, 426, 686, 1004.

Morality

664. Some people seem to think that Christian morality consists in not doing wrong—as if an automobile that never went a mile would be considered good because its motor never knocked. A man whose morality is only "nots" has not Christian morality. Goodness is not purely negative. *References:* Matt. 19:16–22; Luke 10:25–28; 18:18–23; James 4:17.

665. Charles Colson wrote about the bewildering paradox that one-third of all American adults claim to be "born again" (according to a Gallup poll) and yet fail to impact our society. It becomes sicker and more corrupt by the day. There is much talk about religion, but morality is down. *References:* Ps. 78:35–36; Matt. 7:21; Mark 7:6; Luke 6:46; Titus 1:16; 1 John 3:18.

666. MacLaren says: "There are many men that say, 'Give us the morality of the New Testament; never mind about the theology.' But you cannot get the morality without the theology, unless you like to have rootless flowers and lamps without oil. If you want men to live as Paul enjoins, you will have to get them to yield to the mercies of God, which Paul pleads as the motive for all holy life." (*A Year's Ministry,* First Series, p. 316.) *References:* John 8:11; 13:34; Rom. 6:4; 12:1–2; Eph. 4:1; 1 Peter 2:9–11.

Related illustrations: 63, 293, 294, 309, 406, 840.

Murder

667. Murderous King Herod. The hand that had not shrunk from murdering his own sons and wife, and of whom the Roman emperor is said to have remarked, "Better to be Herod's swine than Herod's son," surely would not shrink from crushing a newborn babe. *Reference:* Matt. 2:16.

Music

668. Music, the handmaiden of godliness, has been seduced by Satan to become the slave of iniquity. It is the duty of the church to rescue her and restore her original position of pious service. *References:* 1 Chron. 9:33; 15:16; 25:6–7; 2 Chron. 20:21; Ps. 150; Eph. 5:19; James 5:13.

669. Taylor: "We have fallen into the grievous error of supposing that the music of the sanctuary is for human ears more than for the ears of God." Hence,

> Some to the church repair,
> Not for the doctrine, but the music there.
> (Pope).

References: Ps. 98:1–6; 144:9; 149:1; 150; Is. 42:10; Rev. 5:9.

670. Luther's Influence. The Protestant world and even the Roman Catholic Church have learned congregational singing from Martin Luther, and the greatest musicians of the world received their highest inspiration from him. "If they had not been inspired by the grandeur and beauty of Lutheran church music, Bach, Mendelssohn, and Brahms could not have written their great choral and organ works in which they glorify the doctrine of Scripture," says one authority, Reuther. *References:* Ps. 95:1; Eph. 5:19; Col 3:16.

671. When the ancient Greek philosopher Aristotle was asked what he thought of music, he replied, "Jupiter does not sing, neither does he play the harp." He seems to infer that music is unbecoming to deity and therefore also unprofitable to humanity. The true God, on the other hand, before whom the morning stars sang together at the creation and around whose throne the cherubim and seraphim sing their glory songs, is a lover of music. *References:* 1 Chron. 15:16; Ps. 81:1; 95:1; 98:1; 144:9; 150:3–5; Eph. 5:19.

672. Luther: "Music is one of the fairest and most glorious gifts of God, to which Satan is a bitter enemy, for it removes from the heart the weight of sorrow and the fascination of evil thoughts. It is a kind and gentle sort of discipline; it refines the passions and improves the understanding. Those who love music are gentle and honest in their tempers. I always loved music and would not for a great matter be without the little skill I possess in the art." *References:* Ps. 95:1; Is. 30:29; 1 Cor. 14:15; Eph. 5:19; James 5:13.

Mysteries

673. Great mysteries are in the Book of God of necessity; for how can the infinite God so speak that all His thoughts can be grasped by finite human beings? But it is the height of folly to discuss these deep things and to leave plain, soul-saving truths in abeyance. It reminds one of the two philosophers who debated about food and went away empty from the table, while the common countryman in the corner asked no questions but used his knife and fork with great diligence and went on his way rejoicing. Thousands are now happy in the Lord through receiving the Gospel like little children, while others who can always see difficulties or invent them are as far off as ever from any comfortable hope of salvation. (Spurgeon) *References:* Gen. 2:17; Deut. 29:29; Job 11:7; Matt. 11:25; Mark 10:13–16; John 16:12; Rom. 11:33; 1 Cor. 13:12.

674. Gotthold in his *Emblems* tells that one day in his study he lifted his eyes from his book and to his terror and consternation saw his boy standing on the outside window ledge in imminent peril of falling to the ground and being dashed to pieces. The lad had been anxious to know what his father was doing so many hours of the day in his study and had at last by a ladder managed with boyish daring to climb up. And as Gotthold trembling helped the little boy into the room, he said, "So have I often tried to climb into the council chamber of God to see why and wherefore He did this and that, and thus I have exposed myself to the peril of falling to my own destruction." If we could only say, "I will trust in the Lord with all my heart and lean not on my own understanding"! *References:* Ps. 73:26; Prov. 3:5–6; Hos. 10:13; 1 Cor. 1:18–25; 3:19–20; 2 Cor. 1:12.

675. To be sure, God does some unexpected things. Voltaire and Goethe both said that they lost faith in God because He permitted the Lisbon earthquake. And modern skeptics point to the wars of our generation and demand: "Why does not God prevent such catastrophes?" One of the mistakes of the skeptic is in judging God's plan for the world by the very small section of the world's history of which he happens to be a part. If you were to stop reading *Macbeth* at the second act, or if you were to see Raphael's *Madonna* one-third finished, would it be fair to pass judgment? We see just small bits of God's plan for the world at a time, but God knows, say the Scriptures, "the end from the beginning." *References:* Job 11:7; 33:13; Eccl. 8:17; Is. 55:8–9; Hos. 14:9; Rom. 11:33–34; 1 Cor. 2:16.

Related illustrations: 318, 392, 394, 937.

N

Nature

676. The Empire State Building in New York is but a toy beside the cathedral spires of Zion National Park or the great Half-Dome of Yosemite. The Panama Canal is but a scratch on the surface compared with the Grand Canyon of the Colorado. No artist's brush can reproduce the silvery halo of circling mists that sometimes crown the head of Mount Whitney in the morning light or catch the sunset glow that loves to linger in the tips of the giant sequoias and sets the clouds on fire long after the shadows have begun to lengthen below. The mysteries of the mineral kingdom, the wonders of plant and animal life, the world and all that dwell therein all proclaim the glory of God. *References:* Ps. 8:3; 19:1; 40:5; 139:14; Eccl. 3:11; Rom. 1:20.

Nearness of God

677. A learned scholar went to a Copenhagen church to see Thorvaldsen's famed statue of Jesus Christ called *Come unto Me.* As he stood looking at the statue, disappointment seemed to creep into his face.

A little boy, standing near, said: "Sir, you must go close to Him. Kneel down before Him, and look up into His face."

The scholar walked forward and did as the little boy had suggested and found the wondrous beauty in the Master's face, not known by those who remain at a distance.

How true this is for all of us! It is when we go close to Him, kneel down before Him, and look up into His face, that we find the light. (Clara Bird Kopp in *Christian Advocate*) *References:* Ps. 34:18; 51:6; 138:6; Is. 57:15; 66:1–2; Joel 2:13; James 4:6; 1 Peter 5:5. *Related illustration:* 547.

New Life

See also **Abundant Life**

678. When the first disciples of Jesus Christ remained together in Jerusalem during the early days of the church, they were called "followers of *the Way.*" In life and conduct they represented a new Way. The Christian faith meant a *Way of life* distinct from that of the people around them. *References:* John 10:1–9; 14:5–6; Acts 2:37–47; 4:32–35; Rom. 5:1–2; Eph. 2:18.

679. Gaining by Losing. We gain life by losing it in service to God and to others. We might think of the Arkansas River in Colorado. Formerly it flowed down a steep mountainside past a desert that lay parched for centuries. Year after year it deepened its own channel as it sped on its way to the ocean and oblivion. One winter a dam was built across the dry channel of the summer stream, stopping the flow of the water. Unable to follow its usual course, the river formed a lake from which the water was channeled and ditched into the desert. The former arid region now produces fields of waving grain. The free life of the stream was sacrificed, but it found itself again in the golden harvest. Those who live only for themselves are losing their lives. Those who live for Christ and for others are finding real life—a full, happy, eternal life of loving service. *References:* Matt. 16:25; 19:21, 29; Mark 8:35; John 12:24; 1 Cor. 10:24; Phil. 2:4; 3:8.

680. J. S. Stewart reminds us of a night when Henry Drummond lectured to a group of students at Edinburgh University. As part of his lecture, he read the letter of a man who signed himself "Thanatos," the Greek word for "death." The man described himself as a miserable failure socially, morally, and spiritually. He stated that there was no way out but suicide. Henry Drummond shrugged and said, "I don't know what to tell this man; he's beyond my help." A year and a half later, Henry Drummond lectured again to the students at Edinburgh. Once more he drew a letter from his pocket. "Some of you will remember a letter I read from 'Thanatos.' I have here another letter from him." And he read a portion that heralded: "I am a new man—in Jesus Christ!" *References:* Ezek. 37:1–14; Rom. 6:4; 8:11; 2 Cor. 5:17; Eph. 2:1–6; Col. 3:1.

Related illustrations: 128, 209, 430, 711.

New Year

681. The word *January* is taken from the Latin *janua,* door or portal, from which one may look both ways, and from *Janus,* the Roman god of beginnings, who faced in both directions. As we stand at the threshold of each new year and look back over the way we have come, we see our record of imperfect endeavors, our shortcomings and sins, which the blood of Christ must cover up. But we also see a future bright with promise, like the bud of a rose that has not yet unfolded its petals. *References:* Is. 43:18–19; 65:17; Lam. 3:22–24; 2 Cor. 5:17.

Neglect

682. When Marie Antoinette came from Austria to Paris as bride of Louis XVI, she gave orders that no beggars or anything unsightly or depressing dare be seen along the route by which she entered the capital.

All who have this outlook do not want to face the realities of life or assume any responsibilities as they go through the day. They live in a dream world. *References:* Ps. 69:20; Prov. 21:13; 25:20; Ezek. 34:4; Matt. 25:43; Luke 10:30–32.

683. Neglect by Leaders. We stand aghast at the unconcern of human leaders in the pivotal moments of history. When Rome was besieged by Alaric and his Goths, Emperor Honorius was more concerned about the safety of his prize poultry than the destiny of the imperial city. After a panting messenger brought the news that Rome was lost, he sighed in relief when he learned that it was not his favorite pullet named "Rome" but the capital that had been destroyed. Louis XIV gorged himself with imported delicacies, while his miserable peasants existed on carrion and parched barley.

There have always been those who have been indifferent when they should have led the forces of righteousness and truth, procrastinating when they should have marched as a vanguard for Christ's kingdom, hesitating when they should have been bold to prepare people's hearts to receive Christ as Lord. *References:* Neh. 3:5; Prov. 21:13; Is. 47:8–11; Amos 6:1; Zeph. 1:12–13; Matt. 25:41–46.

Related illustrations: 380, 498, 544, 858.

O

Obedience

684. Wicked persons obey from fear, the good from love. (Aristotle) *References:* John 14:15–21; 1 John 5:2; 2 John 6.

685. When George Washington was 15 years old, his brother obtained for him a midshipman's warrant in the British navy. His kit was already on board when a messenger brought his mother's final word not to go. Though he had set his heart on going to sea, George went back to school and mathematics, which he did not like. His mother gave him a good penknife, saying, "Always obey your superiors. God will not let your filial affections go unrewarded." (Dallmann) *References:* Ex. 20:12; Prov. 1:8–9; 6:20–23; 23:22–26; Eph. 6:1–3; Col. 3:20. *Related illustration:* 329.

Obsession

686. For Wealth. Those who live for mammon are like the diabetic who always feels hungry. When it comes to money, there is always more, but it is never enough, and finally it is never all. "Once I get the car paid off, I should have just enough to make the payments on . . ."

In Milton's *Paradise Lost* we meet the angel Mammon, who, even when he lived in heaven before he fell into perdition, was stooped and hunched over. When he walked about the golden streets, Milton tells us, he kept his eyes fixed on the pavement on the chance of finding some coin or mislaid treasure. Jesus does not say, "Thou shalt not serve God and money." The statement is not in the imperative but indicative—a statement of fact. "You cannot serve both God and Money." *References:* Prov. 1:19; 15:27; Eccl. 5:10; Hab. 2:9–10; Matt. 6:24; 1 Tim. 6:9,10; James 5:3; 2 Peter 2:15.

Old Age

687. Never Too Old to Learn. A person is never too old to learn. Socrates was an old man when he began to play musical instruments; Cato was 80 when he began his study of Greek; Plutarch was in the upper 60s when he undertook to learn Latin; the *Canterbury Tales* were begun by Chaucer when he was 45 and finished when he was 61. Michelangelo worked till the day of his death; when he was 90, he painted himself as an old man with an hourglass and with the inscription: "Ancora imparo"—"I am still learning." *References:* Deut. 34:7; Joshua 14:6–13; Ps. 37:25; Luke 2:36–37.

Omniscience of God

688. When a Greek sculptor was asked why he wasted so much time on the parts of a statue that no one would ever see, the heathen replied, "The gods will see." We work for God. "Thou, God, seest me." Milton worked "as ever in his great Taskmaster's eye." (Dallmann) *References:* Deut. 10:12; Is. 40:27–31;

Matt. 6:1–6; Rom. 12:11; Eph. 6:5–8; Col. 3:22–24.

689. Skillful counselors have brought people to face themselves and see the false defense they have built up to protect their egos. "Truth serum" has been used successfully in psychiatric wards to discover what is bothering a person when neither the counselor nor the patient has been able to discover it. The lie detector of the police laboratory indicates by a change of heartbeat whether a person is speaking the truth. But God needs none of these devices. The psalmist recognizes this: "O LORD, you have searched me and you know me." *References:* 1 Sam. 16:7; Job 34:21–22; Ps. 139; Prov. 5:21; Jer. 16:17; 17:10; 32:19; John 2:23–25.

Opportunities

See also **Hardness of Heart**

690. A Fleeting Chance. The ancient Greeks had a statue called *Opportunity*. It stood on its toes to show how quickly it might pass by. It had wavy hair in the front that people might grasp it by the forelock. But it was bald in back to show that, when it had once passed, it could not be caught. *References:* Ps. 32:6; 95:7–11; Is. 55:6–7; Mark 7:24–30; Luke 18:35–43; 2 Cor. 6:2; Heb. 3:7–15.

691. The Opportunity to Repent Is Now. Dr. R. A. Torrey tells of a worker in Brighton, England, who was eating in a restaurant. He felt the urge to speak to the waiter about his soul but kept putting it off. After the meal he went outside and decided to wait for the waiter and then speak to him about Jesus. After he had waited for some time, the proprietor appeared and asked, "Are you waiting for someone?" "Yes," replied the worker, "I want to speak to the man who waited on me." Said the proprietor, "You will never speak to that man again. Af-

ter waiting on you, he shot himself." Men and women, there are opportunities open to us today that will be gone before another day dawns.

Dwight Moody was once preaching in Chicago to a great crowd of people when he thundered, "I give you one day to repent of your sins." That same night the great Chicago fire broke out, and some of the very people to whom Moody had preached were burned to death. Said Moody many times later, "I have asked God to forgive me for giving these people one day to repent. I should have said, 'Now! Now is the accepted time!'" *References:* Ps. 95:7–8; 145:18; Is. 55:6–7; Jer. 23:23; Hos. 10:12; Zeph. 2:1–3; Acts 17:27; 2 Cor. 6:2.

692. Marvelous opportunities are present at our work. Imagination and faithfulness can bring thrilling rewards. While Eli Whitney was visiting the South a century ago, some of the cotton planters told him of their difficulty in extracting the seeds from raw cotton. If someone could only devise a machine to do that laborious work! That night Whitney lay awake thinking of the problem. Long after midnight he went to the window to get a breath of fresh air. There in the moonlight was a cat that had killed a chicken and was trying desperately to pull it out of the coop. But the space between the slats was too narrow, and every time the cat's paw came out it clutched nothing but a mass of white feathers.

Whitney turned backed to bed and began to think more vigorously than ever. Why not build an iron claw that would pull the cotton fibers through a fine mesh, leaving hard seeds behind? A week later Whitney had worked out the first rough sketch of his cotton gin. *References:* Matt. 11:16–24; 25:27, 37–40; Luke 4:35; 19:41–42; Acts 24:25. *Related illustrations:* 205, 384, 435.

Original Sin

See also **Depravity, Sin**

693. A theologian of the church has stated it clearly and forcefully: "Our first parents are the proximate cause of the original blemish, from whose impure nature the original stain has flowed into our hearts. Everything follows the seed of its own nature. No black crow ever produced a white dove, nor does a ferocious lion beget a gentle lamb, and no man polluted with inborn sin ever begets a holy child." Jesus unequivocally declares, "Flesh gives birth to flesh." The judgment of the Scriptures is that "every inclination of [man's] heart is evil from childhood." And if we are honest, we must admit that our own experience corroborates it. *References:* Gen. 8:21; Ps. 51:5; John 3:6; Rom. 5:18–19; 1 Cor. 2:14; Eph. 2:3.

694. For being part of humanity, you share in the radical depravity and perversion from God that we call "sin." In *Our Faith,* Emil Brunner says that we are all connected by hidden roots, like the runners of a strawberry patch, all of whose plants have developed from the one parent stock. There is a kind of common sin fluid that flows through the whole root system, and yet each individual knows it to be his or her own guilt. *References:* Ps. 51:5; 53:3; Prov. 20:9; John 3:6; Rom. 3:23; 5:18–19; Gal. 3:22; Eph. 2:3.

Related illustrations: 242, 587, 863.

Overcoming Failure

695. Years ago George Frederick Handel was alone in his room, weary, sick of soul, and depressed. A few days earlier, his orchestra had been thrown into the street after rehearsal. The next day, a concert audience jeered his music. He was sure that he was a failure and that nothing remained except for him to leave London. Suddenly a knock at the door interrupted his desperate thoughts. A friend had come with a manuscript for an oratorio, and he asked Handel to write the music. At first he refused, but when he saw the title—*Messiah*—and read its opening pages, the love of Christ struck him, and he fell to his knees, beseeching the Lord's help. Then he started to work, and for three weeks with scarcely an interruption he concentrated his efforts on producing the *Messiah*. Beholding his Redeemer, he finished, declaring, "I have never been so happy as I am now."

And when the *Messiah* was first sung in Dublin, and "The Hallelujah Chorus" reechoed throughout the concert hall, the audience rose to its feet to pay unstinted tribute to the masterpiece of a composer who only shortly before had branded himself a failure. *References:* Is. 57:10; 61:1–3; Rom. 10:8–15.

P

Parents

696. When Oliver Wendell Holmes was once asked, "What is the most important factor in a man's success?" he answered, "He must choose the right parents." *References:* 1 Kings 9:2–5; 2 Chron. 26:4; 27:2; Prov. 23:22; 2 Tim. 1:5.

697. An old Spanish proverb reads: "An ounce of mother is worth a pound of clergy." *References:* 2 Chron. 22:3; Prov. 22:6; 2 Tim. 1:5.

698. "A good mother," it has been remarked, "is worth a hundred schoolmasters." *References:* 2 Tim. 1:5; 3:14–15.

699. Thomas Edison was considered to be a dull scholar, but later in life he confessed, "My mother was sure of me; I could not fail." *References:* 1 Sam. 2:19; Eph. 6:4; Col. 3:21; 2 Tim. 1:5.

700. When Napoleon, alarmed at the moral degeneracy of his day and the frightful economic conditions, was asked, "What does France need most?" he answered, "Mothers." *References:* Prov. 22:6; Is. 28:9; 2 Tim. 1:5.

701. A little boy who was told by his Sunday school teacher that God made people good replied, "Yes, I know; but mothers help a lot." *References:* 1 Sam. 1:24–28; Prov. 31:25–50; 1 Tim. 1:5.

702. Poor Parental Influence. John Locke once said: "Parents wonder why the streams are bitter when they themselves have poisoned the fountain." But what if the fountain were full of true faith and prayer? Do you think we would then have homes that have lost their love, churches that have lost their power, and a world that has lost its mind? *References:* 1 Sam. 3:13; 1 Kings 22:52; 2 Chron. 22:3; Prov. 13:24; Jer. 9:14; Ezek. 20:18; Amos 2:4; Matt. 14:8.

703. Careless Parents. A police captain late one evening telephoned a father and asked him to come at once to the station house, where the man's 15-year-old son was held on the charge of stealing a car. The police officer quickly understood why the boy had gotten into trouble when the father casually replied that he was too busy playing cards with his friends and could not come until the next morning. Another father let his son burn up the highways in hot rods. When summoned by the state trooper to the scene of an accident where the mangled body of his dead son lay amidst the wreck of his demolished car, the father just shook his head and said, "I had a feeling my son would end up in this way." *References:* 1 Sam. 3:13; Prov. 13:24; 29:15; Eph. 6:4; Col. 3:21.

704. Napoleon the Great once said, "My opinion is that the future good or bad conduct of a child depends entirely on the mother." The pages of history and biography furnish countless proofs of this. Who, for example, is surprised that Lord Byron of England, that brilliant genius, led a dissolute life that brought him to the grave at age 36, when we know that his mother was a vain, violent, revengeful woman, so devoid of sympathy as to jest at the child's natural infirmity? On the other hand, recall Hannah's strength of character, and you have the secret of her son Samuel's life. *References:* 1 Sam. 1:24–28; Prov. 31:25–30; Matt. 14:8; Eph. 6:1–3; 2 Tim. 1:5.

705. Anna Jarvis, the originator of Mother's Day, writes: "The man who does not esteem some good woman as mother is to be pitied, not only because he has missed life's crowning joy, the inspiration of a mother's love, but because his manhood has lost a gentleness and a sympathy and a reverence that ennobles in a way nothing else does. A man without mother love is next in isolation to a man without a country." *References:* 1 Sam. 1:22–28; 2:19; Luke 2:35, 51; 2 Tim. 1:5.

706. For the Love of a Pious Mother. John Wanamaker, near the close of a successful life, was not ashamed to admit his debt of undying gratitude to the influence of his mother's love in the words: "My first love was my mother, and my first home was on her breast. My first bed was on her bosom. Leaning little arms on her knees, I learned my first prayers. A bright lamp she lit in my soul that never dies down or goes out though the winds and waves of fourscore years have swept over me. Sitting in my mother's armchair, which she loved because her first-born son gave it to her 40 years ago, I am writing this with the evening twilight coming on. With the darkness falling, I seem to lose myself in the flood of memories and to feel that the arms of the chair have loosed themselves to become my very own mother's arms around me again, drawing me to her bosom, the happiest place on earth, just as she used to do in the days and nights long gone by. I feel the touch of her little hand on my brow, and I hear her voice as she smooths my hair and calls me her boy, her very own boy." *References:* Ex. 2:3; 1 Sam. 2:19; 1 Kings 3:26; Is. 49:15; 66:13; 2 Tim. 1:5.

Related illustrations: 96, 601, 685.

Partiality

707. Partiality is common in society everywhere. More than a decade ago Michael Harrington in *The Other America* documented discrimination against the poor. He pointed out that poverty is often an incitement to arrest, that policemen are much more careful with well-dressed, educated persons who might have important connections than they are with the poor. Since the poor do not have money for bail or lawyers, they usually receive more severe punishment. They are also at the mercy of unscrupulous employers, crooked unions, and racketeers. And not only the poor but also other minority groups in our country receive less than fair treatment when it comes to housing and jobs. That's the way it is with people. They show partiality.

It is not that way with God. God is not influenced by such things as race, social standing, or good looks. *References:* Job 34:18–19; Acts 10:34; 15:8–9; Rom. 2:11; 10:12; Gal. 2:6; Eph. 6:9; James 2:2–9.

708. God is not deceived. He does not regard the outward appearance of people. The very attempt some make to impress Him already reveals the guilt they are trying to cover up. They want to be wise like God. But the verdict is that they are dirt, destined to return to the dirt from which they were taken. The verdict still stands. Try if

you wish. Buy that $20,000 leopard coat, and when you die, have yourself buried in it. After a couple of years, if somebody should dig you up, you know what he would find. A grinning skeleton, a handful of dirt, and a leopard coat that isn't worth $20,000 any more—if it ever was! *References:* Matt. 5:45; Acts 10:34; 15:7–11; Rom. 2:11; 10:12; Gal. 2:6; Eph. 6:9.
Related illustration: 612.

Peace, Spiritual

709. Our soul, says Augustine, was created *by* and exists *for* God and is therefore never quiet till it rests *in* God. It is with a person's soul as with Noah's dove in the Deluge. The dove, after it left the ark, found no rest for the sole of its foot in the world till it returned to the place from which it had come. So there is no sure rest for the fallen soul in the world till it returns to Him from whom it came. (Gataker) *References:* Ps. 42; Is. 43:25; 55:1–7; Hos. 6:1–2; 14; Joel 2:13; Matt. 11:28–30; Luke 15.

710. The peace of God is the inward tranquility that knows no disturbance even though the outward life is agitated by fierce storms. Deep in the center of the ocean the waters lie quiet, although the wildest tempests are raging above and the fiercest currents are running. *References:* Ps. 4:8; Is. 26:3; John 14:27; 16:33; Rom. 5:1; Phil. 4:7; Col. 3:15.
Related illustrations: 66, 83.

Pentecost

711. In the spring as we water the new flowers and sprinkle the newly seeded lawn, we have little doubt that come June the flower beds will be filled with red petunias and the lawn will be a lush mat of green grass. When you have water and sunshine, things grow; past experience is ample assurance of this. Pentecost has a point or two of comparison with the spring grass and red petunias. Pentecost concerns growing things—people, to be exact. Pentecost speaks about the coming of the Spirit to grant us new, fresh life. On Pentecost God poured out His Spirit like water to germinate a fresh life in His chosen disciples. Like dead seeds coming to life in the soil, many a dying faith rebounds to new life as the Spirit of God fills the heart. *References:* Is. 32:12–15; 44:1–6; Acts 2:16–17; Rom. 8:11.

Persecution

712. Persecution has been powerless to destroy the church of Christ. The Christian church is an anvil that has been beaten on by many heavy hammers, and it has worn them all out. (MacLaren) *References:* Matt. 16:18; Luke 21:16–18; Rev. 12:13–17.

713. Conviction on the Persecutor. Sir Walter Scott one day threw a rock at a dog, intending to shoo it away. He threw the rock straighter and harder than he had meant to, with the result that he broke the dog's leg. Instead of running away, the dog came crawling up to him and licked the hand that had thrown the rock, as if to say, "Tell me, what great wrong have I done, sir, that I should be so painfully punished!" That was a sermon Sir Walter Scott could never quite get over or forget. *References:* Ps. 69:4; 119:161; Matt. 27:23; John 15:18–25; 19:6; Acts 7:54–60.
Related illustrations: 279, 642.

Perseverance

714. A soldier who had served his country for a time in the army by deception had his name returned on the roll as dead. He was so reported from his company to his regiment and from his regimental headquarters to the general government. In the great records of the nation "Dead" was written

against his name. After the war was over and peace had been restored, the government began to dispense its bounties and pensions to those who had fought its battles and borne its burdens. The runaway soldier who had deserted the service and caused a false report to be returned, appeared for a reward at the hands of the government. The books were examined, the name was found, but "Dead" was written against it. The government acted according to its official records; in the knowledge of the government he was a dead man and not a living claimant. (Selected from Denton, *Topical Illustrations*) *References:* Luke 11:24–26; 14:28–30; 16:12; Heb. 4:1–11; 10:38; 2 Peter 2:20; Rev. 2:10.

Related illustration: 162.

Philosophy

715. John Dewey makes this confession: "A certain tragic end seems to attend all intellectual movement." History bears this out. One philosophy supplants another; one scientist throws overboard the scientific claims made by another. But the Christian stands on solid ground, saying, "I know in whom I have believed." *References:* Acts 17:18–23; 1 Cor. 1:18–25; 2:1–8; Col. 2:6–9; 1 Tim. 1:12–13.

716. Fatalism: A Philosophy of Despair. The October 1980 *Smithsonian* carries the story of identical twins, James Lewis and James Springer. They were separated in infancy, raised apart, and then reunited 39 years later. The parallels in their lives are striking.

Not only had both been named James by their adoptive families, but they discovered that both had been married twice, that both of their first wives were named Linda and both of their second wives Betty. Lewis had three sons, one of whom was named James Alan; Springer had three daughters and

a son, James Allan. Both had at one time owned dogs named Toy. The twins both have similar workshops in which they make similar things. They both had what they thought were heart attacks, both have intense recurring headaches, and their brain waves are identical.

While these findings are not open to dispute, many may conclude by virtue of scientific authority that people are genetically programmed to be what they are and do what they do, and there is little about them that environment or any other influence can fundamentally alter. Nobel laureate William B. Shockley has already concluded that some races are innately superior, and his proposal for change is the high-IQ "sperm bank." What is can't be changed. We can only alter through genetic manipulation what will be. Such a philosophy is a prescription for despair. *References:* Prov. 23:7; Acts 17:28; 1 Tim. 2:4.

Pleasures, Worldly

717. Xenophon's *Memoirs* contain a striking story told by Socrates, "The Choice of Hercules." Young Hercules, emerging from boyhood into manhood, is pondering how he is to shape his life. Two women appear before him, one voluptuous in form and luxurious in dress, the other severe and strict in appearance and clothed in a simple white garment. The name of the one is Pleasure, the name of the other is Virtue. Pleasure promised to lead young Hercules by the shortest road and without any toil to the enjoyment of every pleasure. Virtue beckons him along a path on which he will experience labors and suffering, but where alone he shall find a beautiful and good life worthy of his manhood. *References:* Deut. 30:19; Joshua 24:15; 1 Kings 18:21; Matt. 7:13–14; 16:24–26; 27:17–21; John 6:66–68.

Related illustrations: 450, 505.

Politics

718. When Abraham Lincoln came to Washington as president, he is said to have declared, "I wish to find a church whose clergyman does not preach politics." Millions of people today want pastors who will give them spiritual comfort and eternal truth rather than party programs and campaign promises. *References:* Ezek. 3:17; John 12:21; Acts 10:36; 17:2–3; 2 Cor. 4:5; 2 Tim. 4:1–2.

Popularity

719. The old Romans used to say: "The voice of the people is the voice of God." This maxim is far from true. Often the voice of the multitude, the voice of the people, is not the voice of God but the voice of sin, the voice of Satan. *References:* Num. 14:6–10; 1 Sam. 8:19; Ps. 2:1–6; Matt. 27:20–25; Mark 15:14–15; Luke 23:18–23; John 19:14–15.

720. After having read nothing but laudatory epitaphs in a certain cemetery, a child turned to his mother and asked, "Mother, where is the other cemetery?" "Which one, my child?" "The cemetery in which the bad people are buried?" *References:* Prov. 24:24; Luke 6:26; 1 Thess. 2:3–6.

721. Following the Crowd. Martin Luther said of his time: "Sectarianism is rampant, and few there are who contend against it and preserve the true doctrine; their names could all be written on a little card." Think of that stupendous scene where a lonely monk faced the combined powers of church and state. The central doctrine of Scripture, *justification by faith, without the deeds of the Law,* was regarded as an insult to human wisdom. Fearing to be ridiculed by the classes and hissed by the masses, Erasmus and others preferred to be popular and let truth take care of itself. They forgot what others have forgotten since that day: "Do not follow the crowd in doing wrong" (Ex. 23:2). *References:* Ex. 23:2; 34:12; Ps. 1:1; Prov. 4:14; 24:1; Rom. 3:4; 1 Cor. 5:11; 2 Cor. 6:14.

Related illustrations: 371, 748.

Praising God

722. C. S. Lewis says that when he first became a Christian, he found one of the biggest stumbling blocks to his faith in the repeated statements of Scripture that we should praise God. "We all despise the man who demands continued assurance of his own virtue, intelligence or delightfulness," Lewis wrote, "and these words of Scripture sounded hideously like God was saying, 'What I want most is to be told that I am good and great.' " It also seemed as though the psalm writers were bargaining with God, saying, "You like praise. Do this or that for me, and You shall have some." Well, the answer, as C. S. Lewis figured out, is that only in the act of worship and praise can a person learn to believe in the goodness and greatness of God. God wants us to praise Him, not because He in any sense needs or craves our flattery, but because He knows that praise creates thankfulness and joy, and joy must automatically overflow into praise. *References:* Ps. 13:5–6; 95; 96; 98; 113; 148; 149; 150.

Prayer

723. Peter Marshall, the late chaplain of the U.S. Senate, once said in a prayer, "O Lord, forgive us for thinking that prayer is a waste of time, and help us to see that without prayer our work is a waste of time." *References:* Ps. 127:1; Luke 18:1–8; John 3:27; 15:5; 2 Cor. 3:5; Phil. 4:4–7; 1 Thess. 5:17.

724. MacLaren: "If a care is too small to be made a prayer, it is too small to be made a burden." *References:* Luke 10:41; John 15:7; Phil. 4:6; 1 Peter 5:7; 1 John 3:22.

725. How can we expect God to be present in our prayers if we ourselves are absent from them? (W. F. Besser) *References:* Is. 29:13; Matt. 6:7; 15: 7–9.

726. William Proctor once said, "Many of our prayers fail to enter heaven for the same reason that a whole generation of Israelites failed to enter Canaan—because of unbelief." *References:* Is. 29:13; Jer. 29:12–13; Mark 11:24; Luke 11:1; John 15:7.

727. The bishop to wayward Augustine's mother, Monica: "Go on praying; the child of so many prayers cannot perish." *References:* Matt. 15:21–28; Mark 7:24–30; Luke 18:1; John 16:23–24.

728. Prayer Goes with Action. Dwight L. Moody on a trip across the Atlantic helped the crew and other volunteers put out a fire in the hold of the ship. A friend said to Moody as they stood in the bucket line, "Let's go up to the other end of the ship and pray." Moody, the common-sense evangelist, said, "No, sir, we will stand right here and pass buckets and pray hard all the time we are doing so." Prayer and action go together. *References:* Ps. 91:14–15; Is. 58:6–9; Matt. 6:12; John 15:7; Phil. 4:4–7; 1 John 3:22.

729. Temple said: "Prayer which is mainly occupied with a result to be obtained is comparatively powerless to obtain results." The Lord's promise of answer to prayers is found in the passage "If you remain in me and my words remain in you, ask whatever you wish, and it will be given you." Augustine comments here: "For, abiding in Christ, how can they wish for anything but what befits Christ?" Sir Wilfred Grenfell says of prayer: "His answers I never venture to criticize; it

is only my part to ask. It is entirely His to give or withhold as He knows best. If it were otherwise, I would not dare to pray at all." *References:* Deut. 3:23–26; 2 Sam. 12:16–23; Matt. 6:10; 26:39; Mark 14:36; John 15:7; 2 Cor. 12:7–10.

730. Vain Repetition in Praying the Lord's Prayer. Luther once said, "The Lord's Prayer is the greatest martyr on earth. Many pray the Lord's Prayer a thousand times a year, and though they have prayed it a thousand years, yet have they not properly prayed one letter thereof." This great prayer of our Lord is often abused by vain repetition. I have often heard someone say at the end of a meeting, "Let's close by reciting the Lord's Prayer." By reason of its very familiarity all of us are in danger of letting this prayer degenerate into a mere recital of words. Whether it be in the church service or at your family worship or when you place your head on your pillow at night, the use of the Lord's Prayer can become merely a routine exercise. *References:* Ps. 78:35–36; Is. 29:13; Ezek. 33:31–32; Matt. 6:7–13; 7:21; 15:7–8; Mark 7:6; Luke 11:2–4.

731. Continuous Prayer. To be a praying Christian does not simply mean to pray occasionally but to pray continually. No one can live by taking a breath only once in a while. A person cannot read by a light that flickers on and off. A ship cannot sail with only an occasional puff of wind. So also a Christian cannot maintain spiritual life and health by praying only once in a while. *References:* 1 Chron. 16:11; Luke 18:1; 21:36; Eph. 6:18; Phil. 4:4–6; Col. 4:2; 1 Thess. 5:17.

732. Meaningless Prayers. In Tibet and Mongolia people use prayer wheels, wheels inscribed with prayers, which they deem efficacious when the wheel is turned. One who stands at the wheel and turns and turns for a long time is regarded as a man of prayer. Let us take care lest our prayers become mechanical, vain repetition of words, a grinding of just so many words. We must not merely say our prayers but pray them. Worse than worthless are all prayers that are said without devotion, prayers of the mouth and not of the heart. *References:* Is. 29:13; Matt. 6:7–8; 15:7–9; 23:14; 2 Tim. 3:5.

733. What Keeps People from Prayer? Many people have little heart for prayer because they have never spent enough time in fellowship with God, with His Word, and in seeking His will in prayer to ever get used to it. They are strangers to spiritual things, and that's why prayer is so tough for them. They are like the eight-year-old child of a psychology professor, who, when asked why he never did his homework, replied, "I've adjusted myself to inferior grades." *References:* 1 Chron. 16:11; Luke 18:1–8; 21:36; Eph. 6:18; Phil. 4:4–6; Col. 4:2; 1 Thess. 5:17.

734. G. S. Bowes: "A holy boldness, a chastened familiarity, is the true spirit of right prayer. It was said of Luther that, when he prayed, it was with as much reverence as if he were praying to an infinite God and with as much familiarity as if he were speaking to his nearest friend." *References:* John 16:24; Eph. 3:12; Heb. 4:14–16; 10:21–22; James 4:8.

735. Admiral James Kelly, navy chief of chaplains, tells that the members of the *Pueblo* crew began to pray more and more as the weary months of their captivity dragged on. At mealtime the men would bow their heads ever so slightly and thank God for the food before them. But when the Communist guards would spot them, they would

scream, "This is not a church! This food is a gift from the Democratic People's Republic of North Korea!" At night they dared not kneel beside their bunks, but they prayed as they were lying on their backs in the bunks. The men had a name for it, they called it COMMWORLDFLT, capital letters standing for "Commander of the World's Fleets." In prayer, they felt they were making contact with the Supreme Commander of all things, and they were under His protection and care. *References:* Ps. 91; Is. 58:9; Jer. 33:3; Luke 18:1–8; Eph. 6:18; Phil. 4:4–7; 1 Peter 5:6–7.

736. Prayer No Substitute for Good Sense. Though we urge the sick to pray, we are far removed from the view of those who hold that nothing but believing prayer is necessary to effect a cure. When we pray, "Give us this day our daily bread," we are not such simpletons as to expect that now we may lay our hands into our laps and God will feed us without the use of means. He has indeed on extraordinary occasions, as in the case of the Israelites in the wilderness, supernaturally provided bread for people. And we know that He could do so again. But He has not promised us that He would. And to believe what God has not promised is just as wrong as not to believe what He has promised. That is superstition and presumption; this is unbelief. Sober Christians do not trust in prayer alone any more than they trust in the means alone. Their confidence is in God's blessing on the means. *References:* Luke 10:34; Col. 4:14; 1 Tim. 5:23.

737. Monica, the mother of the illustrious church father Augustine, had a heathen husband who by his violent and vicious conduct caused her much grief. Yet she did not murmur but bore her burden with great patience, hoping that in the end she might win her husband for Christ. It is said that she talked more with God about her husband than with her husband about God. *References:* Ps. 40:1; Luke 18:1; Rom. 12:12; 1 Cor. 7:13–16; 2 Thess. 1:4; James 5:7.

738. A young mother was alone with her three children on a remote farm in central California. The three children had been swimming in their pool, when the mother suddenly noticed that the two-and-a-half-year-old was at the bottom of the pool. She got the child out as quickly as she could, and just then a neighboring farmer came by. He immediately began the tedious and fearful process of mouth-to-mouth resuscitation to try to save the child. After several minutes life stirred in the little form, and after a later examination the doctors said that they were sure there had been no brain damage.

In the days following, people who heard of the child's rescue from drowning would comment to the father or mother, "You sure were lucky! You sure were lucky!" But the father told his pastor, "When people would say that to me, I replied, 'It wasn't luck at all. My wife and daughter were on their knees praying while our friend was working on my son.' " And he concluded, "What a wonderful opportunity I had for witnessing to Christ again and again as my friends spoke to me about my son being saved." *References:* 2 Sam. 22:7; Ps. 18:6; 20; 91:15; 118:5; Jer. 33:3.

739. Before the surrender of Weinsberg the women of that besieged city asked the enemy to let them carry at least their most precious possessions with them. The permission was granted. But who can describe the open-mouthed astonishment of the victors when the good women of Weinsberg, with a shrewdness as great as

their love, came plodding through the gates of the city with their husbands, sons, and brothers astride their shoulders? May many women similarly succeed in carrying their dear ones out of this world on the shoulders of their prayers! (W. F. Besser) *References:* Mark 2:3–5; Rom. 9:3; 1 Cor. 7:12–16; 9:22.

740. Prayer: An Identifying Mark of a Christian. It was once as common for Christians to give thanks before meals as it was for them to eat. An incident from the Thirty Years' War is fitting. Two or three of the Protestant officers were hiding together in a cave to which day by day a little girl was sent with goods from the nearest farm. One day a stranger who happened to be walking through the woods joined them, and they were naturally suspicious of him, but he talked so much like one of themselves that all their doubts were removed. After a while the little girl came with their supplies, and with genuine politeness they offered food to the stranger first. To their surprise he began to eat without giving thanks. That omission revealed the true character of the man. He was what they had suspected, a spy, and they barely had time to make their escape from the papal dragoons with whom he was in league. Prayer is one of the identifying marks of a Christian household. *References:* Eph. 6:18; Phil. 4:6; Col. 4:2; 1 Thess. 5:17; 1 Tim. 2:8.

741. A Confession of Helplessness. Dr. O. Hallesby in his classic *Prayer* says, "Prayer and helplessness are inseparable. Only he who is helpless can truly pray" (p. 17). Again, "Prayer (therefore) consists simply in telling God day by day in what ways we feel helpless. We are moved to pray every time the Spirit of God, which is the spirit of prayer, emphasizes anew to us our helplessness, and we realize how impotent we are by nature to believe, to love, to hope, to serve, to sacrifice, to suffer, to read the Bible, to pray and to struggle against our sinful desires'' (p. 25). *References:* Gen. 32:9–12; 2 Sam. 22:7; 1 Kings 3:7–9; Ps. 34:4–6; Jer. 10:23; Mark 10:23–24; 2 Cor. 3:5; 12:8–10.

742. Sir Walter Raleigh came, as he frequently had done, to Elizabeth, queen of England, with a certain petition. The queen, somewhat indignant, remarked, ''Sir Walter, when will you ever stop to approach me with petitions?'' Raleigh quickly replied, ''When the queen will stop to grant me my petitions.'' So it should be with us Christians. As long as the promise of God, our heavenly Father and Sovereign, that ''it will be given to you'' stands, we should pray without ceasing. *References:* 1 Chron. 16:11; 2 Chron. 7:14; Is. 55:1–6; Matt. 7:7; Mark 11:24; Luke 18:1; 1 Thess. 5:17.

Related illustrations: 621, 639, 814.

Preaching

743. Preachers are like wind instruments; the breath that is blown through them is that of the Holy Spirit in the Word. (MacLaren) *References:* Acts 1:8; 2:4; 4:20.

744. Richard Baxter, the 17th-century Puritan divine, described the seriousness of the preacher's task with the couplet:

> I preach as never sure to preach again
> And as a dying man to dying men.

References: Eccl. 9:10; Is. 62:6; Ezek. 3:17; 33:6; Matt. 10:27–28; John 9:4; 1 Cor. 9:16; 2 Tim. 4:1–5.

745. A great preacher once said that there is one preacher who is always up to date—the man who preaches to aching hearts. *References:* Is. 40:1–2; 66:13; Matt. 5:4; 1 Thess. 4:18.

746. ''*Rash* preaching,'' said Rowland Hill, ''disgusts; *timid* preaching

leaves poor souls fast asleep; *bold* preaching is the only preaching that is owned of God.'' *References:* Jer. 1:7; Matt. 10:27; Mark 16:15; Acts 5:20; 2 Tim. 4:2; Titus 2:15.

747. To preach more than half an hour a man should be an angel or have angels for his hearers. (Whitefield) *References:* 1 Cor. 2:1; 3:2.

748. Preachers are to be like needles of compasses, which always point in the same direction regardless of weather conditions or the position of the instrument. Preachers are not like weather vanes, letting the wind of popular opinion and the spirit of the times to turn them about. (W. F. Besser) *References:* Is. 62:6–7; 1 Cor. 1:23; 2:1–5; 2 Tim. 4:1–5; Heb. 13:17.

749. A village church in one of the Tyrolese valleys is noted for one piece of art. On the pulpit is an outstretched arm, beautifully carved in wood, the hand of which holds up a cross. The emblem is a permanent reminder to the one in the pulpit that his ministry should be and must be a holding up of the cross of Christ as the only hope of the world for the hearers. *References:* Matt. 16:21–23; Acts 8:29–35; 1 Cor. 1:17–23; 2:2; Eph. 2:13–18.

750. Reaching into the Enemy's Camp. George Gobel once closed his weekly telecast with the statement: ''This program is being broadcast throughout the world to the armed forces—of our enemies!''

This unusual twist on a familiar line might offer a serious reminder to the Christian church regarding its preaching. The purpose of Christian preaching—if it is really preaching in the New Testament sense of the term—is always a conscious reaching into the camp of the enemy. The real struggle of preaching does not consist primarily in planning the preaching program, in finding time to prepare the sermon, or in developing more effective delivery, important as all of these considerations may be. Finding the point of closest contact with the enemy constitutes the real problem. *References:* 2 Sam. 12:1–14; 1 Kings 18:17–24; Ps. 2; Acts 2:14–40; 3:11–26; 17:22–31; 2 Tim. 4:1–5; Rev. 2–3.

751. Jean Baptiste Massilon, who did honor to his name as a great preacher, was selected to preach at the court of Versailles during the Advent 1699. Louis XIV confessed to him, "When I listen to other preachers, I am usually very much satisfied with them. When I hear you, I become very much dissatisfied with myself." *References:* Ps. 141:5; Prov. 15:5; Eccl. 7:5; Is. 58:1; Eph. 5:11; 2 Tim. 4:2; Titus 2:15; Heb. 12:5.

752. Preach to Be Understood. Put yourself for a moment in the place of the people in the pew, who throughout the week may have had little contact with things spiritual. Words like *grace, sin,* and *righteousness* whistle past their ears. They think they know what the preacher is talking about, but they are not quite sure. Then all of a sudden the word *justification* whips by. Now they know for sure. They *don't* know what the preacher is saying.

A few inquirers will insist on discovering the meaning of what they do not understand. Others will respond the way Leo Durocher did the first time he faced the youthful Bob Feller in spring training. After watching two fast balls split the middle of the plate without offering to strike, Durocher shouldered his bat and started for the dugout. The umpire called out to him that he had another strike coming. Durocher called back, "That's all right. I'm not interested anymore." *References:* Ps. 119:130; Matt. 11:25; 1 Cor. 2:1–4; 9:19–23; 2 Cor. 1:12.

Related illustrations: 449, 569, 718, 828.

Prejudice

753. Deception of Outward Appearances. There is a well-known legend about Da Vinci's *The Last Supper.* The painting was complete except for the faces of Jesus and Judas Iscariot. Da Vinci looked a long time for a face that would serve as a model for Jesus. One day in the quiet of St. Peter's in Rome he saw a young man. His face indicated peace and inward joy. This young man became the artist's model for the face of Jesus.

For years Da Vinci looked for a model for Judas. He was looking for a face that would describe the horror and the treachery of Judas's heart. At last he found a beggar in Florence. His face fairly shrieked with all that is sinful, vile, evil, and corrupt. It spoke of blasted years and crushed hopes. Da Vinci rushed the beggar to Milan and painted the face of Judas. When he had completed his work, the beggar turned to him and said, "You do not know me. I am Bandinelli. Fourteen years ago you painted the face of Jesus from my face." *References:* 1 Sam. 16:7; John 7:24; 2 Cor. 5:12; 10:7; James 2:2–4 (one cannot judge a person by outward appearances). 1 Sam. 15:5 (Saul); 2 Sam. 12:7–10 (David); 1 Kings 11:1–15 (Solomon); Matt. 26:69–75 (Peter) (sin defiles the best of people).

754. The Irony of Bigotry. A tragic instance when blood could have saved a person's life took place on April 1, 1950. Dr. Charles Richard Drew, a black physician and scientist, was killed in an auto accident on that day, and his life might have been saved if the door had not been closed to him at the all-white hospital that had a blood bank. But he was denied help and died—at the age of 46.

The irony was that his research on "banked blood" had earlier contributed much to plasma research and saved countless lives. But he was denied the benefits of his own discoveries—because he was "different."

Our Lord also was engaged in "blood research." His life's blood has given new life to millions. Because of His "donation," people will live forever. But He was rejected because He was "different." *References:* Matt. 13:53–58; Mark 6:1–6; Luke 9:51–53; John 7:52; 8:48.

755. Persecution of Jews. The Jewish people have been persecuted more than any other people in history. One of the main causes for the persecutions has been the accusation that the Jews were responsible for killing Christ. Although prejudice against the Jews developed over the years after the crucifixion, it reached serious proportions in A.D. 613 when the Jews in Spain were given the option of either being baptized or leaving the country. A few years later those who remained were declared slaves and given to pious Christians. Children under seven years old were taken away from their parents and given to Christian families to provide a Christian education.

In 1121 the Jews were driven from Flanders, which is now a part of Belgium, and were not allowed to return until they repented of the guilt of killing Jesus Christ. The persecutions spread. Jews were killed, burned at the stake, and tortured in the inquisitions. They were driven from most countries in Europe. The climax was reached when Hitler came to power in Germany and began his persecution of the Jews in 1933, resulting in the murder of 6 million Jews by the Nazis. *References:* Matt. 27:25; Acts 3:13–26; Rom. 9:1–5.

Related illustration: 479.

Pride
756. Moody once said, "Strife is knocking another down; vainglory is setting oneself up." *References:* Phil. 2:3; 2 Tim. 2:24; James 3:14.

757. Alexander the Great, seeing Diogenes looking attentively at a parcel of human bones, asked the philosopher what he was looking for. "That which I cannot find—" was the reply, "the difference between your father's bones and those of his slaves." *References:* 2 Sam. 14:14; Ps. 89:47–48; Eccl. 3:19.

758. A certain braggart, after enumerating what he considered to be some of his outstanding achievements, exclaimed, "I'll have you know that I'm a self-made man!" One of those who heard him remarked, "Well, I'm glad to hear that! It certainly relieves the Creator of a tremendous responsibility!" *References:* Prov. 25:14; 26:12; Is. 5:21; 1 Cor. 8:2; Gal. 6:3; James 4:16.

759. There's an old fable about two ducks and a frog who lived in a farmer's pond. The ducks and the frog were the best of friends; they played together all day long. But when the hot summer days came, the pond began to dry up. The ducks realized that they would have to move. They could easily fly away to another place, but what about their friend, the frog?

Finally the ducks decided to put a stick between them. Each would hold one end in its bill while the frog hung on to the stick by its mouth. So the three friends set out for another pond. As they were flying, the farmer saw them and said, "How clever! I wonder who thought of it." The frog said, "I did." And that was the end of the frog. "Pride goes before the fall," the proverb says. *References:* Prov. 11:2; 16:18; 28:25; Obad. 4; Hab. 2:4; Matt. 23:12; James 4:16.

760. Tragic Results of Spiritual Pride. A Danish fable tells of a young spider who lived in a large barn. One day, while crawling about on the ceiling, he looked down and saw a spot that seemed just perfect for a new home. So he came down on a thin filament of web until he reached that wonderful spot, and there he created a huge, beautiful web. He grew slick and prospered. One day, while walking about his domain, he saw that thin filament of web reaching up into the darkness above and thought to himself, I have no need of this, and so he cut it. The whole web (spider and all) came crashing to the ground and a big cow stepped on him! How much we are like that young spider! We are quick to declare our independence from God— sometimes with pride, but always with tragic results. *References:* Deut. 8:11–14; Prov. 3:5–7; 16:18; 26:12; Is. 1:2–3; Luke 12:16–20; 1 Cor. 8:2; Rev. 3:17.

761. When Napoleon I was about to begin his campaign against Russia, someone tried to dissuade him and remarked, "Man proposes, but God disposes!" whereupon Napoleon arrogantly replied, "I dispose as well as propose!" A Christian lady heard this blasphemous answer and said, "I believe this to be the turning point in Napoleon's career. God cannot permit any of His creatures to arrogate to themselves His prerogatives with impunity." And she was right. From that time Napoleon's star began to wane and soon turned to darkness. (Dallmann) *References:* Job 24:24; Ps. 20:7–8; Prov. 16:18; Is. 10:12–19; 14:11–23; 26:5; 40:21–25.

762. The Great Sin. One chapter of C. S. Lewis's book on morality, *Christian Behavior,* is titled "The Great Sin." We might imagine that it would deal with murder or adultery. Instead it describes "pride," or "self-conceit," as the great sin. (He makes the same point in *Mere Christianity.*) "And the devil did grin, for his darling sin is pride that apes humility" (Coleridge). With God's gracious help we can heed the Scriptural admonition "Clothe yourselves with humility toward one another, because, 'God opposes the proud but gives grace to the humble' " (1 Peter 5:5). *References:* Prov. 11:2; 16:18; 26:12; Obad. 4; Matt. 23:12; Luke 14:11; 1 Peter 5:5.

763. It is extremely hard to accept a gift. Our pride and suspicion always stand in the way. A few years ago there was a popular TV program called "Candid Camera." One night the producer of the show tried to give away various articles to people who were passing by. With very few exceptions he found it almost impossible to give away money, perfume, billfolds, cigarette lighters, and even flowers. People were suspicious of gifts from a stranger. They reasoned that people simply don't give anything away without expecting something in return. It's hard to give something away. People don't want to be in debt to anyone. Our pride says to us, "Stand on your own two feet, be your own man, don't get burned." *References:* Luke 4:16–29; John 3:16–19; 4:10; Rom. 5:15–17; 6:23; Eph. 2:8–9.

Related illustrations: 452, 471, 846, 907.

Profanity

764. George Washington gave this order to the Continental Army on August 3, 1776: "The General is sorry to be informed that the foolish and wicked practice of profane cursing and swearing, a vice heretofore little known in the American army, is growing into fashion; he hopes the officers will by example as well as by influence en-

163

deavor to check it, and that both they and the men will reflect that we can have little hope of the blessing of heaven on our arms if we insult it by our impiety and folly; added to this, it is a vice so mean and low, without any temptation, that every man of sense and character detests and despises it.'' *References:* Ex. 20:7; Lev. 19:12; Matt. 5:34; 12:36–37; James 1:26; 5:12; 1 Peter 3:10.

765. One day during World War II a detachment of American soldiers on Guadalcanal was startled to read the following announcement posted at the entrance to their mess hall: ''American soldiers are requested please to be a little more careful in their choice of language, especially when natives are assisting them in unloading ships and trucks and in erecting abodes. American missionaries spent many years among us and taught us the use of clean speech. Every day, however, American soldiers use bad words, and the good work your missionaries did in our midst is being undermined by your careless profanity.'' To the greater shame of the Americans this notice was signed by a Polynesian chief. *References:* Ex. 20:7; Lev. 19:12; Matt. 5:34; 12:36–37; James 1:26; 3:9–10: 5:12; 1 Peter 3:10.

Related illustration: 583.

Progress

766. Dr. John Rilling in *INSIGHTS into Preaching* points out that life is lived in a resisting medium. It always requires effort to reach goals. The slogan of my graduating class in the eighth grade was ''Rowing, not drifting.'' Progress requires effort. Doing nothing usually results in slipping back, away from the goal. *References:* Matt. 7:13–14; Acts 20:24–31; 1 Cor. 9:24; Phil. 2:12; 3:12–15; 2 Tim. 4:5–8; Heb. 12:1–2; 2 Peter 1:5–10.

767. In Arizona there is a river whose bed is filled with quicksand. You may walk in safety over the bed of that river provided you keep moving forward. But the moment you stop, the treacherous quicksand will begin to pull you down. How like the world that river is! Go forward or be lost! *References:* Prov. 4:25–27; Ezek. 1:12; Luke 9:62; Phil. 3:13–14; Col. 2:6; Heb. 12:1.

768. Fear of Progress. In a cookbook published toward the end of the 19th century, a footnote to directions for reducing tallow and making candles in the home informed the housewife that in some sections of the country gas was being used for light but was probably too dangerous for general home use. It added that the latest experiments with electricity for this purpose also did not promise much success, and besides, light from an electric bulb was harmful to the eyes. It was feared that street lighting would aid only the criminals, and besides, God intended the night for sleep. Today the high school physics student can tell you all about the laser beam. *References:* Eccl. 1:11; Dan. 2:20–21; 1 Cor. 7:31.

Prophecy

769. Jesus' Prophecy of the Temple's Destruction. The second thing that was to happen was the destruction of the temple. It has never been rebuilt. Even though a Roman emperor made five attempts to rebuild the temple and therewith to prove the prophecy of the Bible untrue, he never succeeded. Earthquakes and fire made the attempts futile. *References:* Is. 64:11; Micah 3:12; Matt. 24:1–2; Mark 13:1–2; Luke 21:5–6.

770. Prophetic Vision of Malachi. Martin Luther lived about as long before our time as Malachi lived before the birth of Christ. Luther with all his gifts and learning could not possibly know that a new empire would arise on this continent to outshine the Old World or that North America would be nominally Protestant and South America overwhelmingly Roman Catholic. We may speak of men with forethought and vision, yet the keenest minds cannot penetrate the mists that hide the events and possibilities of future ages. We cannot even strip aside the veil of tomorrow and know whether banks will open or close, whether stocks will rise or fall, or whether we shall live or die. Yet Malachi boldly undertakes to foretell future events. He definitely assures the people that the Lord, the Messenger of the Covenant, would suddenly come to His temple and that He would not come alone would but have a forerunner, a messenger, to prepare the way for Him. (See also Is. 40:3.) *References:* Is. 40:3; Mal. 3:1.

Punishment
771. Chrysostom: "To be separated from God is greater punishment than a thousand hells." *References:* Matt. 8:12; 13:49; 22:13; 25:41–46; Luke 13:25–28; 16:26; Rev. 22:14–15.
Related illustration: 588.

Purpose in Life
772. There is a pleasing story of how the father of Matthew Henry, the Bible commentator, won his bride. He was a minister, she an only daughter and the heiress of a considerable fortune. Her father objected. "You see," he said to his daughter, "he may be a perfect gentleman, a brilliant scholar, and an excellent preacher, but he is a stranger, and we do not even know where he comes from." "True," replied the girl with all the insight that her great son afterward displayed, "but we know where he is going, and I should like to go with him." *References:* Matt. 8:5–12; Luke 7:36–50; 16:19–25; 23:39–43 (not where you're

from but where you're going that counts). Gen. 24:3–4; Deut. 7:3–4; Neh. 13:25–27; 2 Cor. 6:14–18 (the benefit of marrying a believer).
773. Rachel Carson in *The Sea Around Us* describes the microscopic plant life of the sea that provides food for many of the ocean's smallest creatures. These little plants drift thousands of miles, wherever the current takes them. They have no power or will of their own to direct their destiny. They are called "plankton," a Greek word that means wandering or drifting. *Plankton* is an accurate term to describe the aimless life of many people of our century, people who have lost a sense of direction, who are powerless to direct their own destiny, and who wander through life without a purpose. These people are subject to the shifting wind of every fad. They struggle to find a purpose for their lives either in some sort of pleasure or in one of the new religious movements or mind control efforts. *References:* Ps. 1:4–6; Ezek. 13:10–11; Matt. 7:26–27; Phil. 3:19.
774. Our Need for Meaning. Dr. Albert Einstein once said, "The man who regards his own life and that of his fellow creatures as meaningless is not merely unhappy but hardly fit for life." More recently the great Viennese psychiatrist, Dr. Viktor Frankl, concluded that one of the most basic of all human needs, driving people at least as strongly as sex or hunger, is what he calls "the will for meaning." One can endure almost any suffering, says Dr. Frankl, if there is a purpose or meaning in it. Conversely, we will be miserable even amidst great luxury if we cannot relate our life to some larger context that makes it meaningful. It would seem that what Dr. Frankl is saying in psychological terms was said by St. Augustine in spiritual terms

some 15 centuries ago: "Thou hast made us for Thyself, O God, and our hearts are restless until they find their rest in Thee." *References:* Joshua 24:15; John 4:34; Acts 20:24; 1 Cor. 9:24–27; Phil. 3:13–14; 2 Tim. 4:7–8.

Related illustration: 25.

R

Reason

775. Reason is a beautiful light, but it will not light the way to salvation. Candles are useful enough to brighten up rooms, but do not expect them to illuminate heaven and earth. We have the sun for that. And we have God's Word to show us the way to salvation. But moles and bats, that is, the worldlings, think little of this light. (Luther) *References:* Is. 29:14; Matt. 11:25; 1 Cor. 1:18–23; 3:19–20; 2 Cor. 10:5; Col. 2:8; James 3:15.

Related illustrations: 832, 886.

Receiving Christ

776. In Holman Hunt's picture *The Light of the World,* an august person stands with a lamp in his hands under a midnight sky, on the outside of a walled enclosure, the entrance gate of which is barred. He has knocked again and again but has received no answer; the wild vine and bramble have grown over the gate, showing how long and resolutely it has been closed. So Christ stands outside the temple of our hearts, willing to enter and consecrate them, if we will but open the door. *(Biblical Treasury) References:* John 10:27; 18:37; Eph. 3:17–19; 1 John 3:24; Rev. 3:20.

Related illustration: 823.

Reconciliation

See also **Forgiveness**

777. Paul Tournier in *A Doctor's Case Book* tells of a girl he had treated unsuccessfully for several months for anemia. Finally, he referred her to a medical officer to get permission to refer her to a mountain sanatorium. A week later he received a note from the medical officer indicating that the blood figures did not agree with the ones Dr. Tournier had mentioned. He took a fresh sample, rushed to the lab, and was amazed at the change. He sought information from the patient about what had happened. She replied, "I have suddenly been able to forgive someone against whom I bore a nasty grudge. Now at last I can say yes to life." For our own spiritual, mental, and physical health we need to be reconciled to people, to live in an attitude of acceptance and friendship with people. *References:* Prov. 11:17; Matt. 5:7, 23–26; Luke 6:36; Gal. 6:1–2; Eph. 4:31–32; Col. 3:13.

Related illustrations: 363, 570.

Redemption

778. The Lord Jesus is everything in redemption, for He is both the buyer and the price. *References:* Rom. 3:24–25; Gal. 3:13; Heb. 9:12.

779. A lad spent a lifetime constructing a replica of a ship he had once seen docked in the harbor near his home. Every sail was intricately cut and sewn exactly to scale and perfectly placed, and every plank was carved and then fastened precisely as it should have been. Finally the time came for the grand launching on a small creek just the right size for such a small craft. During the first moments the ship slid gracefully over the water and rode the slow current the way a finely crafted vessel should. But then without warning the current quickened, and suddenly the improbable happened. A gust of wind caught the sails, and the ship darted completely out of reach. In a few moments it bobbed out of sight in the widening stream. The boy was crushed.

Some months later he spotted it in the window of a hobby shop—his ship! The very ship he had fashioned so painstakingly was for sale. The price was steep, and even though it belonged to him already, he was willing to pay anything to get it back. To him it was a "pearl of great price." So he scraped together every last penny and bought it. It was his again. And this time it would not get away.

The whole world is God's by right of creation. He built it, and it was "very good," precisely as He wanted it. It is also His by right of "purchase." He bought it. It is His twice—all of it, including you and me. *References:* Gen. 3:15; 1 Chron. 17:21; Ps. 77:13–15; Is. 43:1–4; Rom. 3:23–25; 1 John 2:2.

Rejected for Christ's Sake

780. Fanny Foster was a brilliant writer. She was greatly admired by many. She became the rich queen of society. Then she married Adoniram Judson, the great missionary to Burma. She had to learn a strange language. She was forced to live in a dreary climate. She had to make her home among a people largely uncivilized. In fashion circles they whispered, "She is mad." But was she? *References:* John 10:20; Acts 26:24–26; 2 Cor. 5:13–14 (mad for Christ). Is. 66:5; Luke 21:15–17; John 15:18–19; 1 John 3:13 (rejected for the Gospel).

781. When Robert Short, author of *The Gospel According to Peanuts* and *Parables of Peanuts,* spoke at Concordia Teachers College, Seward, Neb., he disclosed that as a high school student in Midland, Tex., he became an agnostic, although he had been raised in a Methodist home. He became president of the science club, whose activity caused such a stir that the high school principal complained to his parents. He remembered sitting across the table from his mother as she spoke to him. Tears were running down her cheeks as she said, "I thought we raised you right. I never thought it would come to this: our son an agnostic."

During his college years Robert Short, through contacts with a campus pastor, found a new relationship to Jesus Christ and decided to become a minister. He went home to tell his mother about his decision. They were sitting at the same table. Again tears rolled down her cheeks as she said, "I never thought it would come to this: my son a religious fanatic." *References:* Matt. 10:34–36; Luke 12:51–53; 21:16.

Related illustrations: 536, 944.

Religion

782. To the unconverted all religions are alike, just as all colors are alike in the dark. (Wm. Taylor) *References:* Is. 42:8; 45:20; 1 Cor. 2:14–15.

783. Religion should be a power in our daily lives. But many carry it as a church carries its bells—high up in a tower to ring out on holy days, to strike for funerals, or to chime for weddings. All the rest of the time it hangs high above daily affairs—silent, voiceless, dead. (Beecher) *References:* Is. 58:1–7; Ezek. 33:31–32; Luke 6:46.

784. All religious preachers may be divided into two classes: those who seek their own glory and those who seek the glory of Him whose ambassadors they are. *References:* Obad. 4; Matt. 23:12; John 7:18; Rom. 10:3.

785. Not Really Alike. At an international gathering in New York, a young American asked a cultured young woman from Burma about the religion of her country. She said that most of her people were Buddhists. The young man said rather casually, "Oh, well, I don't suppose that matters much. All religions are about the same anyway." She looked directly at him and said, "If you had lived in my country, you would not say that. I have seen what centuries of superstition, fear, and indifference to social problems have done to my people. We need the truth of Christianity. When I became a Christian, it cost me something. I suffered loss of friends, income, and social standing. If your religion had cost you more, it might mean more to you too. My country needs Christ." *References:* Deut. 7:25; 11:16; Prov. 14:12; Is. 45:20; Rom. 1:22–23; 1 Cor. 8:1–6; 12:2; 1 John 5:21.

786. Sad it is, indeed, that altogether too many in our day have lost their first love for the work of the Lord. They let religion become a "spare-tire religion." How? Every motorist generally carries a spare tire. Although it is not a necessary and immediate part of the machine, it becomes necessary when you have a puncture or a blowout. It provides insurance against being stranded on the road. The religion of too many within the church is no more than a spare tire. They belong to the church and support it in a way, but their religion is not really a part of their life. It is a "spare." *References:* Judg. 4:1–6:1; 1 Kings 18:21; Jer. 3:10; Luke 6:46; 1 Cor. 15:58; Rev. 2:4.

787. Religious Syncretism. Another Baal that tempts us is religious syncre-

tism, watered-down religion in general, the cultural religion of America. Although America has been "Christianized," Christianity has also been Americanized. Religion has so accommodated itself to our environment that it has degenerated to nothing more than a national cult, a civil religion. The church in America may be a rock, but even rocks are subject to erosion: the erosion of doctrinal clarity, the smoothing of the edges of witness, the loss of religious content. Scriptural precision is challenged by blurry, generalized religion; distinctive witness is dulled by our attempts to be nice to all religions whether true or not; theological content is corrupted and often replaced by mere sentiments about religion. Many people believe, but they don't know what they believe. At best, the god of religion-in-general is mild and manageable. He's just like one of us, too much like one of us—an American jolly good fellow. *References:* Deut. 12:30; Is. 45:20; John 17:15–17; Acts 2:40; Rom. 12:2; Heb. 11:24–25; 1 John 2:15.

788. Do-It-Yourself Religion. Some time ago we read of a do-it-yourself funeral. The lips of the corpse in the casket were motionless on the day of this funeral of a 79-year-old Denver newspaperman, but his own voice, the voice of the deceased, filled the air of the funeral home. Before his death he had recorded the message he wanted people to hear at his funeral.

That Denver newspaperman may have been the first person ever to arrange for a do-it-yourself funeral, but he was not the first to have a do-it-yourself religion. Through all ages many have made only do-it-yourself preparations for their entry into Paradise. The sermon they want to be preached at their funeral might well be titled: "What a Good Boy Am I!" *Ref-*

erences: Matt. 19:16–26; Rom. 3:10–24; 9:30–33; Gal. 2:16; 3:1–5; Eph. 2:8–9; 2 Tim. 4:3–4; Titus 3:4–5.

789. Somebody once asked Samuel Taylor Coleridge, the famous British poet, "Is Christianity true?" The poet answered that question with two little words: "Try it." A Hindu convert to Christianity once declared, "If I were a missionary, I would not argue the question of religion; I would give people the New Testament and say, 'Read that.'" *References:* Is. 1:18; John 1:46; 20:27; Acts 26:28–29; Rev. 22:17.

790. Major William E. Mayer, army psychiatrist, interviewed 200 American soldiers whom the Chinese released after the Korean War. He is said to have studied all the official records of 800 other American former prisoners from Korea. He concluded that it was possible for the communists to brainwash about one-fourth of the American prisoners because they first of all lacked religious conviction. *References:* Ps. 17:3; 34:19–20; Luke 6:47–48; 1 Cor. 10:13; 2 Cor. 12:9; 2 Peter 2:9; Rev. 2:10.

Related illustrations: 106, 120, 148, 199, 277, 370, 474, 493, 550, 665, 834, 917, 950, 996, 1013.

Repentance

791. The cry of "Fire! Fire!" at midnight may sometimes startle a sleeping person rudely, harshly, and unpleasantly. But who would complain if that cry was the means of saving one's life? The words "except ye repent, ye shall perish" may at first seem stern and severe. But they are words of love and may be the means of delivering precious souls from hell. (Ryle) *References:* Eccl. 7:5; Is. 58:1; Luke 13:3–5; 17:3; Eph. 5:11; 1 Thess. 5:14; 2 Tim. 4:2.

792. Henry Ward Beecher was talking about all of us when he said, "Some men, when they attempt to reform their lives, reform those things for which they do not much care. They take the torch of God's Word, and enter some indifferent chamber, and the light blazes in, and they see that they are sinful there; and then they look in another room, where they do not often stay, and are willing to admit that they are very sinful there, and they leave unexplored some cupboard and secret apartments where their life really is, and where they have stored up the things which are dearest to them, and which they will neither part with nor suffer rebuke for." *References:* 1 Chron. 28:9; Ps. 44:20–21; 139:23–24; Jer. 17:10; 23:24; Amos 9:3; Rom. 8:27.

793. A Special Day of Repentance. Let us search and try our ways, trace them whither they lead, test them whether they have been good or evil. Let us be thorough in such searching and trying. Such a searching is necessary, and it is a good custom to observe a special day for such conscientious examination of our whole life. A merchant keeps his books in good shape all the year round, but at the close of the year he will make a special audit of them in order to see how he stands. A housewife sweeps and cleans every day, and still she finds it necessary to institute a special annual house cleaning. In like manner our whole life should and must be a constant searching of our ways, and still it is necessary and profitable for us to set aside a special day for special searching. *References:* Lam. 3:40–41; Matt. 7:5; 1 Cor. 11:28; 2 Cor. 13:5.

794. J. B. Phillips tells us about a children's book called *The Wind in the Willows* with various animals as human characters. There's Toad, a very conceited chap who loves to rush all over the country in his car and is always singing his own praises. Toad gets into a mess through his conceit and selfishness, and his friends Mole and Rat get Badger (who is a rather stern type) to give him a good talking to. In Badger's living room Toad breaks down and admits all his folly and guilt, and he promises complete reform. So Badger lets him go, an apparently repentant character. But a few moments later, Toad is found outside throwing his weight around just as before. Rat and Mole are horrified. "What!" cries Badger. "You backsliding animal! Didn't you tell me just now in there . . ." "Oh, yes, yes, in there. But I've been searching my mind since, and I find I'm not a bit sorry or repentant really, so it's no earthly good saying I am now, is it?"

There are many people who can be made to *feel* guilty by a parent or teacher or pastor. They may even admit it and promise all sorts of things. And the tragedy is that many think that this feeling of artificial guilt is Christian faith. *References:* 1 Sam. 24:16–17; Ps. 78:35–36; Ezek. 33:31–32; Matt. 7:21; 18:23–28; 23:29–35.

795. Confederate General Robert E. Lee once told his soldiers, "We poor sinners need to come back from our wanderings to seek pardon through the all-sufficient merits of our Redeemer. And we need to pray earnestly for the power of the Holy Spirit to give us a precious revival in our own hearts and among the unconverted." *References:* 2 Chron. 7:14; 30:9; Ps. 51:10–13; Is. 55:1–7; Jer. 3:12; Ezek. 18:21; Luke 15:7; Acts 2:38.

796. Some years ago an American journal of some importance offered valuable prizes in a contest of original poetry. Lo and behold, the judges gave first prize to a "poet" who had written a most disgusting and suggestive lampoon entitled *King David*. The satire dealt at great length with the immoral relations of David and Bathsheba, constantly interweaving in a most cunning and devilish manner quotations from the psalms of David. It is true what Nathan said to David: "You have made the enemies of the LORD show utter contempt." But be not deceived, God is not mocked. While such frank revelations of sinful human depravity will continue to be a stumbling block to the ungodly readers of the Bible, children of God see in them a warning in which they clearly read the divine lesson, "If you think you are standing firm, be careful that you don't fall." The story of the fall and rising again of King David does not give us occasion to blaspheme in secret joy and laughter, but it is for us *a most solemn call to repentance. References:* 2 Sam. 12:1–14; Ps. 40:13–17; 70; Ezek. 25:1–7; 1 Cor. 10:12; Gal. 6:1.

797. False Repentance. A hospital chaplain kept a record of some 2,000 patients whom he had visited, all apparently in a dying condition, and who showed signs of repentance. But among those restored to health, he felt that only two really showed a marked change in their spiritual lives after their recovery.

A physician kept similar record of 300 persons, among whom only 10 showed evidence of spiritual as well as physical recovery after their return to health.

Whatever criteria these men used to determine "repentance" or "spiritual recovery," the point at stake is intriguing. Have you ever known anyone in a serious accident or in the hospital for a long time who expressed profound sorrow over the past and made fervent promises to change but some months later was observed by someone who said, "You know, Bill hasn't really changed a bit, has he?'' *References:* Judg. 3:5–12; Matt. 3:7–8; 18:23–25.

Related illustrations: 237, 435, 630, 691, 855, 887.

Responsibility

798. Daniel Webster: "The most important thought I ever had was my individual responsibility to God." *References:* Ezek. 3:17–21; 33:7–11; Matt. 18:23; 25:19; Luke 12:48; 19:15; Rom. 14:12.

799. Shirking One's Responsibilities. "There is a French folk tale about a small village which had just been assigned a new priest. The village decided that each would bring some wine to be put into a large barrel which would be presented to the priest. The village blacksmith, being a wise and frugal man, decided that since the rest were bringing wine, he would bring water. No one would know the difference anyway. So when it came his turn to put the contents of his jug into the barrel, he poured in the water. The time came for the big presentation, and when they turned the spigot on the barrel, out came pure water. All the villagers had been 'wise and frugal'; each had depended on the others to do his job." (Paul Simon, "Your Election Responsibilities," *Cresset* [January 1957]) *References:* 1 Sam. 15:21; Luke 14:18–20; Gal. 6:2–5; 1 Thess. 4:11–12; 2 Thess. 3:11–12.

800. Our Responsibility Against Error. Charles Porterfield Krauth pressed home our responsibility when he wrote, "A church which contends for nothing either has lost the truth or has ceased to love it. Warfare is painful, but they whose errors created the necessity for it are responsible for all its miseries." Luther had sharp words to speak to George Major on the subject: "A teacher who keeps silent on errors and wishes still to be known as

an orthodox teacher is worse than a manifest fanatic, and does more damage with his dissembling than a heretic and is not to be trusted. He is a wolf and a fox, a hireling and a belly server." *References:* Acts 20:27–30; Gal. 1:6–9; Eph. 5:11; 1 Tim. 5:20; 2 Tim. 4:2; Jude 3.

Related illustrations: 280, 282, 295, 380, 566, 579, 682.

Resurrection of Christ

See also **Easter**

801. The Empty Tomb. In *Therefore Stand* Wilbur M. Smith notes that "of the four great religions of the world resting directly upon personalities, rather than upon some philosophical system, the Christian religion is the only one that even talks about an empty tomb in relation to its founder." *References:* Matt. 28:1–6; Mark 16:4–6; Luke 24:1–6; John 20:1–3; 1 Cor. 15:17–20.

802. Resurrection Silences All Vain Arguments. Before the Communists seized control of Russia, it had been a long-established custom for relatives and friends to exchange verbal Easter greetings. An unnamed priest once availed himself of this usage to win a debate. Lunatscharsky, the Bolshevik commissar for popular education, delivered a public lecture in a large Moscow auditorium. He said that the Christian religion was now completely overthrown and that the Bible could be easily disproved. He felt so sure of himself that he challenged anyone in the audience to find a flaw in what he had just presented.

A young priest came forward, turned to the audience, and said, "Brethren, *Christos woskresse*—Christ is risen!" (This was the usual Easter greeting.) With one accord the vast audience cried out, "*Woistinu woskresse*—He is risen indeed!" (the customary reply).

"I have finished," said the priest. "I have no more to say." The meeting was closed at once. Lunatscharsky's eloquence and flowery language had availed him nothing. *References:* Job 11:2–6; Is. 36–37; Titus 1:10–11 (the vain arguments of the ungodly avail them nothing). Ps. 2; Acts 26:19–28; 1 Cor. 15:12–20 (Christ's resurrection silences all vain arguments).

803. An Englishman named Frank Morison was a non-Christian and quite proud of it. He went to Palestine with the aim of researching the resurrection story in order to disprove it, for then the whole structure of Christianity would come toppling down. He searched for the chunk of evidence that would refute it all, for collateral explanations to account for the claims of Easter Sunday morning. But the more he examined the evidence, the more interesting and impressive he found it, and the more tired he grew of his naturalistic explanations. Ultimately, he shed his agnosticism and became converted to Christianity, finding the resurrection account too difficult to disprove. He gave a briefing on the whole experience in *Who Moved the Stone? References:* Matt. 12:38–40; 28:11–15; Luke 24:44–47; Acts 1:3; 3:25–26; 26:22–28; 1 Cor. 15:3–20.

804. In his last book, De Wette, the well-known Bible critic and leader of skepticism in the past century, made this concession: "The fact of the resurrection, though it may be shrouded in impenetrable mystery, cannot be questioned any more than the assassination of Caesar." *References:* Matt. 28:15; Acts 3:14–15; 10:39–41; 1 Cor. 15:12–20.

Related illustrations: 157, 283, 983.

Resurrection of Man

805. A Universal Hope for the Hereafter. Cicero, the noted Roman writer, assures us that there is nothing so well established as belief in the immortality of the soul. He finds that the Greeks as well as the Romans placed lighted candles in the tombs of their departed dead. The Persians left their graves partly open. Even the most barbarous nations had customs that expressed or implied a hope of life after death. *References:* Eccl. 12:7; Dan. 12:2; Matt. 25:32; Acts 24:15; Rom. 8:19–23; Heb. 9:27.

806. In the laboratory of the scientist Faraday a highly prized silver goblet was dropped by a careless workman into a vat of acid. Immediately the substance attacked the silver, eating it atom by atom, until is disappeared from view, held in solution by the clear liquid. The workman was in despair, but the great chemist, assuring him that all would end well, set about to recover the treasure. To the uninitiated the goblet was lost, but the scientist knew that, although it was no longer visible, its form had only been changed—the silver was all there and could be recovered.

The scientist then poured the right chemicals into the solution, and the silver was quickly precipitated. Then it was gathered together and sent to a silversmith with the proper designs. In a few days the goblet was in its place again, none the worse for its strange experience.

If that great chemist, under all the limitations of the flesh, could gather together the atoms of that scattered silver goblet, how much easier will it be for God Almighty to gather the scattered elements that once made up a human being, set them in order again, and give the person a better and higher life! *References:* Job 19:26; Dan. 12:2; John 5:28–29; 1 Cor. 15:42, 51–52; Phil. 3:21; Rev. 20:13.

Related illustrations: 157, 539.

Revenge

807. He who takes revenge is like the bee, which by stinging others loses not only its sting but often also its life. (Stock) *References:* Prov. 20:22; Matt. 5:39; 1 Peter 3:9.

808. Divine Vengeance: Reaping What One Sows. Sometimes our gracious God uses children to teach a lesson to their parents. In an old fable, a married couple forced the grandfather of the household to sit in a corner and eat his gruel out of a wooden bowl because he spilled so much and broke so many dishes at the table. One day their young son was whittling on a block of wood. When asked what he was doing, he replied simply and directly, "I'm making a wooden bowl for you when you get old." *References:* Matt. 7:2; 2 Cor. 5:10; Gal. 6:7; Rev. 20:12.

809. Revenge Satisfied by Kindness. In South Africa two men lived at enmity with each other. They spied on each other to find opportunities to avenge themselves. One day one of them met the daughter of his enemy, a little girl, while she was picking berries in the forest. Seizing her, he cut off both her hands, and crying triumphantly, "Now I am avenged!" he sent her home.

Many years passed. The girl had grown to womanhood and had moved to another community with her father. One day a gray-headed beggar came to her door asking for food. She immediately recognized him as her father's enemy, who had so cruelly mutilated her. Going into the hut, she bade her servant take as much bread and milk to the poor wretch as he was able to eat. She watched him as he ate ravenously of the proffered food. When he was satisfied, she dropped the cloth that covered the stumps of her arms and said to him, "Now I am avenged." *References:* Lev. 19:18; Prov. 20:22; 25:21; Matt. 5:44; Rom. 12:17–20; 1 Thess. 5:15; 1 Peter 3:9.

Righteousness of God

810. Imputed Righteousness. The crucial text for Martin Luther was Romans 1:17: "The righteous will live by faith." In 1519, two years after he nailed the theses to the church door and two years before he made his "Here I stand" confession at the Diet of Worms, Luther preached on "Two Kinds of Righteousness." He said, "Just as a bridegroom possesses all that is his bride's and she all that is his—for the two have all things in common because they are one flesh—so Christ and the church are one spirit. Thus the blessed God and Father of mercies . . . granted to us very great and precious gifts in Christ. . . . Everything that Christ has is ours, graciously bestowed on us unworthy people out of God's sheer mercy, although we have rather deserved wrath and condemnation in hell. . . . Through faith in Christ, Christ's righteousness becomes our righteousness and all that He has becomes ours; rather, He Himself becomes ours. . . . He who trusts in Christ exists in Christ; he is one with Christ, having the same righteousness as Christ." *References:* Jer. 23:6; Rom. 1:17; 3:21–26; 4:5–9; 9:30–31; 2 Cor. 5:21; Gal. 3:6.

Righteousness of Men

811. Being on God's Side. During the dark days of the Civil War, Abraham Lincoln happened into a church service during which the minister was asking the Lord to be on "our side" and to give the victory to "our side." After the service was over, Lincoln said to his companion, "As for me, I have learned to ask but one thing of the Lord—not that He may be on our side, but that I may be on His side." To be on the Lord's side is to be on the right side, the safe side, the winning side in the end. To be on the Lord's side should be a nation's first concern. (Lenski) *References:* Ps. 33:4; Jer. 42:3; John 15:4–5.

812. Better to Suffer with the Righteous. Some centuries ago as the Arctic winter closed in on Hudson Bay, mutinous sailors put their captain Henry Hudson overboard in a rowboat. As they were about to sail away leaving him to almost certain death in the great frozen north, the ship's carpenter demanded to be put in the rowboat, too. "But you can stay with us," the mutineers told him. He answered, "I'd rather trust myself to the mercy of God and stay with my dear master than be safe and warm with companions like you." *References:* Ps. 35:19–28; Matt. 5:10–12; Luke 6:20–26; Rom. 8:18; 2 Tim. 2:12; Heb. 11:26.

813. When an African chieftain asked the queen of England what the secret of Britain's greatness was, she handed him an English Bible, saying, "Here is the secret of England's greatness."

"Righteousness exalts a nation" (Prov. 14:34). *References:* Prov. 11:11; 14:34; 16:12; 25:5; 28:2; 29:4. *Related illustration:* 187.

Rogate

814. A Special Sunday for Prayer. In A.D. 466, when there was great distress throughout Europe as the result of earthquakes and other calamities, Bishop Claudius of Vienna decreed that the first three days before the Ascension festival should serve as a period of prayer and processions in the churches and on the fields to call on God to remove the sufferings of the people. Gradually this custom came into usage in other places, and in 591 it was prescribed for the whole Christian church. Thus the Sunday before Ascension Day (known as "Rogate") became the special prayer Sunday of the year, and the week beginning with this Sunday became the week of prayer. *References:* 2 Chron. 7:14; Is. 55:6–7; 56:7; Acts 1:14; 4:24; 12:12; James 5:16.

S

Sacrifice

815. David Livingstone, missionary-explorer to Africa: "People talk of the sacrifices I have made in spending so much of my life in Africa. Can something be called a sacrifice that is simply paid back as a small part of a great debt owed to our God that we can never repay? . . . I never made a sacrifice." *References:* Ps. 116:12–14; Luke 17:10; Rom. 12:1–2.

816. At the close of World War II Winston Churchill paid tribute to the Royal Air Force by saying, "Never have so many owed so much to so few." Looking at Jesus Christ as He hangs on the cross, we must declare, "Never has humanity owed so much to One." *References:* Is. 53:5–6; John 12:23–24; Rom. 5:6–8; 2 Cor. 5:15; Heb. 2:9; 1 Peter 2:24; Rev. 1:5; 5:9.

817. Going the Extra Mile. In the Roman Empire any official of the state or an officer of the army could draft any citizen into any kind of service needed for the moment. But the official could not compel the draftee to go more than one mile out of his way to perform the service. You recall that Simon of Cyrene was forced by the centurion to take up the cross of Jesus and carry it to Calvary. Since the centurion called on him to carry the cross, Simon could not refuse. Calvary was less than a mile away, and the officer had the legal right to press him into service.

In the Sermon on the Mount Jesus urges us to do more than the Law requires. He asks us to do the extra, to be ready to sacrifice time and energy to be helpful to those who are in need. The Christian does not take a yardstick or a measuring rod and say, "Here ends the mile, and I will go no farther." *References:* Matt. 5:38–42; 22:34–40; Luke 10:33–35.

818. When Sevastopol was besieged in the Crimean War, Prince Menshikov sank 100 ships across the entrance of the harbor to keep the enemy out. Shall we not be ready to deny ourselves, take up our cross, and follow Christ? Shall we be unwilling to sacrifice a few things, to forgo certain advantages, profits, companionships, and pleasures in defense of the citadel of our faith and for the extension of God's kingdom? Jesus said, "If your right hand causes you to sin, cut it off and throw it away" (Matt. 5:30). *References:* Matt. 5:30; 19:21, 39; Mark 8:35; Rom. 6:6; 8:13; Phil. 3:7–8; Col. 3:5.

819. Self-sacrifice is what makes Jesus more than a great teacher, more than a religious leader; it makes Him the Redeemer of all people. But are you just as ready to make this the mark of your ministry? For Paul, getting up out of the dust of the Damascus road meant giving up prestige, honor, career, and even life. For Luther it meant giving up safety and the quiet life of a monk. For William Carey, the inspired cobbler of London, it meant more of the scorching sun of India instead of a chair at Oxford University. For Livingstone it meant leaving his bones in some forgotten kraal in Africa. For Chalmers it meant a bloody end on the coast of New Guinea.

Are you willing to step in behind that glorious army whose unfaltering marching feet in all ages, in all places, and under all sorts of conditions were ready to follow their great Captain into the jaws of death because they, too, bore in their bodies His mark of self-sacrifice? *References:* Matt. 16:24; Mark 10:21; Luke 14:26–27; 18:28; John 11:16; Rom. 12:1–2; Gal. 5:24; Phil. 3:8.

820. But Christ Died for the Ungodly. Many people have been willing to die for the good. A Greek story tells of the devotion and loyalty of Damon and Pythias. Dionysius of Syracuse had condemned Pythias to death. Pythias begged and pleaded to be set at liberty for a short time so that he might arrange his affairs. Damon pledged his life for the return of his friend. And Pythias faithfully returned before the appointed hour of execution, as he had promised. The tyrant was amazed at the devotion and loyalty of these two and begged to be included in their friendship. They were good men, and each was ready to die for the other. But seldom is a person willing to die for someone who is of no account. No one wants to identify with a criminal, with the ungodly. *References:* John 15:13; Rom. 5:6–8; 1 Cor. 15:3; 2 Cor. 5:15; Gal. 1:4; Col. 1:21–22; 1 Tim. 1:15.

821. No Sacrifice. James Chalmers, missionary to New Guinea, was clubbed to death and eaten by cannibals. During his lifetime given in service to Christ, a lifetime in which Christ worked through him, he wrote, "The word *sacrifice* should never be used in Christ's service." It is no sac-rifice for us to give of our time in order to visit someone whose name we have requested from the pastor in order to invite him or her to come to church next Sunday. It is no sacrifice for us to give our earthly goods in order that our church may educate ministers and missionaries and send them all over the world. *References:* Deut. 10:12; Mal. 3:8–10; Luke 17:7–10; Rom. 14:8; 1 Cor. 4:2; 6:19–20; 9:16.

822. The Lamb of God. A traveler in Europe once spied a carving of a lamb high up on a stone near the top of a church tower. He had seen such carvings of a lamb before, but never in such a place. Asking for an explanation, he was told that in the days when the church was being built, one of the workmen lost his footing and fell from the scaffolding just when that particular stone was being laid. His fellow workmen hurried to the ground and were shocked to see the man standing there brushing the dust from his clothes. He had fallen into the midst of a flock of sheep, and pointing to a lamb at his feet, he said, "That lamb was crushed, but I live." The workmen carved a lamb on that stone so that all might remember the miraculous escape of the workman. But more than that, it also points everyone to "the Lamb of God, who takes away the sin of the world" (John 1:29). *References:* Gen. 3:15; Is. 53:7; John 1:29; 1 Cor. 5:7; 1 Peter 1:18–19; Rev. 5:5–10; 12:11.

Related illustrations: 16, 107, 178, 382, 530, 589, 601, 679, 785.

Salvation

See also **Justification**

823. Salvation Offered to All, Rejected by Many. In 1829 or 1830, a certain George Wilson in Pennsylvania was sentenced to be hanged for robbing the mails and for murder. President Andrew Jackson pardoned him. But

SALVATION

Wilson refused the pardon and insisted that it was not a pardon unless he accepted it. That was a point in law never before raised in the United States. The attorney general said the law was silent on the point. The president was urged to call on the Supreme Court to decide the point at once because the sheriff must know whether to hang Wilson or not. Chief Justice John Marshall, one of the ablest lawyers, handed down the following decision: "A pardon is a paper the value of which depends upon its acceptance by the person implicated. It is hardly to be supposed that one under sentence of death would refuse to accept a pardon, but if it is refused, it is no pardon. George Wilson must hang." Who was responsible for his death? No one but the man himself. The Supreme Court decision illustrates the truth that the atonement of Christ, although providing for the salvation of the whole world, is beneficial only to those who receive the benefits of His salvation by faith. *References:* Mark 16:15–16; John 1:11–12; 3:16–18; Acts 10:34–35; Rom. 10:11–21; Heb. 4:1–11; 1 John 2:2; Rev. 14:6.

824. False Saviors. People have sought and trusted in other helpers, but to no avail. In his better moments even the Roman Emperor Nero, notorious for his brutal disregard for human life, looked about him for a savior. For a time he chose Seneca, the sage, to be his teacher. But preserved in the museum of Naples is a caricature of a butterfly holding the reigns of a dragon, representing Seneca trying in vain to curb the passions of Nero, that profligate and brutal ruler, with the velvet wings of his philosophy. So must ride to ruin today on the dragon of selfishness and greed and unhallowed pleasure and usurped power and science falsely trusted for solutions to every problem those who trust in other help-

ers and refuse to give the reigns of their life into the hands of God. *References:* Ps. 46:1–3; John 6:68; Acts 4:12; Rom. 8:3; 1 Cor. 3:11.

825. Quit Struggling to Save Yourself. A drowning boy was struggling in the water. On the shore stood his mother in an agony of fright and grief. By her side stood a strong man, seemingly indifferent to the boy's fate. Again and again the suffering mother appealed to him to save her boy. But he made no move. By and by the desperate struggling began to abate. He was losing strength. Presently the boy rose to the surface, weak and helpless. At once the strong man leaped into the stream and brought the boy in safely to the shore.

"Why did you not save my boy sooner?" cried the now grateful mother.

"Madam, I could not save your boy as long as he struggled. He would have dragged us both to certain death. But when he grew weak and ceased to struggle, then it was easy to save him."

To struggle to save ourselves is simply to hinder Christ from saving us. Only when we "cease from our own works" and depend helplessly on Him do we realize how perfectly able He is to save without any aid from us. (James H. McConkey) *References:* Rom. 3:20; 11:6; Gal. 2:16; 3:1–3; Eph. 2:8–9; Titus 3:4–5.

826. Joy of Salvation. In 1675 the white settlement at Brookfield, Mass., was suddenly attacked by a large force of Indians. All the cabins of the village were burned except the last one, in which Captain Hutchinson and his men had taken refuge. After several desperate attempts, one brave fellow finally succeeded in getting through the lines of the Indians under cover of darkness and rushed off to Providence to spread the alarm. For three days the

178

Indians attacked the cabin, but after every attack, bodies of Indians were left lying on the ground of the clearing. Finally, on the evening of the third day, the besieged within the fort heard the shouts of friends rushing to their rescue. Major Willard of Boston had been apprised of the siege at Brookfield and with all possible haste rushed to the aid of the brave men, whose ammunition and energies were by this time almost completely exhausted. You can imagine the joy and the thanksgiving in the hearts of the besieged when the Indians were dispersed and driven into the woods.

Thus we, once held in bondage and sitting in the shadow of death, have been delivered from sin, death, and hell when we despaired of all help. While we sat helpless and hopeless, our great Deliverer and Savior came. *References:* Is. 9:2–7; 40:9–11; 42:5–9; 52:7–10; Luke 1:67–80; 2:25–32.

Related illustrations: 317, 322, 397, 506, 528, 549.

Sanctification

See also **Holiness, Servanthood**

827. God's Unfinished Work. Like Michelangelo's partially completed statues, we are all unfinished products—spiritually. As we take time for the Lord's Word and Sacrament on a regular basis, we are also giving the Holy Spirit, the heavenly sculptor, opportunities to work on us. He wants to continue to chip away at us and shape us so that we more fully resemble the image of Christ. He may have to cut or chisel deeply at times to achieve desired results. Lumps of pride may have to be hacked away until God-pleasing humility reveals itself. He may have to sandpaper us at times. This may prove painful, but it will produce a more polished Christian personality. *References:* Eph. 4:11–15; Col. 1:28; 1

Thess. 3:12; 2 Peter 1:5–7; 3:18; 1 John 3:2.

828. Prof. George Stoeckhardt of Concordia Seminary, St. Louis, once said to his students, "Sermons on sanctification serve their purpose only if they call to the remembrance of Christians that they can do what they are told to do. In order that the Gospel may prevail, tell them, 'You are free. Prove that you are by successfully resisting sin.'" *References:* John 8:31–36; Rom. 6:5–7; 2 Cor. 9:8; Gal. 5:24; Phil. 4:13; 1 Peter 2:24; 1 John 5:4.

Related illustrations: 93, 180, 188, 462, 556.

Science

829. Walter Hearn, associate professor of biochemistry at Iowa State University, has said, "Science tells us what we *can* do, but it does not tell us what we *ought* to do. In my own life ultimate personal questions find their solution in my relationship to God through the person of Jesus Christ." *References:* John 3:8–12; 14:6; 18:37; Eph. 4:17–24.

Related illustrations: 228, 277, 715, 716.

Scoffers

See also **Infidels**

830. David Hume, the historian, philosopher, and skeptic, spent his life in traducing the Word of God. In his last moments he joked with those around him, but the intervals were filled with sadness. He wrote, "I am affrighted and confounded with the forlorn solitude in which I am placed by my philosophy. When I turn my eye inward, I find nothing but doubt and ignorance. Where am I and what? I begin to fancy myself in the most deplorable condition imaginable, environed in the deepest darkness." *References:* Ps. 73:6–28; Prov. 1:7; Is. 5:18–24; Jer. 17:15–18; 2 Peter 3:3–4.

831. What of the future of the church, its growth and continued existence? Enemies prophesy its speedy downfall. Diocletian, after a general persecution, had medals struck: "Christianity now at last extirpated." Voltaire, father of modern infidels, said in 1758, "In 20 years there will not remain a single altar to the God of the Christians." The blatant Ingersoll said, "In 10 years no more churches will be built." Your neighbors may say, "The Church cannot hold its own. The Gospel has outlived its usefulness. The passing of the old members will mark the end of the church." *References:* Deut. 18:21–22; Joshua 1:5; 23:9; Matt. 16:18; 1 Cor. 2:14; 1 John 4:1.

832. We live in a world in which selfish, proud, and conceited people place themselves and their own reason above God's Word and thereby assail our faith with all manner of doubt. They tell us that the immortality of the soul and the resurrection of the body is nothing more than wishful thinking, a sort of "pie in the sky when you die" philosophy. This godless thinking is not something new or peculiar to our day and age. Back in the 11th century an old Persian cynic and poet, Omar Khayyam sang in his *Rubaiyat:*

> Some for the glories of this world; and some
> Sigh for the Prophet's Paradise to come;
> Ah, take the cash, and let the credit go,
> Nor heed the rumble of a distant drum!

A thousand years before Omar Khayyam our Lord Himself was forced to contend with the same erroneous and harmful thinking. *References:* Ps. 73; Prov. 1:24–30; Acts 13:38–41; 2 Peter 3:3–10 (godless cynics are nothing new). Eccl. 2:1; Is. 22:13; Amos 6:3–8; Acts 17:18; 1 Cor. 15:32 (Epicureanism).

Related illustrations: 649, 802.

Second Coming of Christ

833. Some years ago a tourist was traveling along tne shores of Lake Como in Northern Italy. He wanted to visit especially one castle called Villa Arconti. When the tourist reached the castle, a friendly old gardener opened the gate and showed the tourist the grounds, which this old man kept in perfect order.

"How long have you been here?" the tourist asked. "Twenty-four years," replied the gardener. "And how often has the owner of the castle been here during that time?" "Four times." "When was he here the last time?" "Twelve years ago." "Never since then?" "Never." "Does he write to you?" "No." "From whom then do you get your instructions?" "From his agent at Milan." "Does this agent come out here quite often?" "Never." "Who, then, comes here?" "I am almost always alone—only once in a great while a tourist comes here." "But you keep this garden in such fine condition and take such excellent care of all the plants, just as though you expected your master to come tomorrow." "Today, sir, today," the old gardener promptly replied.

This answer made a deep impression on the tourist. How faithful that old man was to his trust! Day after day his thought was not "Tomorrow the master may come" but "Today, sir, today." Oh, how the Lord of heaven appreciates such faithfulness on the part of the workers in His vineyard that will always think: Today my Lord may return. I must work and be ready. *References:* Matt. 24:42–47; 25:1–13; Mark 13:32–35; Luke 12:35–40; 1 Thess. 5:5–6; Rev. 16:15.

834. The grandmother looking out the front-room window for the family to arrive for dinner on Christmas Day is not going to be nearly as ready as the grandmother basting the turkey in the kitchen and only now and then listening for the car coming into the driveway. You cannot always be looking heavenward for the personal appearance of our Lord, but it is possible for you to be prepared and ready for His coming. *References:* Matt. 24:37–46; 25:1–13; John 9:4; 1 Cor. 15:58; Heb. 6:10–12; Rev. 2:10.

Seeking God

835. Some years ago Roger W. Babson told of a visit he once paid to the president of the Argentine Republic. They sat in the sun parlor, overlooking a river. The president spoke: "Mr. Babson, I have been wondering why it is that South America, with all its natural resources, is so far behind North America, despite the fact that South America was settled before North America." The president went on to tell how the forests of South America had 286 kinds of trees that could be found in no book of botany. He spoke of the many ranches that had thousands of acres of alfalfa in one block. He mentioned the iron, coal, copper, silver, and gold mines of that continent. He pointed out that South America's great rivers had water power that rivaled Niagara. With all this as a prelude, the president asked: "Why is it that, with all these natural resources, South America is so far behind North America?"

Mr. Babson knew the answer, but being a guest, he wanted the president himself to answer the question. "I have come to this conclusion," the president said: "South America was settled by the Spanish, who came here in search of gold, but North America was settled by the Pilgrim Fathers, who went there in search of God." *References:* Deut. 4:29; 2 Chron. 7:14; Ps. 105:4; Prov. 8:17; Is. 55:6; Hos. 10:12; Acts 17:27; Heb. 11:6.

Related illustration: 829.

Self-centeredness

836. The ancient Greeks had a legend that Narcissus, the son of the river god, had fallen in love with himself after seeing his image in a pool of water. A seer had told his mother that her son must never see himself if he was to mature into manhood. For this reason everything that threw off a reflection, such as metal, was removed. But one day he found a spring that formed a pool filled with crystal-clear water. As Narcissus stooped to drink, he saw his reflection in the pool. He fell desperately in love with himself, and seeking to embrace himself, he fell into the water and drowned.

Everyone is more or less in love with self. The Bible says, "No one ever hated his own body, but he feeds and cares for it" (Eph. 5:29). And Jesus tells us that if we want to love someone very much, we must love him as much as we love ourselves. "Love your neighbor as yourself." But many people fall in love with themselves to such an abnormal extent that they become extremely selfish and self-centered, that they lose all interest in others or use them only as tools to obtain greater advantages for themselves. *References:* Prov. 12:15; 20:6; 26:12; Luke 18:10–12; 2 Cor. 10:12; Phil. 2:3.

837. A New York telephone company analyzed 500 telephone conversations and discovered that the most frequently used word was "I." It was used more than 4,000 times in those 500 short conversations. By nature we are all this way. We put "I" at the center. What we do is determined by what "I" want. *References:* Is. 14:13–14; Matt. 23:12; Luke 12:17–19.

Related illustration: 850.

Self-denial

838. Luther once said, "If someone

were to knock on the door of my heart and ask who lived here, I would say, 'Martin Luther used to live here, but he moved out, and Jesus Christ has moved in.' " *References:* Deut. 32:6; Song of Sol. 2:16; Rom. 8:9; 14:8; 1 Cor. 3:16; 6:19–20; 7:23.

839. As the body of David Livingstone was being brought back to London to be buried in Westminster Abbey, throngs lined the streets along the route. One man was obviously much moved. Someone standing next to him asked, "You knew the missionary well?"

"Yes," was the reply. "David and I were boyhood friends. Later we went to Africa together. David went for Africa's souls, and I went for Africa's gold. And today I realize I concentrated on the wrong world!" *References:* Matt. 5:11–12; 10:39; 19:29; 2 Cor. 4:11; 12:10; Phil. 1:21; 3:7–8.

840. Popular Christianity is an easy-fitting garment; it is like an old shoe that you slip off and on without any difficulty. But a religion that does not put up a strong barrier between you and many of your inclinations is not worth anything. The mark of a message from God is that it restrains and coerces, forbids and commands. (MacLaren) *References:* Prov. 16:32; 25:28; Rom. 6:12; 1 Cor. 6:12; 2 Peter 1:5–7.

841. Baron von Welz, who renounced his title and estates and went as a missionary to Dutch Guiana, where he filled a lonely grave, said as he gave up his title, "What to me is the title 'well-born' when I am born again in Christ? What to me is the title 'lord' when I desire to be a servant of Christ? What is it to me to be called 'Your Grace' when I have need of God's grace, help, and succor? All these vanities I will do away with, and all else I will lay at the feet of Jesus, my dearest Lord, that I may have no

hindrance in serving Him aright." Just so all God's children, intent on serving their Lord, remove their hearts from the world, its honor and glories, and their own selfish satisfactions and set them on things above. *References:* Matt. 20:25–28; Rom. 12:1–3; Phil. 3:13–14; Col. 3:1–4; Heb. 11:24–25; 1 John 2:15.

Selfishness

842. He who lives to benefit himself confers a benefit on the world when he dies. *References:* Prov. 11:26; Hab. 2:6–8.

843. The selfish person has a heart that, like a man's coffin, is just his own measure—long enough and broad enough comfortably to hold him with no room for anyone else. (Guthrie) *References:* Zech. 7:6; Luke 12:16–21; 16:19–22.

844. A Lonely Harvest. Don't look out for your interest too sharply, and do not take undue or unfair advantage of other people's generosity or use other people for your own ends. Viewed from this angle, no career offers a better example than Napoleon's. He was a good soldier but a fool in many ways, a selfish fool. He ended in exile on the island of St. Helena. But that is not the point. The question is, Who was there to share his exile? His wife? No. She returned to her father. Berthier, his lifelong comrade in success? No. This comrade deserted him without saying good-by and became a captain in Louis XVIII's bodyguard.

Two of Napoleon's trusted marshals openly insulted him at the end. Even the servants who had slept across his bedroom threshold for years left him flat. "Ingratitude!" you say. Oh, no. Napoleon himself set the example. Let me quote him in his heyday of pomp and power.

"After all," said he, "I care only for people who are useful to me, and so long as they are useful." Or again: "I have made courtiers. I never pretend to make friends."

There is a public monument to Napoleon in Paris now. But those who knew him best when he lived raised no monument to him on St. Helena. The epitaph of this miserable, selfish man might be: "I care only for people who are useful to me." Don't let that be yours! *References:* Gen. 4:9; 1 Sam 25:10–11; Is. 56:11; Matt. 23:4; 25:41–46; Luke 10:31–32; Phil. 2:21. *Related illustrations:* 624, 836, 848.

Self-righteousness
See also **Works-righteousness**
845. People have gone down into hell, as the Pharisee did to his house, thanking God that they are not like others. (Guthrie) *Reference:* Luke 18:11–12.

846. The well-known habit of the hen is that when it has laid an egg, it announces the fact by loud cackling. The spiritually proud and self-righteous are like that. (Scriver) *References:* Ps. 49:6–7; James 3:5; 4:16.

847. Can you identify the speaker of the following quotation?

I have spent the best years of my life giving people the lighter pleasures, helping them to have a good time, and all I get is abuse, the existence of a hunted man.

Who was this man—some public servant from the world of politics, sports, mass media, or business? No. It was Al Capone. At one time America's Public Enemy Number One, Capone actually regarded himself as a public benefactor, one who was unappreciated and misunderstood.

Lewis Lawes, who for many years was America's most famous warden, once stated:

Few of the criminals in Sing Sing regard themselves as bad men. They are just as human as you and I. So they rationalize, they explain. They can tell you why they had to crack a safe or be quick on the trigger finger. Most of them try by fallacious and illogical reasoning, to justify their antisocial acts even to themselves, consequently stoutly maintaining that they should never have been imprisoned at all.

References: Is. 5:23; Amos 5:6–7; Matt. 7:21–23; Luke 18:11–12.
Related illustrations: 479, 506, 788, 867.

Servanthood
848. Height of True Nobility. *Ich dien'* (I serve) is the proud motto of the Prince of Wales. We read and ponder and are startled. How these words clash with the attitude that people commonly take toward life! Out in the world we see how people make every effort to fling themselves into positions where they are able to command and force others to serve them. They are willing to serve, but only themselves. Selfishness has ever afflicted the world of sinners; it is the besetting sin of our age. *Ich dien'*—I serve. The person whose heart speaks these words rises to heights of true nobility. *References:* Matt. 20:25–28; 23:11; Luke 22:26; 1 Peter 2:11–20; 5:5.

849. Our Top Priority. Some years ago someone asked John Wanamaker, "How do you find time to manage a Sunday school of four thousand children in addition to the business of your two stores, your work as postmaster-general, and other obligations?" Instantly Mr. Wanamaker replied, "Why, the Sunday school is my business! All the other matters are just things." *References:* 1 Sam. 7:3; 2 Chron. 15:15; Matt. 4:10; 6:19–24; Luke 2:49; John 9:4.
Related illustrations: 34, 141, 143,

249, 396, 679, 839, 841, 897.

Sex

850. A college boy in an eastern school was quoted as saying, "Sex is conquest, love is surrender. Who wants to surrender?" *References:* 1 Cor. 5:1–2; 6:18; Eph. 5:2–3.

851. There is considerable talk about how premarital sexual relations are valuable, if not indispensable, ways to test compatibility in marriage, to find out ahead of time if one is suited biologically. Here I would agree with Waldo Beech when he suggests that "this is one of the flimsiest rationalizations on the campus market today." It would be bought only by people who measure marital compatibility solely in physical folklore. In fact, statistically speaking, chances for a durable marriage are higher among those who have not gone in for sexual experimentation before marriage than among those who have (although durability of marriage is dependent on many other factors than the sexual one). *References:* Rom. 6:11–13; 13:14; 1 Cor. 9:24–27; Gal. 5:16, 24; Col. 3:5; 1 Thess. 4:1–3; 1 Peter 2:11.

Signs

852. An ancient allegory told of a man who had made a contract with death that the latter was not to appear until he had sent three messengers. The man felt quite secure and gave no thought to his death. One day he fell ill; the doctor had to be called and pronounced his condition serious. His wife told him that his condition alarmed her. Asking for a mirror, he corroborated the judgment of his wife. Still he did not feel any anxiety because he felt that death would have to send his three messengers before he could approach him. All of a sudden the dreaded visitor entered. When the man remonstrated, death pointed to his three messengers:

the physician, the wife, and the man himself. He had been given the promised warnings but had not recognized them as such. Let us not make the mistake of overlooking the signs of the Last Day that God places around us in such abundance. *References:* Matt. 24:36–51; Mark 13:32–37; Luke 19:41–44; 21:35.

853. A proverb of the Greeks insists: "The feet of the avenging deities are shod with wool!" But the feet of our God are not thus shod. There was no deceiving noiselessness in the approach of His judgment on these Christ-rejecting communities. Before He struck, Jesus sounded His trumpet: "Woe to you, Korazin! Woe to you, Bethsaida! . . . And you, Capernaum . . ." *References:* Ezek. 33:11; Matt. 3:1–3; 11:20–24; John 16:7–11; Acts 2:37–40; Rom. 1:18–20; 2 Peter 2:20.

Simplicity

854. "Simplicity," said Longfellow, "is the supreme excellence in character, in manners, in style, in all things." *References:* Ps. 116:6; Matt. 5:3; 11:25; Mark 9:35–37; 10:15; Luke 9:46–48; 18:17; 2 Cor. 1:12.

Sin

See also **Depravity, Original Sin**

855. Sin is like the descent of a hill; every step we take increases the difficulty of our return. (Guthrie) *References:* Rom. 1:24–32; 2 Tim. 3:13; 1 Peter 2:11.

856. The error of neither knowing nor understanding what sin is usually brings with it another error, that of neither knowing nor understanding what grace is. (Luther) *References:* Ps. 32:5; Rom. 2:1–4; 5:20; 1 John 1:9.

857. Whoever finds pleasure in evil and pain in virtue is a novice in both. *References:* Prov. 2:10–22; Jer. 14:10; 2 Thess. 2:11–12.

858. Sins of omission are no less

deadly than sins of commission, even as hunger, if unfed, is no less deadly than sickness. *References:* Matt. 23:23; 25:45; James 4:17.

859. Of the Righteous. If a shoe is covered with mud, a splash or two more or less will make no difference; but if it is polished and clean, one speck shows. (MacLaren) *References:* Ps. 32:1–5; Rom. 7:19–25; 1 John 1:8–10.

860. When we get the prize for our wrongdoing, we find that it is not as all-satisfying as we expected it would be. As the proverb has it, "The chase is a great deal more than the hare." (MacLaren) *References:* Ps. 36:1–2; Micah 6:5; 1 Tim. 6:9–10.

861. There is perhaps no clearer proof that people are bad than the sort of people whom they consent to call good. (MacLaren) *References:* Is. 5:20; Mal. 2:17; Luke 6:26.

862. Dwight L. Moody used to say that if we had to go about with a glass window over our hearts, we would all want that window to be stained glass, for our hearts are rotten to the core. *References:* Ps. 53:3; Eccl. 8:11; 9:3; Is. 64:6; Jer. 17:9; Mark 7:21–23; Heb. 3:12.

863. When water of its own accord rises above its fountain, then may Adam's children boast of a nature loftier than his. The tree is diseased not at the top but at the root. (Guthrie) *References:* Ps. 51:5; 58:3; Ezek. 18:2.

864. A rattlesnake is a rattlesnake whether it be a foot or a yard long. As the gravest sin is pardonable under the Gospel, the smallest sin is damnable according to the Law. (Nitzsch) *References:* Matt. 5:19; James 2:10.

865. You take a tiger cub into your house. It is graceful in its motions, playful, and affectionate. But it grows up and becomes your master—if not your murderer. Keep little sins out of your heart! (MacLaren) *References:* Prov. 28:13; Rom. 1:18.

866. Hammarsten: "A single sin, whatever its name, may enslave you for life. A single wrong turn of a railroad switch may cause a great disaster. A single leak in a ship may cause it to sink beneath the waves. It does not require many sins to ensnare the soul." *References:* Gen. 2:16–17; Num. 20:7–13; 1 Sam. 13:13–14; Rom. 5:12.

867. How idle to talk of other men being greater sinners than we are—to flatter and deceive ourselves with that! A person who has his or her head beneath one inch of water drowns as surely as the one who, with a millstone hung round the neck, has sunk a hundred fathoms down. (Guthrie) *References:* Ps. 130:3; Prov. 20:9; Rom. 3:19.

868. Sin's Besetting Nature. We once saw the ruins of a latticed window that eloquently portrayed the nature and the power of sin. A strong vine several inches thick had completely wrecked the once beautiful window and held a few remnants of the latticework in a viselike grip. Can you not picture the encroaching, the besetting, the destroying work of that vine? At some time, when the window still had its original beauty, a tiny, tender tendril found its way into the lattice. Had it been removed at that time, it would have worked no harm. But it was not removed. It was permitted to stay and to twine itself through the lattice. How aptly this describes the besetting nature and the power of sin! Sin also approaches us as something soft, sweet, and most desirable. If met at once with the weapons that God's Word supplies, it can be shaken off before it gains a deadly hold. But if left unmolested to stay, to grow, and to entwine itself into the heart of a person, it grows stronger and stronger, until it thoroughly wrecks the person's heart and life and leads to eternal ruin. *References:* Prov. 1:10–19; Rom. 6:12–14; 7:11; Heb. 3:13; 12:1; James 1:14–15.

869. An Epidemic. In 1868 a Frenchman imported a few gypsy moths to this country to crossbreed them with silkworms. One night a few of them escaped from the cage at his home in Melrose, Mass. He was terrified and notified the neighbors of his alarm. They laughed him to scorn. But 20 years later every bit of green foliage for miles around Melrose was devoured, and today we spend $75,000,000 every year just to keep the "gyp" under control in New England. Sin is like that. "Sin entered the world through one man, and death through sin, and in this way death came to all men." *References:* Ex. 20:5; Is. 43:27–28; Jer. 7:26; 16:12; Lam. 5:7; Rom. 5:12; 1 Cor. 5:6.

870. The Great Enemy. A pastor, as was his custom, was holding the annual examination of his flock, at which both old and young were asked to express the hope that was in them. Asking which were the greatest and most terrible enemies of the human race, he received the answer, "Sin, death, and the devil." He now turned to a child and asked which one of these was the greatest enemy. The child answered, "Death. I do not wish to die and be buried in the grave." He then turned to a man and asked the same question, and the reply was, "The devil; for when I think of hell, a shudder comes over me, and my hairs stand on end." Finally he accosted an old woman who was well versed in the Word of God, and she answered, "Sin; for if this enemy had not first bound us with his chain, death and the devil could have no power over us." *References:* Gen. 3:19; Joshua 7:11–12; Prov. 8:36;

Ezek. 18:4; Rom. 5:12; 6:19–23; 2 Thess. 2:11–12.

871. On a cold winter day a man was watching the rapids above Niagara Falls. He noticed the carcass of a sheep floating along in the swift current. Presently he saw an eagle swoop down on the carcass to feed. The eagle was aware of the falls, but it had no fear, for when it got to the brink, it could lift its powerful wings and fly away in safety. But the eagle had not considered one thing, namely, the paralyzing power of frost. At the last moment it lifted its wings to fly, but its feet were frozen fast to the sheep's fleece, and so this "king of birds," in spite of its powerful wings, went over the falls and was dashed to pieces on the rocks below. *References:* 1 Kings 11:4–8; 1 Chron. 10:13; Rom. 3:23; 6:19–23; 8:12–13.

872. Sin's Allurement. During the Middle Ages, when an apostate church was persecuting the people of God, the Spanish inquisitors used an instrument of torture called "The Virgin." It had the form of a beautiful woman dressed in gorgeous robes with an inviting smile on her face and arms outstretched. Into those arms the poor victim was pushed in order to kiss "The Virgin." By means of a secret mechanism, her arms enclosed him in a deadly embrace, and he was pierced through with a hundred hidden knives.

Certainly sin is always like that "Virgin." It puts on a beautiful exterior and smilingly invites us to take its arm and walk along the paths of worldly delight. Sin always offers its victims the fairest propositions and most alluring prospects, but once those proposals and pleasures are accepted, it leaves its victims deceived and condemned to eternal death. *References:* Gen. 3:6; Joshua 7:20–21; 1 Kings 11:1–4; Prov.

9:17–18; 14:2; James 1:14–15; 2 Peter 2:18.

873. The Deep Darkness of Sin. We are quite simply "in the dark." Our condition is far more critical than being without physical light. It cannot be penetrated by spotlights or laser beams. It is the darkness that Jesus describes when He says, "If then the light within you is darkness, how great is that darkness!"

The only fitting comparison to our condition is what astronomers have termed a "black hole." Their theory suggests that deep in space there are collapsed stars so dense and with such strong gravitational pull that they literally swallow up everything—planets, moons, and stars. They all disappear into this dark abyss, and not even light can escape.

Such a black hole is right here, as the Lord says, within us. It's the black hole of our sin. It's the darkness of death itself. Pointing to the heart of our problem, the psalmist cries: "Some sat in darkness and the deepest gloom, prisoners suffering in iron chains, for they had rebelled against the words of God and despised the counsel of the Most High" (Ps. 107:10–11). *References:* Ps. 107:10–11; Is. 9:2; 60:2; Matt. 6:23; John 3:19; Rom. 13:12; Eph. 5:8.

874. Our One Great Problem. That we do not need a new gospel is illustrated by an incident at the University of California. A thorough study was made of termites, and the findings were printed in a pamphlet, *The Control of Termites.* Thousands of these pamphlets were produced and stored on shelves. When they were to be distributed, it was discovered that termites had eaten the whole stack hollow.

This illustrates what is happening in our nation and in the whole world. All the latest discoveries will not help us if sin is eating away at our hearts and destroying our moral fiber. What the community needs more than anything is the Spirit of God working in the hearts of men and women. *References:* Eccl. 2:11; Is. 5:1–2; Matt. 16:26; Mark 8:36; Col. 3:2; Rev. 3:17.

875. Sinful Human Inclination. A cat goes up quickly into the topmost branches of a tree, but it does not come down so quickly. It cannot come down head first. Its claws were made to work the other way, and it has to turn around and back down. It is just the opposite with people. It is a great deal easier for them to come down than to go up; they incline to sin and evil. (Beecher) *References:* Ps. 52:3; Micah 7:2–4; Mark 7:21; Rom. 5:12.

876. Sin is a dangerous playmate. A performer used to demonstrate his power over a boa constrictor. Keeping the snake's head before him and under the constant control of his eyes, he would let it coil around his body to the amazement of onlookers. But on one occasion he made the fatal mistake of taking his controlling gaze from the snake before it had entered its hidden cage. Thinking that his pet was safely in the cage, he turned to acknowledge the prolonged applause of the audience. The reptile, noting its opportunity, quickly and quietly returned and, taking the performer by surprise, coiled itself around his body, this time free of the controlling eye of its master. The spectators, thinking that this was still part of the act, applauded and did not realize the seriousness of the situation until the agonizing cries of the performer and the cracking of his bones convinced them that he had fallen prey to his pet.

Thus sin, petted and played with and seemingly under the control of the sinner, will eventually ensnare and crush its victims and drag them into the bottomless pit of hell. *References:* Prov.

14:9; 26:11; 28:26; Eccl. 10:1; 1 Cor. 5:6; 10:12.

877. Everyone's Business. A minister was speaking in a college chapel when one student asked another, "What is this business of sin he's talking about?" The other replied, "I think it has something to do with Adam and Eve." The first student concluded, "Oh, then it doesn't have anything to do with us." But I assure you, this business of sin does vitally pertain to you and me. *References:* Ps. 53:3; Prov. 20:9; Micah 7:2; Rom. 3:23; Gal. 3:22.

Related illustrations: 124, 242, 349, 417, 464, 561, 563, 617, 753, 895, 924, 948.

Slander

See also **Lying**

878. When someone complained to President Coolidge about the slanderers of George Washington, Coolidge looked out of the White House at the monument erected in honor of Washington and said, "I see his monument is still standing." *References:* Ps. 31:13–16; 101:5–6; Prov. 10:18.

879. Alexander the Great used to hold one ear closed when someone was accused, saying it was reserved for the absent one. (Dallmann) *References:* Ps. 31:13; Jer. 9:4.

880. Emperor Theodosius commanded that no one who spoke against him should be punished; "for what was spoken lightly," said he, "was to be laughed at; what spitefully, pardoned; what angrily, to be pitied; and if truly, he would thank him for it." (Spencer) *References:* Matt. 5:38–39; Luke 6:27–35; Col. 3:13.

Social Concerns

881. Of the Churchgoer. Gordon Allport in *The Nature of Prejudice* reports on some studies of the relationship between a person's churchgoing and concern for oppressed minorities. The findings present a paradox. Churchgoing people are both *more* concerned and *less* concerned than nonchurchgoing people. Allport explains that churchgoing people whose relationship to the church is purely institutional are *less* concerned for oppressed minorities than are nonchurchgoers. They regard their churchgoing as a safe and social thing to do. On the other hand, churchgoing people who have taken seriously the teachings of Jesus on love and brotherhood are far *more* concerned for oppressed minorities than are nonchurchgoing people. Once again, the deeper our faith and identification with Christ, the greater will be our concern for people, and the greater our concern for people, the greater also will be our sorrow when we see these people suffer. *References:* Deut. 15:7–11; Ps. 82:3–4; Matt. 19:21; 25:31–46; Acts 20:35; Gal. 6:10; 1 Tim. 6:17–18; James 1:27.

882. In 1966 the manuscript of *In His Steps,* the 1896 novel credited with helping revolutionize the nation's and the church's attitude toward social problems, was sold for $4,500. It was the most widely read religious novel of all time. The story begins with a minister trying to write a sermon on the basis of 1 Peter 2:21. He is interrupted by a shabbily dressed man who asks for help in finding a job. The pastor excuses himself from offering any help because he has a sermon to write on this Friday morning. The man shows up in the kindergarten class taught by the pastor's wife. He shows up in the Sunday morning worship service and dies of a heart attack.

Before he dies he talks to the congregation about the songs they had been singing—songs that spoke of taking the cross of Jesus and leaving all and following Him; of giving their all for Jesus, all their powers and thoughts, all they did all the days and hours of their life. The shabbily dressed man, about to die, conjectures about what Jesus would do and wonders out loud before the congregation about the big churches and good clothes and nice houses, the money spent for luxuries and summer vacations by members of the churches while people outside the churches by the thousands died in tenements, walked the streets for jobs, never had a piano or picture in the house—not even one painted by numbers—and grew up in misery and sin. Ask yourself, "What would Jesus do?" *References:* Ex. 23:11; Ps. 41:1; Prov. 19:17; Is. 58:7; Matt. 25:31–46; Luke 10:25–37; Acts 20:35; 1 Peter 2:21.

Related illustrations: 158, 280, 357, 441, 460, 461, 615, 707, 874.

Solitude

883. "You see," said an Ozark blacksmith to a traveler, pointing to the front axle of a farm wagon in his shop, "these axles last. My father cut this from the heart of a hickory tree 20 years ago, and it is still good. It does not bend or crack or break. It was taken from a lone tree. My father used to travel over the hills in search of sound lumber, and if he found a good tree, he would purchase it as it stood and cut it into timbers for his shop. By experience he found that the strongest wood was taken from trees that stood alone. So he would select hickories that grew in open space, and of these he would make his best axles and wagon tongues. Those trees that stood alone proved to be by far the strongest. They had stood up under the storms where there was no protection, and their wood was of the finest grain and as strong as steel. You can't break those tongues and axles."

So it is better to stand alone than to make unsound compromises. (Th. Graebner) *References:* Ex. 23:2; Ps. 1; Prov. 4:14; 24:1; Jer. 15:15–21; John 15:19; 16:32.

Sorrow

884. May Lead to Ultimate Blessings. In the Church of St. Nicholas in Amsterdam, Holland, there is a wonderful chime of bells. If you go into the tower of the church, you will see a man with wooden gloves on his hands pounding on a keyboard. As you listen, you hear nothing but the clanging of the keys and the harsh, deafening noise of the bells over your head. From that position the bells seem to have no harmony or meaning whatever.

But if you were standing out on the street a few blocks away, you would be entranced by the beautiful harmony of the bells.

So it is with the sorrows of life. They often seem harsh, cruel, and inexplicable. But in later years they will have an entirely new meaning. We will see then that the omniscient hand of God was producing sweet and harmonious music in our lives, and we did not know. (*Light on the Gospels*) *References:* Is. 51:3; 61:1–3; John 16:19–23; Rom. 8:22–28; 1 Cor. 13:12; 1 Thess. 4:13–18; 1 Peter 1:3–9; Rev. 7:9–17.

885. The Mystery of Sorrow. The famous artist Thomas Nast once sought to explain the mystery of sorrow. With rapid strokes of his brushes he painted a beautiful country scene on a canvas— green meadows, fields ripe with grain, a house and barn, a rippling brook, birds in the trees, and a bright, blue sky with fleecy clouds. He stepped back from the easel, and the audience applauded loudly. It was a wonderful, peaceful scene.

"But," he said, "the picture is not

finished," and turned to brush it with dark, somber colors. Sweeping the canvas with apparent recklessness, he made daubs and blotches such as a child might make in smearing. Out went the blue sky and peaceful countryside until only a patch of each was left at the top and bottom. "Now," he said, "the picture is finished and perfect." No one applauded. All sat puzzled and doubtful.

Then the artist turned the picture on one end, and the whole crowd gasped in amazement, for now they saw a beautiful, dark waterfall, masses of water pouring over moss-covered rocks and raising rainbow hues in the air. He had changed the first quiet scene into the rich, beautiful second one while the audience thought he was ruining the canvas. (*Day Dawn*, p. 146) *References:* Ps. 30:5; Is. 25:8–9; 35:1–10; John 14:1–2; 1 Cor. 15:50–58; 2 Cor. 4:17; Rev. 21:4.

Soul
886. Carnal reason cannot understand how a soul can subsist after its separation from the body. But eagles see more than owls. *References:* Eccl. 12:7; Matt. 10:28; Rev. 20:4.

887. Giving One's Soul to the Devil. Luther had a maid in his house named Elizabeth, who, contrary to his wishes, left his service and became so wicked that she gave her soul to the devil. Not long after, she was stricken with a serious disease and became very despondent. At her request Luther was called to her bedside. When he arrived, Elizabeth confessed to him that she felt very sorry for what she had done and also revealed to him her greatest grief, namely, that she had given her soul to the devil.

"That is nothing," replied Luther. "Listen, if you had given all my clothes to a stranger when you were

still in my service, would that have been a valid transaction?" "No," answered the maid. "Well," Luther replied, "thus it is here. Your soul does not belong to the devil, but to Jesus, your Lord. You cannot give away what does not belong to you. Go therefore to your Lord and ask Him to receive again what belongs to Him; but cast the sin that you have committed back on the devil, because that belongs to him." The maid did as Luther advised and soon thereafter was found calm and happy. (Rodenmeyer) *References:* Is. 15:21–28; 43:1; 55:6–7; 2 Cor. 5:18–19; Col. 1:20.
Related illustrations: 125, 503.

Soul Saving
See also **Witnessing**
888. A real fisherman with very crude tools often catches more fish than the city "dude" with every angler's appliance at his disposal. The theologically and doctrinally trained student is not always the best soul winner. *References:* Eph. 4:11; Jude 22–23.

889. Don't Lose Heart. Robert Morrison, the pioneer Protestant missionary in China worked there for seven years before he baptized his first convert, and during his 27 years of service he won only 10 converts, but they were the firstfruits of a great harvest. *References:* Matt. 28:19; Mark 16:15; Gal. 6:9.

890. When Dr. John Broadus, great preacher of the last century, was converted as a little boy, he went to one of his schoolmates, Sandy Jones, a red-haired chap, and was instrumental in bringing him to Christ. At the close of the service in which he confessed Christ, Sandy came to his friend and said, "Thank you, John! Thank you!" Dr. Broadus later left that little town and became the president of a large seminary. Every summer when he went home, an awkward, red-headed farmer in plain clothes and with red mud on his boots would come up and stick out his big bony hand and say, "Howdy, John. Thank you, John! Thank you for telling me about Jesus!" His friends tell us that when Dr. Broadus lay dying and his family was gathered around him, the doctor said, "The sweetest sound I expect to hear in heaven, next to the welcoming voice of Him whom, having not seen, I have tried to love and serve, will be the welcome voice of Sandy Jones, saying, 'Howdy, John, and thank you, John!' "

When I enter that beautiful city,
And the saved all around me appear,
I want to hear somebody tell me,
It was you who invited me here.

References: Ps. 126:6; Luke 15:6–7; Acts 15:3; Phil. 2:16; 1 Thess. 2:19–20; Heb. 12:2.

891. Some years ago the *Walther League Messenger* told a most touching story of an aged minister who was informed by one of his deacons that there was something radically wrong with his preaching because only one person had been added to the church in a whole year, and that person was only a boy. But was his service in vain? Years later, when the minister had already gone to his heavenly reward, that one boy, now a man, returned to London from Africa as a missionary whom the entire nation revered. Not only had he brought to Jesus one of the most savage African chiefs, but he had also translated the Bible into African dialects, so that the Word of God might become known to them. And so it may be with you, my dear friends. The one soul you bring to Jesus may serve the kingdom of God better than the crowds. *References:* John 1:40–42, 45; Acts 9:17.

892. Are you saved, seated above the boiling sea of guilt, safe on the Rock of Ages? Then reach down your hand to pull up this and that other drowning wretch! I would rather see people with eager eyes and outstretched arms bending down to draw others up on the rock than to see them on their knees thanking God for their own escape and safety. (Guthrie) *References:* Is. 52:7; Hos. 2:23; Matt. 24:14; 28:19; Acts 1:8; Rom. 10:13–15; 15:9.

893. A young artist named Tucker painted the picture of a forlorn mother and child in a storm. This vision took such hold on him that he laid aside his pallette and brush and said, "I must go to the lost instead of painting them." He became the great bishop of Uganda, Africa, and one of the "Who's Who" in the mission world. It is well to give for missions; it is better to tell of Jesus. It is the personal contact that wins the soul.

Passing through a slave market at Rome, Augustine of Canterbury saw a group of fair-haired Saxons on sale. On being told that they were "Angles," he remarked, "Not Angles, but angels," and set forth to evangelize Britain. *References:* Matt. 9:35–38; 10:5–15; Luke 10:1–12; 15:1–6; Acts 8:26–38.

Sovereignty of God

894. German Lutheran Bishop Hanns Lilje, rudely arrested and thrown into prison by the Nazis during World War II, describes his impressions when the guards would scamper for cover as the Allied bombers dropped their deadly load: "When the guards had fled and we were alone up there in the darkness, we felt as if their power had been removed; for a few moments, at any rate, we felt the pressure of their authority lifted, and we knew ourselves to be in the hands of the Lord of life and death, whose sovereignty was exercised over them and us alike." (Hanns Lilje, *The*

Valley of the Shadow [Philadelphia: Muhlenberg Press, 1950], p. 75.) *References:* 2 Chron. 20:6; Job 12:19; Ps. 2; 10:16; Dan. 7:14; Rev. 17:14; 19:6.

Spiritual Death

895. As an Indian evangelist was preaching, a flippant youth interrupted him. "You tell about the burden of sin. I feel none. How heavy is it?" The preacher answered, "Tell me, if you laid four hundred pounds weight on a corpse, would it feel the load?" The youth replied, "No, because it's dead." The preacher said, "And that spirit, too, is dead that feels no load of sin." *References:* Jer. 6:15; 8:12; Zeph. 3:5; 1 Tim. 4:2; 5:6.
Related illustration: 395.

Spiritual Gifts

896. A $50,000 violin hanging silently and dusty on the wall is not worth as much as a kitchen spoon that is used. *References:* Matt. 25:14–30; Luke 19:11–26; Rom. 12:13; 1 Peter 4:10.

897. Discovering Your Gift. The life of Gladys Aylward has become an inspiration to many through the book *The Small Woman* and the movie *The Inn of the Sixth Happiness.* A native of Britain, she went to China in 1920, "bought" orphans who were being discarded, and made a home for them. When the Japanese invaded, she had to flee with 100 children and ended up on Formosa, continuing to devote her life to raising children who knew no other mother. She explains, "I did not choose this. I was led into it by God. I am not really more interested in children than I am in other people, but God through His Holy Spirit gave me to understand that this is what He wanted me to do, so I did."

As you try various forms of service, you gradually discover the special gift that God has given to you, and you can also say, "This is what God wants me

to do." *References:* Rom. 12:3–8; 1 Cor. 4:7; 12:4–12.

898. Making the Best of What You Have. When Cathy Rigby, one of the gymnasts on the United States Olympic Team in Munich in 1972, failed in her dream to win the coveted gold medal, she was crushed. She sat down with her parents ready for a big cry and faltered, "I'm sorry. I did my best." Her mother echoed to her the word she had heard from her mother, "You know that, and I know that, and I'm sure God knows that, too. Doing your best is more important than being the best." God doesn't expect you to be the best in the church in terms of accomplishing the most or having the most attention. He only expects that you do the best with the gift He gives you. Discover that gift and use it for Him. *References:* Prov. 22:29; Eccl. 9:10: Matt. 25:14–30; Rom. 12:4–8; 1 Cor. 4:2; Heb. 6:10–11; 2 Peter 1:10; 3:14.
Related illustrations: 477, 957.

Spiritual Growth

899. When Thorvaldsen, the great Norwegian sculptor, had finished his masterpiece, he examined it carefully. He found no flaw, nothing to improve. Then he burst into tears. Since the work he had completed was flawless as far as he could tell, further growth for him was impossible. Henceforth his powers would decline.

It is human nature to try to improve, to develop one's powers, and to grow. The possibility of growth is the inspiration of life, something that makes living really worth while. *References:* Eph. 4:15; Phil. 3:12–14; Col. 1:10; 1 Thess. 3:12; 4:10; Heb. 6:1; 1 Peter 2:2; 2 Peter 3:18.

900. A man who had previously taken little interest in his religious faith once said to Dwight Moody, famed evangelist of yesterday, "I attended one of your meetings a year ago, and I was saved." "That's interesting," Moody replied, "but what is more interesting is what happened since. What progress have you made in your Christian life?" It was the same Mr. Moody who, in speaking of the struggles of the Christian life, said: "I have had more trouble with Dwight Moody than with any other man I know." This is what Paul is describing to the Philippians: "Not that I have already obtained all this, or have already been made perfect, but I press on" (1959, p. 147.) *References:* 1 Cor. 14:20; Eph. 4:14–15; Phil. 3:12–14; 1 Thess. 3:12; 4:10; Heb. 5:12–6:1; 2 Peter 1:5–6; 3:18.

Related illustrations: 52, 93, 128, 173, 290, 430.

Spiritual Power

901. Joe DiMaggio, one-time home run hitter for the New York Yankees, once asked his teammate, Lefty Gomez, what to say when sportswriters asked where his great power came from. "Don't worry about that," Gomez replied. "It's when they ask you where your power went that it's time to worry." We may not be able to explain or understand how God's power helps us to resist temptation and to choose loyal service to Him. That's not our concern. But when people can no longer see that power at work in and through our lives, then we need to be concerned that we are somehow blocking the power of God's love from working for us. *References:* Eccl. 11:5; John 3:8; Rom. 11:33.

902. Jesus, Our Power Source. The great Scottish preacher, George Jeffrey, once told of his visit to Niagara Falls. He reported that even more impressive than the great flow of Niagara's mighty waters was the small power station he inspected at the edge of the falls. In this quiet place one heard only the faint hum of the dynamos. No more than a trickle of Niagara's waters had been harnessed, and yet this station supplied light and power for miles around. In a very similar way, each Christian serves as a conductor of God's power as we minister to one another's needs. And yet that power can never be exhausted, for it has its foundation not in our good intentions or our own human resources; it has its foundation in Jesus Christ. It is a power that only persistent faith can apprehend.

> His love has no limits, His grace has no
>   measure,
> His power no boundary known unto
>   men,
> For out of His infinite riches in Jesus
> He giveth and giveth and giveth again.

References: Mal. 3:10; Matt. 28:18–19; Luke 6:38; 2 Cor. 12:9–10; Eph. 3:14–21; Phil. 4:13, 19; 2 Tim. 4:17–18.

Related illustration: 209.

Stewardship
See also **Giving**

903. One day a meat packer was asked, "What is your business?" He answered, "I am a Christian." Rather puzzled and perplexed over the answer, the inquirer continued, "Sir, you evidently did not understand me. I mean, what is your daily business in life?" "My daily business is to be a Christian. I pack meat to pay the expenses." *References:* Matt. 6:24; 22:37; Eph. 6:5.

904. There is an old legend—and it is, of course, merely a legend—that after Jesus had ascended into heaven, the angel Gabriel asked Him, "Who is going to carry on Your work now?" And Jesus answered, "I have left it to John and Peter and Andrew and the others." Gabriel then asked, "What if they don't do it?" Jesus answered, "I have made no other plans."

Christ has no hands but our hands
 To do His work today;
He has no feet but our feet
 To lead men in His way;
He has no tongue but our tongues
 To tell men how He died;
He has no help but our help
 To bring them to His side.

References: Is. 6:8; Luke 4:43; John 15:16; Acts 1:8; 2 Cor. 5:19; Col. 1:25–29; 1 Tim. 1:11; Titus 1:3.

905. There are two seas in the same country, both within a short distance of each other, both fed by the same stream of water. But they are as different from each other as day and night. One is the Sea of Galilee, the other the Dead Sea. The river is the Jordan. The one is alive and fresh, its waters sweet and pure, a home of fish, a bearer of commerce. Vegetation crowds its shores. It gives as much as it receives and seems happy in the giving. Having taken into itself the waters of the Jordan, it generously sends them on again into the valley to the south toward the other sea.

The second body of water lies in a sunken valley, dead and still. There is no fish life in its salty waters; no commerce moves on its glassy bosom. No vegetation carpets its bleak shores. It swallows up all the water brought to it by the stream that feeds it, but not a drop does it give off or send on, and it remains what it has been for centuries—a lifeless, barren, watery waste.

This illustrates the difference between those who take but do not give and those who build a life of service and stewardship out of what is given. The same stream of bounteous divine blessings feeds both, and the latter become sources of joy and good things to others, but the former end up being curses even to themselves. *References:* Ps. 41:1–3; Prov. 3:9–10; 11:25; Mal. 3:8–12; Luke 6:38; 14:12–14; 2 Cor. 9:6–8.

Related illustrations: 180, 491, 939.

Straying from God

906. In 1845 a Texas pioneer named Sam Maverick accepted a herd of four hundred cattle in payment of a debt. He put them under the care of one of his men on his nearly 400,000-acre ranch. Here they were neglected and allowed to run wild. When calves were born, they were unmarked and consequently appropriated by neighboring ranchers, who immediately branded them. Their ownership could no longer be disputed, because the brand was the legal mark of identity. From this event developed the term *maverick*—an unbranded animal found straying and appropriated by the first finder.

That seems to mirror the history and character of humanity. "We all, like sheep, have gone astray," wrote Isaiah; "each of us has turned to his own way" (Is. 53:6). While under the ownership of God, humanity, including you and me, strayed away—became "mavericks." And invariably we are branded by other gods, the innumerable idols of this world. *References:* Is. 53:6; Jer. 50:6; Ezek. 34:6; Matt. 9:36; Mark 6:34; Eph. 2:12; 1 Peter 2:25; 2 Peter 2:12–15.

Related illustration: 99.

Strength

907. God Not on the Side of the Strong. Napoleon insolently sneered, "I observe that God is usually on the side of the strongest battalions." And how did God answer the taunt? In 1812 the glittering ranks of France and its tributary kings—numbering some 600,000 men—crossed the Niemen to invade Russia. They captured Smolensk, won the bloody battle of Borodino, and approached Moscow. Then God sent down on them the soft, feathery flakes of feeble, innocent snow. The snows of God, the soft snows that a breath can melt, were too strong for the mightiest battalions. The French soldiers perished by thousands, and the Cossacks with their lances thrust out the miserable, frozen, famine-stricken remnant that the northern winter had not slain. God was not on the side of the strongest battalion that time. Alexander of Russia knew to whom he owed the victory, if Napoleon did not, and on his commemorative medal were the words, "Not to us, O LORD, not to us but to your name be the glory" (Ps. 115:1). *References:* Ps. 20:7–8; Is. 10:12; 14:11–15; 26:5–6; 36:11–37:7; 60:14; Matt. 11:23; Luke 1:50–53.

908. As the Lutheran *Weimer Bible* tersely puts it, "When Samson had been shaved, he was not strong as before, not because his strength was actually in his hair, but because God had sustained him with extraordinary strength only so long as he was true to his vow." Always his special strength was entirely from the Lord. *References:* Num. 6:1–5; Judg. 16:17; 2 Sam. 22:40; Is. 40:31; 41:10; Dan. 11:32; Zech. 4:6; Eph. 3:16.

Success

909. Success depends on backbone, not wishbone. *References:* Deut. 29:9; 1 Chron. 22:13; 2 Chron. 31:21.

910. Success is 10 percent inspiration and 90 percent perspiration. (Thomas Edison) *References:* 1 Cor. 9:24; Phil. 3:13–16; Heb. 12:1.

911. A Right Cause Better Than a Successful One. President Woodrow Wilson suffered a blow from which he never recovered when his dream of a League of Nations was crushed by the refusal of the U.S. Senate to ratify American participation. But even during his final illness, Wilson could say, "I would rather fail in a cause I know will one day triumph than to succeed in a cause I know will one day fail."

We may fail many times as we struggle through life, but the cause will win. There is nothing visionary in the words of Paul: "Thanks be to God! He gives us the victory through our Lord Jesus Christ" (1 Cor. 15:57).

Missionary Alan Gardiner, dying in far-off Patagonia after a lifetime of suffering, closed his diary with the words: "I am overwhelmed with a sense of the goodness of God." That's the real vision. *References:* Ps. 75:4–7; Matt. 5:11–12; 1 Cor. 15:57; Heb. 11:13–16, 32–40; 1 Peter 4:12–16; Rev. 2:8–11. *Related illustration:* 889.

Superficiality

912. Meaningless Pat Answers. A Sunday school teacher tells the story of the day and mentions the wonders of creation. "What's a foot or so long, has a bushy tail, climbs trees, and saves nuts?" was one of her questions. None of the little children would answer. Three times she repeated the question and pleaded for the obvious answer. Finally, one little boy got enough courage to reply: "It sounds like a squirrel to me, but I'm sure it's supposed to be Jesus." How often the pat, easy, obvious, and even trite little Sunday school answers represent our faith. *References:* Matt. 7:21–23; Luke 3:8; 10:25–28; Titus 1:16.

913. Sunday Christians. We laugh at the little boy who spent 20 cents of his allowance for chewing gum and gave only five cents in Sunday school because, as he put it, "we chew gum all week long and have religion only on Sunday." You can't be lost all week long and expect to make up for it all on Sunday. *References:* Ps. 78:35–36; Ezek. 33:31–32; Matt. 7:21; Mark 7:6; Luke 6:46; Rom. 2:24; Titus 1:16; 1 John 3:18.

914. In the early days of railroading, every main railroad crossing had a crossing guard, who was to signal with a lantern that a train was coming. One night a crossing guard fell asleep in his shack but woke up and ran out with his lantern just seconds before the train came. There was a terrible accident. At the investigation, he was asked, "Were you present at your job?" "Did you have a lantern?" The crossing guard was exonerated of any blame. He later said, "No one asked me whether or not the lantern was lit."

There is much superficiality in religious matters for those both inside and outside the church—partial questions and pat answers. People seem to be right on the track as far as ethics are concerned but are not in the Kingdom because they have missed the Gospel, or because the Gospel itself has become a pat answer. Jesus is indeed the answer, but the answer to what? One cannot know the fullness of Jesus and have faith in Him until one understands the problems and questions for which He is the answer. *References:* John 6:25–36; Acts 8:9–24; 19:13–16.

915. Our Superficiality in Judging Others. Though we have often been disappointed with some free soap or cereal, we find it hard to resist the next offer of free soap or cereal, so strong is our trust in appearances. C. S. Lewis calls this "our peculiar inability to disbelieve advertisements" no matter how often they have proved misleading. A higher salary has the image of bringing happiness. A beautiful girl seems to have the makings of a good wife, though really she has more the makings of a tyrant. Since neatness and cleanliness are equated with goodness, the washed are reckoned more important than the unwashed. *References:* 1 Sam. 16:7; Matt. 23:27; John 7:24; 2 Cor. 5:12; 10:7; James 2:2–4.

Related illustrations: 657, 786.

Superstition

916. Credulity is as real a sin as unbelief. (Trench) *References:* 2 Thess. 2:10–12; 2 Tim. 3:13; 4:3–4.

917. Open biographical volumes wherever you please, and the person who has no faith in religion is the one who has faith in a nightmare and ghosts. (Bulwer) *References:* 2 Thess. 2:10–12; 2 Tim. 3:13; 4:3–4.

918. Superstition and Unbelief. Unbelief and superstition are closely allied. Religion is so essential that if its form can be set aside, some false form will be eagerly seized to fill the aching void. Just as a sailor, looking out into the night over a solitary, islandless sea, sees shapes and makes land out of fog banks, so people shudderingly look into the dark unknown, and if they do not see their Father there, they will either shut their eyes or strain them in gazing it into shape. The sight of Him is religion; the closed eye is infidelity; and the strained gaze is superstition. (MacLaren) *References:* Deut. 18:10–12; 1 Kings 20:23; Jer. 10:2–6; Matt. 14:2; Rom. 1:21–23; 2 Thess. 2:10–12; 1 Tim. 4:7; 2 Tim. 4:3–4.

Related illustration: 736.

Sympathy

919. Sympathy of Jesus. A drummer boy in Napoleon's army lost his footing and slipped into a chasm in the Alps as the army was marching. He was not seriously hurt but was unable to extricate himself without help. He began to beat on his drums to attract attention. His comrades heard him, but they could not break rank without orders from the commander. Such orders never came. The drummer boy finally began beating out his own death march. Hardened soldiers could not keep from sobbing as they passed by, but Napoleon was not moved. He was

SYMPATHY

too busy conquering the world to remember an insignificant boy who had been clumsy enough to lose his footing. Thank God, Jesus is not like that.

References: Matt. 15:21–28; Luke 8:43–48; 13:11–15; 18:35–43; 19:5; Heb. 4:15.

Related illustrations: 357, 639.

T

Temptations

920. The devil tempts everyone, but the lazy person tempts the devil. *References:* 2 Thess. 3:10–11; 1 Tim. 5:13.

921. No one is ever in greater danger than the person who thinks he or she can no longer be tempted. *References:* Matt. 26:33–41; 1 Cor. 10:11–13; 1 Peter 5:8.

922. We cannot prevent the birds from flying over our heads, but we can prevent them from building nests in our hair. (Luther) *References:* 1 Cor. 10:13; James 1:2–12; 4:7.

923. According to the Greek myth, Achilles, the great hero of the Trojan War, was dipped as a child in the waters of the river Styx by his mother, Thetis, to make him invulnerable. The result of that plunge was that every spot on Achilles' body was protected against wounds except the heel by which his mother had held him. For many years Achilles escaped unhurt, but at last the poisoned arrow of the Trojan Paris found the weak spot and inflicted the death wound there. So Satan tempts Christians where they are the weakest. Having found their pet inclinations, passions, and desires, he attacks them at their weak spots and is unusually successful. Therefore, to resist his efforts through the power of God, Christians not only in general strive to be sober and vigilant, but they above all guard the weak spots of their nature. (Rodenmeyer) *References:* Matt. 26:41; 1 Cor. 10:6–13; Gal. 5:16–17; Eph. 6:11–18; James 1:13–16; 1 Peter 5:8.

924. "Do you know what happens to little boys who tell lies?" mother asked Billy. "Sure," said Billy, "they get into the movies for half price." Many are not even interested in trying to resist temptation. The trouble often is that the results of their choices may not become clear until Judgment Day. As Aldous Huxley once put it, "Life is not what happens to a person, but what a person does with what happens." *References:* 2 Sam. 11:2–5; James 1:13–14; 4:2; Jude 16.

925. The Devil Made Me Do It. A mother, on leaving home to go downtown, told her little son, "Johnny, while I am gone, don't get into the jam." "No, Mother, I won't," he promised.

When she returned, the mother noticed jam between Johnny's fingers and in the corners of his mouth. "Didn't I tell you not to get into the jam, Johnny?" "Yes, Mother, you did." "Johnny, didn't I tell you that when Satan tempts you, you should tell him to get behind you?" "Yes . . . but when he got there, he pushed me right on in." So it is with many a child of God who casts side-glances at and in the heart ponders temptations to partake of the allurements of the world. *References:* Matt. 5:29–30; 18:8–9;

Rom. 13:14; Gal. 5:16; James 4:7.

926. With their beautiful songs the sirens lured the sailors to shore and then killed them. When Ulysses came near their island, he lashed himself to the mast so that when he was tempted to rush toward his ruin, he could not even if he wanted to. Similarly, we owe it to ourselves to prepare against temptations and to put ourselves in such a position that we cannot fall even if we want to. If our eye would tempt us to sin, let us pluck it out; for it is better to go to heaven with one eye than go to hell with two eyes. If you, for instance, find your business is keeping you away from God, get out of the business, even though you lose heavily; for it is better to go to heaven poor as Lazarus than to go to hell rich as Dives. (Dallmann) *References:* Matt. 5:29–30; 18:8–9; Rom. 13:14; 1 Cor. 9:27; Gal. 5:16, 24; 1 Peter 4:2.

927. Oscar Wilde once said, "When fleeing temptation, always be sure you leave a forwarding address, for the only real way to get rid of temptation is to yield to it." Despite the humor of that statement we need to recognize that temptation will never leave us peacefully. *References:* Matt. 12:43–45; 26:41; 1 Cor. 10:12; 1 Peter 5:8; 2 Peter 3:17.

Related illustrations: 244, 245, 331, 613, 872, 1002.

Tempting God

928. In 1929 Samuel Whitaker, convicted of hiring a thug to kill his wife, cried out in court, "If I am guilty, I hope God will strike me dead before I reach my cell!" The judge, unimpressed, sentenced him to San Quentin. En route he became ill and was taken to the prison hospital. He seemed to improve, and a cell was prepared for him, but before he could enter it, he fell dead. *References:* Ex. 20:7; Lev.

19:12; Matt. 4:6–7; 5:34–37; Acts 12:21–23; James 5:12.

Thanksgiving Day

929. In 1621, "after the ingathering of the first harvest in a new world," Governor Bradford of the Plymouth Colony invited the Pilgrims to keep "a day of prayer, praise, and thanksgiving." In 1789 President George Washington issued the first *national* thanksgiving proclamation in the United States. In 1863, after the bloody Battle of Gettysburg, President Lincoln urged the entire nation to observe a day of prayer and thanksgiving on the last Thursday in November. Since then this particular Thursday has been America's annual Thanksgiving Day. *References:* Lev. 23:39; Deut. 8:10–11; Ps. 67:5–7; 92:1.

Related illustration: 421.

Thoughts, Human

930. Said Emerson, "The thought is the ancestor of the deed." Long before Emerson, the inspired writer said, "As a man thinks in his heart, so is he." *References:* Prov. 23:7; Jer. 4:14; Matt. 9:4; 15:19; Mark 7:20–21.

931. As water cannot rise above its source, so our words and deeds cannot rise above our heart. *References:* Prov. 23:7; Matt. 7:17–20; 15:18–19; Luke 6:43–45; James 2:18.

Time

932. Vitellius, a famous spendthrift Roman who lived in the first century (68 A.D.) offered the priests of the province of Flamen two hundred and fifty million dollars for one minute of time. But the best they could do for him was to turn the clocks back. Time itself cannot be reversed. (1948, p. 556.) *References:* Ps. 90:10–12; Matt. 6:27; 1 Cor. 7:29–31; Eph. 5:15–16; Col. 4:5; James 4:14.

Tolerance of Others

933. Christians often find themselves

in a dilemma. There are two different opinions about how something should be done. How do you reconcile them? Maybe you can't. There is a story about a hippopotamus that fell in love with a butterfly. The hippo related his problem to an oracle. The oracle thought about it for an hour or so and then told the hippo to turn himself into a butterfly. The hippo went off deliriously happy—until he discovered he didn't know how to turn himself into a butterfly. So he rushed back to the oracle and said, "I don't know how to turn myself into a butterfly." The oracle replied, "Well, that's your problem. I just make policy; I don't carry it out." The point is, not all differences of opinion can be reconciled, any more than a hippopotamus can turn himself into a butterfly. *References:* Eph. 4:2–3; Phil. 2:3; Col. 3:13; 2 Tim. 2:14; James 3:13–15.

934. A mature Christian realizes that God created a world of infinite variety in which no two snowflakes or sunsets or persons are ever exactly alike. We differ when we come into the world; we have different training, different experiences, different reactions.

A priceless old story tells of two gladiators who met at a beautiful statue in ancient Athens. One said, "This is certainly a gold statue!" The other responded emphatically, "Gold? Don't be silly! It's silver!" The argument that ensued became so heated that they decided to settle the matter by dueling with swords—as though that would settle anything! One gladiator was killed and the other mortally wounded. The statue was not affected. As the wounded gladiator crawled slowly past the statue, he made a startling discovery. The statue was gold on one side, silver on the other. Each had been right from his own narrow viewpoint; each had been wrong in that his view did not

encompass all sides. *References:* Matt. 7:3; Rom. 14:5–7; 1 Tim. 6:4. *Related illustration:* 4

Tradition

935. Ernst Kasemann in his little book of essays entitled *Jesus Means Freedom* (Philadelphia: Fortress Press, 1970, pp. 115–16) brings this kind of discipleship to account:

> What human beings can never do, Christians must never even wish to do, namely, build impregnable citadels on earth, take their stand on what is conventional so as to abandon the future for the sake of the past. Every one of us is called every day to an exodus, as Abraham had to migrate from his father's house into an unknown country. Anyone who will not join in the march loses touch with God's people, even if he dwells in temples.

Speaking of the church as nothing more than a band of disciples, Kasemann goes on to say:

> What is true for the individual is no less true for the church as a whole. It, too, is constantly being called to break camp, and it has to leave behind what was once its gain; otherwise it is ruled not by the Spirit but by its own tradition. A continual exodus is the reverse side of Christian freedom. To be free one must be able to give up what is old, and so answer God's will today and tomorrow.

References: Is. 42:9; 43:18–19; 65:17; Matt. 15:3; Mark 7:7–8; 2 Cor. 5:17; Col. 2:8, 20–22.

Tribulations

See also **Affliction**

936. One troubled soul asked a friend, "What shall I do in all my troubles?" They both stood by a cow that was looking over a stone fence. The troubled soul was asked, "Why is this cow looking over the fence?" His answer: "Because she cannot look through it." This is a fine example for us in all our troubles: Look over them and up to God, because we can never look through them. *References:* Ps. 34:4–5; 121; 123:1; Is. 40:26; Dan. 4:34; John 17:1; Acts 7:55.

Related illustrations: 18, 536, 790.

Trinity, Holy
937. A man attended an evening service in a certain church. The pastor preached about the Triune God—that there are three Persons but only one Godhead. After the service the man approached the pastor and said, "I enjoyed your service, but I am not convinced of what you said. I just cannot get it through my head that there are three Persons and yet only one God."

The pastor asked the man, "What size hat do you wear?" The man replied, "6⅞—but why do you ask?" The pastor replied, "I was just wondering how you expected to get this great and almighty and majestic God of heaven and earth into 6⅞!" Yes, how can a little human being hope to comprehend the great God? *References:* Gen. 1:26–27; 11:7–8: Matt. 28:19; John 14:26; 15:26; 2 Cor. 13:14; 1 Peter 1:2 (Holy Trinity). Job 11:7; 33:12–14; Rom. 11:34; 1 Cor. 2:16 (incomprehensibility of God).

Related illustrations: 392, 394.

Trust
938. Trust in a God Who No Longer Is Our Judge. The scene is a courtroom. The judge, robed in a black gown, has taken his seat. A prisoner, handcuffed, is led into the room. As he sees the judge, his heart quakes, and he is filled with fear. He has good reason to fear, since the judge must pronounce sentence on him for his crime. Then suddenly, a young boy enters the same room, makes his way through the seats filled with spectators, runs up to the judge and whispers something into his ear. The judge reaches into his

pocket and gives the lad a coin, and the boy exits in a happy mood. The boy had no fear of the man robed in black. The judge was his father.

And so it is with us. In Christ God is not our Judge. In Christ God is to us what the judge was to the little boy—our Father—and we can approach Him fearlessly; He will provide for all our needs. *References:* Ps. 68:5; Is. 63:16; Matt. 6:9; 7:11; John 1:12; Rom. 8:14–17; 2 Cor. 6:18; Gal. 4:4–7.

939. When the saintly Theresa of medieval times was ridiculed for planning to found an orphanage with nothing but a penny in her hand, she calmly said, "With a penny Theresa can do nothing, but with God and a penny there is nothing Theresa cannot do." (M. Sommer) *References:* Ps. 37:5; 40:4; 118:8; Prov. 3:5–6; Is. 26:3–4; Matt. 19:26; Mark 10:27; Phil. 4:13.

Related illustration: 674.

Truth
940. Athanasius: "If the world goes against the truth, then Athanasius goes against the world." *References:* Prov. 23:23; Rom. 3:4; Titus 1:2; Heb. 6:18.

941. Luther: "Peace if possible, but truth at any rate." *References:* Prov. 12:19; 23:23; John 18:37; Rom. 3:4.

942. In 1 Esdras, one of the apocryphal books dating from between the Old and the New Testaments, is the legendary story of a feast of King Darius of Persia. He gathered 127 governors from India to Ethiopia for a grand celebration.

Part of the festivities was a contest among four young wise men who were to describe in one sentence the strongest thing in the world. Each wrote his sentence and submitted it. When they were read, each young man explained why he chose his subject. The first one said, "Wine is the strongest." The second, the king; the third, women; and the fourth, truth. The fourth wise youth explained his reason like this: "Wine, the king, and women are strong, but they are also wicked, and they perish. But truth endures forever. It is the source of justice and order. It is the strength, kingdom, power, and majesty of all ages." Christ said, "I am the way and the truth and the life. No one comes to the Father except through me." *References:* Deut. 32:4; Ps. 146:6; Prov. 12:19; 23:23; John 14:6; Rom. 3:4.

943. Truth may be suppressed for a time, but it always rises from its apparent grave. Savanarola and Huss were burned, but the Reformation was not prevented. Stephen sank in blood, but his place was taken by the young man who stood by to incite the murderers. Four years after Jesus had died on the cross, Stephen was stoned to death for being His disciple; 30 years after the death of Stephen his deadliest opponent died for the same holy faith. (Farrar) *References:* Prov. 12:19; John 8:32; Acts 6:8–9:30; Rom. 3:4; Eph. 6:14.

944. Commenting on the "excuse" that the chief priests and Pharisees gave for seeking to kill Jesus, George Stoeckhardt writes, "That was mere pretense. They themselves did not actually believe that Jesus from a political point of view was a dangerous man. But He did not contribute to their prestige among the people. They hated Him because He had told the truth. In the same way the world considers Christians to be disturbers and rebels. Those who speak thus usually know very well that Christians are harmless people. But the Christians are disliked by them and are seen as obstructionists because they tell the truth and rebuke them because of their sins." (*Biblische Geschichte*, N.T., p. 227.) *References:* Matt. 24:9; Luke 6:22–23; John 8:31–36; 11:47–53; 15:18–25; 16:1–3; Acts 7:51–60; 1 John 3:12–13.

Related illustrations: 192, 436, 446, 689, 800, 955, 959.

U

Unbelief

945. The body of an unbeliever is the walking coffin of a dead soul. (Bovee) *References:* Gen. 2:17; John 3:18; Rom. 8:6; 1 Cor. 2:14.

946. We are thinking of the many unfortunate souls who are without hope in the world. With the German philosopher they express their hopelessness in the empty prayer, "O God, if there is a God, have mercy on my soul, if I have a soul." *References:* Eccl. 11:5; Is. 59:8; Jer. 5:4; Micah 4:12; Rom. 10:3; Eph. 4:18.

947. They Too Shall Acknowledge Christ. Jean Jacques Rousseau, unbeliever though he was, said, "Socrates died as a man, but Jesus died as God." *References:* Matt. 27:54; Mark 15:39; Luke 23:47; Phil. 2:10–11.

948. Sin is a stream, unbelief its source; the stream will not cease to flow till the source has been stopped. Unbelief is an evil root, all other sins being but its sprouts. Nothing is accomplished if the sprouts are cut off and the root is not removed. From the evil root new sprouts will shoot up. *References:* John 3:18; 8:24; 16:8–9; 2 Thess. 2:12; Heb. 3:12–13; Jude 4–5.

949. Most Unbelievers Are Not Actually Atheists. The image that the playwrights and the philosophers of our day project is of people tormented and frustrated by the absence of God. Tennessee Williams confronts us with it in *Sweet Bird of Youth.* Through the heck-ler he says, "I believe that the long silence of God, the absolute speechlessness of Him, is a long, long, an awful thing that the world is lost because of." A German existentialist, Martin Heidegger, directs us to the same experience. "I do not deny God," he writes. "I state His absence." This is the problem of our world. *References:* Is. 1:3–4; Jer. 5:4; Micah 4:12; Rom. 1:28; 10:3; Eph. 2:12; 4:18.

950. Hopeless Prospects. The mother of David Hume, the infidel philosopher, was once a believer. Misled by the philosophy of her son, she followed him in the ways of unbelief and lost her faith. Years passed, and she approached the gates of death. From her deathbed she wrote to her son: "Dear son, my health has forsaken me. I am failing rapidly; I cannot live much longer. My philosophy affords me no comfort in my distress. I have lost the hope and comfort of religion and am sinking into despair. You can offer me something that will replace the hope of religion that I have lost. Hurry home, I beseech you, to comfort me, or at least write me what consolation you can afford in the hour of death."

But the philosopher had no comfort for his dying mother. Such is the bankruptcy of unbelief. (*Der Lutheraner* 65:25.) *References:* Ps. 73:17–19; Prov. 14:12; Ezek. 7:26; Amos 8:11; 1 Cor. 2:6–16; Eph. 2:12; 1 Thess. 4:13.

951. Unbelief is the child of ignorance. For example, a woman asked her friend, "Do you have any religious views?" She thought for a while and then finally said, "No, but I have some dandy snapshots of Niagara Falls." *References:* Ezek. 8:12; Micah 4:12; Matt. 13:15; John 15:21; Rom. 1:21–28; 10:3; Eph. 4:18; 2 Peter 3:5.

Related illustrations: 1, 232, 433, 726, 918.

Unchurched

952. Goodness Without Godliness. J. Russell Hale, in his study "Who Are the Unchurched?" (Glenmary Research Center, 4606 East-West Highway, Washington, DC 20014), has interviewed a number of these people. He describes them as "Anti-Institutionalists, the Boxed-In, the Burned-Out, the Cop-Outs, the Happy Hedonists, the Locked-Out, the Nomads, the Pilgrims, the Publicans, the Scandalized, the True Unbelievers, and the Uncertain." One intriguing discovery in his interviews was that many people considered themselves Christians but just didn't see the need for the church and all that the Christian faith involves.

But this diffidence, indifference, and lack of commitment to the way of our Lord Jesus Christ is "goodness without godliness." *References:* Jer. 2:35; Matt. 7:21–23; 15:7–9; Luke 14:15–20; John 9:41; 2 Cor. 10:12; Rev. 3:15–18.

Understanding

953. People often use the same words but have entirely different meanings in mind. For example, Johnny Carson, on the day after the World Series was concluded, asked band member Tommy Newsom: "Well, Tommy, what do you think of the Cincinnati Reds now?" Tommy answered, "I just don't like Communists! I don't care where they live!"

Something like this happened between Pilate and Jesus. Each had a completely different concept of what Jesus' kingship meant. *Reference:* John 18:33–37.

954. Knowledge Does Not Assure Understanding. Survey data is often relied on to note or to forecast a trend. Politicians rely on polls and samplings to get a feel of where they stand with the voting public. But the data is not absolute. It can be misread or misinterpreted. A good example of this is the story of the lioness and the fox in a little book called *Aesop Without Morals.* The fox keeps chiding and belittling the lioness because she can produce only one cub at a birth. The lioness replies, "Yes, this may be so, but remember, it is a lion." The fox failed to read this simple bit of data correctly. He failed to grasp the impact of what it means to be a lion.

In a sense the disciples on the Emmaus road were like the fox. They didn't seem to fathom the uniqueness of Jesus. They had many facts and batted them around like a Ping-Pong ball, but they didn't know how to interpret the data of all that had taken place in Jerusalem over the past days. *References:* Is. 6:9; Luke 18:31–34; 24:13–27; John 3:9–10.

Unionism

955. There can be no true love where there is not also true hatred—no love of truth without abhorrence of error. (Krauth) *References:* Ps. 119:104; Prov. 8:13; Rev. 2:6.

956. A prominent evangelist said, "When you get to heaven, you will be ashamed of your denomination. There are no Baptists, Methodists, Presbyterians, Congregationalists, or United Brethren. We are all one. If there is anything in your church which keeps you from sitting down with me at the

Lord's Table, it is wrong. Or if there is anything in my church which keeps me from sitting down with you, it, too, is wrong." That view is unionism.

True, in heaven the church will no longer be divided. The light of glory dispels all error. But here on earth people maintain error. What must be our attitude? May we hold church fellowship with those who deny Biblical doctrine? Dare we practice pulpit or altar fellowship? Unionism says yes. *References:* Rom. 16:17; 2 Cor. 6:14–17; Eph. 5:11; 2 Thess. 3:6; 1 Tim. 6:5; 2 Tim. 3:5; 2 John 10.

Uniqueness
See also **Tolerance of Others**
957. Unique in the Same Spirit. You may pluck a hundred leaves from the same branch and not find two alike. They will all follow the same general pattern but differ in size, vigor, shade, and shape, and not one will be geometrically perfect. Yet on the bough they looked graceful and symmetrical enough.

We sometimes forget that Christians retain their individuality, that though they all have the same Spirit, they differ in the degree of gifts, knowledge, love, labor, talents, responsibilities, and temptations. We cannot establish a rule of uniformity. All the saints are led in a right way, but no two of them are precisely the same way. *References:* Matt. 25:15; Rom. 12:6; 1 Cor. 4:7; 12:4; Eph. 4:11.

Unity
958. For wolves to devour sheep is no wonder, but for sheep to devour one another is monstrous and astonishing. (Salter) *References:* Acts 20:30; Phil. 2:3; James 3:14–16.

959. If two work the same problem and both get the *right* answer, both will also get the *same* answer; they need not try to harmonize their answers afterward. Just so all those who teach the truth will agree with others who teach the truth without trying to agree. The truth is one and always agrees with itself. Unity and union will take care of themselves if all teachers of God's Word are faithful and loyal to the truth. (M. Sommer) *References:* Ps. 119:142; Prov. 23:23; John 14:6; 17:17; 18:37; Rom. 3:4.

Unworthiness
960. It was an honest man who wrote this epitaph for his own tombstone: "Anthony Benezet was a poor creature, and through divine favor was enabled to know it." *References:* 2 Sam. 12:13; Luke 15:18; 18:13; 23:41; Rom. 7:24; 1 Tim. 1:15.

W

Watchfulness

961. There are critical times of danger. After great services, honors, and consolations we should be on our guard. Noah, Lot, David, and Solomon fell in these circumstances. Satan is a highwayman. A highwayman will not attack a person going to the bank but on the return with pocket or purse full of money. (Newton) *References:* Matt. 16:13–23; Luke 18:9–14; 1 Cor. 10:12.

962. Frederick Forsyth's intriguing fictional account of *The Day of the Jackal* illustrates the painstaking way in which a potential rebellion, the assassination attempt on a top French political figure, had to be put down. The authorities worked around the clock. They followed up every clue. They put into effect every conceivable restraint and eventually, just in the nick of time, thwarted the assassin's assault on Charles DeGaulle.

With equal fervor you and I must root out every rebel force within that seeks to minimize God's Word or reject His authority and then step out to accept His good gift of forgiveness and healing. *References:* Rom. 16:17; 1 Cor. 1:18–24; 2 Tim. 4:3–5.

Related illustrations: 171, 544, 645.

Wealth

See also **Greed**

963. You may know how little God thinks of money and riches by observing on what bad and contemptible characters He often bestows them.

(Guthrie) *References:* Eccl. 2:6; Luke 12:18–20; 1 Tim. 6:9.

964. What would you think of a man who voluntarily sells himself into abject slavery to his own servant? Well, the miser has done just that. *References:* Prov. 15:27; Eccl. 5:10; 1 Tim. 6:9–10.

965. "How much did he leave?" asked a man of the friend who had told him about the death of a wealthy merchant. "Hm, all he had," was the significant reply. The rest was silence. *References:* Ps. 49:10; Jer. 17:11; 1 Tim. 6:7.

966. A man was visiting a Texas land baron. After dinner the host took the guest out on the front porch to show him the view. Waving his arm toward the horizon, he said, "Everything you see belongs to me. Those oil wells on the horizon—they're mine. That golden grain on the hills—that's mine. Those cattle in the valley—mine, all mine. Twenty-five years ago when I came out here, there was nothing, and I had nothing. But now I own everything you see."

The host waited for a word of praise. But the visitor waved his arm toward the heavens and said, "And what do you own up there?" *References:* Eccl. 2:4–11; Matt. 4:8–10; 6:19–21; 16:26; Luke 12:15; 1 Tim. 6:7–10; Heb. 13:5; James 5:1–3.

967. When the Roman Church stood at the heights of glory and prestige and wealth, one of the popes exclaimed, "No longer can the church say, 'Silver and gold have I none.' " But a wise counselor significantly replied, "Can it still say, 'In the name of Jesus Christ of Nazareth, rise up and walk'?" *References:* John 14:13; 20:31; Acts 1:8; 3:6; 1 Cor. 2:1–5.

968. No Joy in Wealth. A great Muslim caliph, 'Abd ar-Rahman III, who attained great power for the Muslim empire in Spain and accumulated fabulous wealth for himself, is said to have confessed shortly before his death, "Fifty years have passed since I became caliph. Riches, honors, pleasures—I have enjoyed all. In this long period of seeming happiness I have numbered the days on which I have been happy. They amount to twenty. And even then I was not completely happy." *References:* Job 27:16–17; Ps. 62:9–10; Eccl. 2:26; Jer. 17:11; 1 Tim. 6:9–10; James 5:3.

969. The days of prosperity that came to the church during the reign of Constantine would have been an unmixed blessing to the Christians of that day if they had not also brought with them the temptation to become secure and indifferent. As it was, an era that was very favorable to the dissemination of the Gospel and the extension of the Kingdom also saw the sowing of the seed from which the papacy later sprang. Times of material well-being are never conducive to the strengthening of the inward life of the church and the individual Christian. *References:* Ps. 17:10; Ezek. 16:49; Hag. 1:6; Luke 6:25; 12:21; 1 Tim. 6:7; Rev. 3:17.

970. The Poorest of God's Gifts. Riches are the pettiest and least worthy gifts that God can give a person. What are they compared with God's Word, yes, even with physical gifts such as beauty and health or with the gifts of the mind such as understanding, skill, and wisdom? Yet people toil for them day and night and take no rest. Therefore our Lord commonly gives riches to foolish people to whom He gives nothing else. (Luther) *References:* Ps. 49:10; Prov. 23:4; Eccl. 2:26; 5:10–20; Matt. 19:23; Mark 4:19; 1 Tim. 6:7–10.

Related illustrations: 98, 414, 426, 427, 686, 999.

Witnessing

971. The best advertisement of Christianity is a good life. People read us a great deal more than they read the Bible. They see us; they only hear about Jesus Christ. (MacLaren) *References:* Matt. 5:13–16; 2 Cor. 9:2; 1 Thess. 1:8.

972. On a Southern battlefield a soldier had an artery of his arm lacerated severely by the fragment of a shell and was fast bleeding to death. A passing physician bound up the artery and saved his life. As the physician was leaving, the man cried, "Doctor, what is your name?" "Oh, no matter," said the doctor. "But, Doctor, I want to tell my wife and children who saved me." So when Christ has come binding up broken spirits and saving life eternally, may there be a burning desire to tell others what He has done for us. *References:* Is. 52:7; 63:7; Matt. 10:32; Mark 5:18–20; Luke 12:8; John 4:29; Acts 4:20; 1 Peter 3:15.

973. A Task for All. Sidney Powell said, "The world will never be converted by the ministers because there are not enough of them." The only way we can ever hope to reach every individual in our community with the Gospel is that every Christian be a witness. *References:* Ex. 19:6; Is. 43:10; 61:6; Acts 1:8; 1 Peter 2:9; Rev. 1:6; 5:10; 20:6.

974. A Soul-Saving Work. Dwight

L. Moody once said that his favorite picture was of a girl clinging to a cross-shaped rock in the midst of the storm-tossed sea. Clinging tightly with both hands she was saved.

Another picture was found that made this first seem almost meaningless by comparison. The picture was almost the same—the same girl, the same storm-tossed sea, the same rugged, crosslike rock. But now the girl clung to the rock with only one hand and with the other reached out to save another from the sea. This is witnessing. This is sharing Christ today: clinging to Christ's Word tightly and sharing it freely that all may hear and by God's grace believe and live. *References:* Ps. 66:16; Is. 62:6; Matt. 4:19; Mark 5:18–20; John 15:27; Acts 1:8; 1 Peter 3:15; Jude 23.

975. And having provided the opportunity, God wants us to be ready to speak anywhere and everywhere. The great evangelist of the past, Dwight L. Moody, was once heard to remark that the most cherished epitaph on his tombstone would be: "A young man walking about the streets witnessing to Jesus."

A converted charwoman, who spoke to as many as possible about Jesus, once began witnessing to a wooden Indian in front of the little drugstore. When she was told how ridiculous that looked, she answered, "My eyesight isn't as good as it used to be, and I guess that's why I made this mistake. But this isn't nearly as bad as the wooden Christians, who don't speak to anyone about Jesus." *References:* Is. 62:6; Jer. 20:9; Acts 4:20; 2 Tim. 1:8; 1 Peter 3:15 (readiness to witness). Prov. 29:25; John 7:13; 12:42; 19:38 (wooden Christians).

976. Taking Christ to the World. In the downtown section of St. Paul, Minn., some years ago was a church known as the People's Church. At one time it was filled with throngs of expectant worshipers, but as the business district closed about it, the worshipers dwindled until only a handful came there to worship and pray. One night the old church caught fire. Before the firemen could extinguish the blaze in the sub-zero temperature, a large part of the church had been burned.

An eight-foot, life size marble statue of Thorvaldsen's "The Appealing Christ" had occupied a central place at the altar. During the blaze it had fallen into the basement but by some miracle was undamaged. After the ruins had cooled, the firemen placed the statue of Christ with arms outstretched on the sidewalk beside the church. The next morning the throngs that passed by on their way to work, most of whom had never been inside the old church, saw the figure of Christ in a gesture of gracious invitation.

This incident is a striking illustration of the task of the church today. It must take the Christ of the church out into the world where people are. And that's your task and mine as Christians. *References:* Matt. 24:14; 28:19; Mark 13:10; 16:15; Luke 24:47; Acts 1:8; 26:17–18; Rev. 14:6.

977. When Dr. Lyman Beecher was asked the secret of his success, he replied, "I preach to my people on Sunday, and they go out and preach all week, so that there are at least 688 sermons preached through my parish each week." There is an urgent need in the church today for more Christians who will speak for Christ and thus daily witness for Him. *References:* Ps. 107:2; Matt. 5:13–16; Acts 2:46–47.

978. A Sunday school teacher told me about a session in which she had been talking about the Gospel with her class. She had told the children, "If you believe that Jesus died for your sins, you'll have everlasting life. You'll go to heaven." A little girl in the class thought about that for awhile and finally said to her teacher, "I do believe that. But teacher, if that's so, why don't I just die right now and go right to heaven? Why am I here?" Why are we here? We are here so that the water of life might well up in our lives and overflow and splash across us into the lives of others. *References:* Matt. 5:13–16; 28:19–20; Mark 16:15–16; Luke 24:47; Acts 1:8; Phil. 1:21–24.

979. In Krishnasamadrum, India, lived an old, blind Christian teacher, whose heart burned for the Savior. Because his soul had seen the salvation of the Lord, he went and told others. And one day the missionary came that way. He found 26 converts ready for Baptism, brought to Jesus by the ministry of the old teacher. A little congregation was organized. It grew till the name of the place was changed from "the City of Krishna" (the heathen god) to "the City of Christ," Kristasamadrum. *References:* Mark 5:18–20; Luke 1:40–42, 45–46; Acts 9:17–18.

980. O may it not be said of us what Wu Ting Fang said of Christians in our country: "I met Christian missionaries in China and became impressed with their religion. When my country sent me as its ambassador to Christian America, I made up my mind to become a Christian and join the first Christian church that asked me. I have been here three years, and no one has asked me. Now I shall not come." *References:* Is. 6:8; Matt. 9:37–38; 28:19; Luke 14:21; Acts 1:8; 22:15; 1 Thess. 2:8.

981. Let us remember that education and training are no more necessary for the Christian witness than they are for the witness in the courtroom. People are not called to the witness stand because they have the training or education necessary to be doctors, professors of ancient history, or engineers, but because they have seen and experienced something that is important to the case being tried. *References:* Is. 43:10; Mark 5:18–20; John 1:40–46; 4:28–29; Acts 1:8; 4:8–13; 1 Peter 3:15; 1 John 1:1–3.

982. Where Is Our Samaria? Have we a Samaria today? I shall never forget the eloquent plea of Missionary Lazos of Mexico City, begging us not to forget our Samaria—Mexico. We must bear witness also in hostile quarters, among those whose enmity consists in unbelief, rationalism, or a false trust in science, and among those who call themselves Christians but are not. *References:* John 4:5–42; Acts 1:8; 8:5–17.

983. A cub reporter was assigned to cover a bridge-opening ceremony. He came back empty-handed and explained to his editor that he couldn't get the story because the bridge collapsed. The reporter forgot his real task: reporting the news.

The Christ movement seemed to collapse with Jesus' death and would scarcely have been reported but for His resurrection. The church does not forget its assignment to publish good news. *References:* Is. 52:7; Matt. 9:10–13; Luke 24:25–27, 44–48; John 12:47; 18:37.

Related illustrations: 110, 165, 312, 313, 579, 655, 738, 1017.

Women

984. Woman was taken out of man—not out of his head to rule over him, nor out of his foot to be trampled on, but out of his side to be near him, under his arm to be protected, and near his heart to be loved. (M. Henry) *References:* Gen. 2:21–24; Eph. 5:25–29; Col. 3:19; 1 Peter 3:7.

985. Their Prominence in the Church. Why do Hindus teach that woman has no soul and do not permit her to read the Veda or to eat at the same table with her own husband? Why is it that the Muslims do not educate their women, do not permit them to enter a mosque, and make them serve as concubines? Why did Buddha say that a wise man should avoid married life as if it were a pit of burning coals and that the Buddhist religion has 18 special hells for its Buddhist women? Why does Confucianism consider woman a necessary evil, buy and sell her for domestic services, the stage, and immoral purposes, and let her kill her girl babies? It is because these religions consider women to be far inferior to men.

The high honor and respect that the Christian woman enjoys in the church, in the home, and in society wherever Christian influence is felt is due to the Christian teaching that women are co-heirs of eternal life with men. Husbands and wives, says Peter, are "heirs with you of the gracious gift of life." The Christian religion gives women an important place in the church. *References:* Prov. 31:10, 30; Matt. 27:55–56; Luke 1:28–30; 21:2–4; Acts 16:14–15; Rom. 16:1–4; 2 Tim. 1:5; 1 Peter 3:7.

986. Made to Be Man's Helper. Under the old Roman law a husband had absolute power of life and death over his wife and absolute control of her property. The Athenian woman was treated throughout her life as a minor and under constant tutelage, being subject at various times to the authority of her father, brother, grandfather, husband, son, or guardian; she had practically no authority except in the sphere of domestic economy. The Scriptures make the woman "a helper suitable for" the man (Gen. 1:27–28; 2:18).

Her relation to the man is not to be coordinate or subordinate, but she is to be his auxiliary. (P. E. Kretzmann) *References:* Gen. 1:27–28; 2:18; Prov. 31:10–31; Luke 8:2–3; 1 Peter 3:1–7.

Work
See also **Labor, Stewardship**

987. Leisure has destroyed more lives than labor. Do not be afraid of doing too much. *References:* Prov. 6:6–11; 10:5; 20:13; Eccl. 9:10; 1 Thess. 4:11–12; 2 Thess. 3:10–13.

988. A former president of the United States, when asked what his coat of arms was, said, "Two arms with sleeves rolled up." *References:* Prov. 6:6–11; 13:11; 20:13; Eccl. 9:10; 1 Thess. 4:11–12; 2 Thess. 3:10–13.
Related illustrations: 766, 904, 1017.

Works-righteousness

989. Dr. Luther: "Works without faith is idolatry." *References:* Matt. 19:16–26; Rom. 3:20; 9:32; 10:3; Gal. 2:16; 3:10; Eph. 2:8–9.

990. To oppose God's wrath with our good works is like trying to extinguish a fire by throwing straw on it. (Luther) *References:* Rom. 9:32; 10:3; Gal. 3:10.

991. George Bernard Shaw, the doctrinaire playwright, is reputed to have remarked, "Forgiveness is a beggar's refuge; a man must pay his debts." People of such a mind hold that their good deeds will conceal their evil deeds just as credit cancels debt. *References:* Luke 18:9–14; Rom. 3:20; 9:32; 10:3; Gal. 2:16; 3:10; Eph. 2:8–9; Titus 3:4–5.

992. There has been a rumor abroad in the human race for centuries that entrance into heaven could be obtained by presenting a satisfactory work record on earth. That is similar to a rumor that spread in the United States in 1947 that the Ford Motor Company would give a Ford in exchange for every copper penny dated 1943. The rumor spread so fast that Ford offices throughout the country were jammed with requests for information, and in spite of a telephone strike thousands of inquiries came in by telephone as well as by telegram and mail. It all turned out to be a joke. The records of the mint show that in 1943 there was no copper available for coinage and that 1,093,838,670 pennies were minted of zinc-coated steel; none were made of copper (Donald Grey Barnhouse, *Let Me Illustrate* [Westwood, N.J.: Fleming H. Revell Company, 1967], p. 356).

Rumors so often prove to be wrong. Forgiveness of sins is not received in exchange for the proper amount of good works that are performed here on earth, no matter how sincerely they are done. *References:* Matt. 7:22–23; Rom. 3:20; 9:32; 11:6; Gal. 2:16; 3:10; Eph. 2:8–9; Titus 3:4–5.

993. No Grounds for Boasting. Dwight Moody once said, "It is well that man cannot save himself; for if a man could only work his own way to heaven, you would never hear the last of it. Why, if a man happens to get a little ahead of his fellows and scrapes a few thousands of dollars together, you'll hear him boast of being a self-made man. I've heard so much of this sort of talk that I am sick and tired of the whole business; and I am glad that through all eternity in heaven we will never hear anyone bragging of how he worked his way to get there." *References:* Matt. 7:22–23; Rom. 3:20; 11:6; 1 Cor. 1:26–31; Gal. 2:16; Eph. 2:8–9; 2 Tim. 1:9; Titus 3:4–5.

994. A Subtle Form of Universalism. In *Bridging the Generation Gap* Merton P. Strommen reports on a survey of Lutherans in which 70 percent of young people agreed with this statement: "God is satisfied if I live the best

life I can." This is a subtle form of universalism that somehow each one of us wants to believe; that is, if our neighbors are good people and live good lives, they are going to make it. They are going to be all right somehow. Or as I think about my Jewish friends, I would like to believe that they can be saved through the Old Testament; then I don't have to share Jesus Christ with them. *References:* John 3:16–17; 8:24; Acts 4:12; Rom. 3:23; 1 Cor. 3:11: Eph. 2:8–9.

995. A Pretense of Piety. Helmut Thielicke tells that he once was hospitalized and was cared for by a nurse who had worked for 20 years on the night shift. When he asked her whether this was perhaps too great a strain that would eventually wear her out, she replied with a radiant look in her eyes, "Well, you see, every night I put in sets another jewel in my heavenly crown, and already I have over seven thousand of them." And right there, Thielicke says, his appreciation for the services of this nurse went down. The nurse was using the patients in the hospital to serve her own ends.

This is the kind of person Jesus calls a hypocrite, literally an actor who covers or conceals his true nature. Using another person to serve one's own ends Immanuel Kant called the greatest immorality. It is just as immoral when someone encourages another to believe that thereby he or she wins brownie points in heaven. *References:* Matt. 6:1–6, 16–18; 23:15.

996. A prominent historian who made a thorough study of the various religions of the world summarized their chief doctrines briefly as follows: The Greek says, "Man, know thyself." The Roman says, "Man, control thyself." The Confucian says, "Man, improve thyself." The Buddhist says, "Man, destroy thyself." The Brahman says, "Man, absorb thyself." The Muslim says, "Man, submit thyself." But Jesus says, "Without Me ye can do nothing." (Abendschule) *References:* Lam. 5:21; John 6:44, 65; 15:5; Rom. 5:6; 7:18; 2 Cor. 3:5.

Related illustrations: 322, 788, 825.

World

997. Not Your Home. An old Norwegian catechism says that God our Father called us aside one day in the home palace of heaven and sent us out to this "island colony called the earth." After describing what our life would be like here, our Lord ends by saying, "The greatest danger is that you may fall in love with this island so that you will not care to return to the home kingdom. Love the island because it is My possession, but do not love it because it is your home. It is not your home. Your home is here in the palace with Me." (Alvin N. Rogness, *On the Way* [Minneapolis: Augsburg Publishing House, 1942]). *References:* John 14:3; 17:14; 1 Cor. 7:31; 2 Cor. 5:6–8; Phil. 1:21–23; 2 Tim. 2:4; Heb. 11:13–16; 1 John 2:15.

998. Its Doom. This world often seems like a rock at sea on which, eager to escape the jaws of death, more drowning people seek standing room than it offers. And when the few who have risen on the shoulders of the many who sink have gained for themselves the wealth or power or pleasure they desire, they have only reached an unsheltered, slippery rock, from which the giant wave of death presently sweeps them to their doom. (Guthrie) *References:* Ps. 121; Eccl. 3:12–17; Matt. 16:26; 1 Cor. 7:31; Col. 3:12; James 4:4; 1 John 2:15.

Related illustrations: 127, 773.

Worldly Cares

999. In the ruins of Pompeii was found the petrified body of a woman holding in her hands her jewels, which she had tried to gather up instead of fleeing from the doomed city, thus losing both her jewels and her life. Thus many today want both the pleasures of the world and the treasures of heaven but in the end will lose both. *References:* Deut. 12:30; Matt. 16:25–26; 24:17–18; Luke 21:34; Titus 2:12; James 4:4; 1 John 2:15–17.

1000. Luther was for a time in gloomy spirits. In vain did Kate, his beloved wife, try to cheer him. At last she put on a widow's garment and went around the house in deepest mourning. When Luther observed this, he asked, "Who is dead?" "God," replied Kate. "Don't talk so foolish!" retorted the great Reformer. "Well, my dear Doctor," answered Kate, "you are so downhearted that I concluded God must be dead, and so I put on my mourning apparel." Luther understood the lesson his good wife wished to teach him, embraced her, and forgot his cares. *References:* Ps. 115:12; Matt. 6:32; 11:28–30; Luke 12:7; John 14:1; Phil. 4:6; 1 Peter 5:7.

1001. A ship with about a hundred passengers was wrecked on a South Seas island. Fortunately, all lives were saved, together with sufficient food for several months' existence and several sacks of seed for springtime sowing. But the men had hardly reached shore when someone discovered gold. The men began to dig and pan furiously for gold, heaping it up for themselves and forgetting all about the seed and the need to plant and harvest. When the fall winds began to blow and the cold of winter settled on them, they died of hunger and starvation.

Oh, how many there are today who feverishly dig in the gold mines of this world, goaded wholly by greed and selfishness, forgetting all about God, His Word, His church, and the needs of their soul, only to die the eternal death when the raw winds of life overtake them. *References:* Ps. 127:1–2; Matt. 16:25–26; Luke 12:16–21; 16:19–31; 1 Tim. 6:6–19.

1002. One of Aesop's fables says, "A pigeon oppressed by excessive thirst saw a goblet of water painted on a signboard. Not supposing it to be only a picture, it flew toward it with a loud whirr and unwittingly dashed against the signboard and jarred itself terribly. Having broken its wings by the blow, it fell to the ground and was killed by a bystander." The mockeries of the world are many, and those who are deluded by them not only miss the joys they sought but in their eager pursuit of vanity bring ruin on their souls. We call the dove silly to be deceived by a picture, however cleverly painted, but what epithet shall we apply to those who are duped by the transparently false allurements of the world? (C. H. Spurgeon) *References:* Prov. 1:19; Eccl. 2:1–11; Jer. 17:11; Mark 4:19; 1 Tim. 6:9–10; James 5:3.

1003. Worldly Noise Drowns Out the Gospel. If you stood on a street corner where the traffic is abundant and incessant, where the constant thunder of rumbling wheels creates a din, it would be hard to preach so as to command an audience, for the abundant sound would prevent all hearing. To a great extent the mass of humanity is in that condition as far as the joyful sound of the Gospel is concerned. The rumbling of the wheels of commerce, the noise of trade and the cries of competition, the whirl of cares, and the riot of pleasure—all these drown the persuasive voice of heavenly love so that people hear no more of it than they would hear of a pin falling in the midst of a hurricane at sea. Only when the ear shuts out the distracting noises of the world around can the heart hear and

absorb the still small voice of the Gospel. *References:* Num. 9:8; 1 Kings 19:9–12; Ps. 4:4; 46:8–11; Eccl. 4:6; Luke 8:7–14; 21:34; 1 Peter 3:4.

1004. A False Perspective. The laws of perspective are such as that a minute thing near at hand shuts out the image of a massive thing far off, and a hillock by my side will hide the Himalayas at a distance, and a piece of money may block out God, and "that which is least" has the diabolical power to seem greater to us than—and to obscure the sight of—"that which is most." (MacLaren) *References:* Ps. 49:10; Prov. 27:24; Matt. 13:22; Mark 4:18–19; Luke 8:14; 12:16–23; Col. 3:2; James 5:3.

1005. If my hands are laden with pebbles, I cannot clasp the diamonds that are offered to me. Unless you fling out the sandbags, the balloon will cleave to the earth, and unless we turn the world out of our hearts, it is no use to say, "Come, Lord Jesus." There is no room for Him anyway. (MacLaren) *References:* 1 Sam. 7:3; Prov. 21:17; Matt. 6:24; 16:24–26; Luke 12:16–21; 16:13; James 4:4–8.

Related illustration: 144.

Worry

1006. Bruce Barton: "There is a difference between the man who does not worry and the man who does not care." *References:* Matt. 6:25–34; Luke 10:38–42; 12:29; 21:34; 1 Peter 5:7.

1007. One of the French kings built himself a palace that he called "Sans Souci," which means "without care, without worry." But the king soon discovered that he could not close out the cares and worries of the state, because he carried them in his heart and mind. *References:* Ps. 127:2; Matt. 6:25–34; 14:30–31; Luke 10:41; 21:34; Phil. 4:6; 1 Peter 5:7.

1008. The United States Public

Health Service issued a statement some time ago about the tendency of worry to weaken and shorten life. It reads in part: ''So far as is known, no bird ever tried to build more nests than its neighbor. No fox ever fretted because it had only one hole in which to hide. No squirrel ever died of anxiety, lest it should not lay by enough for two winters instead of one, and no dog ever lost any sleep over the fact that it had not enough bones laid aside for the declining years.'' Worry wreaks havoc. It makes you ineffective and inefficient. It weakens you for the long pull. *References:* Ps. 127:2; Eccl. 1:13; Matt. 6:25–34; 13:22; Luke 21:34; Phil. 4:6; 1 Peter 5:7.

1009. The Needless Pain of Worry. One dark, pitch-black night a man was walking down an unfamiliar road. On either side was a deep ravine. Suddenly he stepped into space and began to fall. Thinking he was falling to certain death, he began flailing his arms and clutching for anything he could get his hands on. He was able to grasp a bush along the side, and he held on for dear life. It was agony. His body became numb. At last in weakness and despair, he let go and dropped—six inches to the bottom of the ditch. Think of the needless agony he went through because he didn't let go sooner. Think of the needless agony you go through in the midst of your worries because you don't let go and let God. *References:* Eccl. 2:26; Matt. 6:25–33; 13:22; Luke 10:40–41; 1 Cor. 7:32; Phil. 4:6; 1 Peter 5:7.

Worship

1010. When Sir William Cecil, sometime Lord Treasurer of England, went to bed, he would throw off his official robe and say, ''Lie there, Lord Treasurer,'' bidding adieu to all state affairs so that he might more quietly rest. So when we engage in any religious practice, whether hearing, praying, or coming to the Lord's Table, we should put aside all affairs of this life so that we may concentrate fully on the worship of God. *References:* Ps. 46:8–11; Matt. 6:31–33; Luke 10:38–42; 12:29–31; Phil. 4:6.

Related illustrations: 529, 722, 1003.

Y

Youth

1011. Tell me the prevailing sentiments that occupy the minds of your young people, and I will tell you what is to be the character of the next generation. (Burke) *References:* Eccl. 11:9; Lam. 3:27; Titus 2:6–7.

1012. Luther was not yet 34 when the blows of his hammer on the church door of Wittenberg reverberated throughout the civilized world. Gustavus Adolphus, the savior of Protestantism, whose heroism lifted prostrate Germany to its feet, was only 21 when his military career began. And when the Saxon immigrants came to this country, some of their notable leaders were young in years and experience. Dr. Walther, for instance, was only 27 years old when he arrived in Perry County. Friedrich Wyneken began his work in Baltimore when he was 28. These and others might have objected with Jeremiah: "I do not know how to speak; I am only a child." But they rose to the opportunities of the crises in which they found themselves, and the church owes an infinite debt to their youthful leadership. *References:* Gen. 41:46; Judg. 6:15–16; 1 Sam. 17:33–37; 2 Chron. 24:1–3; Jer. 1:6–7; Luke 2:49; 1 Tim. 4:12.

Related illustration: 517.

Z

Zeal

See also **Religion**

1013. Religious zeal without knowledge is like speed to a man in the dark. (J. Newton) *References:* Matt. 23:15; Acts 26:11; Rom. 10:2–3.

1014. How perverse the human heart is! Paul said the Jews "are zealous for God, but their zeal is not based on knowledge." Of many of us the apostle might complain, "They have knowledge of God, but without zeal." (W. F. Besser) *References:* Eccl. 9:10; Rom. 10:2–3; 2 Tim. 1:6.

1015. Zealous Soldiers of the Cross. When the ancient Spartans marched into battle, they advanced with cheerful songs, willing to fight. But when the Persians entered the conflict, you could hear, as the regiments came on, the crack of whips by which the officers drove the cowards to the fray. No wonder that a few Spartans were more than a match for thousands of Persians, that in fact they were like lions in the midst of sheep.

So it is with the members of Christ's church. There is no need to drive them to action, but full of irrepressible life, they long to overcome everything that is contrary to God and His Word. As such enthusiastic soldiers of the cross, we are like lions in the midst of herds of enemies, and with God's help noth-ing can stand against us. (Spurgeon) *References:* Ps. 40:8; 100:2; Luke 10:17; Eph. 6:10–18; 1 Tim. 1:18–19; 6:12.

1016. The spurious zeal that is excited by other stimulants than the Word will do more harm than good. It will be not like the river that flows deeply but gently, bringing fertility and freshness, but like the furious torrent of the spring that sweeps away the soil and leaves behind only barren rock. (MacLaren) *References:* Jer. 5:3–4; Matt. 7:21–23; 13:20–21; Mark 4:17; Rom. 10:2–3; 2 Cor. 13:5; 1 Peter 2:2.

1017. Because children of the world do everything in the sphere of their interests, they have been called wiser than the children of light. Their lesson to us is a challenge that we need not be ashamed to accept. We have reason to work with even greater energy than the Greek runner Pheidippides, who fell dead after he had run from the plain of Marathon to bring the tidings of victory to the triumphant Athenians. The tidings that we bear to a waiting world are the eternally glad tidings of a crucified Redeemer, who conquered sin, death, and hell for us that we might live. *References:* Is. 62:1; Luke 8:39; 16:8; Rom. 10:15; 1 Cor. 14:12; Heb. 12:1; 2 Peter 3:14.

SCRIPTURAL INDEX

220

223

4—162
4:1—111
4:2–3—108

Matthew
1:1—122
1:18–23—135
1:18–25—136
1:20–23—131
1:23—204
2:1–2—132
2:1–11—133
2:1–12—303, 304
2:16—667
3:1–3—853
3:2—189
3:7–8—797
3:7–9—346
3:7–12—486
3:9—102
3:9–10—295
3:10—373
3:11–12—430
3:12—448, 515
3:13–15—489
4:1–11—450, 613
4:3–10—246
4:4—409
4:6–7—928
4:8–10—966
4:10—849
4:18–20—352
4:19—974
4:23—438
5:3—854
5:3–5—478
5:4—745
5:5—428
5:6—92
5:7—640, 777
5:7–9—445
5:9—437
5:10–12—812
5:11–12—254, 656, 839, 911
5:13–16—143, 276, 313, 655, 971, 977, 978
5:16—502, 579, 584

5:18—75
5:19—561, 864
5:22—36, 451
5:23–26—777
5:25–26—437
5:27–30—243
5:29—81
5:29–30—925, 926
5:30—818
5:32—626
5:34—764, 765
5:34–37—928
5:36—372
5:38–39—880
5:38–42—817
5:38–48—518
5:39—807
5:39–48—298
5:43–44—297
5:43–48—368, 398, 641
5:44—809
5:45—603, 708
5:46—612
6:1–6—688, 995
6:5–13—90
6:7—725
6:7–8—732
6:7–13—730
6:9—395, 938
6:10—262, 548, 729
6:12—364, 728
6:12–14—360, 366
6:16–18—995
6:19–21—307, 426, 966
6:19–24—849
6:23—873
6:24—351, 508, 509, 661, 686, 903, 1005
6:25–33—1009
6:25–34—578, 1006, 1007, 1008
6:27—372, 932
6:30—164
6:31–33—83, 182, 1010
6:32—85, 468, 1000
6:33—2, 180, 307
7:1–5—339, 340, 342, 437
7:2—808

7:3—934
7:3–5—341
7:5—793
7:7—742
7:11—938
7:13–14—717, 766
7:15—645
7:15–20—87, 200
7:15–23—335, 373
7:15–27—299
7:17–20—931
7:18—441
7:21—199, 665, 730, 794, 913
7:21–23—114, 400, 615, 847, 912, 952, 1016
7:22–23—992, 993
7:23—490
7:24—72, 293, 321, 569
7:24–25—211
7:24–27—307
7:26–27—773
8:1–4—461
8:5–12—772
8:8—415
8:8–10—620
8:11–12—588
8:12—233, 771
8:13—401
8:17—83, 541
8:19–20—253
8:21–22—252
8:23–37—320
8:26—354
9:4—930
9:9—352
9:10–13—482, 606, 983
9:35–38—893
9:36—906
9:37–38—300, 980
10:5–15—893
10:8—188, 376, 377, 379, 381
10:16—116, 567
10:16–22—631
10:17–18—459
10:22—162, 254, 329, 642
10:27—746

228

233

10:27–28—260, 352
10:28—266
11:1–46—649
11:3—94
11:16—329, 819
11:25–26—220
11:25–27—284
11:27—388
11:47–53—944
12:20–22—658
12:21—529, 718
12:23–24—107, 112, 816
12:24—679
12:35–36—580
12:37—433
12:40—240
12:42—146, 238, 975
12:46—318
12:47—983
12:48—299
13:1—601
13:4–15—482
13:4–17—34
13:5—480
13:15—499, 500, 501
13:34—368, 405, 666
13:34–35—82, 609
13:35—4, 611, 615
14:1—1000
14:1–2—885
14:1–3—215
14:2–3—220, 224
14:3—997
14:5–6—678
14:5–9—534
14:6—259, 829, 942, 959
14:7–9—387
14:8–11—319
14:13—967
14:15–21—684
14:15–23—69
14:17—463
14:22–23—613
14:26—463, 465, 937
14:27—66, 710
15:1—373
15:2–7, 95
15:3—107

15:4–5—372, 534, 811
15:4–7—159, 634
15:5—191, 260, 723, 996
15:6—369
15:7—724, 726, 728, 729
15:9—368
15:9–12—405
15:9–17—610
15:12—4, 82, 611
15:13—106, 112, 600, 601, 820
15:16—542, 904
15:18–19—780
15:18–21—642
15:18–25—713, 944
15:19—125, 137, 144, 883
15:21—44, 436, 951
15:25–27—299
15:26—937
15:27—974
16:1–3—631, 944
16:2—459
16:3—436
16:6–7—37
16:7–11—853
16:8–9—948
16:12—442, 673
16:13—463
16:13–15—69
16:19–23—884
16:23–24—727
16:24—734
16:32—586, 883
16:33—66, 127, 710
17:1—936
17:3—321, 549, 552
17:4—250, 556
17:5—387
17:14—997
17:14–17—192
17:15–17—787
17:15–18—137
17:16—125
17:17—63, 959
18:15–27—630
18:33–37—114, 953
18:36—546

18:37—353, 776, 829, 941, 959, 983
18:38—192
19:1–16—195
19:6—713
19:14–15—719
19:30—250
19:33–34—202
19:38—238, 975
19:38–39—146
20—283
20:1–3—801
20:1–18—285
20:16–17—286
20:20–27—530
20:21—26
20:24–28—278
20:25—206
20:27—789
20:28—388
20:28–31—179
20:29—319
20:31—103, 967
21:15—100, 370
21:15–17—99, 630, 647
21:15–18—445
21:15–19—483, 656
21:16—615
21:22—352

Acts
1:3—803
1:6–11—194
1:6–14—37
1:8—121, 281, 651, 653, 655, 743, 892, 904, 967, 973, 974, 976, 978, 980, 981, 982
1:10—605
1:14—814
2—653
2:4—743
2:4–11—140
2:14–40—750
2:16–17—711
2:36—109, 113, 387
2:36–37—177, 429
2:37–40—853

234

2:37–47—678
2:38—54, 632, 795
2:40—205, 787
2:42—148, 595
2:42–47—153
2:46—139, 150
2:46–47—977
2:47—422
3:6—967
3:11–26—750
3:13–26—755
3:14–15—804
3:22–26—122
3:25–26—803
4:7–13—166
4:8–13—981
4:11—105
4:12—103, 106, 824, 994
4:13—104, 265
4:18–20—323
4:19–20—282
4:20—110, 743, 972, 975
4:24—814
4:31—166
4:32–35—212, 383, 678
4:32–37—153, 188
4:33—653
4:34—382
4:34–35—379, 384
5:1–2—380, 657
5:3–4—463
5:20—746
5:31—113
5:34–39—618
5:34–42—508
5:41—194, 536
6:5—458
6:8–9:30—943
7:51—433
7:51–60—944
7:54–60—713
7:55—936
7:59—216
7:59–60—368
7:60—398
8:5–17—982
8:9–24—914
8:26–38—893

8:29–35—749
8:33—480
8:36—54
8:37—388
9:1–22—81, 483
9:15–16—656
9:17—891
9:17–18—979
9:29—166
10:19–20—463
10:34—612, 641, 707, 708
10:34–35—305, 823
10:36—718
10:39–41—804
10:44—465
10:44–48—55
11:27–30—379
11:29–30—384
12:7—34
12:12—814
12:21–23—928
13:2—463
13:14—151
13:27—61, 74
13:38–41—832
13:47—313
14:3—166
14:15—78
14:15–17—555
14:17—391
15:3—890
15:7–9—612
15:7–11—708
15:8–9—708
16—457
16:14–15—985
16:19—425
17:2–3—718
17:11—70, 88, 511
17:18—292, 832
17:18–23—715
17:22–31—344, 392, 555, 750
17:23—44, 390
17:27—691, 835
17:27–29—547
17:28—716
17:30–31—205

18:24—34
18:26—89
19:8—166
19:13–16—914
19:19—516
20:7–12—47
20:24—250, 331, 556, 774
20:24–31—766
20:27–30—800
20:27–31—163, 646
20:28—647
20:28–30—330
20:28–31—351
20:29–30—41, 144
20:29–31—645
20:30—958
20:35—188, 357, 382, 383, 881, 882
21:13—329
22:15—980
22:16—54
24:15—539, 805
24:25—235, 237, 317, 413, 692
26:11—1013
26:17–18—976
26:22–28—803
26:24–26—780
26:28—317
26:28–29—789
27:23—34
28:10—422
28:19–28—802
28:23—89
28:27—512, 553
28:30–31—166

Romans
1:3—533
1:11–18—564
1:14–15—281
1:16—65, 76, 77, 322, 565
1:16–17—401, 407, 620, 632
1:17—318, 810
1:18—865
1:18–20—853
1:18–23—555

235

236

11:32—95
12:1–11—5
12:2—785
12:4—957
12:4–12—897
12:13—54, 55
12:27—138
13:1—484
13:1–2—615
13:1–8—610
13:4–8—614
13:5—338
13:8–11—648
13:11—173
13:11–12—568
13:12—319, 442, 443, 554, 673, 884
14:12—1017
14:15—672
14:20—73, 88, 900
15:1–8—284
15:3—820
15:3–6—198
15:3–20—803
15:10—490
15:12–20—802, 804
15:17–20—801
15:20–28—223
15:32—832
15:42—806
15:42–44—219
15:50–52—219
15:50–58—885
15:51–52—142, 806
15:51–58—223, 283
15:54–55—214
15:55–57—217
15:57—911
15:58—139, 162, 282, 331, 396, 556, 786, 834
16:2—188, 381

2 Corinthians
1:3—155
1:3–4—127
1:12—674, 752, 854
2:7–8—154
3:1–3—306

3:5—78, 372, 634, 723, 741, 996
3:5–6—430
3:15—74
3:17—571
3:18—276
4:1—251
4:4—81
4:5—718
4:6—186
4:6–12—194
4:6–18—656
4:8–10—254
4:8–12—629
4:8–14—284
4:11—190, 212, 326, 619, 839
4:11–12—203
4:13—140
4:16–18—251
4:17—3, 7, 17, 19, 21, 22, 80, 224, 284, 885
4:17–18—469
4:18—299, 504
5:1–4—219
5:1–8—224
5:4—83
5:6–8—997
5:8—220
5:10—538, 808
5:11—174
5:12—488, 753, 915
5:13–14—780
5:14—405, 572, 599, 610
5:14–15—178, 601, 613
5:14–16—479
5:15—107, 358, 816, 820
5:15–20—652
5:17—128, 187, 209, 417, 680, 681, 935
5:17–21—407
5:18–21—570
5:18–19—887
5:19—904
5:20—26
5:21—489, 541, 810
6:2—435, 690, 691
6:6—614

6:10—12, 16, 536, 537
6:14—628, 721
6:14–17—956
6:14–18—772
6:18—938
7:1—462
8:1–5—34, 188, 384
8:1–6—382
8:1–8—657
8:1–9—383
8:8—377
8:9—480, 482, 533
8:12—402
9:2—313, 971
9:6—382, 383
9:6–7—188, 379
9:6–8—905
9:7—375, 376, 377, 378, 381
9:8—2, 828
10:5—775
10:7—488, 501, 753, 915
10:12—274, 342, 836, 952
12:7–9—19
12:7–10—80, 257, 729
12:8–10—741
12:9—536, 790
12:9–10—23, 902
12:10—656, 839
12:14—96, 336
12:20—48, 318
13:5—793, 1016
13:14—937

Galatians
1:4—820
1:6–9—800
1:6–10—335
1:6–12—200
1:8–9—206
2:6—612, 707, 708
2:11—330
2:14—507
2:16—462, 788, 825, 989, 991, 992, 993
2:20—5, 104, 112, 190, 207, 210, 212, 386, 405, 600, 601, 610, 613

238

239

3:3—261
3:5—605
3:6—956
3:6–9—502
3:9—313
3:10–11—920
3:10–13—25, 494, 987, 988
3:11—49
3:11–13—492

1 Timothy
1:6–7—452
1:11—904
1:12–13—715
1:12–17—476
1:15—416, 471, 603, 820, 960
1:18–19—1015
2:3–4—397
2:4—597, 716
2:8—740
3:16—387
4:1—273
4:1–3—144, 452, 516
4:2—175, 895
4:6—87, 198
4:7—918
4:7–9—289
4:12—313, 1012
4:16—200
5:1–4—517
5:6—895
5:13—49, 920
5:20—330, 800
5:21—305
5:23—439, 736
6:1–2—557
6:3–5—452
6:4—340, 934
6:5—110, 956
6:6–10—28, 183, 577, 660
6:6–19—1001
6:7—229, 426, 662, 965, 969
6:7–10—966, 970
6:9—427, 963
6:9–10—332, 333, 334,

686, 860, 964, 968, 1002
6:10—661, 663
6:11–12—646
6:12—116, 1015
6:15—115
6:17–18—881
6:17–19—188
6:19—211

2 Timothy
1:5—291, 337, 517, 696, 697, 698, 699, 700, 704, 705, 706, 985
1:6—1014
1:8—975
1:9—993
1:10—214, 217, 223
1:12—269, 324
2:1–3—646
2:4—125, 997
2:9–12—22   *38, 326 327*
2:11—190, 619
2:12—812
2:14—933
2:15—73, 496, 567, 569, 646
2:19—211
2:21—181
2:24—756
2:24–26—659
3—335
3:1–5—527
3:1–7—39, 564
3:2—101, 525, 526
3:3—577
3:5—497, 732, 956
3:7—290, 310, 553, 554
3:7–9—40
3:12—459
3:13—855, 916, 917
3:13–14—144
3:14—291, 511
3:14–15—698
3:14–17—73, 277
3:15—72, 293
3:15–17—56, 57, 60, 62
3:16—73, 550
3:16–17—67, 197, 275

3:16–4:5—198
4:1–2—645, 718
4:1–5—158, 642, 646, 744, 748, 750
4:1–8—116, 300
4:2—746, 751, 791, 800
4:3—144, 516
4:3–4—294, 788, 916, 917, 918
4:3–5—335, 962
4:5–8—766
4:6–8—216, 221, 250, 629
4:7–8—556, 774
4:10—53, 172, 173, 371, 486
4:17–18—902
4:18—361, 604

Titus
1:2—940
1:3—904
1:6—657
1:9–2:1—277
1:10–11—802
1:13—330
1:15—175
1:16—114, 485, 665, 912, 913
2:1–7—517, 646
2:6–7—1011
2:7—502
2:7–8—200
2:9—557
2:11–12—428
2:11–14—605
2:12—999
2:15—330, 746, 751
3:2—48, 49
3:4–5—788, 825, 991, 992, 993
3:4–8—189, 400
3:5—416, 638

Hebrews
1:1–11—393
1:5–13—387
1:10–12—504
1:12—532
1:14—34

241

2:1–3—413
2:9—489, 816
2:9–10—107
2:9–11—178
2:14—217, 223, 283
3:1–2—500
3:7–15—690
3:12—862
3:12–13—948
3:12–15—278
3:13—139, 435, 868
4:1–2—316
4:1–7—435
4:1–11—714, 823
4:6—61
4:8–11—221
4:9–11—224
4:12—61, 70, 77
4:14–16—37, 361, 639, 734
4:15—204, 480, 919
4:15–16—85, 403
4:16—604
5:7–9—184
5:12—86, 409
5:12–14—73
5:12–6:1—900
5:12–6:3—88
6:1—899
6:4–6—294
6:8—233
6:10–11—898
6:10–12—834
6:12—492
6:18—940
6:18–20—117
8:6–13—560
9:12—778
9:14—189
9:27—227, 230, 234, 539, 805
9:28—201, 541
10:17—367
10:19—361
10:21–22—734
10:22–23—38
10:23—261, 331

10:25—145, 149, 150, 151, 152, 348
10:27—344
10:34—536
10:38—53, 173, 714
11:1—320
11:1–6—318
11:6—323, 462, 835
11:8–16—160
11:13—216, 221, 319
11:13–16—125, 224, 443, 469, 911, 997
11:24–25—787, 841
11:24–26—306
11:26—812
11:32–40—631, 911
11:37–12:1—459
12:1—86, 767, 868, 910, 1017
12:1–2—161, 250, 329, 766
12:1–3—118, 178
12:2—354, 501, 535, 890
12:2–3—25
12:5—17, 751
12:5–8—523
12:5–11—95
12:6—94
12:11—7, 9, 14, 17, 18, 21, 22, 23, 284
12:17—237
12:25—413
12:25–28—75
13:1–2—82, 611
13:2—143, 544
13:3—141
13:5—159, 966
13:5–6—261
13:6—134, 604
13:8—213, 504, 532
13:12–13—178
13:15—422
13:17—748
13:20–21—263

James
1:2–3—11
1:2–12—922
1:3–4—10

1:5—68, 92
1:8—508, 509
1:13–14—924
1:13–16—923
1:14—244
1:14–15—450, 617, 868, 872
1:15—242
1:19—581
1:26—764, 765
1:27—141, 460, 881
2:1–4—603
2:1–7—312
2:2–4—488, 753, 915
2:2–9—707
2:4–5—305
2:8—4
2:10—561, 563, 864
2:17–18—399, 462
2:17–26—400
2:18—323, 931
3:2—350
3:5—846
3:6—49
3:9—308
3:9–10—765
3:13–15—933
3:14—301, 756
3:14–16—958
3:15—775
3:17—293
4:1—242
4:2—924
4:3—262
4:4—144, 998, 999
4:4–8—1005
4:6—677
4:7—247, 922, 925
4:8—508, 509, 734
4:10—477, 478
4:10–12—341
4:11—48, 49
4:14—234, 574, 575, 576, 932
4:16—758, 759, 846
4:17—566, 664, 858
5:1–3—966

5:3—332, 334, 686, 968,
1002, 1004
5:7—659, 737
5:10—194, 254, 329
5:10–11—10
5:12—764, 765, 928
5:13—621, 668, 672
5:14—119
5:16—814
5:20—185, 367

1 Peter
1:2—937
1:3—157
1:3–7—19, 537
1:3–9—884
1:6–7—17, 22, 469
1:6–9—21
1:7—14, 18
1:8—535
1:8–9—319
1:13—162, 250
1:18–19—822
1:22—4, 63, 82, 579, 607,
608, 611
1:24–25—299
1:25—58, 72, 75, 550
2:2—67, 73, 93, 409, 899,
1016
2:5—307
2:6—105, 211
2:9—86, 126, 148, 264,
651, 652, 654, 655, 973
2:9–10—263
2:9–11—666
2:10—55
2:11—851, 855
2:11–20—848
2:12—399, 400
2:16—417
2:17—410
2:18—557
2:19–21—20
2:21—178, 254, 352, 499,
501, 882
2:24—109, 201, 212, 358,
438, 489, 541, 816, 828
2:25—490, 906

3:1–7—627, 986
3:3—39
3:4—428, 1003
3:7—984, 985
3:8—141
3:9—298, 363, 807, 809
3:10—764, 765
3:15—116, 655, 972, 974,
975, 981
3:18–22—109
3:20—205
3:22—113
4:2—926
4:7–11—25
4:8—338
4:10—896
4:12—18
4:12–13—3, 16, 19, 80,
536, 537
4:12–16—911
5:2—647
5:5—474, 477, 677, 762,
848
5:6–7—735
5:7—78, 85, 269, 468,
639, 724, 1000, 1006,
1007, 1008, 1009
5:8—171, 921, 923, 927
5:9—282

2 Peter
1:5—289
1:5–6—10, 52, 900
1:5–7—543, 827, 840
1:5–10—766
1:10—898
1:10–11—397
1:19—62, 76
1:19–21—465, 550
1:21—72
2:1–2—248, 273
2:1–3—452
2:9—790
2:10–12—527
2:12–15—906
2:15—28, 332, 333, 425,
661, 686
2:18—872

2:18–19—244, 583
2:20—50, 53, 714, 853
3:3–4—830
3:3–5—498
3:3–7—45, 111
3:3–10—832
3:5—951
3:7—449
3:8–10—35
3:9—205, 397
3:14—249, 898, 1017
3:17—927
3:17–18—499
3:18—73, 88, 568, 827,
899, 900

1 John
1:1–3—981
1:3—104
1:3–7—153
1:5–7—580
1:6–10—169, 429
1:7—189, 349, 595
1:7–9—549
1:8—239, 341, 342
1:8–10—859
1:9—170, 408, 856
2:2—476, 606, 779, 823
2:6—501
2:9—437
2:15—125, 428, 787, 841,
997, 998
2:15–17—999
2:15–19—144
2:17—213
2:19—486
2:22—45
2:23—167
2:27—465
3:1—600, 602, 605, 609
3:1–3—38
3:2—263, 319, 442, 443,
469, 827
3:5—541
3:12–13—944
3:13—780
3:14—445, 615

TOPICAL INDEX

Numbers refer to illustrations, not pages. Words in bold type are subject headings found in the table of contents.

abundant blessings 79
Achilles 923
Adams, John Quincy 46
Aesop 405, 1002
Alexander the Great 28, 30, 109, 205, 229, 236, 324, 757, 879
allurements (**Temptations**) 450, 929, 1002
"Amazing Grace" 416
Androclus and the lion 640
Antionette, Marie 682
apathy 86
appearances 753
Aquinas, Thomas 280
Archelaus 454
Aristotle 671
Arnold, Benedict 588
articles of faith 70
astrology 495
Athanasius 330, 940
Augustine, St. 190, 359, 362, 394, 709, 727
Augustine of Canterbury 893
avarice (see **Greed**)
Aylward, Gladys 897

Bacon, Lord 67
Barclay, William 454
Beecher, Henry Ward 792
Bible difficulties 68
Bible manuscripts 72
bigotry 754, 755
boldness 361, 746
Bonhoeffer, Dietrich 80, 140, 141, 643

boredom 47
Bread of life 132, 270
brotherhood 611, 615
Brunner, Emil 558, 694
Bryan, William Jennings 309, 310
Bugenhagen, John 622
Bunyan, John 83
Burr, Aaron 498
Byrd, Adm. Richard 76

Caesar, Julius 30
Capone, Al 847
Carey, William 616, 653, 658
Carpenter, Scott 639
Carson, Johnny 953
ceremonial laws 560
Chalmers, James 656, 821
Chesterton, G. K. 535
Christ, the Rock 105, 213, 532
Chrysostom, St. 196, 627, 671
church activities 139
church and state 144, 167, 411, 412
Churchill, Winston 194, 816
Cicero 503
cleansed from sin 351
Clement of Alexandria 458
Cleopatra, queen of Egypt 591
Coke, Sir Edward 195
Colgate, William 383
Colson, Charles 665
Columbus. Christopher 142
Communion, Holy (see **Lord's Supper**)
confidence 324, 325, 361, 397, 605
Constantine, Emperor 108, 144
Copernicus 415
corruption (see **Depravity**)
Cortez, Spanish explorer 252

245